The Middle East
after Iraq's Invasion
of Kuwait

The Middle East after Iraq's Invasion of Kuwait

EDITED BY ROBERT O. FREEDMAN

University Press of Florida

GAINESVILLE/TALLAHASSEE/TAMPA/BOCA RATON

PENSACOLA/ORLANDO/MIAMI/JACKSONVILLE

Library of Congress Cataloging-in-Publication Data

The Middle East after Iraq's invasion of Kuwait / edited by Robert O.
    Freedman.
        p.   cm.
    Includes bibliographical references and index.
    ISBN 0–8130–1214–7 (alk. paper). — ISBN 0–8130–1215–5 (pbk. :
alk. paper)
    1. Middle East—Politics and government—1979-   I. Freedman,
    Robert Owen.
    DS63.1.M4844   1993   93–18252
                                        CIP

The University Press of Florida is the scholarly publishing agency for the
State University System of Florida, comprised of Florida A & M
University, Florida Atlantic University, Florida International University,
Florida State University, University of Central Florida, University of
Florida, University of North Florida, University of South Florida, and
University of West Florida.

University Press of Florida
15 Northwest 15th Street
Gainesville, FL 32611

To my secretary,
ELISE BARON,
for her many years of dedicated service

CONTENTS

PREFACE

The Middle East has long been one of the most volatile regions on the globe. Wars, coups d'état, rapid shifts in alliances and alignments, numerous intra-Arab, intrastate, and regional conflicts, and constant intervention by the superpowers have wracked the region since the first Arab-Israeli war in 1948. In an effort to increase public understanding of this complex region, the Center for the Study of Israel and the Contemporary Middle East of Baltimore Hebrew University was founded in 1977 and has held a series of conferences bringing together Middle Eastern specialists from various perspectives to analyze and discuss the region.

The first conference, held in 1978, examined the impact of the Arab-Israeli conflict on the Middle East, and the papers were later published as *World Politics and the Arab-Israeli Conflict*, edited by Robert O. Freedman (New York: Pergamon, 1979). The second conference, held in 1979 (two years into the administration of Israeli Prime Minister Menachem Begin), made a preliminary analysis of the dynamics of the Begin regime. Following the Israeli election of 1981, the papers were updated and published as *Israel in the Begin Era*, edited by Robert O. Freedman (New York: Praeger, 1982). The third conference, which took place in 1982, dealt with Middle Eastern developments in the period between the Camp David agreements of 1978 and the Israeli invasion of Lebanon in 1982. These papers were published as *The Middle East since Camp David*, edited by Robert O. Freedman (Boulder, Colorado: Westview Press, 1984). Just as the Camp David agreements marked a major turning point in the Middle East, so too did the Israeli invasion of Lebanon. For this reason, three years after the invasion, a fourth conference was held at Baltimore Hebrew University to analyze the impact of the invasion on the Middle East. The papers were published as *The Middle East after the Israeli Invasion of Lebanon*, edited by Robert O. Freedman (Syracuse: Syracuse University Press, 1986). The Iran-Contra affair was yet another key event in Middle East politics with major ramifications throughout the region, and a fifth conference was held at Baltimore Hebrew University in 1988 to assess its impact on the course of Middle East history. The conference papers were published as *The Middle East from the Iran-Contra Affair to the Intifada*, edited by Robert O. Freedman (Syracuse:

Syracuse University Press, 1991). In December 1989, with the Intifada
(Palestinian uprising) entering its third year, a conference was held to
analyze its impact. The papers presented at that conference were
published as *The Intifada: Its Impact on Israel, the Arab World, and
the Superpowers*, edited by Robert O. Freedman (Miami: Florida International University Press, 1991).

The Iraqi invasion of Kuwait, which took place in August 1990, was
another seminal event in Middle Eastern affairs, and 15 months after
the invasion, in November 1991, with the Madrid Arab-Israeli peace
talks having just begun, a conference was held at Baltimore Hebrew
University to assess the impact of the Iraqi invasion and the Gulf War
which followed it. This book, the seventh in our series on the Middle
East, is the outgrowth of that conference.

Many individuals and institutions should be thanked for their help
in making possible both the conference and the book that emerged
from it. First and foremost, generous grants from Baltimore Hebrew
University, the Baltimore Jewish Council, and the Jack Pearlstone Institute for Living Judaism provided the financial support for the conference. The president of Baltimore Hebrew University, Leivy Smolar,
has been a strong supporter of the Center for Israel and the Contemporary Middle East, and I would like to offer him special thanks.
Second, assistance was provided by the Baltimore Jewish Council,
which cosponsored the conference. Third, the director of Baltimore
Hebrew University's library, Arthur Lesley, and his staff assistant,
Jeanette Katcoff, provided special assistance in expediting publication
of the book, as did Rosa Zumer, my administrative assistant, who has
helped to maintain the center's research files on the Middle East.
Finally, special thanks are also due to my secretary, Elise Baron, who
typed the manuscript while also maintaining the Graduate Office of
Baltimore Hebrew University in an exemplary manner.

Robert O. Freedman

INTRODUCTION

The Iraqi invasion of Kuwait in August 1990 set in motion a number of forces whose ultimate impact on the Middle East is yet to be seen. First, the power of Iraq and its aspirations to be a Middle East superpower received a major blow, yet its leader, Saddam Hussein, has remained in power more than a year after Iraq's disastrous defeat ("the Mother of all defeats") and continues to pose a potential threat to his neighbors. Second, building upon the influence it had obtained by leading an Arab/European/Moslem coalition against Iraq, the United States proved able, for the first time, to organize a multilateral Arab-Israeli peace conference, with the participation of not only Israel and its immediate neighbors (Jordan, Syria, Lebanon, the Palestinians, and Egypt) but also Saudi Arabia, the European Community, and Japan, although success in the negotiations has yet to be achieved. Third, the Gulf War saw a tremendous decline in the Middle East influence of the Soviet Union which, less than ten months after the end of the Gulf War, would cease to exist as a unitary state. Its successor states, led by Russia and the Ukraine, are so preoccupied with internal economic problems and territorial claims against each other that they have little capacity to play active roles in the Middle East. Indeed, the Moslem Central Asian states of the former Soviet Union have become objects of an influence competition featuring Iran, Turkey, Saudi Arabia, Pakistan, and Israel, as well as the United States, Germany, Japan, England, France, and South Korea. Finally, both Iran and Syria, in difficult straits prior to the Gulf War, were able to use the conflict to improve their economic and political positions, although the ultimate directions of their policies remain in doubt.

Thus, while the Iraqi invasion of Kuwait certainly had a major impact on the political geography of the Middle East, the ultimate political fallout of the war remains to be determined. Nonetheless, a number of new trends have set in, and each of the specialists contributing to this volume analyzes the changes in his or her country of specialty in the period 1989–92. Prior to introducing their analyses, however, a brief overview of Iraqi policy from the end of the Iran-Iraq War to the invasion of Kuwait will be presented, to provide a background for the later analyses.

Iraq on the Eve of the War

Following the end of the Iran-Iraq War, there had been expectations of a move toward democracy in Iraq, with a permanent constitution, a multiparty system, and freedom of the press. These expectations were quickly suppressed by President Saddam Hussein. In addition, a drop in the standard of living because of a sharp jump in inflation and shortages of basic commodities, coupled with postwar unemployment, added to the strain on the regime. So did an apparent failed military coup in January 1989, which was followed by the suspicious death of the Iraqi defense minister, Adnan Talfah, in a helicopter crash in May.[1] Saddam Hussein also faced rising opposition from Iraq's Kurdish population, which he drove out of areas bordering Iran and Syria in an effort to create an eighteen-mile-wide security belt along Iraq's borders with the two countries.

Saddam's domestic problems were exacerbated by foreign policy concerns. First, his huge foreign debt was estimated by the end of 1989 to be as much as $90 billion, half of which was owed to Arab countries.[2] Given the fact that Saddam was continuing to pour Iraqi resources into building up a sophisticated arms industry, Iraq had little left over to pay the interest on the debt, let alone begin repaying the capital or meet the needs of the Iraqi people for civilian goods. Consequently Saddam sought to negotiate new repayment arrangements with his Western creditors, and while he succeeded in doing so with France and Britain few new credits were forthcoming. Compounding the problem was a scandal over Italy's Banca Nazionale del Lavoro (BNL), whose U.S. branch in Atlanta had secretly approved $3 billion in credits to U.S. and European companies to finance sales to Iraq. These sales, instead of being consumer goods, turned out to be, in part, machinery and chemicals which enabled Iraq to build poison-gas facilities and long-range missiles.[3] The revelation of the true purpose of the BNL's activities complicated relations between Iraq and both the United States and Italy and also revealed hitherto secret Iraqi attempts to build up its arms industries.[4]

Soviet-Iraqi relations had also chilled by the time of the invasion. Although the USSR continued to supply Iraq with high-quality weaponry, including T-72 tanks and SU-24 fighter-bomber aircraft,[5] political relations deteriorated, especially after the conclusion of the Soviet-Iranian arms agreement of June 1989 which Iraq feared would strengthen Iran's military-political position in the Gulf. Indeed, *Al-Iraq* lambasted Gorbachev for his "opportunistic" behavior and his failure to respect the Soviet-Iraqi treaty, because selling arms to Iran was no longer "a purely Soviet affair" but something that also concerned Iraq.[6]

If Iraq had problems with the Soviet Union and the West, it did not fare much better in the Arab world. Although Iraq, along with Jordan, Egypt, and Yemen, had formed the Arab Cooperation Council in February 1989, its efforts to use the organization as a means of pressure against Syria failed because of the growing Egyptian-Syrian rapprochement. In addition, Iraq clashed directly with Egypt over the mistreatment of Egyptian citizens working in Iraq, many of whom were forced to flee back to Egypt. While there was an improvement of ties with Saudi Arabia (an agreement on noninterference in internal affairs and nonuse of force was signed in March 1989),[7] Saddam remained unable to pressure Kuwait into signing an agreement to lease the islands of Warba and Bubiyan. As a result, Iraq continued to be cut off from the Gulf because Iran refused to allow the opening of the Shatt al-Arab until the other outstanding questions between Iran and Iraq were solved: the exchange of prisoners; Iraq's withdrawal from occupied Iranian territory; and the final border demarcation in the *thalweg* (midpoint) of the Shatt al-Arab.

Given his domestic and foreign problems, and possibly fearing that what had happened to the Ceausescu regime in Romania might happen to him, Saddam Hussein, by the beginning of 1990, decided to radicalize Iraq's foreign policy in an effort both to divert attention from the growing economic crisis in Iraq and to capture the leadership of the Arab world in order to legitimize his subsequent invasion of Kuwait. To do this he adopted a virulently anti-British, anti-U.S., and anti-Israeli position while at the same time making concessions to Iran so as to protect his flank as Iraqi troops moved into Kuwait.

Saddam's anti-U.S. policy was initiated in a speech to the Arab Cooperation Council on February 24, 1990, in which he demanded that the United States pull its forces out of the Gulf (a position also calculated to gain both Iranian and Soviet support). Saddam noted that as a result of the erosion of the power of the USSR, which had been "the key champion of the Arabs in the context of the Arab-Israeli conflict," the United States, "with its known capitalist approach and its imperialist policies," was now able to penetrate the Arab world further and commit "follies against the interests and national security of the Arabs" while building "an aggressive Israel to serve its needs in the region."[8] Saddam also deliberately provoked England, the former colonial overlord of Iraq, by executing, over British protests, an Iranian-born British journalist, Farzad Bazoft, who had been investigating an explosion at one of Iraq's military factories. As Saddam sought to bolster his anti-imperialist credentials in the Arab world by lambasting the United States and Britain, he also began a series of verbal attacks on Israel, calling for the "liberation of Palestine" and threatening Israel with Iraqi reprisals ("We will burn half of Israel") should Israel attack Iraq's scientific and military installations as it had the Osirak nuclear reactor in 1981.

In taking these steps to challenge both Israel and the West, Saddam did what no Arab leader had done since Gamal Nasser in the 1950s and 1960s: as the first half of 1990 wore on, the Iraqi leader was to try to rally the Arab world around Iraq as its new leader since Iraq, because of its military might, was able both to "stand up to the imperialists" and to lead the Arab world in its confrontation with Israel. Unfortunately for Saddam, and particularly for the people of Iraq, Saddam, just as Nasser, was to overreach himself and get involved in a conflict which badly damaged Iraq and terminated its hopes to lead the Arab world.

As Iraq was preparing to use its enhanced position in the Arab world as a cover for the invasion of Kuwait, Saddam, realizing the need to protect his flank against Iran, began in April 1990 to hint at a compromise on the Shatt al-Arab while urging Iran to join in a common anti-Israel and anti-U.S. front on the basis of Islam, noting that "true struggle makes Arabism and Islam one thing rather than two separate things."[9]

Iraqi pressure against Kuwait began to mount in July with Iraqi accusations that, acting in U.S. interests, Kuwait had exceeded its OPEC oil quota and was artifically keeping oil prices low, thus badly hurting Iraq. In addition, Kuwait was accused of stealing Iraqi oil from the Rumeilia oil field and encroaching on Iraqi territory.[10] As pressure on Kuwait built up, the Bush administration, perhaps continuing to see Iran as the greater danger and hence not wishing to alienate Iraq, took a neutral position. U.S. Ambassador April Glaspie, in a meeting with Saddam several days before the invasion, said "We have no opinion on Arab-Arab conflicts like your border disagreement with Kuwait."[11] Consequently, undeterred by the United States, Iraq sent its forces into Kuwait on August 2, 1990. In the short run, Saddam's move appeared at one stroke to have solved many of Iraq's problems. First, Kuwait was a quick source of food, consumer goods, and cash for the hard-pressed Iraqi economy. Second, by occupying Kuwait, Saddam doubled Iraq's oil reserves, and he now controlled 20 percent of the world's total reserves. Third, the occupation and subsequent troop deployment on Saudi Arabia's borders ended pressure to demobilize the million-man Iraqi army. Finally, Kuwait gave Iraq strategic access to the Persian Gulf, thus enabling Saddam to compromise on the Shatt al-Arab with Iran. Unfortunately for Iraq, these were to be only short-term gains, far outweighed by the losses they were to suffer as the result of the war that followed the invasion five and one-half months later.

Analyses of the Contributors

The war itself was almost a textbook example of the advantages of a mobile force confronting defenders stuck in fixed positions. In this book's first chapter, Professors of the National War College Bard O'Neill and Ilana Kass note that Saddam Hussein made a series of strategic mistakes, first by calculating that he could inflict heavy casualties on the Allied forces that would be unacceptable to Western publics and political leaders ("The Vietnam Syndrome") and second by assuming that the United States would engage in frontal attacks on the fortified Iraqi positions, as Iran had done in the Iran-Iraq War. What the United States did, in fact, was to seize the strategic initiative, first by pounding the command and control facilities of the Iraqi army and then by outflanking the fortifications. O'Neill and Kass attribute the U.S. success to the post-Vietnam transformation of the U.S. military forces in the areas of organization, training, and combat capability. They note that in the Persian Gulf, "in obvious contrast to Vietnam—political considerations, both domestic and international were consistent with sound military objectives. As a result, military power was used effectively, efficiently, and with almost total public support." The authors are critical, however, of the decision to end the war so early before key Republican Guard divisions had been destroyed. They consider this "a clear case of misplaced kindness, particularly in light of their [the Guards'] subsequent savage action against the Shiia in the South and the Kurds in the North."

An analysis of U.S. policy during the Gulf War and its aftermath is presented by Robert E. Hunter of the Washington-based Center for Strategic and International Studies. After pointing out the blunders of U.S. policy makers in totally misunderstanding Saddam's

policy on the eve of the Iraqi invasion of Kuwait, he gives high marks
to President George Bush's skillful organization of the coalition,
made up of the United States, Britain, France, and Arab and non-Arab
Moslem states, to fight against Iraq. He also notes that had the war
lasted longer, or had the United States driven to Baghdad in an attempt to oust Saddam Hussein physically, not only would U.S. casualties have been greater but the carefully crafted coalition might have
fallen apart. He also cites U.S. concern for the interests of allies Saudi
Arabia and Turkey as the main reason it did not come to the aid of
the Kurdish and Shiite uprisings in Iraq which Bush himself had
urged. In looking to the future of U.S. policy toward the Gulf, Hunter
argues that for the interests of long-term regional stability, an improved U.S. relationship with Iran was essential.

Hunter also praises the Bush administration for its skillful exploi-
tation of the Gulf War to begin multilateral talks on solving the
decades-long Arab-Israeli conflict and notes that, if the effort is successful, it will blunt some of the appeal of Islamic fundamentalism.
He concludes by urging the Bush administration to work harder to
curb the sale of all kinds of weaponry to the Middle East—not just
weapons of mass destruction—and asserts that it is in the long-term
interest of the United States to promote the development of representative institutions in Middle Eastern states, even at the risk of Islamic
fundamentalists coming to power in democratic elections in some of
these states.

While Robert Hunter describes the policies of the United States as
the preeminent outside power in the Middle East, whose influence—
and responsibilities—are growing in the region, Robert O. Freedman
of Baltimore Hebrew University describes the collapse of Soviet
power and influence in the region. In a detailed study of Soviet behavior during and after the Gulf War, he notes that the brevity of the war,
coupled with Gorbachev's unwillingness to support actively the U.S.-
led coalition, as well as his wartime efforts to save Saddam Hussein,
marginalized the Soviet role in the region at the close of the war. Initially, following the war, Gorbachev sought to shore up the Soviet position and to prevent the United States from dominating both the
Gulf and the Arab-Israeli peace process by adopting positions that,
while on the surface were supportive of U.S. aims, still subtly reinforced anti-U.S. forces in the region. In the Gulf, Moscow both supported Iran's call for Gulf security to be a matter for the regional
states themselves and continued to try to protect Iraq from further

U.S. military intervention. In the Arab-Israeli peace process, Freedman notes that Moscow first gave tacit support to the hard-line position of Hafiz Assad. But when Assad in mid-July 1991 opted for the U.S. peace plan, Moscow quickly sought to make the best of the situation by emphasizing the fact that the U.S. peace initiative called for joint U.S.-Soviet sponsorship of the peace conference. Following the abortive coup of August 1991, with the removal of a number of hard-liners from the Soviet leadership, Gorbachev moved to shore up his position by cooperating even more closely with the United States, whose leader, George Bush, held him in far greater respect than did his Soviet countrymen. Thus he removed the last obstacles in the Soviet-Israeli relationship by agreeing to join the United States in denouncing the UN General Assembly resolution equating Zionism with racism. He agreed to allow direct flights of emigrants between the USSR and Israel and established full diplomatic relations with the Jewish state. He also signed an agreement with the United States cutting off arms to Afghanistan and agreed, albeit in a limited way, to curtail arms shipments to the Middle East. Finally, he aided, although only marginally, the convening of the Madrid Peace Conference in the expectation that he could use the occasion both to elicit more economic aid from the West and to demonstrate domestically that he was still a major actor on the world scene.

Unfortunately for Gorbachev, all his efforts to use Middle East events to shore up his domestic political position proved futile, and less than two months after the Madrid Peace Conference the Soviet Union fell apart. The policies of the successor states of the Soviet Union toward the Middle East remain open questions.

Unlike either the United States or the Soviet Union, Japan, despite its massive economic strength, was not a major player in the Gulf War. Eugene Brown, of Lebanon Valley College, seeks to explain the passiveness of Japan during the crisis which he calls "an acutely painful episode" in Japan's "nascent effort to define its proper international role and responsibility." Based on a series of interviews he conducted in Japan, as well as a close reading of the Japanese press, Brown concludes that the Iraqi invasion of Kuwait precipitated five different Japanese elite views as to the desirability and level of Japanese participation in the anti–Saddam Hussein coalition. He describes these schools of thought as the *minimalists*, who urged Japanese autonomy from the United States and minimal participation in the U.S.-led anti-Iraq effort; the *realists*, who argued that the Gulf crisis required Japan to wield greater international clout because of the imperatives of the state system; the *moralists*, who advocated a policy of activism grounded in the principle of "right vs. wrong"; the *utilitarians*, who saw the crisis as an occasion for Japan to enhance its international stature; and the *bilateralists*, who urged robust Japanese efforts in order to strengthen Japan's most important foreign relationship—that with the United States. After describing the five different schools and their main proponents, Brown concludes that Japan is likely to undertake a more active international political role as a result of the Gulf War.

The central question for Laurie Mylroie of the Naval War College in her study of Iraq is how Saddam Hussein has been able to remain in power despite his massive defeat in the Gulf War. She notes that, although Saddam has been able to stay in power, his control over the Shiia regions in southern Iraq and the Kurdish areas of northern Iraq has been greatly weakened. Mylroie sees four reasons for Saddam's ability to remain in power in central Iraq: poor U.S. postwar planning, which left Saudi Arabia in charge of dealing with the Iraqi opposition (the Saudi decision to back an individual who, likely, was an Iraqi double agent was therefore counterproductive to U.S. interests); Saddam's brutal treatment of the Iraqi opposition and his ability to suppress the Kurds and Shiia; the relative weakening of the Iraqi army—a likely source of a coup attempt—compared to the more pro-Saddam Republican Guards as a result of U.S. military action during the war; and Saddam's efforts to curry favor within the army by means of awards and other forms of recognition.

While, as a result of the Gulf War, the Iraqi middle class has been decimated, Mylroie notes that the elite around Saddam has actually benefited from the widespread economic dislocation and suffering, which Saddam has also used to try to rally support among the Arab masses to pressure their governments to lift economic sanctions. Mylroie concludes that the Iraqi dictator, surrounded by a "sycophancy born of terror, ambition, ignorance and isolation," has sought, albeit not too convincingly, to demonstrate that by staying in power he was, after all, the victor in "the Mother of all battles."

While Iraq suffered badly as a result of the war, even if Saddam has managed to stay in power, Shireen T. Hunter of the Center for Strategic and International Studies demonstrates how Iran's clever diplomacy during the Gulf War enabled it to improve its position in the Gulf greatly, primarily at the expense of its long-time rival, Iraq. She also discusses the rise in influence of Iran's new moderate president, the

Ayatollah Rafsanjani, but notes that despite his victory in the April 1992 Majlis elections, the radical opposition, which opposes his efforts to improve ties with the West, still has positions of power in the bureaucracy, the Revolutionary guards, the press, and the student body. Indeed she sees the hand of these radical elements in the assassination of Iran's former prime minister Shapur Bakhtiar in August 1991, an event that severely damaged ties between Iran and Western Europe.

Nonetheless, despite the Bakhtiar murder and the continuation of the death sentence against author Salman Rushdie for alleged "blasphemy," Hunter sees a clear trend toward moderation in Iran's domestic and foreign policy, which, she notes, increasingly reflects the principle of "statism" where state interests are given priority over other considerations—including Islam—even if the state interests are rationalized by religious terminology. The clearest example was Iran's refusal to join Saddam Hussein's self-proclaimed Jihad against the West following his invasion of Kuwait, as Iran, tacitly cooperating with the U.S.-led Allied coalition, greatly benefited from Iraq's weakening during the war.

After Iraq and Iran, the third most powerful state in the Gulf is Saudi Arabia, the leader of the six-nation Gulf Cooperation Council (GCC). F. Gregory Gause, of Columbia University, analyzes Saudi policy during the Gulf War and concludes that while little has changed in the basic Saudi approach to regional security and Saudi-U.S. relations, changes in domestic politics in Saudi Arabia may have a longer-lasting impact. Gause sees three sets of interrelated issues which Saudi leaders must balance to assure their long-term security: increasing the size and structure of their own armed forces and those of their GCC allies; developing security relations with Gulf War allies Syria and Egypt so that they would be available if again needed; and developing enhanced security relations with the United States in such a way that it could once again come to Saudi aid in time of need—but not at the domestic political cost of allowing it to permanently station troops in the kingdom. In trying to balance these activities in the post–Gulf War period, Gause notes that the Saudis have talked about—but not implemented—universal conscription to beef up the size of their armed forces; that they have retreated from earlier plans for close security cooperation with Egypt and Syria, making the postwar Damascus declaration essentially an "academic" document; and that, while not allowing U.S. troops to establish a permanent military base in Saudi Arabia, the Saudis have tacitly supported an enlarged

U.S. military presence in smaller Gulf states such as Kuwait and Bahrain, a move that brings to Saudi Arabia the security benefits it wants while limiting negative domestic and regional repercussions for the desert kingdom. Gause also points out that while Saudi-Iranian relations have clearly improved in the post–Gulf War period (as Saudi Arabia follows a policy of balancing off Iran against the Syrian-Egyptian axis), Saudi-Yemeni relations have deteriorated in part because Saudi Arabia sees a security threat from the newly united Yemen and in part because Yemen backed Iraq during the Gulf War. Gause also asserts that Saudi Arabia wanted to aid the Shiia rebels in Iraq during their uprising following the end of the Gulf War, while it was the United States that opposed such an action.

In terms of domestic politics, Gause notes that the reforms of March 1, 1992, were the most important such reforms in Saudi Arabia in thirty years, as a "Basic System of Government" and a Consultative Council were established, along with a system of regional government for the country's fourteen provinces. Gause cautions, however, that the key to understanding the significance of the reforms is how they will be interpreted and implemented.

While the main impact of the Iraqi invasion of Kuwait centered in the Gulf, the states of the eastern Mediterranean (Israel, Syria, Jordan and Egypt), along with the Palestinians, saw their political positions significantly affected by the Gulf War.

Israel, well before the Gulf War, had been going through a major transformation, as Marvin Feuerwerger of the Washington Institute for Near East Policy indicates in his study of Israel in the period 1989–92. He cites the collapse of the Soviet Union (the superpower supporter of Israel's main Arab enemies—Syria, Iraq, and the PLO) and the influx of more than 300,000 Soviet Jews from October 1989 to September 1991. While these new immigrants initially favored the parties of the right, the Shamir government's failure to provide sufficient housing and jobs moved them to the left, a move that was to be a significant factor in Israel's 1992 elections.

Feuerwerger points out that while the Shamir-led Likud party dominated the National Unity government that was formed following the 1988 elections, and then formed the most right-wing government in Israel's history in June 1990, following the collapse of the National Unity government, its failure to make significant progress on the Arab-Israeli peace process was to lead to a clash between it and the

United States in 1991 and 1992. While Shamir acceded to Bush's request not to retaliate against Iraq for the thirty-nine SCUD missiles
launched against Israel during the Gulf War, U.S.-Israeli relations
were to deteriorate sharply following the war because of the Israeli
government's decision to rapidly expand Jewish settlements in the
West Bank and Gaza and the U.S. decision to suspend $10 billion in
loan guarantees to help Soviet Jewish resettlement until Israel stopped
building the settlements. Despite the U.S. commitment of Patriot
missiles and U.S. soldiers to man them during the Gulf War, U.S.-
Israeli relations hit a new low in 1992. This was a major problem for
the Shamir government as it embarked on the 1992 election campaign
and was one of the reasons for its defeat.

While the Shamir government complained about the deterioration
of its relations with the United States, so too did the PLO. In an analysis of Palestinian politics in the period 1988–92, Helena Cobban, of
the Washington-based Institute for Peace and Cooperation in the
Middle East, notes that the political dialogue that had begun between
the United States and the PLO following the November 1988 Palestinian National Council declaration of a two-state solution to the Israeli-
Palestinian conflict had ended by June 1990, when PLO leader Yasser
Arafat refused to denounce an abortive terrorist attack on a Tel Aviv
beach. At the same time, the Palestinian population in the occupied
territories became increasingly disenchanted with the failure of the
peace process to make progress. These conditions set the stage for
Arafat's enthusiastic embrace of Saddam Hussein during the Gulf
War. Cobban gives three possible reasons for Arafat's association with
Saddam: to deflect criticism within the PLO that he was selling out
the Palestinian cause by associating himself with an Arab leader who
was voicing increasingly loud denunciations of Israeli and U.S. policy;
to build up an Iraqi counter to the pressure that Palestinians saw
coming from Cairo to accede to U.S. and Israeli demands on the peace
process; and to gain badly needed financial support.

Whatever the reasons, Arafat's backing of Saddam was a major blow
to the Palestinian cause, as noted by several other top PLO leaders
who sharply criticized Arafat's alignment with Saddam. The weakened
PLO leader had no choice but to enter the postwar Middle East peace
process orchestrated by the United States on U.S. and Israeli terms (no
PLO representation, no Jerusalemites, and no exiles), although important segments of the PLO, like the Democratic Front for the Libera-

tion of Palestine (DFLP) and the Popular Front for the Liberation of Palestine (PFLP) opposed the move, as did the Islamic fundamentalist Hamas movement.

While the PLO was severely weakened by the Gulf War, Syria made significant gains. Alasdair Drysdale, of the University of New Hampshire, notes that, as a result of the Gulf War, Syria was able to emerge from a position of isolation in the Arab world to a position of significant influence. Similarly, Syria's relations with both Western Europe and the United States, which had been severely strained before the war, improved markedly as a result of both Syria's behavior during the war and its willingness to join the U.S.-led Middle East peace talks following the war. Given the collapse of the USSR and the Communist regimes in Eastern Europe, which had been Syria's main outside supporters, Assad had little choice but to move toward the West. Syria's participation in the Allied war effort, which, Drysdale notes, "provided legitimating Arab nationalist cover for Western intervention in the Gulf," brought major gains. First, Assad was able to crush the forces of General Aoun in Lebanon, thus removing the last major anti-Syrian figure in that country, an action that paved the way for complete Syrian hegemony over Lebanon. Second, Syria obtained $2 billion in economic aid from the GCC states. Finally, not only did Britain agree to resume diplomatic relations with Syria, but the European Community lifted economic sanctions against it, President George Bush met Assad in Geneva, and Syria, which had been isolated in Arab affairs because of its support for Iran in the Iran-Iraq War, moved to center stage in Arab diplomacy, thanks to its new alignments with Egypt and the GCC states.

If Syria clearly benefited from its participation in the Allied victory over Iraq, Jordan, whose regime was seen as closely allied to Saddam Hussein, was a clear loser. Adam Garfinkle of the Philadelphia-based Foreign Policy Research Institute analyzes Jordanian policy from the outbreak of the Intifada in December 1987 to the beginning of the Madrid Arab-Israeli peace talks in October 1991, a period of Jordanian foreign policy that he likens to "a long and frightful roller coaster ride." Garfinkle notes that because of the economic crisis that beset Jordan in the late 1980s, King Hussein sought to divert public pressure by allowing parliamentary elections, only to find that Islamic fundamentalists had gained 40 percent of the vote. These militants, together with Palestinian nationalists emboldened by the Intifada, created a strong pro-Iraqi and anti-Israeli atmosphere following the

Iraqi invasion of Kuwait. And although Jordan suffered severe economic dislocations as a result of the Iraqi invasion, the king had no choice, according to Garfinkle, but to adopt a pro-Iraqi and anti-U.S. position during the crisis if he wished to stay in power. Garfinkle also notes, however, that after the war, Jordan quickly embraced the U.S.-led peace process, and he lists six reasons: to beat down an already weakened PLO, which the king continued to see as a rival for the loyalty of Palestinians living in Jordan; to check the Syrians, whom he continued to distrust; to get renewed financial aid from the United States and, the king hoped, from U.S. ally Saudi Arabia; to protect Jordan from Israeli threats of "transfer" of West Bank Palestinians; to isolate the Islamic forces in Jordan; and to move toward peace, which Jordan desperately needs.

Like Syria, but unlike Jordan and the PLO, Egypt gained significantly from the Gulf War, which symbolized Egypt's return to the center of Arab and Middle East diplomacy. Louis Cantori, of the University of Maryland, Baltimore County, examines the role of Egypt as a potential hegemon in the region. But he notes that the increased influence of Syria and Saudi Arabia, plus Egypt's decision to cooperate closely with the United States in the unipolar post–cold war world, could prevent Egypt's becoming the regional hegemon. Cantori notes that one of Egypt's central objectives in the period 1989–92 was to draw closer to the United States in order to gain economic and military advantages. By participating in the Gulf War, Egypt indeed did gain an advantage: one-half of its $40 billion debt was forgiven ($7 billion from the United States), thus saving Egypt $1 billion per year in debt service payments, and it also obtained $10 billion in compensation for economic war-related losses and $9 billion in new loans from the International Monetary Fund. Egypt did not, however, obtain a permanent security role in the Gulf after the war, as Cantori notes that the Saudis preferred an over-the-horizon presence of the now-proven U.S. army to Egyptian (and Syrian) troops on its soil. Cantori concludes by warning that if the Arab-Israeli peace process—in which Egypt has been active since 1989—founders, then "the volatile factors of the economic have-nots of Algeria, Tunisia, Morocco, Yemen, and Sudan, and the Islamic trend could come together to destabilize and radicalize the region."

In sum, the contributors to this volume have examined the consequences of the Iraqi invasion of Kuwait from a number of different perspectives: those of external powers, those of the Gulf states, and those of Israel, the Palestinians, and the Arab states of the eastern Mediterranean. While the outcome of many of the trends set in motion by the Iraqi invasion of Kuwait and the subsequent Gulf War are not yet clear, it is hoped that this book will aid both students and policy makers toward a better understanding of this complex period of Middle East politics.

Notes

1. *Al-Iraq*, July 1, 1989, cited in Ofra Benjio, "Iraq in 1989," *Middle East Contemporary Survey (MECS)* 1989, ed. Ami Ayalon (Boulder, CO: Westview Press, 1990), p. 381.

2. Ofra Benjio, "Iraq in 1990," offprint of the chapter on Iraq in *MECS 1990*, ed. Ami Ayalon (Boulder, CO: Westview Press, 1991) (hereafter *Benjio, 1990*), p. 5.

3. *MECS 1989*, pp. 409-10.

4. The Bush Administration chose, however, to continue to aid Iraq in what has become known as the "Iraq-gate" scandal. See the report by Elaine Sciolino, *New York Times*, May 22, 1992 and the article by Eugene Robinson and R. Jeffrey Smith, *Washington Post*, November 24, 1992.

5. See *Middle East Military Balance 1988–1989*, ed. Shlomo Gazit (Boulder, CO: Westview Press, 1989), pp. 179–81.

6. *Al-Iraq*, July 1, 1989, cited in Benjio, "Iraq in 1989," p. 408.

7. *Al-Thawra*, March 17, 1989, cited in *MECS 1989*, p. 404.

8. Amman TV, February 24, 1990, cited in Benjio, 1990, pp. 9–10.

9. INA, June 26, 1990, cited ibid., p. 17.

10. Ibid., pp. 20–21.

11. *New York Times*, September 23, 1990, cited ibid., p. 23.

One

THE MILITARY AND POLITICAL DYNAMICS OF THE GULF WAR

1

THE PERSIAN GULF WAR:

A POLITICAL-MILITARY

ASSESSMENT

Bard E. O'Neill and Ilana Kass

Our purpose here is to provide a political-military assessment of the Persian Gulf War. To do so, we shall examine the interests, goals, policies, and strategies of the main antagonists, the United States and Iraq. Any judgments about success or failure must be based on an understanding of the adversaries' initial political and military objectives, for ultimately all wars are evaluated in terms of their aims. Thus, while battlefield outcomes may determine "winners" in Hollywood, political consequences define victories in the international arena.

With this in mind, we begin with a summary account of U.S. and Iraqi postures on the eve of the conflict. We will assess the dynamics of the war—its conduct and termination. In doing so, we return to the goals of the two sides and attempt to provide a balance sheet of gains and losses from both regional and global perspectives. Finally, we assess the impact of the war on the region overall, focusing on four major problems brought to the fore during the conflict: economic maldistribution, political participation, proliferation, and the Arab-Israeli conflict.

Note: The views in this paper are solely the authors'. They do not necessarily represent those of the U.S. Government or Department of Defense.

The Prewar Setting

U.S. INTERESTS AND GOALS

Of the various types of interests the United States has in the Middle East, two have been consistently deemed major or vital since at least 1973—security and economic. Remarkably, these interests have remained paramount despite the dramatic changes throughout the globe.

As far as security interests are concerned, prior to the upheaval in Eastern Europe, U.S. foreign policy stressed containment of perceived Soviet threats through a balance of power structure, which was gradually in transition from loose bipolarity to multipolarity. Since the Soviet Union maintained impressive military forces and was engaged in sustained competition and rivalry with the United States, it was viewed as the central threat to global stability.

The Middle East played an important part in U.S. security calculations since events there could adversely affect the psychological, economic, and military elements of the overall balance of power. Psychologically, there were two issues. The first had to do with perceptions of which side in the cold war was gaining in terms of what the Soviets called the correlation of forces; the second had to do with credibility. By the time Ronald Reagan came to office, there was great concern that the relative decline in U.S. power, coupled with increasing Soviet ability to project its might—even use its foothold in Afghanistan to expand into the oil-rich Gulf—had put the United States in a reactive posture. Under such conditions, U.S.-Soviet competition was viewed in zero-sum terms (i.e., gains by one side were, ipso facto, a loss for the other). Within this conceptual context, the expansion of Soviet influence into the Middle East was considered threatening because it lent credence to Moscow's claims of gradual ascendancy. Fortunately for Washington, it soon became evident that such Soviet claims were hollow.[1]

Although the growing recognition of Soviet domestic problems eliminated fears about Soviet preeminence, it by no means removed concerns about Moscow's military capability and opportunism. This, in turn, meant that U.S. credibility (living up to its commitments) remained important. Essentially, the concern was that a failure by the United States—whether actual or perceived—to fulfill its obligations, especially those related to the security of friendly states, would encourage Soviet ambitions and discourage allies, perhaps in critical areas of the world such as Europe. In the Middle East, this concern translated into a requirement to assure the security of Israel and Saudi Arabia against threats from both the Soviets and their regional proxies. To do any less would invite Soviet aggression in the region and elsewhere.

The economic aspect of power also came into play in the Middle East. This was no small matter, since the United States had achieved most of its objectives during the cold war through various economic means. As U.S. economic problems began to mount in the 1980s, the prospect of a major oil crisis was hardly welcome. The oil glut of the 1980s provided little comfort to strategists concerned with the future, especially given recurrent warnings that the primacy of Persian Gulf oil supplies would reemerge sometime in the 1990s.[2] The fear was simple: a major disruption in the flow of Gulf oil during a period of greater dependency and worsening U.S. economic problems would severely undermine U.S. capability to wield the economic instrument of statecraft. (In this context, the projected Soviet decline as both an oil producer and exporter was perceived by the United States as an added problem.)

The prospect of a future oil crisis portended grave problems for military power. In the short term, it could reduce operational readiness on land, at sea, and in the air, and it could place great strain on the Western alliance—as indeed happened in 1973. Over the long haul, the resultant exacerbation of U.S. economic problems might lead to cutbacks in and a diversion of resources that would substantially damage the industrial underpinnings of military strength.

As if the potential impact of a major oil crisis in the Persian Gulf on U.S. security interests was not troubling enough, there were also substantial worries over the possible effects on the international economic system and the U.S. economy. Renewed inflation and steadily, if not sharply, climbing deficits could quickly derail the efforts to spur productivity, improve education, and increase savings that economists argued were essential to resuscitate the U.S. economy, improve its competitiveness, and reduce its external deficit. Beyond that were the inevitable and incalculable social costs that would be visited on various segments of the population such as the poor, the homeless, the sick, the elderly, and so forth. In short, when one looked past the oil glut of the 1980s and contemplated potential and unforeseen problems associated with the projected renewed dependency on Persian Gulf oil in the 1990s, there was cause for great concern.

If there were any doubts about the importance of security and economic interests in the Persian Gulf, these were dispelled by President Jimmy Carter in 1979 when he responded to the turmoil in Iran and, particularly, to the Soviet invasion of Afghanistan by warning that U.S. vital interests would compel it to resist any efforts by outside powers to control the area. Several years later, similar fears about the expansion of Soviet influence led the Reagan administration to extend naval protection to reflagged Kuwaiti oil tankers during the Iran-Iraq War, believing that if the United States did not act the Soviets would and, thereby, would gain a new foothold in the Gulf. Shortly thereafter, however, fears about the Soviet threat changed dramatically.

In the Soviet Union, a looming economic crisis convinced Soviet leader Mikhail Gorbachev that economic restructuring was essential, that reform necessitated an opening up of the political system, and that both required improved relations with the West, especially the United States. A foreign policy of compromise and accommodation gradually unfolded. It was within the context of this "new thinking" that the Soviets withdrew from many of their Third World outposts and allowed the rapid dismantling of their control of Eastern Europe.

The disintegration of the Soviet empire, along with a more congenial atmosphere in U.S.-Soviet relations and an evolving effort to resolve superpower competition in several areas of conflict, led, quite naturally, to a reassessment of the threats to U.S. interests around the world. It was during this period of transition and strategic reassessment that Saddam Hussein invaded Kuwait.

As might be expected in such a context, the identification of threats to U.S. interests was marked by uncertainty and ambiguity. Although Soviet behavior had sharply changed, there was a residual fear that the shift was reversible; specifically, a failure by Gorbachev to deal with the domestic crisis might lead to a resurgence of Soviet hard-liners that could result in time in a renewed competition and conflict with the West. The Soviets aside, U.S. national security elites began to warn in general terms about threats to U.S. interests that might be posed by increasingly better-armed regional powers. Yet the identification of potential adversaries and conflict issues was not set forth with great exactitude. In a nutshell, the United States saw future threats to its interests emanating from either a reactionary, resurgent Soviet Union or from regional powers—and perhaps from both.

In order to advance its national interests and to protect them from threats, the United States pursued a number of identifiable global and regional goals. Two long-standing global goals that would take on special significance when Saddam moved into Kuwait were maintaining a favorable international balance of power and fostering world order. Although balance of power calculations, especially during a period of transition, were hardly precise, there was a growing sense that the relative decline in U.S. power had to be arrested and that the principal arena for such an effort was economic rather than military.[3] Thus Saddam's seizure of the Kuwaiti oil fields—and the possibility of Iraqi dominance over oil supplies and prices resulting from a threat to Saudi Arabia—could cause economic havoc and thereby alter the global balance of power to the detriment of the United States.

As for world order, the United States had long subscribed to the principle of peaceful change, even though, as critics were apt to point out, its own behavior was at times inconsistent with the idea. Be that as it may, Saddam's open aggression against a member of the United Nations was a demonstrable challenge to the goal of world order. Worse yet, it occurred at a time when changes in the Communist bloc and improved relations among the major powers engendered hopes that real and important advances might be made with respect to peaceful and orderly change. What Saddam's actions suggested instead was that the improved climate of major power relations could just as easily be conducive to regional violence as to regional accommodation.

U.S. regional goals in the Middle East were long-standing and familiar to students of the area, even though they appeared in various formulations when articulated to the world, Congress, or the public in general. Four goals captured the thrust of U.S. policy in the Middle East: assuring adequate supplies of petroleum at reasonable prices; maintaining and enhancing regional stability; guaranteeing the survival of Israel; and achieving an Arab-Israeli peace settlement. A fifth traditional goal—namely, containing the USSR—has been rendered irrelevant by dynamics internal to the Soviet Union.

In sum, while the effectiveness, accomplishments, and even morality of U.S. policy in pursuit of these goals are certainly open to debate, the often-articulated criticism that the United States did not have clear objectives in the Middle East is simply groundless.

INSTRUMENTS OF STATECRAFT

If, over the years, the United States failed to attain many of its regional goals, it could hardly be blamed for insufficient effort or unwillingness to expend resources. Countless hours were devoted to

the preparation and execution of diplomatic tasks; extensive information campaigns were undertaken; and billions of dollars were provided
in various forms of economic and military assistance. In addition, to
support its diplomacy, the United States maintained naval contingents in and around the Persian Gulf and the eastern Mediterranean
Sea. The limited success of traditional U.S. policy in the Middle East
was, in part, attributable to the fact that its efforts never coalesced
into a sustained, coherent regional strategy (to say nothing of a grand
strategy). In other words, the United States never had a grand scheme
for systematically orchestrating the integrated use of the instruments
of statecraft to achieve its goals and serve its interests. Whether such
a strategy was ever feasible is perhaps questionable, given the multi-
plicity of regional factors (disruptions caused by socioeconomic
change and ideological, nationalist, and religious fervor) that limited
the influence of outsiders, as well as the crucial impact of American
domestic politics.

The problems of devising and implementing a coherent regional
strategy were reflected in and exacerbated by the inherent tension
generated by Washington's goals. Thus, for example, the goals of assuring adequate oil supplies and fostering stability often clashed with
the goals of assuring Israel's survival and settling the Arab-Israeli conflict. Arms sales to friendly Arab states on behalf of the first two goals
were opposed by Israel because they threatened its security, while aid
and political support to Israel in pursuit of the latter two goals were
denounced by the Arabs. U.S. diplomatic, economic, informational,
and military efforts rarely, if ever, were simultaneously applauded by
both Israelis and Arabs. Instead, the norm was that whatever the
United States did to support one side was frequently castigated by the
other. This situation was impossible to resolve, since the foreign policies of Israel and the Arab states were frequently determined by internal considerations that, more often than not, gave intransigent
hard-liners inordinate leverage.[4] A specific outcome, of course, was
the continuation of the Arab-Israeli conflict and the failure to resolve
the Palestinian issue.

Frustrated by a failure to make headway on the Arab-Israeli problem in 1990 and increasingly preoccupied with fast-breaking developments in Europe and the Soviet Union, the Bush administration
gradually lessened its attention to the Middle East.[5] Under such circumstances, there was little opportunity for full reassessment of U.S.
relations with a truculent, increasingly threatening Iraq or to deal

with the changing regional balance of power in the wake of the Iran-Iraq War.

IRAQI INTERESTS AND GOALS

Like the United States, Iraq emphasized security and economic interests in its foreign policy calculations. Unlike the United States, the definition of those interests was highly personalized: for Iraq, the primary object of security was the rule of President Saddam Hussein, and everything else was secondary. Since Saddam's rise to power took place in a violence-ridden context—to which he was a notable contributor—and since he had played a key role in toppling the previous regime, Saddam knew full well the vulnerability of any leadership echelon in Baghdad.

To protect his own rule, he sought to avoid the mistakes of his predecessors by skillfully using both carrots and sticks. He was extremely generous to individuals and groups who were loyal and savagely ruthless to those he suspected of disloyalty. His obsession with security—some diagnosed it as paranoia—meant that he trusted few, if any, people. The few he may have trusted were mostly relatives from Takrit; almost without exception, they were in charge of the various security organs with the job of eliminating threats to the regime and keeping watch on one another. To make sure that his allies did not waver in their support, he frequently had them personally murder real or imagined enemies, thereby making them dependent on him for their security against those who might plot revenge. While some segments of the ruling Ba'ath party may have become more pragmatic or liberal over the years, and thus the subject of interesting academic speculation in the West, the essence of the regime had not changed. It remained a highly coercive, one-man rule.

In 1980, Saddam had gone to war with Iran because he believed that its new Islamic government intended to topple him from power. Indeed, it was the calls from Tehran for his overthrow and the subversive actions of Iranian-backed groups like *Al-Dawa al-Islamiyyah* (the Islamic Call) that led him to invade Iran, on the premise that a quick territorial gain would bring down an aggressive group of clerics who had yet to consolidate power. The hoped-for short war became a prolonged and bloody one, thus establishing what would become a penchant for strategic miscalculation on Saddam's part.

Fortunately for Saddam, the Iranian leadership also proved to be inept. Rather than settle for the limited aim of forcing a withdrawal of

Iraqi forces and restoration of the status quo ante bellum, Khomeini personalized the conflict and doggedly clung to the objective of eliminating Saddam. When the fighting finally ended in 1988, Iraq came out the net winner, since Khomeini did not achieve his stated goal. However, given the enormous human and material cost incurred by Baghdad, the victory seemed largely Pyrrhic.

Though the war removed the threat to Saddam from the mullah-cracy across the border, it did not alleviate his security phobias. In fact, within two years Saddam convinced himself that Israel, the West (especially the United States), and the patrimonial regimes of the Gulf were all conspiring against the Iraqi leadership. Frequent warnings by Israeli officials about the threat posed by Iraq's large, battle-tested army and its growing potential to build and deliver weapons of mass destruction were heard in Baghdad. Obviously concerned about a repeat of Israel's 1981 air strike against Iraqi nuclear facilities in Osirak, Saddam threatened to respond by incinerating large parts of the Jewish state.[6]

As the Iraqi leader saw it, the West and the Gulf states were playing a particularly insidious role in the conspiracy. Saddam believed that they intended to squeeze and eventually destroy the Iraqi economy by compelling Iraq to pay off its large debts while at the same time reducing its oil revenues.[7] Specifically, covert overproduction of oil by Kuwait and the United Arab Emirates (U.A.E.) was reducing its price and, hence, the petrodollars flowing into Iraq's coffers. With the Iraqi economy collapsing, there would be pressure to divert resources from the military to improve the standard of living of the professional middle class. Failure to satisfy the conflicting demands of either group could lead to internal unrest. The perceived economic—and, consequently, political—threat was so serious that Saddam portrayed it as a mortal danger both to himself and to his nation.[8]

INSTRUMENTS OF STATECRAFT

Saddam sought to promote his paramount goal of maintaining his power and the Ba'ath regime through skillful orchestration of diplomacy, propaganda, and economic and military power. Thus, he attempted to garner international support, isolate adversaries, and create an atmosphere in which the transfer of highly sophisticated technology to Iraq was facilitated. Although his economic troubles at home were worsening, he provided selected assistance to governments such as Jordan that he considered important. A vigorous information effort, directed mostly at the Arab world, articulated his conspiratorial theory and sought to promote Iraq as a staunch defender of Arab and Islamic interests. Finally, and most important, he maintained large military forces and sought to enhance their quality and lethality by spending billions of dollars, both covertly and overtly, on the latest equipment. Such lethality included an intended biological and nuclear capability and an existing chemical arsenal and ballistic missile program. This military capability provided the means for coercive diplomacy against his neighbors, should the other instruments prove insufficient for his purposes.

By spring 1990, Saddam apparently concluded that such was indeed the case, and he began to rattle his sabers against Kuwait and the U.A.E. The resort to coercive diplomacy was epitomized by Saddam's warning to Kuwait in July that its overproduction of oil was "a poison dagger in Iraq's back" and that if words failed to protect Iraq, something effective would have to be done.[9] Sometime in early summer 1990—the exact date is known only to Saddam—he concluded that coercive diplomacy was not yielding the desired results. The next step was to invade and seize Kuwait.

The Persian Gulf War

The Persian Gulf crisis began on August 2, 1990, when Saddam's forces moved into Kuwait, rapidly overwhelming the surprised defenders. An early, transparent effort (appointing an unknown batch of quislings as a provisional government) to make it seem as if native Kuwaitis were behind the takeover was quickly discredited. Iraq consolidated its brutal control, annexed Kuwait, and deployed forces in menacing positions along the Saudi border. Whether, as some would later claim, Saddam indeed intended to sweep down the coast and occupy Saudi Arabia remains a matter of conjecture. However, it is clear that he had the capability to carry out a significant incursion.[10]

The United States quickly overcame the initial shock of the surprise attack and decided that it could not stand by and gamble that Saddam's ambitions were limited. The immediate and clear threat posed to vital U.S. interests led to a dramatic change in U.S. policy toward Baghdad. A prewar policy drift—characterized by lack of attention by top government leaders, ambiguous warnings to Iraq about its intentions toward Kuwait and Israel, and inadequate control over technology transfer to Iraq—was replaced by confrontation, starting in the diplomatic arena.[11]

COERCIVE DIPLOMACY

Perhaps atypically, the United States rapidly crafted a coherent grand strategy that involved the use of all instruments of statecraft in response to Iraq's invasion. Four political objectives were set forth with rare clarity: immediate, complete, and unconditional withdrawal of Iraqi forces from Kuwait; restoration of Kuwait's legitimate government; security and stability of Saudi Arabia and the Persian Gulf; and safety and protection of the lives of U.S. citizens abroad. The first two objectives were situation-specific and, hence, became the central focus of U.S. policy throughout the crisis; the latter two were really reiterations of traditional, long-term goals. Another objective, reportedly articulated on August 3 by Brent Scowcroft, the president's national security advisor, was to topple Saddam Hussein through covert action. While the central objectives remained consistent throughout the crisis, the aim of toppling Saddam would be waffled in public, presumably because it was not acceptable to all the governments supporting the general U.S. effort.[12]

Diplomatically, the United States moved with alacrity to obtain international backing for Security Council Resolution 660 (August 2), which condemned the invasion and demanded immediate and unconditional Iraqi withdrawal. Intensive global diplomacy on all levels, including energetic personal efforts by President Bush, produced an extraordinary coalition of friends and adversaries that imposed economic sanctions (August 6) and a naval embargo (August 25) against Iraq. To deter a possible Iraqi military move against Saudi Arabia, the United States dispatched air forces and limited ground contingents to the region while laying the groundwork for a war-fighting posture.

The high point of success in the diplomatic arena was reached on November 29, 1990, when the United Nations authorized the use of force if Iraq did not withdraw by January 15. A vigorous informational campaign, directed at many audiences, depicting Saddam as a latter-day Hitler with a record of ruthless violence, prevarication, and hypocrisy, was successfully interwoven with diplomacy to shore up domestic and international public support.[13]

Saddam sought to counter the unfolding U.S. strategy by striking at its perceived weak point—the fragility of the international coalition,

especially the Arab members. Diplomatic and informational undertakings sought to justify Iraq's seizure of Kuwait, initially by pointing
to the hostile oil policies of the emirates and then by stressing the
historical legitimacy of Iraq's claim to Kuwait.[14] Attempting to rupture and destroy the coalition, Iraqi diplomats and spokesmen tried to
convince major powers—for example, the USSR and France—that
their national self-respect was being undermined by slavish subser-
vience to Washington. In the region, the approach was to undermine
those Arab governments supporting the coalition by generating popular protests against them. To galvanize such pressure, U.S. actions
were depicted as being inherently hostile to Islam, pro-Zionist, anti-
Arab, anti-Palestinian, and supportive of regimes that benefited from
gross economic maldistribution in the region.

Although the coalition did not succumb to Saddam's strategy in the
short term, its long-term durability remained in question. Public
commentary and countless hours of expert testimony before Congress
failed to provide any clear-cut answers to the crucial questions: how
long it would take the embargo to break Iraq; how long before the coalition unraveled; and which would happen first?[15] In the absence of a
compelling argument that the coalition would hold until the embargo
was effective, the Bush administration made a major decision in November to establish the capability for offensive military operations.

Unwilling to leave Kuwait under such pressure because it would
discredit him throughout the Arab world, Saddam continued his political and psychological efforts to fragment the coalition. He sought to
portray his policy as one that served Arab and Islamic interests by
linking the issue of Kuwait to an Israeli withdrawal from the West
Bank and Gaza Strip as well as a Syrian withdrawal from Lebanon.
While hinting—supposedly, for example, to Algerian President Chadli
Ben Jedid in December, and to Soviet envoys throughout the crisis—
that he was prepared to be flexible, Saddam refused to discuss withdrawal from Kuwait unless and until these other issues were addressed.[16] Concurrently, the prospect of a comprehensive deal was
juxtaposed with an increasing emphasis on the specter of unacceptable battlefield losses for the Allies in the event of hostilities. No
doubt recognizing that this gambit might fail to dissuade the coalition
from using force, especially in the absence of a clear commitment to
withdraw from Kuwait, Iraqi military leaders prepared for the possibility of war. As they did so, the outlines of their military strategy became apparent.

The Iraqis calculated that the prospect of heavy casualties would be unacceptable to Western publics and political leaders. In the United States, public opinion and Congress were thought to be especially vulnerable because of the continuing impact of the Vietnam syndrome, manifested, most recently, in the October 1983 bombing of the Marine barracks in Beirut. Besides stressing the risk of high battlefield losses, the Iraqis sought to influence Western political calculations by portraying coalition objectives as nothing more than a quest for cheap gas prices and reestablishment of a corrupt, undemocratic, sybaritic government in Kuwait. Casting the aims this way made their accomplishment appear both immoral and insignificant in light of the predicted cost. To influence the "rational calculus" in the West further, the Iraqis tried to strike a resonant chord with neo-isolationists, by claiming that since the Iraqis did not interfere in Western affairs, there was no reason for the West to become involved in an Arab problem, which, in any case, could be solved by the Arabs themselves. Interestingly, all these themes—in countless variations—reverberated in Western media and, subsequently, in congressional debates. Whether, and if so to what extent, the tenor of the Western public discourse reinforced Saddam's preconceived notion that the coalition lacked the will to fight is, of course, impossible to ascertain.[17]

By January 1991, it was becoming apparent to Baghdad that war was a distinct possibility. Accordingly, while Iraq's efforts to influence the U.S. political debate continued, it began to sharpen and clarify the essential components of the military strategy that would be followed in the event of hostilities.

Basically, the strategy had two facets. One was the conduct of a worldwide terrorist campaign, which Saddam referred to as "extending the battlefield outside the Middle East."[18] The second and preeminent aspect was conventional warfare in the Kuwaiti theater. While the Iraqis conceded that they could not win a decisive military victory over the coalition, they asserted that they could prolong the fighting and inflict substantial casualties. Specifically, they hoped to offset their adversaries' technological superiority by several factors: first, the Iraqis had large numbers of battle-tested troops from the war with Iran; second, they would be fighting in a desert environment to which they were accustomed and the Allies were not; third, they would be better motivated because they would be defending Arab land and Islam; and fourth, and perhaps most important, their complex line of defensive fortifications in Kuwait, composed of interlocking fields of fire, extensive mine fields, artillery, and armor, to be reinforced by reserve units farther to the rear, would enable them to inflict heavy losses if the Allies moved to the offensive. The human and material costs to the coalition would, Saddam believed, lead the Allies to cut their losses and accept a settlement short of their stated political objectives. In essence, the loss of will in Vietnam and Lebanon would be replicated on the sands of Kuwait. The fatal flaw in the strategy was the assumption that the coalition's military strategy would be as unimaginative as the Iranians' had been—that is, frontal assaults against Iraqi defensive fortifications.

U.S. Military Response: The Continuation of Policy by Other Means

POLITICAL USE OF MILITARY POWER

In analyzing the U.S. military response to Iraq's invasion of Kuwait, it is useful to differentiate between Desert Shield and Desert Storm and to address both the defensive and offensive operations in the context of established patterns of U.S. use of military power to support its policy goals. This approach will not only provide a clearer perspective on the conduct of the war; it will also set the framework for a comprehensive assessment of the outcome.

Given the scope, importance, and enduring nature of U.S. interests in the Middle East—and the volatility endemic to the region—it is hardly surprising that military power was often used as an instrument of U.S. policy. Most notably, U.S. Marines went ashore in Lebanon in 1958 and again in 1982—albeit under vastly different circumstances and with equally different results. In September 1970, the United States postured its forces to deter a Syrian threat to Jordan. In October 1973, during the Yom Kippur war, the United States placed its forces on worldwide alert to deter Soviet involvement in the conflict. In 1987-88, during the Iran-Iraq War, a joint task force was established to support U.S. reflagging of Kuwaiti tankers and to counter Iranian gunboat and missile attacks on shipping in the Gulf. U.S. combat power was also employed in punitive actions against Libya, Iran, and Syrian forces in Lebanon.

Relative to the Gulf War, these crises were limited in scope and duration, yet each was fraught with the dangers of escalation and wider entanglement. Each also demonstrated the readiness to put U.S. forces in harm's way to support U.S. policy goals.

Perhaps less dramatic but equally reflective of U.S. resolve to deter threats to its regional interests was an extensive network of military cooperation, ranging from arms sales to joint exercises. These programs were significantly expanded following the enunciation of the Carter Doctrine, which designated U.S. interests in the Persian Gulf as "vital"—that is, by definition, interests for which the United States would be ready to fight. Thus, in January 1980, the United States created the Joint Rapid Deployment Force (JRDF), dedicated to Middle East contingencies, and began to pre-position military equipment in the region.

While neither rapidly deployable nor much of a force, the JRDF served as the basis for increasingly robust security assistance. Military presence, however, remained limited by local sensitivities. In January 1983, with regional tensions escalating, the JRDF was upgraded to a Unified Command status and became the U.S. Central Command (CENTCOM). Its commander-in-chief, one of five so-called war-fighting CINCs, was charged with planning for the deployment of U.S. forces into the region—itself a monumental task, given the distances involved and the limited combat power immediately available in theater—and their employment in support of national political and military objectives.

This fairly extensive history of U.S. military involvement in and commitment to the region was critical to the success of the war effort. As the crisis unfolded, the United States could rely on an established command system, advanced planning, and a well-developed infrastructure to support and sustain operations.[19] Less tangible but equally important was the experience of operating in the region and interacting with regional partners, without which it would have been difficult, if not impossible, to create and sustain the multinational coalition.

DESERT SHIELD AND DESERT STORM: PATTERNS OF CONTINUITY AND CHANGE

At first glance, Desert Shield and Desert Storm are merely two sequential stages of the same campaign, involving, respectively, the deployment and employment of military power to achieve policy goals. On closer analysis, however, the two operations are qualitatively different in terms of their objectives, strategy, and implications.

Operation Desert Shield—beginning on August 7, 1990, with the initial deployment of U.S. forces to Saudi Arabia and officially ending at dawn on January 16, 1991—pursued the traditional cold war objectives of deterrence, containment, defense, and restoration of the status quo. Thus, it is consistent with the post–World War II pattern of U.S. crisis response.

Specifically, by deploying a quick-reaction force to the Gulf in the wake of Iraq's invasion of Kuwait, the United States sought to dissuade Iraq from attacking Saudi Arabia by confronting it with the threat of unacceptable cost (classical deterrence) and, should deterrence fail, to defend Saudi territory. Concurrently, Iraq was to be persuaded to withdraw from Kuwait (to restore the status quo ante) by the traditional combination of increasingly painful political and economic pressure, reinforced by the threat of force.

Deterrence, of course, is in the eye of the beholder. As a strategy, it pursues a negative aim: to dissuade an adversary from taking action which he may or may not intend to take in the first place. Its success, therefore, is also measured in negative terms: each day an attack does not happen, is, ipso facto, a victory. However, deterrence leaves the initiative with the opponent. Thus, until the Allied offensive began, it was entirely up to Saddam to attack the initially vulnerable deterrent force, to withdraw peacefully with his army intact, or to stay in place.

When assessed against this backdrop, Saddam's decision to stay the course makes sense. To the extent that one can assume rational decision making in Baghdad, it is likely that he perceived Desert Shield as a mere show of force rather than as a precursor to the use of force. As noted earlier, he did not expect the United States to muster the will to force him out. He remained blinded by this conviction even after the United States doubled its forces in the theater and acquired an overwhelming offensive option.

Operation Desert Storm caught Iraq by surprise precisely because it deviated from the established pattern of deterrence and defense. Instead, military power was used in the classical, Clausewitzian sense: as a "means to impose our will on the enemy" by "disarming him and rendering him defenseless."[20] Not since the Korean War has the United States committed its forces to combat—and led a wartime alliance—with the express objective of rolling back an invasion and destroying the aggressor's war-making potential.

Thus, the transition from Desert Shield to Desert Storm is more than an operational shift from a defensive to an offensive phase—

from establishing and securing a staging base (Saudi Arabia) to its utilization to mount an offensive. The real transformation occurs at the level of strategy and policy. It entails a qualitative change from deterrence to compellance, from containment to coercion, and from leaving the initiative with the opponent to seizing the strategic initiative in order to shape the postwar environment. In this sense, the shift to Desert Storm occurred not on January 17, 1991, but in November 1990, with the president's decision to deploy heavy, offensive forces to the region.

OBJECTIVES AND STRATEGY

Wars are fought for political goals. It is policy that determines the kind of war to be conducted and the level of effort—in terms of blood and treasure—to be committed to the pursuit of its objectives. Simply put, policy sets the ends and provides the means; military strategy is the plan to achieve the desired ends with the available means.

Rarely, however, can the application of military power alone achieve all the goals set by policy. Military strategy, therefore, must translate the political goals into appropriate and attainable military objectives, subordinate to and supportive of the political objectives. Thus, to assess the conduct and outcome of any war, it is crucial, first, to understand the inherently destructive nature of military power and, second, to grasp what military power can—and what it cannot—attain.

Of the four national policy objectives framed by the administration, only one—"the immediate, complete and unconditional withdrawal of all Iraqi forces from Kuwait"—could be (and was) fully attained through the use of force. As regards the remaining two goals—"restoration of Kuwait's legitimate government" and "security and stability of Saudi Arabia and the Persian Gulf"—military power could only assist in the former and contribute to the latter. (The fourth stated objective, "safety and protection of the lives of American citizens abroad," was essentially achieved when the foreign hostages were released and the threatened campaign of terrorism failed to materialize. A main reason that the terrorist campaign did not unfold was the rigorous anticipatory actions by Western intelligence agencies and police forces.) In other words, by destroying the immediate threat and degrading Iraq's ability to wage war again, military power could shape an environment more conducive to the realization of ultimate U.S. goals.

Accordingly, the military objectives for Operation Desert Storm were defined as follows: "neutralization of the Iraqi National Command Authority's ability to direct military operations; ejection of Iraqi forces from Kuwait and destruction of Iraq's offensive threat to the region, including the Republican Guards in the Kuwaiti Theater of Operations (KTO); destruction of known nuclear, biological, and chemical weapons production and delivery capability, to include Iraq's known ballistic missile program; assistance in the restoration of the legitimate government of Kuwait."

These objectives were further rendered into theater military objectives, for execution by the forces under the CENTCOM commander. Thus, coalition forces were ordered to "attack Iraqi political-military leadership and command and control; gain and maintain air superiority; sever Iraqi supply lines; destroy known chemical, biological and nuclear production, storage, and delivery capabilities; destroy Republic Guard forces in the Kuwaiti Theater of Operations (KTO), and liberate Kuwait City."[21]

The internal consistency and coherence are striking, as political objectives are translated into attainable military objectives and then into appropriate operational tasks and missions. Equally remarkable is the fact that the coalition went to war with clearly limited objectives.

Thus, the primary objective was to destroy Iraq's ability to wage war—now and in the future. However desirable or hoped for, the overthrow of Saddam Hussein's regime was never stated as a political goal. Whether it should have been is, of course, a different matter altogether.

Insofar as military operations are planned and executed for political purposes, their effectiveness can only be measured in terms of the objectives they were designed to achieve—not in terms of what might have been, should have been, but ultimately wasn't a criterion for success. The overthrow of an opponent's government—and its replacement with another, more amenable to the overarching goal of peace and stability—is a political objective. Its pursuit by military means would have required a political decision to expand significantly the scope, duration, thrust, and, most crucially, human cost of the operation. That decision was not taken, evidently because the costs and risks were deemed disproportionate to the intrinsic value of the objective.

Military strategy is circumscribed not only by what is militarily suitable and feasible but also by what is politically acceptable, both at home and abroad. Thus, a coalition strategy is almost always based on accommodation and compromise—often on the lowest common denominator.[22] This is particularly true of heterogeneous coalitions, where disparities in capabilities and resources are compounded by real or perceived asymmetries in commitment to the common cause. Furthermore, maintaining cohesion often becomes a goal in and of itself, superseding the objectives that were the coalition's initial raison d'être. Thus, for example, while keeping Israel out of the war never was a stated U.S. or coalition objective, the concern that Israeli retaliation for Iraqi attacks on its cities would fragment the coalition dictated a significant diversion of military effort to the "SCUD hunt," while political capital was invested in convincing the Shamir government that restraint was in its own national interest.

Similarly, perceptions and appearances become critical in a coalition, at times overriding real mission requirements. Thus, contrary to popular belief, the CENTCOM commander had operational control only over U.S., British, French, Italian, and Canadian forces. All Arab and Islamic forces from Afghanistan (guerrillas), Bahrain, Bangladesh, Egypt, Kuwait, Morocco, Niger, Oman, Pakistan, Qatar, Saudi Arabia, Senegal, Syria, and the United Arab Emirates were under the operational control of a Saudi lieutenant general. Within this dual command structure, coalition forces were assigned missions consistent with political restrictions on their use—as well as with their rather disparate capabilities—while maintaining the image that both the glory and the burden are shared equally. For example, both Syria and Egypt stated that their forces would not fight in Iraq but could participate in the fixing force and in the liberation of Kuwait. Similarly, political considerations dictated that the first forces entering Kuwait City be Arab rather than U.S. or Western troops and that Iraqi prisoners of war be surrendered to the Saudis. Overall, according to the U.S. Department of Defense, "The Gulf war presented some unique challenges to the assignment of missions . . . the formal command relationship structure and attendant bureaucracy tended to complicate, rather than simplify the command's ability to prosecute the war. Because the Arab/Islamic Coalition forces were not placed under the operational command of CINCCENT, a multinational coordination center was established as an expedient device to provide necessary unity of command."[23]

Given the brevity of the war, frictions remained manageable and cohesion was not put to a serious test. Early and decisive victories helped to cement the coalition. Nonetheless, its fragility and the tenuous nature of some of the partners' commitment dictated that the war be terminated quickly, with minimal Allied casualties and low collateral damage. By the same token, political sensitivities—particularly the Saudis'—militated against humiliating Iraq with demands of unconditional surrender.

Domestically, the twin imperatives of minimizing casualties and avoiding a prolonged, Vietnam-style imbroglio were key. The daily drumbeat—from legislators, commentators, journalists, and assorted military experts—as to what will happen "when the body bags start coming home" both reflected and reinforced the perception that the domestic consensus was liable to collapse. This dictated that overwhelming force be employed early to produce an almost instantaneous paralysis of Iraq's war-fighting capability. These same imperatives were reflected in the length and intensity of the strategic air campaign, and in the overall reliance on high-tech, precision-guided, stand-off weapons, to save lives and limit collateral damage. Similarly, the final land assault—unleashed only after the air campaign had shattered the Iraqi will and ability to resist—relied on speed, surprise, deception, and maneuver, as well as overwhelming firepower to rout the Iraqis quickly, decisively, and with remarkably low casualties.

In the Persian Gulf—in obvious contrast to Vietnam—political considerations, both domestic and international, were consistent with sound military objectives.[24] As a result, military power was used effectively, efficiently, and with almost total public support.

THE MAKINGS OF VICTORY

The Persian Gulf War might already be the most overanalyzed conflict in human history. More ink than blood has been spilled before, during, and after the war, and the quest for lessons learned has flourished into a veritable cottage industry. This analysis, therefore, seeks to highlight a few of the fundamentals rather than attempt a comprehensive review of the action. Concurrently, our focus is on issues that have been largely eclipsed by the more dazzling aspects of Desert Storm rather than on those that have received extensive coverage in Western literature.

With the initial euphoria of victory having subsided, a new conventional wisdom seems to be emerging. It is based on two interwoven premises: first, that the victory over Iraq was cheap and easy—a "Nintendo war" against an unworthy opponent; second, that the war was so unique—in terms of the enemy, terrain, international constellation, and sheer luck—that few broadly applicable conclusions should be drawn.

It is ironic that many of the same experts who, before the war, predicted catastrophic results in fighting the well-armed, battle-hardened Iraqis now argue that the contest was so lopsided that the outcome was guaranteed before the battle was even joined.[25] This view overlooks the lessons of Vietnam and Afghanistan, namely, that superiority in every single indicator of power is insufficient to produce victory. In this context, it is worthwhile to recall a bitter story that made the rounds in Washington during the closing days of the Vietnam War: "When the Nixon Administration took over in 1969, all the data on North Vietnam and the U.S. was fed into a Pentagon computer: population, gross national product, manufacturing capability, number of tanks, ships and aircraft, size of armed forces, and the like. The computer was then asked, 'When will we win?' It took only a moment to give the answer: 'You won in 1964.'"[26]

Clearly, the Iraqis—like the North Vietnamese—lacked the military means to defeat the most powerful nation on earth. But, like the Vietnamese—or, for that matter, the Chinese, the North Koreans, the Mujahadeen, the Algerians, and the Palestinians—they could have attempted to make the war so protracted and costly as to undermine their opponent's national will. That they failed to do so stems first and foremost from the coalition's success in defeating the Iraqis' strategy through preemption—that is, seizing the strategic initiative and forcing the opponent to fight (and lose) our kind of war. If, as the British strategist Sir Basil Liddell Hart noted, "the perfection of strategy would be to produce a decision without any serious fighting."[27] Allied strategy indeed was the "acme of military skill."[28]

Without a doubt, the Iraqis were singularly inept. The point is that "in war, it is by compelling mistakes that the scales are most often turned."[29]

The coalition's military strategy relied on the time-tested principle of pitting strength against exploitable weakness. The military effort was concentrated on Iraq's "centers of gravity"—those "hubs of all power and movement on which everything depends."[30] Once thrown off balance by the massive application of airpower simultaneously against all its centers of gravity, Iraq was never given the time or the opportunity to recover. Unable to see, hear, speak, or move, the Iraqi army—the world's fourth largest—was rendered unable to fight.

When seen in perspective, the victory over Iraq was neither automatic nor quick and easy. In fact, it was long in the making, costly, and often painful. As one general officer put it, "We didn't start winning this war last August. We started winning this war ten to fifteen, if not twenty years ago."[31]

What this statement captures is perhaps the most commonly over-looked aspect of the Persian Gulf War, namely that both its course and its outcome reflect the post-Vietnam transformation in how U.S. forces organize for combat, how they train, and how they fight. This revolu-tion—largely ignored or misperceived by critics who continued to pil-lory the military as a bunch of bunglers, wasting money on gold-plated weapons that did not work and preparing to fight threats that would never materialize[32]—allowed the United States to field the best-led, best-motivated, and best-equipped force in its history. Unencumbered by political micromanagement and free from cold war constraints, this force could deliver a spectacular—if not bloodless—victory.

More than anything, Desert Storm validates the old adage that sweat in training and innovative thinking in peacetime save blood on the battlefield. In particular, realistic, tough, aggressive exercises, em-phasizing outsmarting—rather than outnumbering or outgunning—the enemy, paid tremendous dividends on the battlefield. So did the sustained quest for technological force-multipliers, designed to save lives and compensate for quantitative inferiority. By the same token, the restoration of the "warrior spirit" to the officer corps and the armed forces at large, coupled with an across-the-board inculcation of sophisticated war-fighting concepts, were critical ingredients of suc-cess. Central to this conceptual arsenal were renewed emphasis in both training and education on joint and combined operations at the operational level of war (that is, the level bridging tactics and strat-egy); recognition of the importance of surprise, deception, and opera-tional security; focus on speed, agility, synchronization, and maneuver; fusion of superior battlefield intelligence with precision-guided weap-ons; and last, but certainly not least, an overarching emphasis on tar-geting the adversary's mind—his strategy, his will, and his perceived ability to fight—so as to produce a battlefield decision through stra-tegic dislocation and disruption rather than through costly attrition.[33]

Desert Storm served as a field test for ideas (and weapons systems) developed in the late 1970s and early 1980s and designed primarily for war with the Soviet Union, most notably, AIRLAND Battle, Follow on Forces Attack (FOFA), and the Maritime Strategy. All are predicated on superior intelligence, technology, and training and capitalize on agility, audacity, and mutually reinforcing operations. All seek to ex-ploit opponents' weaknesses and leverage U.S. advantages—particularly in the air and at sea—to defeat a massive, rigidly controlled land army. And, finally, all are designed to force the opponent to disperse his forces so that he can be defeated in detail.

Undoubtedly in Desert Storm the concepts and systems were applied under ideal conditions. For example, in contrast to the canonical scenarios for war in Europe, where NATO was expected to absorb the first strike, recover, and seek to wrest the strategic initiative from the Warsaw Pact, in the Gulf the coalition determined the time, place, and nature of each engagement. Air superiority—the sine qua non of battlefield success—was achieved more quickly and with fewer losses than might have ever been deemed possible in the skies over Europe. Similarly, Iraqi air defenses snapped under significantly less pressure than would have been required to break the more robust and better-integrated Soviet system. It is also unlikely that the Soviets—or, for that matter, any sophisticated opponent—could have been so completely deprived of the ability to see and control the battlefield. Furthermore, in obvious contrast to European scenarios, Allied rear areas and staging bases were never seriously threatened, permitting full concentration of effort on deep, offensive operations. Finally, and perhaps most important, if history is a guide, the Soviet morale and spirit—the will to fight—would not have collapsed so quickly and thoroughly.

As in any war, terrain was also a key determinant: without air cover, an army in the desert is easy prey. Rommel learned that lesson fighting Montgomery in North Africa; the Israelis revalidated this principle in 1967 and again in 1973. Likewise, geography created a trap for the Iraqis—as it did for the Egyptians in 1973—permitting an envelopment of their entire army.

Thus, while all war are unique, they differ primarily in terms of what Clausewitz termed "the belligerents' dominant characteristics." In other words, while the combatants' strengths and vulnerabilities—and such factors as terrain, weather, and time available—are, indeed, situation-specific, the principle of negating an opponent's will to resist by leveraging strengths and exploiting vulnerabilities is universal. To quote Liddell Hart, again, "The principles of war can be condensed into a single word—'concentration.' But, for truth, this needs to be amplified as the 'concentration of strength against weakness.'"[34]

ANATOMY OF DEFEAT

The amazingly quick Allied success left Saddam defeated and humiliated, although still in power. Politically, he failed to mobilize the Arab world by turning the masses against their rulers, to say nothing of the Islamic world. Several factors accounted for this failure. First, the heterogeneity of the Arab and Islamic worlds was simply not conducive to an easy transnational rallying of the masses. Second, Saddam's ambitions to lead the Arab world collided with the interests of both Syria and Egypt and thereby underscored the historical tripolar rivalry among Cairo, Damascus, and Baghdad. Third, Saddam's own well-known behavioral excesses—ruthless violence, opposition to a role for religion in politics (antithetical to Islamic philosophy), recent conflicts with his neighbors (consistently with Syria and with Egypt until the war with Iran)—were well known on the Arab street.[35] And, fourth, key Arab leaders—as well as the Iranians—effectively exploited these shortcomings in their own propaganda, thus preventing any groundswell of support. In the final analysis, the places where Saddam did get popular support, such as Yemen, Algeria, Morocco, Tunisia, Jordan, and the West Bank, were either marginal or too far removed from the conflict. Emotionally charged demonstrations were never translated into physical power (military or economic) that could be put at Iraq's disposal; eventually, they lost their momentum. Other parts of the Arab and Islamic world were either passively sympathetic to Saddam or overtly opposed to Baghdad.

Whatever hopes Saddam had for overcoming this situation rested on prolonging the conflict, inflicting sizable casualties on the coalition, and achieving some local successes that could be embellished as great victories. However remote, the possibility that Saddam might somehow emerge as politically victorious from the ashes of military defeat— much as Nasser did in 1956—was demolished by the stupendous incompetence of Saddam as both a military commander and strategist.

Iraq's stated objectives of protracting the war and maximizing enemy casualties dictated a strategy of attrition. Incantations about "the Mother of all battles" aside, Iraq simply lacked the wherewithal to pursue a strategy of annihilation. Thus, while the quick buildup of Allied forces had effectively rendered any notion of seizing Saudi Arabia as sheer madness, Saddam still had several options at his disposal. He could have attempted to disrupt Allied preparations and inflict losses through spoiling attacks along the border, commando raids, or air strikes against staging areas. More boldly, he could have attempted to seize the initiative through preemption,[36] with the hope that a limited initial success would produce a favorable political outcome (like the Egyptian and Syrian attack in 1973). Having failed to seize the advantage inherent in striking first, Saddam still could have tried to hinder the ground offensive by employing chemical weapons. Similarly, although his forces were badly mauled by the time the ground war began, he could have still ordered a single massive air and missile strike against Allied forces in the Kuwaiti Theater of Operations (KTO) or in their rear staging areas. The objective of such a suicidal strike would have been similar to the one pursued by the Vietnamese in their 1968 Tet offensive: to shatter the U.S. will to fight—in Washington as well as on the battlefield (CENTCOM was in fact concerned that an "Air Tet" might occur).[37]

As things turned out, Saddam chose the worst course of all—prolonged indecisiveness, which subjected his forces to piecemeal destruction. The only exceptions were the SCUD attacks against Israel and Saudi Arabia and the limited thrust against Khafji on January 29. Despite their negligible military impact, both the SCUD attacks and Khafji benefited from instant worldwide coverage by the media and their effects were thereby magnified. This suggests the very real possibility that a more aggressive use of Iraqi forces might have, in fact, had a major psychological impact favorable to Baghdad. Yet, Saddam failed to seize whatever opportunities there were to operationalize his strategy and exploit his considerable military capability. As a result, the Iraqi military remained paralyzed, with the paralysis quickly becoming rigor mortis.

Iraq's dismal military performance was fatal for its overall grand strategy because any lasting success it might have gained as a result of its diplomatic and informational campaigns ultimately depended on at least a modicum of military success. (The embargo and blockade prevented any meaningful use of the economic instrument during the war.) The total military collapse rendered the much-heralded "Mother of all battles" an object of ridicule in the Arab world and Iraq itself. As for the other instruments of statecraft, Iraqi officials and diplomats did turn out some impressive and polished defenses of their policies. Indeed, many ambassadors and spokesmen came across as urbane and sophisticated in media performances. The problem was that, in the eyes of most of the world, they were defending the indefensible. As President Bush aptly commented in acknowledging Tariq Aziz's impressive performance in his Geneva meeting with Secretary of State James Baker, "he had a bad brief."

On a more specific note, one can question Iraq's early decision to allow the international media, especially CNN, to cover events. While it was clearly in Iraq's interest to portray Allied bombing as indiscriminate and inhumane, initial first-hand reports of precision-guided munitions scoring surgical strikes with little collateral damage left a lasting image, to be subsequently reinforced by Allied film footage. As a result, belated Iraqi informational efforts to garner world sympathy for the "innocent victims" of wholesale destruction came across as disingenuous and crude—the "baby milk factory" being the prime example.[38]

The systematic failure of every single aspect of Iraq's strategy was so thorough that any attempt to orchestrate the instruments of statecraft into a coherent whole—and thereby create the synergy that is the heart and soul of a sound grand strategy—only compounded the disaster. A striking example was Baghdad's behavior at the end of the war, when Iraqi troops ignited Kuwaiti oil fields and increased the repression in Kuwait at precisely the time its diplomats sought to negotiate a cease-fire on favorable terms. Specifically, Baghdad conveyed through the Soviets its readiness to withdraw, provided UN Security Council Resolutions—including 674 and 686—on postwar reparations were dropped. The glaring gap between these diplomatic efforts to minimize Iraq's liability and terrorism against both Kuwaiti civilians and the environment—which only stiffened the world's demands for punishing reparations for damages—was symptomatic of the total absence of coherent thinking on the level of grand strategy.

Yet, Iraq's overall failure and the coalition's success by no means meant that challenges and threats to longer-term U.S. interests and regional goals had been eliminated. To the contrary, several serious problems, some rooted in the way the war was terminated, quickly asserted themselves.

War Termination

The ultimate goal of war is to secure a better peace or, at least, to rectify the conditions that led to the war in the first place. In the final account, therefore, all wars are judged in terms of their political consequences—intended and otherwise.

Before attempting to apply the judgment-by-results criterion to the Gulf War, three caveats are in order. First, our perspective is necessarily limited by the relatively short time that has elapsed since the March 1991 cease-fire agreement. Processes triggered off by the trauma of war are often slow to manifest themselves; the aftershocks might be delayed for some time. Thus, while the general contours of the postwar landscape are already apparent, the final structure remains in flux, complicating both analysis and decision-making.

Second, contrary to popular expectations, the political consequences of war are often less clear-cut than the outcomes achieved on the battlefield. While the resultant ambiguity is frustrating, it is, nonetheless, an integral part of the context within which grand strategy evolves. As such, this ambiguity must also remain a part of our analysis.

Third, the very nature of war creates high hopes for the subsequent peace. War is expected to transform traditional behavior patterns and remedy, once and for all, problems that often have been allowed to fester for years. The postwar settlement is thus expected not only to justify all the sacrifices incurred during the war but also to measure up to a millennial vision of peace. Since the expectations usually far exceed what is realistically attainable—even under optimal circumstances—the aftermath of war often reflects the letdown born of dashed hopes. Wishful thinking, however, is not a relevant measure of merit. Rather, the proper context for appraising what has been achieved and what remains to be done is defined by the goals for which the nation went to war in the first place.

With these caveats in mind, the analysis that follows attempts to set a framework for a precise, sober interpretation of the immediate and longer-term consequences of the Gulf War. We start with a balance sheet of costs and benefits.

The key political objectives of ejecting the Iraqi army from Kuwait and restoring the legitimate government to Kuwait City were accomplished quickly and with remarkably low coalition casualties. Iraq's deployed military might has been shattered, and its war-making potential—indeed, key components of industrial infrastructure—lie in ruins.

The cease-fire terms imposed on Baghdad are among the most severe in history. Stringent economic sanctions remain in effect, dooming the country to continued poverty and impeding internal restoration. Baghdad is not even allowed to export its abundant oil, except under the terms imposed by Security Council resolutions. Specifically, Iraq can export only $1.6 billion worth of oil, provided the sale is supervised by the United Nations and the money paid into an escrow account. After deductions for war reparations, the balance would be used to defray the cost of destroying Iraq's weapons of mass destruction and to buy food and humanitarian supplies for distribution under international supervision.[39]

Furthermore, UN resolutions open Iraq's territory to unprecedented intrusive inspections, with the goal of ferreting out and destroying its nuclear, biological, and chemical (NBC) weapons programs. Overall, the cease-fire terms—backed by both international suasion and U.S. military muscle—effectively deprive Iraq of its sovereignty. Thus, Baghdad is not only isolated and ostracized but completely vulnerable to whatever punishment the coalition might choose to mete out.

Yet the Gulf War failed to rectify the key factor that led to the war in the first place, namely, Saddam Hussein's aggressive behavior. Eight months after one of the most spectacular routs in history, the Iraqi leader is not only alive and well but confident enough to try to try to defy the cease-fire terms imposed on him by the coalition. Indeed, at this writing, military force is being considered once again as a means of ensuring Iraqi compliance with Security Council resolutions.

Furthermore, Iraq was allowed to limp from the battlefield with sufficient military power—Republican Guard divisions, armor, missiles and helicopters—to defeat (at least temporarily) internal threats to the regime and shore up Saddam's grip on power. Indeed, after the cease-fire agreement was signed, it took the coalition's armed intervention and admonishments to save the Kurds and the Shiites from slaughter by the Iraqi army.

Whether this residual force is cohesive enough to serve as a nucleus for reconstituting a credible offensive threat to the region is, as yet, unclear. If the past is a guide, Iraq might prove more resilient and less susceptible to war weariness than generally expected—as was the case after the Iran-Iraq War. And, while any near-term external aggression would be unsustainable and, thus, suicidal, the threat both to Iraq's neighbors and to Israel cannot be dismissed out of hand.

Most ominously, the scope and nature of Iraq's nuclear, chemical, and biological weapons program was grossly underestimated.[40] As a result, a key military objective of Desert Storm—to "destroy Iraq's *known* NBC potential"—has not been fully achieved. Since by definition it is impossible to target unknown facilities, the task of identifying, locating, and destroying what remains of Iraq's arsenal has been left to international inspection teams. Given established patterns of Iraqi subterfuge—and the obvious inadequacy of both international control regimes and Western intelligence collection—Iraq might be able to retain some residual NBC capability, or even to resume covertly its aggressive acquisition program. (Undoubtedly, Iraq would need outside assistance to resume its armament program. In this context, its relations with such known proliferators as Brazil, Germany, China, and North Korea bear watching. Similarly, the potential for uncontrolled proliferation from a disintegrating Soviet Union—perhaps to include migration of weapons experts like the German rocket scientists—is a clear danger.) Thus, the specter of a nuclear Iraq remains a remote but not inconceivable possibility.

This appraisal begs two related questions. Was the war terminated too soon? And was it realistically possible to achieve a more satisfactory outcome within the a priori circumscribed goals of a limited war? While necessarily speculative, the following points are germane to the answer.

First, extending the ground war for another twenty-four to forty-eight hours could have broken the back of the Republican Guard—the true mainstay of Saddam Hussein's regime and the closest contemporary equivalent of the Waffen SS. In hindsight at least, allowing several Republican Guard divisions to escape intact appears as a clear case of misplaced kindness, particularly in light of their subsequent savage actions against the Shiites in the south and the Kurds in the north.[41]

Second, the dichotomy drawn by some analysts between a "hundred-hour war" and "marching to Baghdad" is artificial and misleading. The latter clearly was not—and probably could not have been—a coalition objective. By the same token, however, there is nothing magical about the hundred-hour limit—besides the obvious public relations effect. Thus, continuing the ground war for another couple of days in order to neutralize the Republican Guard would have been fully in line with the overarching goal of quick and decisive victory.

Third, there appears to be a clear disjunction between U.S. public appeals to the Iraqi people to topple Saddam and the decision to terminate the war at the hundred-hour point, with the resultant escape of the Republican Guard. While the appeals implied U.S. support for an uprising, the decision to terminate the war early effectively doomed it from the start. The subsequent decision to allow Iraq to fly helicopters—thus gaining a significant mobility and firepower advantage over the Shiites and Kurds—was extremely damaging to the opposition.[42]

This dissonance in the orchestration of U.S. policy reflects the basic dilemma faced by the Bush administration: its ardent desire to get rid of Saddam Hussein was not shared by all coalition partners, and, worse, it appeared at odds with the long-standing U.S. goal of regional stability. Consequently, the change of regime in Baghdad was never stipulated as a war objective, although it clearly remained a desired outcome.

Thus, the Bush administration was left with a limited range of options, each perceived as holding more peril than promise. Barring Saddam's fortuitous death, and given both his exceptionally effective internal security apparatus and the U.S. prohibition on assassinations, the only mechanism for change was an internal revolt. Insurrections, however, are notoriously unpredictable and difficult to manage. Fomenting and sustaining an insurgency is a long-term, risky venture, particularly for an out-of-area power, with limited ties to and influence over the insurgents.

This universal problem was compounded by circumstances peculiar to Iraq. First, the Kurds and Shiites appeared to lack the organization, unity, and power deemed necessary to topple a weakened but still entrenched dictatorship. This, in turn, conjured up the prospect of a protracted, tumultuous civil war or, worse, dismemberment of Iraq by its regional enemies. Furthermore, given the Shiites' ties to Teheran and the Kurds' linkage with irredentist elements in Turkey and the USSR, a successful uprising threatened to alter the regional balance of power fundamentally, along lines detrimental to U.S. interests.

Daunting as these worst-case projections might have appeared, an equally compelling argument could have been made that, sometimes, poorly organized, ill-equipped insurgents do succeed in defeating an incumbent regime, particularly in the context of military disintegration, economic hardship, and political repression—as was the case in Afghanistan and Ethiopia.

Thus, without both the Republican Guard and air power, the Iraqi army would have been vulnerable to guerrilla attacks that would gradually sap its morale, while sanctions would lead to further economic deterioration and, consequently, growing repression by Saddam's police. As the regime unraveled, the United States could have precluded Turkish and Iranian intervention through diplomacy and, in the case of Iran, threats of punishment, if necessary. Furthermore, it could have been argued that it is fatuous to assume that the Iraqi Shiites would welcome the assertion of control by Teheran, given the historical Arab resistance to Persians (underscored in the Iran-Iraq War). What's more, since the Shiites were divided into many groups, not all of which sympathized with Iran, those groups not closely associated with Teheran might have had little interest in Iranian overlordship.[43]

Faced with the uncertainties inherent in both options, the United States stood aside, effectively allowing Saddam to quell the internal threat to his regime. The unintended—but predictable—consequence of this policy was Saddam's ability to consolidate his grip on power, thus making the prospect of systemic change proportionately less viable.

This assessment of war termination leads to several broadly applicable conclusions. First, as the preceding analysis shows, the decision as to when and how to end a war is at least as difficult—and as momentous—as the initial decision to go to war.

Second, the final outcome of war depends on a wide range of factors, many of them elusive and, thus, difficult to predict, assess, or control. War termination, therefore, is almost always based on "soft" estimates, with ample opportunity for error, deception, and self-delusion.

Third, unless the goal of the war is total annihilation of the opponent and subjugation of his country, it is inherently difficult to determine where and when to cease hostilities. There are no hard and fast rules by which to measure just how much violence is required to produce the desired results. And, as the experience of Desert Storm clearly demonstrates, it is far easier to compel an opponent to sue for peace than to modify his behavior in the aftermath. Thus, the fog of war thickens at war's termination, exacerbating the effort to translate battlefield victories into political realities.

Lingering Issues

In this concluding section, we assess the impact of the Gulf War on four broad issues of enduring importance for U.S. interests and goals in the region: economic maldistribution, political participation, arms proliferation, and the Arab-Israeli conflict.

During the war, the great disparity in wealth between the Arab oil producers in the Gulf and Arab governments elsewhere in the region was frequently cited as a destabilizing force, the notion being that growing numbers of poor, young people in places like Egypt, Algeria, and elsewhere would eventually resort to violence out of frustration and despair with their prolonged deprivations. In this context, major infusions of assistance from the wealthy Gulf regimes were deemed necessary to prevent such violence from erupting and spreading throughout the region. Despite this line of reasoning, however, the heightened attention the redistribution issue received during the crisis faded rather quickly once the guns fell silent. Other than a postwar payoff to Syria in the neighborhood of $2 billion—most of which was used to buy new arms rather than for economic development—

there was neither a sense of urgency nor an inclination to devise a major scheme for the transferal of wealth.

Several factors account for this inaction. First, oil producers, such as Saudi Arabia and Kuwait, had to cope with considerable postwar debts and reconstruction costs of their own. Second, there was and remains a deeply felt bitterness toward Arab governments that procrastinated or supported Saddam Hussein, such as Jordan's. Third, it was not at all clear that restive populations as far away as the Maghreb really posed much of a threat to the oil producers. And, fourth, the infusion of money in the absence of basic psychological and structural changes in the economic sectors of the poor states made aid appear more wasteful than constructive. Accordingly, it is hard to escape the conclusion that the war had little impact on the maldistribution issue. What we will most likely see in the near future is a gradual restoration of the prewar practice of providing bilateral assistance (sometimes covertly) to specific governments considered important for security reasons (such as Syria and Egypt), rather than a grand regional scheme for shifting wealth from the haves to the have-nots.

The question of political participation was also brought to the forefront during the war. Thus, both opposition groups and intellectuals in the Arab world (notably in the Kuwaiti exile community) and Western commentators were quick to argue that, in a new postwar era, nascent demands for democracy would have to be accommodated in the interests of stability. Here again, however, reality proved to be more complex than some advocates of democracy had anticipated. Specifically, several key questions went unanswered: what exactly does participation mean (one man, one vote or a gradual widening of traditional consultative mechanisms to include new people); how many support which version of participation; how intense are their commitments; and how well organized are they? Further complicating matters are concerns that democratization might lead to religious or sectarian strife (as in Yugoslavia and the Soviet Union) and uncertainties regarding the ultimate role of many Islamic extremists who, ironically, are pursuing authoritarian long-term aims (Islamic republics) through emergent quasi-pluralistic political processes in places like Algeria and Jordan. While some believe participation would tame and control the extremists, others warn that experiences elsewhere (e.g., the Weimar republic) and the centuries-old, authoritarian political cultures in the Middle East do not augur well for the future.

In our view, prudent expectations suggest that while limited experiments in pluralist politics—such as Egypt's—will occur, they will be very precarious, especially where there are chronic underlying socio-economic problems, as in Egypt, Jordan, and Algeria. In the Gulf, such experiments will be resisted, and if they are tried they will be circumscribed. What's more, if participation is widened, the main beneficiaries may well be Islamic fundamentalists rather than supporters of Western-style democracy. In view of these uncertainties, it should come as no surprise that the Gulf War's effect on this issue was minimal rather than catalytic.[44]

In contrast, the alarming prospect of an Iraqi nuclear and thermonuclear weapons capability—more advanced and comprehensive than previously assessed—provided a tremendous impetus for regional arms control. As noted in the preceding section, the most immediate concern following the war has been an international effort to eliminate Baghdad's chemical, biological, nuclear, and missile capability. Beyond that, revelations of the role that outsiders, including Western arms merchants, played in building Iraq's arsenal have generated the requirement for a wider, more enforceable arms control regime throughout the Middle East. Precisely what it will consist of, however, is as yet unclear. Efforts to reach agreements among suppliers to limit the types and volume of weaponry are likely to be undermined, at least in the short term, by internal political and economic pressures, as well as by Allied demands for "essential" assistance for defense (e.g., Saudi and Israeli requests to the United States). If anything, the Gulf War has reinforced, rather than undercut, the demand for high-tech weaponry, particularly for those systems that became the instruments of U.S. victory.[45]

Whether the sensitivity to the need for arms control, created by the war, would prove beneficial in the longer term remains to be seen. To succeed, arms control expectations must be realistic and achievable. In the Gulf, explicit U.S. security guarantees, like the September 1991 agreement with Kuwait, may be required in return for clients eschewing certain types of weaponry. In the Arab-Israeli arena, a general understanding regarding the nature of the overall military balance of power must be established. The first order of business will be to preclude the spread of weapons of mass destruction, especially nuclear weapons. This will not be easy as Israel is unlikely to yield its nuclear superiority—its call for a nuclear-free Middle East notwithstanding—as long as Arab states maintain an aggregate quantitative advantage in men and conventional arms. In this context, it is important to note that in the Middle East—in obvious contrast to Europe and the U.S.-Soviet arena—war is still considered a viable instrument of policy. This critical but often overlooked fact does not bode well for attempts to apply the lessons learned from previous successes with arms control to the Middle East.

Consequently, in our judgment, the best one may hope for in the 1990s is continuation of the existing asymmetrical military balance, marked by Arab quantitative conventional superiority, offset by Israel's qualitative advantage that rests, in a major way, on its undeclared nuclear capability. Once that is accepted, such issues as limits on particular weaponry, demilitarized and limited forces zones, prior notification of military exercises, joint patrols, and other confidence-building measures may be addressed. How profound and expeditious the progress will be hinges, in large measure, on the overall tenor of Arab-Israeli relations.

The war clearly created the perception that a new opportunity for progress on the Arab-Israeli question was possible, given the enhanced prestige of the United States, a slightly more forthcoming attitude on Syria's part, and a further diminution of the Palestine Liberation Organization's influence. Yet, while this perception has galvanized energetic diplomatic efforts to arrange a peace conference, it would be a delusion to conclude that such a conference would be anything more than one step in the proverbial "journey of a thousand miles." The war did not remove any of the enduring impediments to an Arab-Israeli settlement, not the least of which is the de facto veto power that maximalists have exerted—the Likud on the Israeli side and Arab radicals dedicated to nothing less than the destruction of Israel—whether through political or violent means.[46] This is not to suggest that the effort to arrange a peace conference is unworthy. In light of regional and international hopes and expectations, failure to exploit the opportunity would be politically unforgivable. But, given the historic record, to expect too much too soon would be intellectually untenable.

The preceding analysis leads to the conclusion that the military and political success of Desert Storm did not usher in a new order in the Middle East. Thus, it did little to facilitate a timely resolution of the enduring, complex problems of economic distribution, political participation, arms control, and the Arab-Israeli conflict. While it is true that the Gulf War enhanced the prestige of the United States as the sole remaining superpower and, thereby, opened a window of opportunity for a comprehensive addressing of these macro issues—especially the Arab-Israeli problem—the actualization of this potential is bound to be a protracted and difficult process. As time goes by, this process will have less to do with the amazing events of 1990–91 than with the domestic and regional exigencies of the moment.

Notes

1. For a well-informed account of recent Soviet policy in the Middle East, see Robert O. Freedman, *Moscow and the Middle East* (Cambridge: Cambridge University Press, 1991).

2. For succinct precrisis assessments of petroleum dependency and the Middle East, see G. Henry M. Schuler, "A Petroleum Forecast: The Impact on U.S.-Arab Relations in the Coming Years," *American-Arab Affairs* (Winter 1986–87): 83–87, and James Schlesinger, "Oil and Power in the Nineties," *The National Interest* (Spring 1990): 111–15. For a quick postwar assessment, see Matthew L. Wald, "Gulf Victory: An Energy Defeat," *New York Times*, June 18, 1991.

3. Whatever the differences among U.S. administrations during the cold war, they all ascribed great importance to the goal of maintaining a favorable balance of international power. See John Lewis Gaddis, *Strategies of Containment* (Oxford: Oxford University Press, 1982). The flavor of the debate over the decline of U.S. power may be captured quickly by looking at Paul Kennedy, "The (Relative) Decline of America," *The Atlantic*, August 1987, pp. 29–38, and Samuel P. Huntington, "The U.S.—Decline or Renewal," *Foreign Affairs* (Winter 1988–89): 76–96.

4. For example, Israel's hard-line policies since 1977 were heavily influenced by the ideological mind-set of the Likud leadership and coalition politics that enabled small, right-wing parties to threaten the breakup of the government in the event of undue concessions to the Arabs. Syria's minority Alawite regime, meanwhile, was also wary of concessions, lest the majority Sunni community portray them as betrayal.

5. Perhaps the clearest manifestation of this growing frustration was Secretary Baker's statement that Israel should give him a call when it is ready for peace.

6. Saddam's warning, delivered to members of the military establishment, was less ominous than reported in the media. Basically, it was a statement of deterrence, not a threat to carry out an unprovoked attack. See the full text in Baghdad Domestic Service, April 2, 1990, in *Foreign Broadcast Information Service-Near East/South Asia* (hereafter *FBIS-NESA*), April 3, 1990, pp. 32–36, especially p. 35.

7. Officials repeated the conspiracy theory ad nauseam throughout the crisis, and it was embellished by Iraqi propagandists. For an early but crude example, see Salah al-Mukhtar, "Why Hostility Towards the Arabs," *Al-Watan Al-Arabi* (Paris), April 27, 1990, in *Joint Publications Research Service–Near East and Asia* (hereafter *JPRS-NEA*), June 29, 1990, p. 19. Not surprisingly, the Arab summit, convened after Iraq's invasion, was dismissed as part of the conspiracy because of its rejection of Iraq's action. See the account of Tariq Aziz's news conference by Baghdad INA, August 12, 1990 in *FBIS-NESA*, August 13, 1990, p. 50.

8. In a speech to an extraordinary Baghdad summit on May 30, 1990, Saddam characterized the oil pricing and production policies of certain Arab "brothers" as a kind of war against Iraq and said the Iraqis had reached a point where they could no longer withstand the pressure. Baghdad Domestic Service, July 18, 1990, in *FBIS-NESA*, July 19, 1990, p. 21.

9. Baghdad Domestic Service, July 17, 1990, in *FBIS-NESA*, July 17, 1990, p. 20. See also the text of Tariq Aziz's scathing criticism of and warnings to Kuwait in a memo to the Arab League in *Al-Dustur* (London), July 30, 1990, in *FBIS-NESA*, August 17, 1990, pp. 21–24.

10. The Iranians claim that a letter from Saddam to President Hashemi Rafsanjani revealed Iraqi intentions to seize Saudi Arabia and other parts of the Gulf and then divide the Gulf with Iran. See *Al-Sharq Al-Awsat* (London), January 28, 1991, in *FBIS-NESA*, February 6, 1991, p. 51. In both Washington and Riyadh, there was great concern about Iraqi intentions shortly after the invasion of Kuwait because they had the capability to invade eastern Saudi Arabia successfully. See Bob Woodward, *The Commanders* (New York: Simon and Schuster, 1991), pp. 263–78.

11. Critical assessments of U.S. policy prior to Iraq's invasion may be found in Paul A. Gigot, "A Great American Screw-Up," *The National Interest* (Winter 1990/91); Don Oberdorfer, "Missed Signals in the Middle East," *Washington Post Magazine*, March 17, 1991; Glen Frankel, "At War, Iraq Courted U.S. into Economic Embrace," *Washington Post*, September 16, 1990, and "How Saddam Built his War Machine," *Washington Post*, September 17, 1990; Leslie Gelb, "Mr. Bush's Fateful Blunder," *New York Times*, July 12, 1991.

12. President Bush's address to the nation on August 8, 1990, revealed an early commitment to use all instruments of statecraft. See "The Arabian Peninsula: U.S. Principles," *Current Policy* No. 1292 (Washington: U.S. Department of State, August 1990). On the objective of toppling Hussein via covert action, see Woodward, pp. 236–37, 282.

13. The effectiveness of propaganda regarding Saddam's ruthless violence was credible because of his well-known proclivity to murder real or imagined political opponents, the gassing of the Kurds after the Iran-Iraq War, his threats to incinerate Israel, and so on. For brief accounts, see *Ma'ariv* (Tel Aviv), April 6, 1990 in *FBIS-NESA*, June 8, 1990, pp. 26–27; Paul Gray, "The Man Behind the Demonic Image," *Time*, February 11, 1991, p. 36.

14. For a most comprehensive statement of the Iraqi case, see Tariq Aziz's explanation of the historical background in *Al-Thawrah* (Baghdad), September 9, 1990, in *FBIS-NESA*, September 12, 1990, p. 26.

15. During the crisis, the staff of Congressman Les Aspin produced excellent summations of the voluminous testimony and discussions in Congress regarding U.S. policy options. See, in particular, Les Aspin, "The Role of Sanctions in Securing U.S. Interests in the Gulf," House Committee on Armed Services, December 21, 1990, esp. p. 26.

16. Saddam told the UN secretary-general on January 13 that the Iraqis would not withdraw because it would be tantamount to victory by the enemy. Although he characterized the possibility of war as being a few hours away, he suggested Iraq was still willing to discuss a comprehensive deal. See the complete text of his meeting with the secretary-general in *Al-Dustur* (Amman), February 9, 1991, in *FBIS-NESA*, February 11, 1991, pp. 25–33, esp. p. 32. For an early assessment of Chadli Ben Jedid's discussions with Saddam and speculation concerning an Arab solution, see "The Diplomatic Round," *The New Yorker*, February 18, 1991, pp. 74–76. For a Soviet view of the lost opportunity for a negotiated settlement, see Yevgenii Primakov, "The War Which Might Not Have Been," *Pravda*, February 27, 28, March 1, 2, 1991, a four-part report by Moscow's chief envoy to Baghdad.

17. That the Iraqis followed the U.S. debate carefully and detected softness and wavering is clear from Iraqi commentaries. See, for example, *Al-Qadisiyah* (Baghdad), November 5, 1990, in *JPRS-NEA*, January 10, 1991, pp. 12–13.

18. In a January 6 speech, Saddam said the battle would not be fought only in its military dimension and that the battlefield would be the world at large. See Baghdad Domestic Service, January 7, 1991, in *FBIS-NESA*, January 9, 1991, p. 26.

19. In late 1989, the United States shifted the focus of its strategic planning to countering non-Soviet regional threats. In CENTCOM's area of responsibility, Iraq was specifically identified as a primary threat. Consequently, CENTCOM developed a concept plan detailing both the force levels and the strategy needed for the successful defense of Saudi Arabia. This plan, reviewed and set up as a war game in July 1990, provided a foundation on which to build specific deployment and employment plans. For further details, see *Conduct of the Persian Gulf Conflict, Interim Report to Congress* (hereafter *Interim Report*) (Washington, July 1991), p. 2-1.

20. Karl von Clausewitz, *On War*, ed. and trans. by Michael Howard and Peter Paret (Princeton, NJ: Princeton University Press, 1976), p. 77.

21. On the military and theater objectives, see Operations Order (OPORD) 91-001, January 17, 1991, quoted in *Interim Report*, pp. 1-1, 1-2, 2-3.

22. The thesis that desirable objectives must often be modified substantially in the context of coalitions is discussed by Robert Carswell, "Economic Sanctions and the Iran Experience," *Foreign Affairs* (Winter 1981–82): 264–65.

Historically, even such cohesive alliances as the anti-Hitler coalition of World War II were plagued by discord over goals and strategies.

23. *Interim Report*, pp. 15-1–15-5.

24. For an excellent analysis of the disjunctions between political goals and military strategy, see Harry G. Summers, Jr., *On Strategy: The Vietnam War in Context* (Carlisle Barracks, PA: U.S. Army War College, 1981).

25. During the period prior to Desert Storm, the media was replete with dire predictions by experts of high Allied casualties and Arab and Islamic worlds engulfed in political flames. Needless to say, neither occurred, nor did exaggerations of Iraqi military capabilities. A welcome departure was the exceptional commentary of the principal CNN military analyst, Maj. Gen. Perry Smith, who avoided immersion in details in favor of providing context and analysis, much of it grounded in his own long military experience. Not surprisingly, he proved to be the most prescient of the various military commentators. For a postwar account of those who fared less well, see Jacob Weisberg, "Gulfballs," *The New Republic*, March 25, 1991, pp. 17–19.

26. Summers, p. 11.

27. Sir Basil Liddell Hart, *Strategy*, 2d rev. ed. (New York: Praeger, 1968), p. 338.

28. The reference here is to a much earlier proponent of the indirect approach, the Chinese philosopher, Sun Tzu. See Sun Tzu, *The Art of War*, trans. Samuel B. Griffith (Oxford: Oxford University Press, 1963).

29. Liddell Hart, pp. 349–50.

30. Clausewitz, pp. 595–96.

31. Lt. Gen. John J. Yoesock, U.S. Army, interview with *Soldiers*, August 1991, pp. 28–29.

32. The best known work in this genre is Edward N. Luttwak, *The Pentagon and the Art of War* (New York: Simon and Schuster, 1984). See also Jeffrey Records, *Revising U.S. Military Strategy* (Washington: Pergamon-Brassey's, 1984).

33. This approach is encapsulated in the U.S. Army's Field Manual (FM) 100-5, Operation, published in May 1986, and in the Air Force's Basic Aerospace Doctrine (AFM 1-1), issued in March 1984 and revised in June 1991.

34. Liddell Hart, p. 3347. For a comprehensive Soviet assessment of the causes of Iraq's defeat, see Marshal of the Soviet Union Sergei Akhromeyev, "Why Baghdad Suffered a Defeat," *Novoe Vremia*, no. 1, March 1991, pp. 22–25. See also, Maj. Gen. G. Kirilenko, "Who was Defeated in Desert Storm: Saddam Hussein or Soviet Military Equipment?" *Komsomolskaia Pravda*, June 4, 1991.

35. Syria's long-standing acrimonious relationship with Iraq is rooted in personal hatreds and competition for dominant influence in the region, particularly over the key instrument for realizing hegemony—the "national command" of the Ba'ath party. The historical setting for current disputes is

the ancient rivalry between Damascus and Baghdad for power and control, dating back to the first great Islamic empires, the Umayyad and the Abbasid. More recent events that have intensified the rivalry include terrorist acts sponsored by each side against the other (often involving Abu Nidal) and Syrian interference with the flow of the Euphrates River. Ideological differences appear less significant and seem to be used as justification for hostile policies adopted due to other factors.

While there were reports of public sympathy for Iraq during the crisis, the Syrian regime's autocratic controls rendered internal opposition negligible. On Syria, see Tony Horwitz, "Many Syrians Believe Assad's on Wrong Side in Persian Gulf Crisis," *Wall Street Journal*, September 27, 1990.

Prior to its war with Iran, Iraq took a leading role in ostracizing and isolating Egypt because of Camp David. Although Egypt later supported Iraq during that war because of mutual fears related to the spread of militant fundamentalism, after the war the Iraqis treated Egyptian workers in Iraq harshly, refusing to pay them and, in several instances, killing those who protested. Despite later efforts by Mubarak to downplay the events, such treatment was well covered by the Egyptian media and was not forgotten. Accordingly, the general lack of sympathy for Saddam and the frequent references to his brutality that observers reported during the crisis were hardly surprising. On the ill treatment of Egyptian workers in Iraq, see the various reports in *Al-Wafd*, *Al-Ahram*, *Al-Akhbar*, and *MENA*, in *FBIS-NESA*, November 14, 1989, pp. 14–25, and Alan Cowell, "Egyptian Laborers Are Fleeing Iraq," *New York Times*, November 15, 1989. During the crisis, the Egyptian population generally backed Mubarak, despite pro-Iraqi sentiments among some Moslem fundamentalists and left-wing intellectuals.

36. The striking success of Desert Storm, especially the ground war, should not lull us into forgetting that Allied forces were extremely vulnerable during the buildup phase from August to December. While this vulnerability would not have resulted in a decisive Iraqi victory, it could have resulted in significant casualties and dramatic media stories to serve Saddam's limited aims. In particular, if he had some limited success early, he could lay claim to the status of warrior-hero, which is highly valued in the Arab political milieu. The term harkens back to the 1973 Arab-Israeli war where both Sadat and Assad were portrayed as heroes because of their early successes. Just as they explained away later reverses on the battlefield as having resulted from U.S. resupply of Israel, Saddam could explain eventual setbacks as the result of unfair odds (Iraq alone against the forces of thirty nations). After the war, Iraq did precisely that. But, without the backdrop of some early successes, it had little effect.

37. *Interim Report*, p. 2–7. For the psychological impact of the 1968 Tet offensive, see Summers, pp. 1–19.

38. Ironically, the building in question might have been a baby milk factory. However, the crude attempts to establish the point—Iraqis with English-

labeled jackets that said "Baby Milk Factory" and cardboard signs in English and Arabic—were received with derision, if not amusement, in the West, partly because of Saddam's earlier clumsy handling of the hostages that was broadcast worldwide. The image of unreliability established by Iraqi propagandists was simply too difficult to overcome. On this general point, see K.J. Holsti, *International Politics*, 5th ed. (Englewood Cliffs, NJ: Prentice Hall, 1988), p. 212.

39. *The Economist*, September 25, 1991.

40. UN inspections in the summer and fall of 1991 revealed a nuclear program that was far more ambitious, advanced, and deadly than originally thought. Current estimates indicate that Iraq was twelve to eighteen months away from producing a deliverable nuclear device. See Michael Wines, "U.S. Is Building up a Picture of Vast Iraqi Atom Program," *New York Times*, September 27, 1991; M. Gergely, "Warn and Threaten," *Profil* (Vienna), July 29, 1991 in *FBIS-NESA*, July 29, 1991, pp. 27–28; William J. Broad, "U.N. Says Iraq Was Building H-Bomb and Bigger A-Bomb," *New York Times*, October 15, 1991.

41. In the closing hours of the war, there was concern in both civilian and military circles over needless slaughter, "turkey-shoots," and the like. Ironically, the potential victims soon became the perpetrators of such attacks, albeit without any restraining rules of engagement or, indeed, without regard to basic human standards. That the Republican Guards would attack civilians with a sociopathic disregard, if ordered to do so, should have come as no surprise to analysts of Iraqi affairs.

42. The effectiveness of helicopters against guerrillas was clearly demonstrated in Afghanistan. Once Soviet helicopter gunships were effectively neutralized by the provision of Stinger and Redeye missiles to the Mujahadeen, the battlefield was transformed radically in the guerrilla's favor and attacks designed to wear down Soviet morale and staging power resumed. Similarly, we believe the neutralization of Iraqi combat and transport helicopters through their destruction in the air or on the ground would have seriously degraded the Iraqi military capability to deal with rebellious Kurds and Shiites. This, of course, does not mean it would have enabled the insurgents to defeat Iraqi forces in conventional engagements. Rather, it would have enhanced insurgent capabilities to wear down their opponents *gradually*.

43. With the partial exception of an excellent report on the Kurds by Alfred B. Prados, there has been little effort to analyze the insurgents in Iraq in a comprehensive and systematic manner. Instead, commentaries in the media and by experts have been fragmentary and impressionistic. Prados's incisive piece may be found in Congressional Research Service Report for Congress, *Kurdish Separatism in Iraq: Developments and Implications for the United States* (Washington: CRS, May 6, 1991). For an example of the kind of comprehensive framework that could be used for a broad, systematic analysis, see Bard E. O'Neill, *Insurgency and Terrorism* (New York: Brassey's, Inc., 1990).

44. For a sensible, straightforward, and balanced assessment of the democ-

ratization issue, see Michael C. Hudson, "After the War: Prospects for Democratization in the Arab World," *Middle East Journal* (Summer 1991): 407–26. For a variety of views that, in the aggregate, are not overly optimistic, see Louis J. Cantori et al., "Democratization in the Middle East," *American-Arab Affairs* (Spring 1991): 1–30.

45. For two thoughtful assessments of the prospects and complexities of arms control following the war, see Geoffrey Kemp, "The Middle East Arms Race: Can It Be Controlled?" *Middle East Journal* (Summer 1991): 441–56, and Janne E. Nolan, "The Global Arms Market after the Gulf War: Prospects for Control," *Washington Quarterly* (Summer 1991): 125–38. A striking example of the difficulty of reconciling security needs with arms control initiatives is Saudi Arabia's desire for huge infusions of weaponry and training from the United States in order to expand its army and acquire the capability to conduct large mobile ground operations. See Patrick E. Tyler, "Gulf Security Talks Stall over Plan for Saudi Army," *New York Times*, October 13, 1991.

46. Throughout 1991, the Likud-led Israeli government made it emphatically clear that it does not intend to trade land for peace or to end the construction of settlements in the territories. This policy was reversed when Labor came to power following the June 1992 elections. On the Arab side, meanwhile, left-wing rejectionists, such as the Popular Front for the Liberation of Palestine (Hawatmeh Wing), have agreed with the militant Islamic neo-rejectionists (Hamas and Islamic Jihad) in opposing participation in a peace conference. Even more troubling, the PFLP and Popular Front for the Liberation of Palestine—General Command have echoed the Islamic groups' call for a return to armed struggle.

Two
THE POLICY OF
EXTERNAL POWERS

2

U.S. POLICY TOWARD THE MIDDLE EAST AFTER IRAQ'S INVASION OF KUWAIT

Robert E. Hunter

When the United States awoke on the morning of August 2, 1990, to learn that Iraq had invaded Kuwait, it found itself in a new era in world history. For some time, U.S. citizens had understood intellectually that the cold war was over and that the United States was achieving a preeminence in global politics that it had never known before—save, perhaps, for a few fleeting moments at the end of World War II. But the shock of Saddam Hussein's aggression against his small neighbor was needed to begin turning the idea of a new era into reality.

The United States was taken by surprise on two levels. Most obvious was a patent miscalculation of Iraqi intentions. In retrospect, Saddam Hussein had made clear his ambitions toward Kuwait and had almost defied the world to do something to thwart them. And he had defined a larger strategic perspective that centered on the collapse of Soviet power, the emergence of the United States "in a superior position," and the risk that the "Arab Gulf region will be governed by U.S. will."[1] When the evidence of Saddam's intentions and the warnings of a few prescient individuals were analyzed, they formed a dismal commentary on the failure of the U.S. government to recognize the obvious.[2] Saddam Hussein, after all, was not supposed to invade Kuwait or take any other action hostile to Western interests. For nearly a decade, he had been a U.S.-chosen instrument in the region, first to prevent an Iranian victory in the war that Iraq had started, then to help obscure the domestic political blunder of the Reagan administration in secretly selling weapons to Iran, putatively in exchange for U.S. hostages held in Lebanon.

Such was the power of myth making, wishful thinking, and a U.S.-

Middle East policy gone wild over the years that Saddam Hussein could even lay down the gauntlet to the U.S. ambassador in Baghdad as late as a week before the invasion, without setting off alarm bells in Washington. The ambassador promptly went on vacation and thus was not on post when the war began.

At a broader level, the United States was taken by surprise by the changed circumstances of East-West relations. During the cold war, an action such as that taken by Saddam Hussein, who was to some degree a Soviet client, was not supposed to happen. By traditional practice, a crisis aborning would have been relatively quickly sorted out by the superpowers, its limits tacitly or explicitly agreed upon, and the offending rascal soon brought to heel. Even though both Washington and Moscow had taken risks in the region on more than one occasion, they had a healthy appreciation of what they could and could not get away with, while preserving their mutual interest, to prevent Middle East events from jeopardizing their broader relationship. Yet by mid-1990, the old rules no longer applied, and perhaps the first person to articulate the new reality was the Iraqi president, in a speech before the Arab Cooperation Council at Amman in February 1990.[3] On that occasion, he said that there was now only one superpower in the region—namely, the United States—and that someone had to counter its hegemonic ambitions in the Middle East.

On the morrow of Iraq's invasion, the United States had rapidly to come to terms both with its miscalculation about Iraq—indeed, with the weaknesses of its overall Persian Gulf strategy—and with the new dimensions of the post-cold war era. To his credit, President George Bush responded vigorously, if a bit uncertainly, during the first few days of the growing crisis. Saddam Hussein could be forgiven, in fact, if he were bewildered by both the alacrity and the strength of the U.S. response. Such a response was not to be expected—had he not recently been assured on this point by the U.S. ambassador to Iraq?—and thus it was doubly unwelcome, having deprived the Iraqi dictator of room to calculate his moves. Similarly, in 1950, Secretary of State Dean Acheson gave a speech that excluded the Korean peninsula from the U.S. security zone, only to have North Korea appear to take him at his word (or his inadvertence) and invade South Korea.

Desert Shield and Desert Storm

On August 6, President Bush ordered a U.S. military buildup in the Persian Gulf that was to reach the level of 500,000 U.S. men and women in the brief period of five and a half months, or about the level of U.S. deployments in Vietnam, which had been achieved over more than five and a half years. Desert Shield, as this buildup was called, was an unprecedented achievement in logistics, with a stunning flow of weaponry, personnel, equipment, and supplies sent a long way in a short period of time. The buildup was aided by the fact that there was no air or sea challenge from Iraq and that there was a ready availability of first-class bases in Saudi Arabia and in some of the smaller Persian Gulf states, but even with these advantages Desert Shield was an impressive feat.

The original declared U.S. strategy, however, was not to use military force to achieve the goal of forcing Iraq's retreat from Kuwait. The military buildup was aptly named: it was to be the shield, the protection for Saudi Arabia in particular, while the sword was to be economic sanctions, endorsed and put in place by the UN Security Council, beginning with Resolution 661 of August 6, the second of fourteen resolutions aimed at Iraq.[4]

Early on in the crisis, it also became clear in Washington that there was virtue in not going it alone in the Persian Gulf. Obviously, such a course was mandated by the decision to impose economic sanctions: their success required widespread cooperation that was secured and that led to modern history's most effective trade embargo against any country. But there were other reasons for the United States to seek cooperation that were not so obvious. The Soviet Union was clearly not going to pose the kind of challenge to U.S. unilateral actions that, prior to the radical internal and external changes set in train by President Mikhail S. Gorbachev, would have been second nature.

Desert Shield may have been represented as defensive, while the offense was composed of economic sanctions, but it did represent incipient conflict and was so understood by the U.S. public. The prospect of open conflict came under intense public scrutiny because of the size of the buildup and the sudden reversal of U.S. policy toward Iraq and because it came in the immediate aftermath of the cold war's end—which had been, in effect, a stunning victory for U.S. and Western policy sustained over more than four decades. Ironically, this scrutiny was applied to an operation whose risks, measured in terms of East-West relations, were far less than many other military activities undertaken by the United States during the cold war.

It rapidly became clear that U.S. popular support for administration policy was more likely to be forthcoming if the United States were joined by other states, especially close allies. What, in fact, was the United States trying to achieve? Or, put another way, if confrontation came to war, for what would the United States be fighting? The Bush administration cited several concerns, including oil, jobs at home, and even the American way of life, but all fell largely on deaf ears. In the post–cold war era, there was suddenly a reversion to an earlier style of popular expectation about U.S. war fighting: now it must be justified in terms of principle, not of realpolitik. But if a fight were truly needed to protect the flow of oil, military action could certainly be justified in terms of critical interests of the United States and its allies; in fact, following the arrival of the first U.S. forces in Saudi Arabia, the basic Western concern was that Iraq's unredressed aggression would give it a whip hand in the politics of oil, if not physical control over that vital Persian Gulf resource.

The Bush administration thus faced two basic requirements. The first was to offset a "democracy gap," the fact that the United States was clearly not acting to secure governments and peoples who fit in the Western camp—a point dramatically borne out by the failure of Kuwait after liberation to move rapidly in the direction of pluralism or democracy. The second was to gain support from traditional U.S. allies which had benefited from U.S. protection throughout the cold war and which, in fact, were far more dependent on Persian Gulf oil than was the United States. To be sure, oil is not fungible, and a threat to the oil supplies of Europe (one-third of whose oil on average comes from the Gulf) or of Japan (two-thirds) would have a devastating impact on the economy of the United States (even though it imports only about one-tenth of its oil from the region).

In the event, the United States gained direct military support in the Persian Gulf from Britain, France (which had not placed its forces under U.S. military command since World War II), and several other European allies. Their willingness to cooperate was facilitated by a critical development: the decision of the Soviet Union not to obstruct U.S. policy and, in the main, to support it—witness Moscow's affirmative votes on all UN Security Council resolutions as well as its general support, at critical times, for overall U.S. policy, despite occasional diplomatic maneuvering. Thus this was the first crisis played out beyond the traditional area covered by the North Atlantic Treaty Organization (NATO) during which the European allies of the U.S. did not have to calculate the potentially negative consequences for East-West détente in Europe if they were to follow the U.S. lead. To underscore this point Secretary of State James A. Baker stopped in Moscow on August 3 and joined Foreign Minister Eduard Shevardnadze in condemning the invasion, and President Bush elicited a declaration of support from President Gorbachev at Helsinki on September 9. No doubt, the Soviets calculated that gaining access to the global economy was more important than pursuing classical regional ambitions, now paling in importance compared with the death throes of an empire. Germany and Japan, however, were constrained by historical memory and legal requirements and did not send combat forces to the Persian Gulf. Rather they acceded to U.S. requests for financial support. (Germany sent some forces to Turkey, within the formal NATO area, and Japan sent some non-combatants to the Gulf.) The aftershocks of this diplomacy are still being felt.

The U.S. forging of a coalition of states to address the crisis in the Persian Gulf also developed a further purpose. Saddam Hussein was not idle while the forces of Desert Shield were being assembled and the sanctions drawn more tightly. Among other things, he countered by attempting to portray himself as the victim of the "imperialists and Zionists," a line he pursued throughout the crisis. Saddam's charges that the crisis was linked to Jerusalem and the Palestinian problem, to the maldistribution of oil resources within the Arab world, and to the presence of Western military forces in Saudi Arabia—the land of the Prophet—found receptive ears in much of the Arab and Islamic worlds. The U.S. countered by broadening the coalition to include several Arab states, four non-Arab Islamic states (Bangladesh, Pakistan, Senegal, and Niger), and other Third World states, for a total of more than thirty countries. The battle of ideas was thus joined, and through its deft diplomacy both bilaterally and at the United Nations the United States made a good showing for itself.

It was never clear how long the United States was prepared to persist with its basic strategy of military shield and economic sword—indeed, how long it could so persist. Debate in the United States was active and vigorous. Proponents of the sanctions strategy argued that a U.S.-sponsored war against an Arab state could lead to a major outpouring of anti-Western sentiment in the so-called Arab street; that the United States could find itself encumbered with a defeated Iraq that it could not hope to administer; that U.S. and other coalition casualties could be high; and that, in any event, sanctions of this unprecedented stringency could work if given time.

Proponents of going to war if Saddam Hussein did not rapidly relent argued principally that sanctions were unlikely to be effective in a reasonable period of time, if at all; that the coalition would inevitably weaken; and that the will of the people would soften as the months passed and a half million troops remained in the desert. Following the war, proponents also emphasized an argument that had had secondary importance beforehand: that it was necessary in order to deprive Saddam Hussein of the opportunity to complete a nuclear weapons program, which, they argued, could never have been stopped by sanctions alone.

A full, public, and widely watched debate in the U.S. Congress led to its endorsement of war, along with that of the UN Security Council. Failing to withdraw from Kuwait—indeed, even to pursue the option of disgorging part of the fruits of his aggression—Saddam Hussein thus brought war upon himself. It began in the early hours of January 16, 1991, soon after the expiration of the period set by the United Nations for the use of only nonmilitary means to force Iraqi compliance with its demands.

The U.S. strategy in the Persian Gulf War, code name Desert Storm, was relatively simple: to exploit vastly superior air power and high technology until Iraq's capacity to resist militarily was severely damaged and only then to expel Iraqi forces from Kuwait physically. In fact, the United States pursued three objectives in the following rough order of priority: to cripple Iraq's future capacity to make war with either conventional arms or weapons of mass destruction; to limit coalition casualties; and to liberate Kuwait. It also had a fourth, undeclared objective of removing Saddam Hussein from power, but it did not elevate this objective to the point of wishing to occupy Iraq. By some calculations—erroneous, as events turned out—the Iraqi dictator's military defeat would inevitably provoke his overthrow by domestic opponents.

The Aftermath

The ground war ended on February 28 with the U.S.-led coalition forces occupying about one-quarter of Iraq and having liberated Kuwait. Afterwards, there was debate about whether the war was halted too soon, especially before the Iraqi Republican Guards had been destroyed. These arguments, however, ignored the potential penalties of U.S. occupation of the entire country, the risks of higher casualties, and the splintering of the coalition if the initial declared and agreed-upon war aims were exceeded. Events that occurred soon after the war's end were more controversial. President Bush had called upon the people of Iraq to revolt against their leader, but when Shi'ites in the south and Kurds in the north did so—representing most of Iraq's population—the United States stood by while Saddam Hussein's forces decimated them. This U.S. policy was adopted in large part at the suggestion of Saudi Arabia, which feared that gains for the Shi'ites would either stir up its own Shi'ite population in the oil-rich Eastern Province or play into the hands of Iran (which in fact provided little or no help to its fellow Shi'ites in Iraq) and in part at the suggestion of Turkey, which feared the impact on its own Kurdish population. Ankara reversed its stance, however, when it became clear that the problem could not be contained, and the United States then sponsored an unprecedented UN-sanctioned mission, Operation Provide Comfort, to protect the Iraqi Kurds for a time against Baghdad.

Saddam Hussein remained in power, however. This became a problem for the Bush administration because of the president's characterization of Saddam Hussein as a Hitler and his pledge that sanctions against Iraq would remain in place so long as the dictator remained in power. In major part, this characterization of Saddam reflected a U.S. tactic to build popular support for Desert Shield and Desert Storm, and, having focused on the role of the Iraqi president, the administration was stuck with its symbol. The dilemma of what to do about Iraq remained unresolved by the end of 1992 and will no doubt complicate U.S. calculations of a viable strategy for the region in the future.

On March 6, 1991, President Bush spoke to a joint session of Congress and presented his postwar strategy for the Middle East.[5] It included U.S. support for regional security efforts—which has come to mean a particular focus on the Gulf Cooperation Council (GCC);[6] some joint military exercises; a continuing U.S. naval presence in the region; a concerted effort "to control the proliferation of weapons of mass destruction and the missiles used to deliver them"; progress in Arab-Israeli peacemaking; and regional economic development. On the last, Secretary Baker proposed a Middle East Development Bank but did not pursue the subject.[7]

Notably, the president was silent on the issue of constraining the flow of conventional weapons to the region; indeed, a new arms buildup began immediately after the war, fueled by recognition of vulnerability plus admiration for the performance of U.S. weaponry. In May 1991, the five permanent powers of the UN Security Council met in Paris to consider the problem, and in December the permanent

members of the UN Security Council approved the creation of a register of worldwide arms transfers.[8] But a U.S.-led policy of permissive-
ness had already guaranteed that, following the collapse of confrontation in Central Europe, the Middle East would remain the most
heavily armed region on earth. Indeed, the United States has been un-
stinting in its arms sales to the region. With the possibility of major
regime changes during the next few years, at least in part as a delayed
reaction to the Persian Gulf War, this lack of U.S. attention to a central aspect of the long-term security structure of the region could be
laying the groundwork for future conflicts.

The Bush administration put far more emphasis on limiting weapons of mass destruction. This was in part a corrective to the failure by
the Reagan administration during the 1980s to respond adequately to
Iraq's use of poison gas against Iran and its own Kurdish population;
in part it was also a reaction to Iraq's use of SCUD missiles against Israel, Saudi Arabia, and U.S. forces during the Persian Gulf War. Thus
under UN mandate, international inspectors carried out a number of
missions to locate and destroy Iraqi facilities for developing and producing chemical, biological, and nuclear weapons as well as ballistic
missiles. Not coincidentally, this emphasis on destroying weapons of
mass destruction, where there is broad international agreement, provided the political basis for sustaining sanctions against Iraq and thus
postponing a day of reckoning for the United States: how to maintain
international support for a policy of keeping sanctions in place as a
means solely of forcing Saddam Hussein from power.

Also absent from declared U.S. policy was recognition of the role
of Iran. In the midst of the war, President Bush did dismiss criticism
of Iranian peace efforts and acknowledge Tehran's positive role during
the crisis and war;[9] indeed, Iran had done virtually everything the
United States had wanted. Nevertheless, it continued to be difficult
for a U.S. administration to hold out the possibility of improved relations, especially against the background of Iran's earlier role in terrorism and hostage-taking, the unresolved hostage crisis in Lebanon, the
competing goals of some U.S. regional partners, and the political memories of the Iran-Contra affair during the Reagan administration. In
December 1991, Iran helped to facilitate the release of the last of the
U.S. hostages, but this aid was not met with a forthcoming U.S. response. Furthermore, the United States was championing Turkey's
role in the six newly independent Moslem republics of the former Soviet Union, hoping thereby to forestall Iranian influence. There was

merit in emphasizing the so-called Turkish model over that of Iran, but there are also long-range risks in encouraging Turkish nationalist ambitions at the expense of the legitimate interests of Iran and of other regional countries. It is a policy that cannot be sustained or at least that could impose major costs and increase the chances of regional turmoil.

In general, a year after Desert Storm, the United States had still not sorted out its long-term security policies toward the Persian Gulf region.[10] The United States voiced support for the GCC, indicated that it would retain some force presence in the region, that it was selling arms to regional countries, and that it was still seeking to contain Iraq. But it had not come to terms with reality: both Iraq and Iran are regional states whose interests must be dealt with. The goal of deposing Saddam Hussein begs the question of what could follow. Some form of pluralism—democracy adapted to regional circumstances—is desirable, but in the short term it could lead to the breakup of Iraq, with unforeseen consequences. The original U.S. hope—that Iraq could be ruled by a military regime without Saddam Hussein—is likely beyond the U.S. ability to engineer, and it is not clear that, from the perspective of regional states, this outcome would be much better than Saddam's rule.

Long-term stability in the region will also require that the United States overcome its reluctance to improve relations with Iran—a goal actually enunciated by President Bush beginning with his 1989 inaugural address. This goal could become possible on the Iranian side with the consolidation of President Ali Akbar Hashemi Rafsanjani's hold on power. Clearly, for long-term stability in the region, Iran's playing a constructive role is essential, and the United States and other Western states have an opportunity to influence its behavior, in part by facilitating its reconstruction after a decade of conflict.

The Arab-Israeli Conflict

U.S. preoccupation with the Persian Gulf during the latter half of 1990 and the first part of 1991 did not mean that it had lost interest in the Arab-Israeli conflict. Indeed, this part of the Middle East was the central focus of the Bush administration's regional policy during 1989–90. The new administration had to address two new basic elements: the continuing Intifada, or uprising, of Palestinians in the West Bank and Gaza, and the declaration by the Palestine Liberation

Organization in December 1988 that it was meeting the three U.S. conditions for opening a dialogue (acceptance of U.N. Security Council Resolutions 242 and 338, recognition of Israel's right to exist, and renunciation of terrorism). The Reagan administration took the PLO at its word and promptly opened diplomatic contacts.

In the early months of the Bush administration, Secretary Baker embarked on a revival of Arab-Israeli peacemaking that turned on the creation of a legitimate authority in the occupied territories for negotiations with Israel. This effort centered on ideas advanced by the United States and the Israeli government, led by Prime Minister Yitzhak Shamir, for elections in the territories. By the time of Iraq's invasion of Kuwait, however, these efforts had achieved little tangible progress.

Following the Persian Gulf War, however, the United States began a diplomatic initiative of a skill and intensity that had not been seen since President Jimmy Carter left office more than a decade before. Most remarkable, perhaps, was the motivation. On the surface, there was no particular strategic rationale for doing so, although the U.S. commitment to gain peace for Israel was still important. With the collapse of the Soviet Union, the so-called Arab confrontation states had lost their superpower patron. Iraq had been defeated in battle. The PLO had supported Saddam Hussein and thus alienated many of its Arab supporters. In sum, there was little risk of an Arab-Israeli war and no risk that the United States and the Soviet Union would find themselves confronting each other.

U.S. motives were thus more complex than they had been in the past. They derived in part from promises made by President Bush during the effort to forge the Desert Shield coalition. In his address to the United Nations on October 1, 1990, the president said that if Iraq withdrew from Kuwait, he believed that "there may be opportunities . . . for all the states and the peoples of the region to settle the conflicts that divide the Arabs from Israel."[11] He reiterated this commitment in his address to Congress on March 6, 1991. But why? The administration was likely responding to U.S. emergence from the Persian Gulf conflict as the unchallenged, preeminent external power in the Middle East, to a degree not rivaled by any other outsider at least in this century. This fact, plus the other developments cited, opened possibilities for Arab-Israeli peacemaking that could take place without opposition from the Soviet Union or unhelpful advice from European friends. Indeed, as part of its overall policy of putting primacy on economic relations with the West, the Soviet Union supported U.S. objectives by permitting the migration of hundreds of thousands of Jews to Israel and by reestablishing diplomatic relations with Israel that Moscow had broken during the 1967 Six-Day War.

In addition, there is the long-term question of the flow of oil, set against the background of incipient political and social changes within the region that were likely given further impetus by the war. U.S. efforts to resolve the Arab-Israeli conflict, certainly one of the principal irritants in U.S. relations with many regional countries, could encounter potentially hostile currents of opinion—including Islamic fundamentalism of various stripes. The revival of the peace process represented one of the few examples of long-range strategic planning in modern U.S. foreign policy.

In comparison with the motives for its strategy, U.S. tactics in peacemaking were simple and straightforward: to pick up both the theory and the practice of the Camp David Accords. The basic theory was that parties to the conflict will be more likely to reconsider rigid positions if they are dealing face-to-face with one another and before their publics; the practice was to proceed step-by-step, pursuing half-measures that could make possible more substantial progress later on.

The centerpiece of the U.S. effort was the Madrid Peace Conference, convened at the end of October 1991. President Bush opened the meeting along with President Gorbachev—the latter present to demonstrate to Arab rejectionists that they had no recourse to the Soviet Union (a point later underscored by Russian officials). In fact, the Madrid meeting fulfilled its purpose simply by opening. In the same room, on global television, gathered Israelis, Palestinians from the West Bank and Gaza, Syrians, Lebanese, and other Arabs, including Saudis as part of a GCC delegation. This gathering sent clear messages in two contexts. First, Syria was accepting Israel's existence, in fact and in politics, if not in law, thus telling all Arabs that the Jewish state was here to stay. Like Anwar Sadat's speech to the Knesset on November 20, 1977, the fact of the encounter spoke louder than the words that, in this case, included a slanging match between Shamir and the Syrian foreign minister, Farouk al-Shara. Second, Israelis and Palestinians were recognizing one another's existence and, further, Palestinians from the occupied territories were acting separate from, if not independently of, the PLO in Tunis.

All else at Madrid was secondary—elaborate diplomatic theater; but the process was well and truly launched in the most important breakthrough since Camp David and for which full credit is due to President Bush and Secretary of State Baker. Following this set of encounters, time would have to work its will, the process itself eventually holding out to the Israeli and Palestinian people the possibility that something could be different, and better, in their relationship. Syria was secondary; change there, in a state dominated by President Hafiz al-Assad, depends almost entirely on calculations of self-interest rather than on the evolution of political possibilities. For now at least, Syria sees its future as constrained by U.S. policy, with no obvious recourse to an alternative, and it has an interest in not being obviously obstructive. Further, Syria's role could be reduced if the other key part of U.S. tactics succeeds.

That U.S. tactic is to focus on direct Israeli-Palestinian negotiations, with Jordan playing an ancillary role in an attempt to establish so-called limited self-rule for the Palestinians in the West Bank and Gaza. A carbon copy of the Camp David concept of autonomy, limited self-rule was designed to alter the relationship between Israelis and Palestinians in the hope that, after the lapse of some years, they will be able to agree on some lasting arrangements to mutual advantage. Today, each claims the territories to the exclusion of the other's interests; tomorrow, perhaps something different can emerge. As Winston Churchill described democracy, this is the worst idea there is for peacemaking—except for all the others. And it has a further advantage: if Israelis and Palestinians can agree on limited self-rule, itself a grinding process, then Syria will lose much of its capacity for obstruction.

Following Madrid, the United States convened several rounds of talks in Washington between the various parties (all of which were essentially inconclusive, although the atmosphere did steadily improve). It also cosponsored in Moscow a brief conference on regional issues, primarily economic in nature. While in the past this agenda has never been able to compete with political issues, it was at least useful to begin the process of looking at the region's future, beyond sterile conflict.

At the same time, the United States and Israel became locked in a bitter struggle over the question of whether the United States would guarantee repayment of $10 billion in commercial loans to Israel to provide housing for Jews migrating from the former Soviet Union. Declaring Jewish settlements in the occupied territories to be "obstacles to peace," the Bush administration refused to provide the guarantees—

which would entail a set-aside of a few hundred million dollars of U.S. appropriated funds—without an Israeli commitment to stop building settlements. Israel's government countered that it could not provide any such commitment without prejudicing its position in negotiations regarding the future status of the territories. Following the Israeli elections in June 1992, this issue was rapidly resolved by the new government of Labour Prime Minister Yitzhak Rabin.

The Emerging Agenda

The aftermath of both the cold war and the Persian Gulf War has left the United States with a greater range of worldwide geostrategic flexibility than it has enjoyed for at least half a century. A partial exception is the Middle East. While the possibility of open conflict is currently remote, old and new problems still require U.S. engagement and enlightened action. Most novel is the requirement to develop sensible and productive relations both with newly independent former Soviet republics in Central Asia and with neighbors contending for influence in them. Risks lie in inadequate knowledge, combined with a temptation to try affecting events beyond U.S. capacity or understanding of alternatives and consequences—practicing geomechanics rather than geopolitics.

Oil also remains a primary U.S. concern, along with the prospect of major changes within regional states—the principal problem for the United States—as opposed to past preoccupation with either regional conflict or intervention from outside. The United States faces a dilemma that often arose elsewhere during the cold war: whether to support current regimes and risk going down with them, or to help foster change and then possibly to find that the outcome is also not salutary. Promoting the development of representative institutions is surely in the long-term Western interest, but there remains the risk that elections will at first produce "one person, one vote, one time." In terms of its basic moral commitments, the United States has little choice: indeed, part of today's dilemma derives from the fact that it and most other Western states for so long fenced off the Middle East from pressures for human rights and democracy because of their overriding concern about Soviet influence and the flow of oil. The price of that historical shortsightedness could be paid in the early 1990s.

Ironically, the United States also faces a greater need for knowledge and understanding about the Middle East now, especially as its prac-

tical confines are extended northward, than during the more dangerous times of the cold war. Greater flexibility in political and other
relationships poses more complex, if potentially less consequential or
risky, demands. This risk will be particularly true in dealing with
deep-seated cultural factors, the most puzzling of which for the
United States is religion, especially the role that Islam will play in different societies. There is still a risk that the United States will
blunder into confrontation with various Islamic states, because of
misunderstanding or lack of adequate leadership to give expression to
common interests. It is remarkable how simple distinctions like that
between Sunnis and Shi'ites are blurred in American commentary, and
fear produced by such ignorance can have unfortunate consequences.

Following the Persian Gulf War, it was possible to argue that U.S.
responsibilities in the region, from taking part in security to prompt-
ing peace between Israel and its neighbors, would decline—possible
but wrong. In fact, by becoming the region's preeminent outside
power, the United States also increased expectations on the part of
regional leaders and peoples about its role, for good or ill. Some view
it as the legatee of Western imperialism and fully expect it to follow
suit; others view it as the ultimate arbiter of all the region's ills.
Neither view is just, but both must be countered by what the United
States does, from taking the lead in controlling the spread of lethal
weaponry, to helping resolve the Arab-Israeli conflict and championing the cause of political and economic modernization, regionwide.
The United States cannot alone be held responsible for advancing this
agenda, but neither can it escape its own essential part in the next act
of the continuing Middle East drama.

Notes

1. Iraqi President Saddam Hussein at the opening of the fourth summit of
the Arab Cooperation Council, Royal Cultural Center, Amman, February 24,
1990, as reported by the *Foreign Broadcast Information Service-Near East/
South Asia (FBIS-NESA)* 90-039, February 27, 1990.

2. See, for example, Shireen T. Hunter, "Iraq Is Not the Lesser of Two Evils,"
Los Angeles Times, July 29, 1990.

3. See note 1.

4. Four days earlier, Resolution 660 demanded Iraq's withdrawal from
Kuwait.

5. For the full address, see *American-Arab Affairs* 35 (Winter 1990–91):
167–71.

6. The GCC, created in 1981, includes Oman, Saudi Arabia, the United Arab Emirates, Bahrain, Qatar, and Kuwait.

7. See "Economic Crisis in the Arab World: Catalyst for Conflict," no. 5 (Washington: Overseas Development Council, 1991), p. 10. See also testimony by Secretary of State James A. Baker III before the House Foreign Affairs Committee, Wednesday, February 6, 1991, and *Congressional Quarterly*, March 9, 1991, p. 613.

8. UN General Assembly Resolution 4636, December 9, 1991, Annex L.

9. "The fact that Iran would like to see the war end is encouraging. And Iran is conducting itself, in my view, in a very credible way here. They've said that those airplanes that come in there are going to be impounded, and we take them at their word on that. They have not been violators of the sanctions that we're aware of. They have wanted to remain neutral. . . . So I have no argument with the way Iran is conducting itself." Presidential News Conference of February 5, 1991, *U.S. Department of State Dispatch*, February 11, 1991, pp. 97–99.

10. For a comprehensive analysis and recommendations for U.S. policy in the region, see *The United States and the New Middle East: Strategic Perspectives after the Persian Gulf War*, Report of the CSIS Aftermath Policy Council, prepared by Robert E. Hunter, CSIS, March 1992.

11. Address before the UN General Assembly, October 1, 1990, in *U.S. Department of State Dispatch*, October 8, 1990, pp. 151–53.

3

MOSCOW AND THE IRAQI
INVASION OF KUWAIT

Robert O. Freedman

One of the central characteristics of Soviet foreign policy in the Gorbachev era was its dedication to the so-called new thinking. However, it was not until the Iraqi invasion of Kuwait on August 2, 1990, and the subsequent war between Iraq and a U.S.-led coalition that Moscow's "new thinking" was put to a major test. In this paper, after briefly examining the principles of Soviet new thinking as they applied to the Middle East, I will examine the degree to which they did—and did not—reflect actual Soviet policy behavior during the Gorbachev era in the pre-invasion period. I will then present an examination of Soviet policy during both the prewar (August 2, 1990 to January 15, 1991) and wartime periods (January 16, 1991 to February 28, 1991) and conclude with an analysis of Soviet behavior from the end of the Gulf War until the collapse of the Soviet Union, less than ten months later. I will also seek to demonstrate how Gorbachev sought to adjust Soviet policy to the rapidly diminishing power and influence of the USSR.

Soviet "New Thinking"

There are five major principles of Soviet new thinking as they applied to the Third World in general and the Middle East in particular:[1]

1. The danger of nuclear war impels the superpowers to realize that human survival should take precedence over the interests of states, classes, and ideologies.
2. There is a need to abandon such concepts as "spheres of influence,"

"vital interests," "positions of strength," and the "zero-sum game" approach to the Third World.

3. A new concept should lie at the heart of international relations, the "balance of interests" that would take into account the legitimate interests of the USSR, the United States, and regional states.

4. Primary reliance should be placed on political means for the resolution of regional conflicts, using the United Nations if at all possible.

5. There is an organic connection between regional conflicts and confrontation between the superpowers, and, hence, there is a need for joint action by the superpowers to settle the most serious regional conflicts because there will be no possible détente in U.S.-Soviet relations if there is no settlement of the most serious regional conflicts, especially in the Middle East.

In looking at the new thinking, it is clear that there is indeed much that is new. First, the linkage between superpower relations and Third World conflicts is a marked departure from the Brezhnev period when the Soviet leadership felt it could act freely in the Third World (in places like Angola and Ethiopia) without having a major effect on détente. Second, there was a downgrading of Marxist-Leninist ideology in Gorbachev's approach to world affairs. Since it did not seem possible to separate ideology's internal role in the Soviet Union as the legitimizer of the rule of the Communist Party, from its role in shaping the Soviet view of world affairs, Gorbachev's domestic critics within the party, already angry at his other reform efforts that threatened their power, took issue with the policy change on ideology. Leaders of self-proclaimed Marxist-Leninist states in the Third World such as Fidel Castro of Cuba and radical Arab states such as Syria and Libya which feared a loss of Soviet support under Gorbachev did the same.

In most parts of the world, Soviet actions in fact reflected the rhetoric of the new thinking. Thus, in addition to acquiescing in the reunification of Germany and the collapse of Soviet control over Eastern Europe (events also protested by his hardline critics), Gorbachev withdrew the Soviet army from Afghanistan and pulled back from such other Third World outposts as Angola, Ethiopia, and Vietnam. In general, in the period 1987–90 the world witnessed the retreat of Soviet power from much of the Third World—although the Soviet Union sought to camouflage the retreat through UN agreements.

However, in the Middle East, not only did Moscow not retreat under Gorbachev in that period; it became much more politically active. And, it was in the Middle East, particularly in the Persian Gulf, in the period preceding the Iraqi invasion of Kuwait, that there were clear limits to Soviet new thinking.

Moscow and the Middle East on the Eve of the Iraqi Invasion of Kuwait

By August 1990, Moscow had sharply improved its relations with two erstwhile Middle Eastern enemies, Egypt and Israel. Gorbachev, seeing the reintegration of Egypt into the Arab world—despite its peace treaty with Israel—as a fait accompli because of the Iran-Iraq War, switched Soviet policy from trying to isolate Egypt in the Arab world, to active cooperation with Egypt. He made this change in part to bring about an international conference on the Middle East to settle the Arab-Israeli conflict, something both Cairo and Moscow wanted.[2]

There was an even sharper improvement of relations with Israel, as consular delegations were exchanged, people to people diplomacy flourished involving athletic, cultural, religious, and academic exchanges, and Moscow allowed the exodus of hundreds of thousands of Soviet Jews to Israel. Gorbachev's motivations for improving relations with Israel were twofold: to improve Moscow's chances of playing a major role in Arab-Israeli diplomacy and to please the United States from which Moscow wanted both new arms control agreements and economic assistance.[3] Moscow's new thinking facilitated the Soviet-Israeli rapprochement. The downgrading of the importance of ideology, removed a major obstacle to the improvement of Soviet-Israeli relations, since Zionism was no longer portrayed as an implacable enemy of the USSR. This, in turn, led the increasingly independent Soviet media to take not only a more balanced view of Israel but also a more balanced approach toward the Arab-Israeli conflict as a whole. In addition, the new Soviet emphasis on a balance of interests in reaching settlements in Third World conflicts became a major theme employed by Gorbachev as a device to entice the United States and Israel to agree to include the Soviet Union in a Middle East peace conference.

While Soviet relations improved with pro-Western Egypt and Israel, its ties to Arab radicals, especially Syria and the Palestine Liberation Organization (PLO), weakened. Both Gorbachev and the Soviet foreign minister, Eduard Shevardnadze, emphasized to Syria's president, Hafiz Assad, that, in the nuclear age, his conflict with Israel had to be solved politically, not by war. Indeed, lessening Soviet diplomatic and military support for Syria—Assad was told he would not get the strategic parity with Israel he had long coveted—was one of the major factors inducing Assad to reestablish diplomatic relations with Egypt in December 1989.[4] At the same time, while PLO leader Yasser Arafat, on a visit to Moscow in April 1988, was told that the USSR still supported Palestinian desires for an independent state, he was also told that Israel had an equal right to security.[5] Soviet influence appears to be one of the factors that (along with the Intifada) induced Arafat and the Palestinian National Council to declare their support for a two-state solution to the Israel-Palestinian conflict in November and December 1988.[6]

While in its attitude toward the Arab-Israeli conflict Moscow's actions were clearly reflective of its new thinking, its policy toward the Persian Gulf and especially the Iran-Iraq War was not so clear-cut. To be sure, Gorbachev, utilizing Soviet-Kuwaiti relations as a model, sought to establish ties with the other conservative Gulf sheikhdoms of the Gulf Cooperation Council (GCC). He proved successful with the agreement of Oman and the United Arab Emirates to establish diplomatic relations with the USSR in 1985, and Qatar followed suit in 1988. Saudi Arabia, however, while intensifying its diplomatic interactions with the USSR (there were frequent diplomatic visits between Moscow and Riyadh), resisted Moscow's efforts to establish diplomatic relations, as did Bahrain. While the Saudi leaders were positively influenced by Gorbachev's February 1988 announcement that he was pulling Soviet troops out of Afghanistan (an action completed in January 1989), the Saudis and other Arabs remained suspicious of the USSR because of its behavior in the late stages of the Iran-Iraq War when, in clearly tilting toward Iran, Moscow seemed to be following the old rather than the new thinking in Soviet foreign policy. Indeed despite all the Soviet rhetoric about new thinking and balance of interests in solving Third World problems, there was far more continuity than change in Soviet policy when one compares Gorbachev's policy toward Iran with that of his predecessors Brezhnev, Andropov, and Chernenko.[7] Thus as Brezhnev first tilted to Iran from 1980 to 1982, then he and his successors Andropov and Chernenko back to Iraq from 1982 to 1985, Gorbachev was to tilt to Iran in 1986, back to Iraq in the first six months of 1987, and then back to Iran again.

In addition, like his predecessors, Gorbachev tried—and failed—to end the Gulf War which caused numerous problems for Soviet strat-

egy in the Middle East, such as dividing the Arab world and enhancing the U.S. political/military position in the Gulf. The cease-fire that
ended the war in August 1988 was due to Iranian war-weariness and
defeats on the battlefield, not to Soviet diplomacy, although the
weaponry supplied to Iraq by the USSR played a role in the Iranian
decision to accept a cease-fire. To be sure, Gorbachev demonstrated
more diplomatic flexibility than his predecessors in dealing with Iran.
Thus in 1986, Iran made a series of gestures to the USSR, such as
agreeing to the reestablishment of direct flights between Moscow and
Tehran, which Moscow eagerly reciprocated, only to find that Iran
had exploited the Soviet drive for influence to mount major offensives
against Iraq. Then Moscow sought to exploit the Iran-Contra affair by
denouncing Iran and championing the Arabs, going so far as to agree
to charter three Kuwaiti tankers. Once the United States moved in a
major way to redeem itself for Iran-Contra by reflagging eleven Kuwaiti tankers and building up its naval armada in the Gulf, however,
Moscow switched positions again, trying to exploit the rise in U.S.-
Iranian tension to enhance its own position in Tehran. Gorbachev's
peace initiative of July 3, 1987, which was marked by anti-U.S. propaganda, and his efforts to delay the imposition of UN sanctions against
Iran (after agreeing to UN Security Council Resolution 598), clearly
reflected the pro-Iranian tilt in his policy. Moscow's policy alienated
the Arab states of the Gulf, while initially winning it very little new
influence in Iran. Indeed relations between the Soviet Union and Iran
appeared to fall to their lowest point since Gorbachev took power
when, in March 1988, the Iranian leadership blamed Moscow for
supplying Iraq with the missiles it used to bombard Tehran.

Soviet-Iranian relations were to improve, however, once the war
came to an end and Moscow pulled its troops out of Afghanistan, and
improved even further following the death of Khomeini in 1989. In
June 1989, the two countries signed a major economic, political, and
military agreement. Two years later Moscow was supplying Iran with
highly sophisticated MIG-29 aircraft.[8] The improvement of ties benefited both countries. For Iran, the USSR was a customer for its oil and
natural gas exports as well as for Iranian consumer goods. Second, the
USSR had become Iran's only source for highly sophisticated combat
aircraft, the lack of which had been a problem for Iran during the late
stages of the Iran-Iraq War. Finally, even in its weakened economic
and political state (a situation that, paradoxically, improved Soviet-
Iranian relations by making Moscow less of a threat to Tehran), Mos-

cow could be a political check against the United States, as U.S.-Iranian relations remained strained, despite the rise to power of the pragmatic Rafsanjani.

For its part, Moscow valued Iran as a source of oil and natural gas (which could be bartered against Soviet aircraft) and as a potential calming influence on the increasingly restive Moslems in the USSR, particularly the Shi'a in Azerbaizhan.[9] In addition, Moscow hoped Iran would use its influence with the Afghan rebels to help free Soviet prisoners of war. Finally, a close relationship with Iran would enhance the Soviet political position in the Persian Gulf which, because of its oil reserves, was the most critical area in the Third World.

As Soviet-Iranian relations improved, Moscow's relationship with Iraq remained "businesslike" if not particularly cordial. The once-close Soviet-Iraqi relationship had waned in the late 1970s. President Saddam Hussein's decision to invade Iran in 1980 caused serious problems for Soviet diplomacy because it led to a sharp improvement of the political/military position of the United States in the Persian Gulf at a time when Moscow was still engaged in a zero-sum competition for influence with the United States in the region. While Moscow, which had cut off arms sales to Iraq at the start of the war, had resumed arms sales to Iraq in 1982, its tilt to Iran in the later stages of the war clearly angered Baghdad, and by the time the war came to an end Soviet influence in Iraq was limited. Nonetheless, there were major areas of mutual interest. Iraq depended primarily on Soviet military equipment, and from the Soviet point of view Baghdad was an excellent customer, paying for Soviet weapons with either oil (which the USSR then sold abroad)[10] or hard currency. In addition, when Iraq invaded Kuwait, 7,830 Soviet economic and military advisers worked in Iraq,[11] and they too were paid in hard currency.

In sum, on the eve of the Iraqi invasion of Kuwait, Moscow's position in the Gulf can be said to have been far better than when Gorbachev took power in March 1985. Three small Gulf sheikhdoms—Oman, the United Arab Emirates and Qatar—had established diplomatic relations with the USSR. Soviet relations with Kuwait had improved by Moscow's chartering of Kuwaiti tankers (although Kuwaiti-U.S. relations had improved even more because of the massive U.S. reflagging and escorting effort). Soviet-Iranian relations had also improved considerably. Moscow and Saudi Arabia had begun to interact diplomatically, although diplomatic relations had not yet been established, and Soviet-Iraqi relations, while not particularly cordial, remained extensive.

The Iraqi Invasion of Kuwait

CENTRAL SOVIET CONSIDERATIONS AT THE TIME
OF THE INVASION

The Iraqi invasion of Kuwait, which Moscow was reportedly not informed of by Baghdad in advance despite explicit provisions requiring such an action in the 1972 Soviet-Iraqi treaty,[12] posed a number of problems for the USSR. On the one hand, it was a clear-cut case of aggression and a major violation of the new world order that Gorbachev was trying to create, under which problems were to be solved politically and not by force. In addition, once the United States committed itself to Saudi Arabia's defense and began to build up its military forces in the desert kingdom, Moscow had to decide whether to support the United States actively to preserve the momentum of superpower cooperation, so that Moscow could continue to benefit from its improved relationship with the United States. A second consideration involved the politics of the Arab world. Egypt and Syria had denounced the Iraqi invasion and had pledged support to Saudi Arabia, as had the other members of the Gulf Cooperation Council. Jordan, newly unified Yemen, the Sudan, and PLO leader Yasser Arafat had sided with Saddam Hussein, while the North African states, except for Morocco, which backed Saudi Arabia, adopted a more neutral position. Here the question for Moscow was whether to continue the Gorbachev policy of improving ties with the conservative Arab regimes, many of whom had money that could be loaned to the USSR (as Kuwait had already done).[13] In the process, by backing the new Saudi-Syrian-Egyptian axis, which seemed likely to dominate the Arab world if Iraq was defeated, Moscow could prevent the United States from becoming the sole superpower guarantor of the region. A related consideration for Moscow was the status of Kuwait itself. Moscow had established diplomatic relations with Kuwait in 1964, and until 1985 it was the only Gulf sheikhdom to have diplomatic relations with Moscow, from which it also bought military equipment. Moscow held out Kuwait as a model and urged the other Gulf sheikhdoms to follow the Kuwaiti example of looking to both superpowers for support in a region in which they might be threatened by more powerful neighbors.[14] As noted, Oman and the United Arab Emirates followed Kuwait's example in 1985, as did Qatar in 1988. Thus, if Moscow did not actively oppose Iraq's annexation of Kuwait, it risked the loss of its ties to the Gulf sheikhdoms; conversely an activist Soviet policy aimed at getting Iraq out of Kuwait might well be rewarded by a Saudi decision to reestablish diplomatic relations with the USSR, long a major Soviet goal.

While issues of U.S.-Soviet and Soviet-GCC relations were important considerations among Soviet decision makers, Iraq was not without its supporters in the USSR. The Soviet-Iraqi Treaty of Friendship and Cooperation signed in 1972 was still operative, Iraq paid hard currency—an increasingly scarce commodity in the USSR—for its arms purchases, and Moscow had 7,830 advisers working in such areas as oil exploration, oil drilling, grain elevator construction, and hydroelectric projects, as well as military advisers in Iraq.[15] Those advisers not only earned hard currency but could also be considered agents of Soviet influence in Iraq. Between 200 and 1,000 of them were what Moscow called military specialists;[16] given Soviet cutbacks around the world, Iraq was one of the few places left where Soviet military specialists could serve under relatively good conditions, and the Soviet military was loath to cut off this relationship.[17] Finally, the "old" thinkers in the USSR grew more influential in the period August 1990 to February 1991, as Gorbachev increasingly turned to the right and abandoned his liberal positions (a development that reached its apogee with the resignation of Foreign Minister Eduard Shevardnadze, warning about a coming dictatorship, in December 1990). The old thinkers felt Saddam Hussein was "standing up to the imperialists who wanted to dominate Middle East oil" and who were "building a major military position near the southern border of the USSR, just as Moscow was pulling out of East Europe, thus decisively altering the balance of power against the USSR." Included in this group were hardliners such as the Soyuz faction of the Supreme Soviet, senior army officers, and Communist Party officials.[18]

In addition, some Soviet specialists argued against actively opposing Iraq because Iraq might emerge from the confrontation with enhanced prestige in the Arab world because it linked its actions in Kuwait to the Palestinian cause.[19] Besides these major considerations, three additional factors permeated Soviet thinking about how to react to the Iraqi invasion of Kuwait. The first might be termed the Afghan Syndrome. Shared by both liberals and hard-liners alike, it was an aversion to sending any Soviet soldiers abroad to fight lest they get mired down in a quagmire like Afghanistan. (It is in many ways similar to the Vietnam Syndrome that affected U.S. policy for many years and was instrumental in Congress's thwarting Henry Kissinger's efforts to support the forces of Jonas Savimbi against the Soviet- and Cuban-backed MPLA in Angola in 1976.) A second factor was the economic crisis that had begun to pervade the USSR. Given Moscow's increasingly serious economic problems (a shortage of food and goods in Soviet stores), there was little inclination to expend Soviet resources on a major commitment of Soviet troops to an anti-Iraqi war. Finally, there was the Moslem factor. While Moslems were on both sides of the Iraqi-Kuwaiti conflict, both Soviet academics and governmental officials feared a negative impact on the increasingly restive Moslems of Soviet Central Asia and Azerbaizhan if Soviet soldiers were seen killing Moslems in Iraq.[20]

Given all these considerations—some of them mutually contradictory—Gorbachev developed what might be called a minimax strategy in the period October 2–January 15. It involved doing the minimum necessary to preserve U.S.-Soviet relations and foster the development of Soviet ties with the GCC states, Egypt, and Syria, while at the same time maximizing the amount of influence Moscow could retain in Iraq. The components of the strategy included supporting the United States in all twelve of the UN resolutions condemning Iraq, denouncing Iraq's seizure of Kuwait and its use of Western specialists as hostages, imposing an arms and economic embargo against Iraq, and supporting the ousted Sabah regime as the legitimate government of Kuwait. On the other hand Moscow also strongly urged a peaceful settlement of the conflict, with the United Nations and the Arab world taking a leading role in the peace effort and delayed action on UN resolutions authorizing force against Iraq. In addition, Moscow committed none of its forces, not even a symbolic hospital ship, to the anti-Iraqi coalition, thereby enhancing its role as a mediator between Saddam Hussein and the Allied forces, and Gorbachev sent a number of diplomatic notes and Soviet diplomatic missions to Iraq to try to persuade Saddam Hussein to withdraw from Kuwait. Finally, Moscow did not withdraw its specialists, especially its military specialists, after the Iraqi invasion, although this policy was to prove somewhat counterproductive to Moscow.

Following the invasion of Iraq, the Soviet government issued a statement on August 2 calling for the "urgent and unconditional withdrawal of Iraqi troops from Kuwaiti territory" and the full restoration of "the sovereignty, national independence and territorial integrity of Kuwait"[21] and announcing the suspension of the supply of military equipment to Iraq.[22] Moscow also joined the United States in approving UN Security Council Resolution 660 the same day, which demanded the unconditional and immediate withdrawal of Iraqi forces from Kuwait.[23] U.S.-Soviet cooperation against the invasion was further underscored on August 3 when Secretary of State Baker and Foreign Minister Shevardnadze, meeting at Moscow's Vnukovo Airport, issued a joint statement condemning the Iraqi invasion and calling on the world community to "take practical steps to respond to it": "Today the USSR and the United States are taking the unusual step of jointly calling on the entire international community to join them in suspending all weapons shipments to Iraq. . . . Governments resorting to flagrant aggression should know that the international community cannot and will not promote aggression."[24] This joint statement, which an *Izvestia* correspondent noted had shown that "the USSR and the United States have acted as allies in the international arena for the first time since World War II,"[25] was followed on August 6 by the adoption of UN Resolution 661, which imposed a trade and financial embargo on Iraq and occupied Kuwait and called for the restoration of Kuwait's legitimate government.[26]

Neither the UN Security Council vote on sanctions nor the decision by the United States the same day to deploy U.S. troops to defend Saudi Arabia had any effect on Iraq which, on August 8, formally annexed Kuwait. This, in turn, led to another Security Council Resolution (662) on August 9 declaring the annexation "null and void."[27] As tensions rose, the Arab League held a meeting in Cairo, where the majority, led by Egypt, Syria, and Saudi Arabia, voted to send troops to Saudi Arabia. A defiant Iraq responded to these moves by the world community by offering to link Iraqi withdrawal from Kuwait to Israeli withdrawal from occupied territories and Syrian withdrawal from Lebanon. Saddam Hussein also moved to protect his flank by agreeing to make peace with Iran on Iranian terms (pulling out of occupied Iranian territory, returning Iranian prisoners of war, and accepting the midpoint of the Shatt al-Arab waterway as the border between Iraq and Iran). He also moved to bring pressure on the countries imposing sanctions by stating that foreign citizens in Iraq (although, initially, not Soviet citizens) would not be allowed to leave until the crisis ended, thus, in effect, making them hostages.

As these events unfolded, Moscow began to move away from its close coordination with the United States. A Ministry of Foreign Affairs statement published on August 10 implicitly criticized the U.S. military buildup while outlining Moscow's approach to solving the conflict:[28]

> The situation in the Persian Gulf region is becoming increasingly dramatic. Since the invasion of Kuwait by Iraqi troops on August 2, such serious events have taken place in this region as the so-called "merger" of Iraq and Kuwait that was announced yesterday and the stationing of American naval and air forces in Saudi Arabia, *which Washington justifies as being in the interests of protecting that country. Unfortunately, the trend toward an escalation of confrontation and a whipping up of passions is continuing to gain momentum rapidly.*
>
> This turn of events is causing alarm and concern in Moscow, since all this is taking place in a region that is already oversaturated with "combustible material" in the form of chronic conflicts, long-standing resentments and mutual territorial claims. At the same time, important political and economic interests of a wide range of states, including the Soviet Union, are closely interwoven there. For this reason, from the very start of the crisis in the Gulf region caused by Iraq's armed invasion of Kuwait, we have firmly and clearly spoken out in favor of extinguishing the conflagration as quickly as possible, restoring the situation that existed before August 2, and drawing the parties involved into a political dialogue aimed at a peaceful settlement of disputed questions.
>
> In addition to efforts within the framework of the Security Council we have had active contacts with the Iraqi leadership, *including an exchange of messages at the level of the Presidents of the USSR and of Iraq, with the aim of channeling the course of events in precisely the direction indicated above.* It seemed to us that this exchange of opinions with the Iraqi side offered hope that things would move toward the fulfillment of U.N. Security Council Resolution No. 660, and thus toward a rapid ending of the crisis.
>
> Regrettably, we are compelled to admit that our hopes have not been borne out. Not only has Iraq not withdrawn its troops from Kuwait, but yesterday it announced the de facto annexation of that country. *It is difficult and distressing for us to give this description of the latest actions of Iraq, a country to which we are linked by long-standing friendly relations. We would like to preserve that friendship.* But in the present situation we cannot take a position of

silence, let alone act against our conscience. Our approach to this question of principle remains firm—the sovereignty, national independence and territorial integrity of the State of Kuwait must be fully restored and protected. The pertinent resolutions of the U.N. Security Council make this same demand.

What is taking place now in the Persian Gulf zone offers particularly clear and convincing evidence of how important it is to display prudence and circumspection in such circumstances and to take no actions that could pour still more oil on the flames. *We would like to point out once again that the Soviet Union is against reliance on force and against unilateral decisions. The experience of many, many years convincingly proves that the surest, most sensible line of action in conflict situations is collective efforts and the full use of UN mechanisms.*

Specifically, we would like to have the Security Council now deal with this extremely critical question on an ongoing basis. *We are also prepared to begin immediate consultations within the framework of the Security Council's Military Staff Committee, which, according to the U.N. Charter, may perform very important functions.*

It seems to us that a special role could be played by the efforts of the Arab countries themselves to prevent the current situation in the Persian Gulf from developing into an even larger military conflict. We have taken note of reports on the emergency meeting of heads of Arab states in Cairo, and we hope that its results will be an important element in overall actions pertaining to the situation around Kuwait.

We would like to emphasize once again that the critical nature and unpredictability of the current situation in the Persian Gulf *urgently require that everyone directly involved in the dangerous confrontation unfolding there show respect for the will of the international community and a sense of lofty responsibility for the fate of peace.* (emphasis added)

What was of particular interest in the statement, beyond Moscow's emphasis on the United Nations and on a peaceful approach to solving the crisis, was its apparent willingness to participate in actions decided by a revived UN Security Council Military Staff Committee, an idea that was to be followed up in Shevardnadze's speech to the United Nations in late September.

As Iraq continued to defy the UN Security Council, the United

States began to urge military action to enforce the sanctions through a naval blockade. Shevardnadze sought to delay such a move, urging the Arabs to take united action to foster a settlement and urging collective action through the Security Council as the proper procedure to settle the crisis.[29] In emphasizing the use of the United Nations, Moscow sought to slow the U.S. move to war and to enhance its own position as a key member of the Security Council. While the USSR joined other members of the Security Council on August 18 to pass Resolution 664 demanding the immediate release of foreigners from Iraq and Kuwait,[30] it also welcomed Iraq's deputy prime minister, Saddam Hammadi, to Moscow for consultations. While Soviet Foreign Ministry spokesman Yuri Gremitskikh, in commenting on Hammadi's arrival, said Iraqi withdrawal from Kuwait was a "necessary element of any political settlement of the crisis in the region,"[31] Shevardnadze commented somewhat favorably on Saddam Hussein's new linkage plan which involved the release of hostages in return for the withdrawal of U.S. forces from Saudi Arabia and an end to the economic embargo against Iraq. This had been strongly rejected by the United States as "rewarding the aggressor." The Soviet foreign minister stated that "there are elements in it which merit serious attention."[32]

With the Security Council now considering the question of enforcing the sanctions through military action, it would appear that one of the goals of Hammadi's trip was to persuade Moscow to veto the sanctions resolution, thereby breaking the united front of permanent Security Council members against Iraq.[33] But his efforts were not successful. Following the failure of an "urgent message" from Gorbachev to Saddam Hussein urging the Iraqi leader to withdraw from Kuwait before the Security Council took "appropriate additional measures,"[34] the USSR voted on August 25 along with the United States in support of UN Resolution 665 which called on UN members with ships in the region to enforce the sanctions by inspecting and verifying cargoes and destinations.[35] Meanwhile, while differing somewhat on the question of how to resolve the crisis, Moscow and Washington appeared to be closely cooperating as the conflict progressed. Indeed, Tass reported on August 22 that the Soviet defense attaché in the United States, Grigoryevich Yakovlev, had visited the Pentagon, and "in response to the request of the U.S. side, he gave some information about the USSR's cooperation with Iraq along military lines."[36] For his part Bush seemed pleased with the degree of U.S.-Soviet cooperation and Tass approvingly cited Bush's comments at a press conference that "there may be some differences, but I have no argument with the way they have cooperated. I can say we are getting superb cooperation from the Soviets."[37]

Nonetheless, as the time for the Bush-Gorbachev summit in Helsinki approached, there were clear differences of opinion between the two superpowers. From the U.S. point of view, the continued presence of Soviet advisers in Iraq, both civilian and military, seemed a violation of the spirit if not the letter of the UN sanctions—a view, incidentally, that was shared by a number of liberals within the USSR.[38] In addition, Moscow's unwillingness to provide troops to the anti-Iraqi coalition or ships to participate in the naval blockade, raised questions in the United States about the depth of the Soviet opposition to Iraq's annexation of Kuwait. Finally, Moscow was much more sympathetic to Iraq's linkage proposal than the United States, seeing it as a face-saving way to get Iraq out of Kuwait. For its part, Moscow was unhappy with what it saw as Bush's overeagerness to use force against Iraq, and a number of Soviet conservatives raised questions about the ultimate purpose of the massive U.S. military buildup in Saudi Arabia. Indeed, Warsaw Pact Chief of Staff General Lobov criticized the buildup as "drastically changing the strategic balance in the region," and since Iraq was only "200 kilometers from the borders of Georgia, Armenia, and Azerbaizhan," the United States would get "an opportunity to exert pressure on events in this region."[39]

These issues were raised at the Bush-Gorbachev summit in Helsinki, and Bush, as he would throughout the crisis, sought both to allay Soviet concerns and to demonstrate that he considered Moscow, whatever its internal political, economic, and nationality problems, a superpower worthy of respect. Indeed, while Bush proved unwilling to allow Saddam Hussein to "save face" in working out a settlement to the conflict lest he "reward the aggressor," he clearly sought to minimize Gorbachev's embarrassment so as to ensure Moscow's even limited cooperation in the coalition effort against Iraq. Thus in their joint statement, Bush agreed to put the emphasis on a peaceful resolution of the crisis, while Gorbachev agreed to consider the possibility of "additional steps consistent with the UN charter" should the peaceful approach fail.[40] Bush also made a gesture toward the linkage that Saddam Hussein was demanding (and which Moscow was now tacitly supporting in its mediation efforts) by agreeing that once the Iraqi forces had withdrawn from Kuwait, "it is essential to work actively to resolve all remaining conflicts in the Middle East and Persian Gulf." Finally, Bush repeated in their joint news conference[41] that he had made it clear to Gorbachev that the United States had no intention of keeping U.S. troops in the area "a day longer than is required."

Then, perhaps to entice Gorbachev into further cooperation, Bush held out economic incentives. In response to a question as to whether or not he was now more sympathetic to suggestions of Western economic aid to the USSR, Bush responded, "I think this convincing cooperation that had been demonstrated by the Soviet Union at the United Nations gets me inclined to recommend as close cooperation in the economic field as possible." While Gorbachev was evidently pleased by Bush's commentary, the Soviet leader for his part was quick to point out that the USSR was not being "bought off" for aid: "I wouldn't want anyone to get the idea from President Bush's answer that the Soviet Union is going to be rewarded with one or another sum for one or another behavior. I think that we are acting in a critical situation and are working to find a solution that would be satisfactory and, most importantly, would safeguard us all from an explosion. In this situation, cooperation—new cooperation in new forms—is becoming a normal element. . . . It would be very superficial and oversimplified to think that the Soviet Union can be bought for dollars."

On the question of Soviet military advisers in Iraq, Gorbachev did not meet Bush's hopes. While Bush stated in the news conference that the pulling out of the advisers would "facilitate things" and that he wanted to see all of them out, Gorbachev was unwilling to do so: "We are in fact talking not about advisers, but about specialists working under contract. Their number is being reduced: Whereas at the beginning of the conflict there were, I think, 196 of them, now there are about 150. And, as a matter of fact, the Iraqi leadership looks at this question from the standpoint that if they have finished their business—this is normal contract work, even though it involves weapons—they leave Iraq. And this process is under way. So I don't think there's a problem there." It seems clear that at this point Moscow still saw the Soviet military and economic advisers as important links of influence to Iraq—and, to a lesser degree, important sources of hard currency. Because of the sanctions, Moscow had lost economically,[42] and Gorbachev, evidently wishing to maintain as much residual influence in Iraq as possible, was loath to withdraw the advisors.

If, on balance, Soviet cooperation was sufficiently strong in the first month of the crisis to prompt Bush to reward Moscow economically, it was also sufficiently strong for Saudi Arabia to reward it politically.

The USSR had long wanted the restoration of full diplomatic relations with the influential oil-rich kingdom, and Saudi Arabia agreed to the Soviet request on September 17. While the joint communiqué emphasized that the two countries "will make active efforts to settle regional conflicts,"[43] Moscow clearly hoped that Saudi Arabia would follow Kuwait's example and become a source of financial aid to the USSR. It would not be long before these hopes were realized. Moscow was to receive a further benefit eleven days later when Bahrain, home to a U.S. military base and the last of the GCC members not to have diplomatic relations with the Soviet Union, also established full diplomatic relations with Moscow.[44]

Buoyed by Moscow's enhanced diplomatic position in the Gulf, while still seeking a peaceful solution to the crisis there, Shevardnadze made a major address to the United Nations at the end of September.[45] First he condemned Iraq's annexation of Kuwait in the strongest terms yet used by a Soviet leader: "Iraq flagrantly violated the UN charter, the principles of international law, universally accepted norms of morality, and standards of civilized conduct. It committed unprovoked aggression, annexed a neighboring sovereign state, seized thousands of hostages, and resorted to unprecedented blackmail, threatening to use weapons of mass destruction . . . a terrorist act has been committed against the emerging new world order."

Then, after warning Iraq that the United Nations was empowered "to suppress acts of aggression," although still urging a peaceful settlement of the crisis, he called for the activization of the Security Council's Military Staff Committee and the examination of "the practical aspects of putting national troop contingents at the Security Council's disposal." He also said that the USSR was prepared to commit its own troop contingent to the Council. Shevardnadze's emphasis on the UN collective use of force seemed aimed at preventing the United States from "going it alone" before all possible peaceful efforts to solve the crisis had been undertaken: "If the Military Staff Committee were operating properly, if the Council had concluded appropriate agreements with the permanent members, and if other organizational questions of countering threats to peace had been resolved, there would be no need today for certain states to be taking unilateral actions."

If Shevardnadze's speech was aimed at slowing down the drift toward war by developing a collective military response for Iraqi-like "acts of aggression," his statement that Moscow might commit its own troops was widely criticized in the Soviet Union.[46] In addition,

Iraq evidently took a dim view both of Shevardnadze's highly critical
speech and the U.S.-Soviet cooperation on the Gulf crisis, because the
Soviet advisers serving in Iraq whom Moscow had hoped would be
agents of continued Soviet influence in that country were transformed, instead, into hostages. Some were harassed, and one was shot
by the Iraqis.[47]

The status of Soviet advisers had become a major concern to Gorbachev in early October, and one of the central reasons Gorbachev's
adviser, Yevgeny Primakov, was sent to Iraq in mid-October was to resolve the question of Soviet citizens working in Iraq.[48] Indeed, accompanying Primakov on his trip was Igor Belousev, the head of the
Soviet interdepartment task force on Soviet workers in Iraq, which
had been formed in mid-August. Adding to the pressure on Moscow
was the Iraqi threat that if the USSR gave the United States any information on Iraq's military potential during U.S. Secretary of Defense
Cheney's forthcoming visit to Moscow, then Iraq would prevent the
return of some of the Soviet advisers.[49] According to Primakov's version of the trip, Saddam, a long-time acquaintance of Primakov, agreed
to the departure of only 1,500 of the specialists.[50] A version of the
visit published in *Rabochaya Tribuna* also noted that the Iraqis demanded the payment of huge "forfeit fees" in the event of the departure of Soviet advisers whose contracts had not been completed.[51]

A second goal of Primakov's visit was to see if Iraq was willing to
moderate its position on the Gulf crisis. Saddam Hussein's hints that
he might be willing to settle for the islands of Bubyan and Warbah
(which block Iraq's access to the Persian Gulf) and the southern section of the Rumelia oil field (about which Iraq and Kuwait had been
in dispute) reportedly led Primakov to be cautiously optimistic about
his visit,[52] although Secretary of State Baker opposed such a deal as
"rewarding aggression."[53]

Nonetheless, nothing concrete came from Primakov's October trip to
Iraq or from his follow-up trip several weeks later despite Gorbachev's
efforts, while on a visit to France, to demonstrate that Saddam Hussein
might be reassessing his position.[54] The crisis continued to get worse.
Moscow did, however, seek to reassure Iraq on one point—the issue of
supplying information about Iraqi military capabilities to the United
States. Foreign Ministry spokesman Genady Gerasimov, just after the
completion of Primakov's first visit to Iraq, told journalists that Moscow had "no intention of sharing military information, since this
would violate existing agreements with Third World countries stipu-

lating that they would keep certain data secret"[55]—a clear reversal of what appeared to be Soviet policy, cited by Tass in mid-August, on sharing military information with the United States at its request.

In addition, Moscow sought to demonstrate to Iraq that it did not have a double standard in treating Middle Eastern events (as Iraq, its Arab allies, and some Soviet hardliners accused the United States of doing vis-à-vis Israel and the occupied territories). It severely condemned the Israeli police killing of seventeen Arabs in an incident on the Temple Mount in Jerusalem on October 8, 1990, which involved Arabs throwing stones at Jewish worshippers praying at the Western Wall just below the Temple Mount. In an official Foreign Ministry statement, Moscow, whose relations with Israel had been steadily improving since 1987, blasted the Jewish state:[56]

> Firmly denouncing this action by Israeli authorities, the Soviet Union believes that the U.N. Security Council should display the same unanimity and consistency in the approach to the situation in the occupied territories as was effectively demonstrated by the Security Council with respect to Iraqi aggression against Kuwait.
>
> We support the idea of sending, as an initial step, a special U.N. mission to investigate the incident.

Iraq, together with the PLO, sought to exploit both the Temple Mount killings and Israel's refusal to allow a UN investigatory mission, to try to divert attention from the annexation of Kuwait, and the issue remained an active one in the United Nations for the next two months. While the pro-Iraqi camp at the United Nations may have hoped that the United States would support Israel and thus perhaps split off the Arab states from the anti-Iraqi coalition, they were mistaken as the United States sided with the critics of Israel, although moderating the language of UN condemnations. Meanwhile, by early November, Iraq still had shown no real inclination to leave Kuwait, and Bush escalated the pressure by announcing on November 8 that he was doubling the size of the U.S. force in Saudi Arabia, thus for the first time giving it an offensive capability against Iraq.[57] While Gorbachev may have hoped that the increase in the size of the U.S. troop deployment would convince Saddam Hussein to withdraw his forces from Kuwait, he also had to realize that the United States was preparing for war. This became evident soon after the deployment decision, as the United States began to press for a formal UN deadline for Iraq to leave Kuwait.[58]

Meanwhile, divisions in the Soviet government over the use of force became more visible. On November 8, the day Bush announced the increased U.S. deployment, Baker met with Shevardnadze who told reporters after the meeting that force might well be required to get Iraq to leave Kuwait: "As for the question of whether or not the use of force could be ruled out, well, probably this could not be ruled out, and a situation may emerge which effectively would require such a move."[59] At the same time, Primakov, in an interview in *Literaturnaya Gazeta*, said that the reason Saddam Hussein was not willing to withdraw was that he feared an attack on Iraq and the continuation of sanctions even if he did comply.[60] One week later, speaking in New York, Primakov called for a "face-saving package" for Saddam, linking a resolution of the Gulf crisis to an overall Middle East settlement, which would include a resolution of the Palestinian problem. Primakov also called for a new security structure in the Middle East designed to stabilize the region, a structure that would guarantee the safety of both Israel and its Arab neighbors.[61] Meanwhile, the most that Gorbachev was willing to say about the crisis was that Saddam Hussein's efforts to weaken international resolve in the Gulf had failed and that the United Nations should now decide how to proceed farther.

As the split over Iraqi policy became more evident at the top echelons of the Soviet government, Baker went to Europe to seek support for a Security Council resolution authorizing the use of force against Iraq if it failed to withdraw.[62] Meanwhile, in mid-November, Moscow sent two additional diplomatic missions to the Arab world, each headed by a deputy foreign minister, to consult with Yemen, Egypt, Syria, Saudi Arabia, the United Arab Emirates, Morocco, Tunisia, the PLO, Libya, and Algeria and to sound out the Arabs about a possible Arab diplomatic solution to the Gulf crisis. Subsequently, the USSR sent a diplomatic mission to Iran as Gorbachev sought to maintain close diplomatic contact with the Rafsanjani regime throughout the crisis. For its part, Iran, which shared the Soviet goal of removing U.S. forces from the Persian Gulf once the crisis was over, publicly stated its willingness to aid the USSR in getting its advisers back home by offering them transit through Iran. While one of the Soviet mission leaders, Deputy Foreign Minister Petrovsky, hailed a Moroccan proposal for an emergency Arab summit to deal with the crisis,[63] little came of the idea, as the Arab world remained badly split.

This was the situation that confronted Gorbachev as he met Bush in Paris for a meeting of the thirty-four-nation Conference on Security and Cooperation in Europe in mid-November. After talking with Bush for two hours, Gorbachev refused to give the U.S. president the necessary assurances of Moscow's support on the UN vote seeking approval for the use of force against Iraq.[64] A similar meeting between Baker and Shevardnadze also failed to bring about an agreement, although Baker sought to put the best possible interpretation on the meeting: "Let me simply say that the United States and the Soviet Union have been united in their approach to this problem, beginning on the 3rd of August. We are united today. President Gorbachev and President Bush have both made it very clear that we intend to be united."[65] As for Bush, all he would say was "be patient and all will be well."[66]

One reason Gorbachev may have delayed voicing his support for a use of force resolution in Paris was that he hoped Saddam Hussein, watching the buildup of pressure against him, might yet reconsider. Indeed, Saddam sent his foreign minister, Tariq Aziz, to Moscow on November 26 for talks with Shevardnadze and Gorbachev in what turned out to be the final Iraqi attempt to convince Moscow not to support the use-of-force resolution. But Soviet opinion was sharpening against Iraq even before Aziz arrived, because Iraq had reneged on the timetable for allowing Soviet advisers working in Iraq to return home. As Vitaly Churkin, the new head of the Soviet Foreign Ministry Information Directorate and an aide to Shevardnadze, warned on the day Aziz arrived: "If the Iraqi side does not immediately remove all the barriers it has artificially erected to block USSR citizens from returning home, and does not ensure their unimpeded departure from Iraq, then that will complicate still further the atmosphere of Soviet-Iraqi relations, and will compel us to adopt an even tougher position on the situation in the Persian Gulf."[67]

While Aziz, in his meeting with Gorbachev, downplayed the delay in the departure of Soviet advisers as due to misunderstandings of a "bureaucratic nature,"[68] he was not willing to make any concessions on Iraq's annexation of Kuwait during what presidential spokesman Vitaly Ignatenko described as a "tough conversation" from which "the interlocutors parted coldly."[69] Following the failure of the talks, Ignatenko stated that the USSR would vote for the UN resolution establishing a "clear deadline" for the Iraqi pullout from Kuwait and the release of hostages.[70] Gorbachev, in an interview broadcast in Arabic to the Middle East following Aziz's departure, blasted Iraq for trying to split the coalition and predicted that the resolution adopted at the Security

Council session "will be, and I am confident of this, very harsh."[71]

Shevardnadze himself headed the Soviet delegation to the Security Council debate on the use-of-force resolution. In his speech at the United Nations, in addition to warning Saddam not to use chemical or bacteriological weapons, he praised the proposed resolution, Security Council Resolution 678, as one "with justice and a high measure of nobility."[72] The resolution authorized member states cooperating with Kuwait to use "all necessary means to uphold and implement Security Council Resolution 660 and all subsequent resolutions to restore peace and security in the area after a pause of goodwill" until January 15, 1991.[73] (Here the USSR won a concession from the United States, which wanted a January 1, 1991, deadline.) Shevardnadze said he viewed the UN deadline of January 15 as a "goodwill pause" which he hoped Saddam Hussein would use "to rise above" his concern about saving face, and to show "wisdom and vision." A Ministry of Foreign Affairs statement issued four days later, following Bush's offer of U.S.-Iraqi talks, emphasized the possibilities for peace inherent in the "goodwill pause." It also praised Bush's offer of talks with Iraq as a "concrete embodiment of Soviet-American mutual understanding on the preferability of resolving the crisis by peaceful means."[74]

In the aftermath of the Security Council resolution and Bush's offer to hold talks with Iraq, the diplomatic situation temporarily improved for Moscow; Gorbachev may have felt that his emphasis on a political settlement to the Gulf crisis was bearing fruit. Thus on December 6, after informing Moscow that all of its citizens could return to the USSR[75]—although Moscow would have to pay for all uncompleted contracts—the Iraqi government announced that all other foreign hostages would be set free. Gorbachev was also strengthened by economic aid that began to pour into the USSR (a good part of it made possible by Moscow's anti-Iraqi stand at the United Nations, although the donors of the aid sought to obscure its political purpose). Thus on November 30 came the announcement in Moscow that the USSR was to receive $3 billion in loans from the United Arab Emirates, Saudi Arabia, and Kuwait.[76] To make Moscow's receipt of the loans more politically acceptable, however, the Kuwaiti ambassador noted that "we are not buying their political stand" because the joint loan had been decided before Iraq threatened Kuwait." He also indicated that Kuwait, in May 1990, had authorized a two-stage $1 billion loan.[77] *Izvestia*, quoting the Kuwaiti ambassador on the combined $4 billion in loans several weeks later, said the purpose of the loans "is to help the Soviet people implement the perestroika that was initiated by USSR President M.S. Gorbachev. . . . We categorically disagree with those who state that the aforementioned loan has been given to the USSR as compensation for its position on the events taking place in the Persian Gulf."[78]

Perhaps even more welcome to Gorbachev was Bush's decision on December 12 to waive the Jackson-Vanik amendment for six months (although the USSR had not yet passed its long-awaited emigration law) to help the USSR meet its anticipated winter food shortages by approving up to $1 billion in federally guaranteed loans to allow Moscow to buy food and other agricultural products.[79] Interestingly enough, just as the Kuwaiti ambassador had denied any political reward for the GCC aid package, so too did Baker, who, together with Shevardnadze, denied that the trade concessions were intended as a payback for Moscow's cooperation on the Persian Gulf.[80]

In addition to the authorization of economic credits, the United States took another action for which Moscow had to be grateful— Baker's invitation for the USSR to send troops, even in token numbers, to participate in the multinational force in Saudi Arabia.[81] Given the fact that for decades a central element of U.S. policy in the Middle East was to keep the USSR out of the region,[82] it had to be gratifying for Moscow to see the United States inviting its erstwhile enemy to send troops to Saudi Arabia, the most important of the oil-rich states in the region. However, sending Soviet troops to the Gulf was a sensitive domestic issue in the USSR, where memories of the decade-long intervention in Afghanistan remained strong. Nonetheless, Moscow's failure to send even a hospital ship seemed to underline its continued efforts to maintain military neutrality if war broke out, thereby preserving its mediating position and the influence that went with it.

Indeed, the chances of war seemed to increase once again soon after Shevardnadze's departure from Washington. Iraq set a date for the visit of Baker so close to the UN withdrawal deadline that Bush put on hold the visit of Iraqi Foreign Minister Tariq Aziz to Washington on December 14, claiming Saddam was not serious in his negotiating.[83] The next day Iraq canceled the Aziz visit to Washington asserting that "Iraq alone" would set the date for the Baker visit.[84] As U.S.-Iraqi tensions escalated, U.S.-Soviet relations also received a blow with the announcement of the sudden resignation of Soviet Foreign Minister Shevardnadze. In his resignation speech, Shevardnadze warned of an approaching dictatorship in the USSR and complained about incessant criticism of his Gulf policy from right-wing elements in the Soviet government.[85] Given the fact that Shevardnadze had developed an extraordinarily close working relationship with Baker, there were concerns that U.S.-Soviet cooperation in the Gulf crisis would suffer.[86] To allay this concern, Vitaly Churkin, in a press conference after the resignation, stated, "We, the USSR Foreign Ministry, are deeply convinced that our foreign policy currently meets the country's and people's fundamental interests. This applies also to the Persian Gulf. We hope that the basic direction of the country's foreign policy will remain unchanged."[87]

Nonetheless, strains between the two superpowers surfaced almost immediately, with Soviet KGB Chairman Vladimir Krychkov asserting that the United States and other Western countries were trying to subvert the Soviet system under the guise of offering economic aid.[88] State Department deputy spokesman Richard Boucher strongly condemned Krychkov's assertion: "We are concerned that such a senior Soviet official would turn to this kind of outdated and inflammatory rhetoric which can only be described as inconsistent with the improvement that has taken place in both the atmosphere and substance of U.S.-Soviet relations."[89] Krychkov's comment that bloodshed might be required to restore order to the Soviet Union[90] further chilled relations, which suffered another blow three weeks later when a bloody Soviet crackdown took place in Lithuania in which fourteen Lithuanian civilians were killed.

As U.S.-Soviet relations cooled, the situation in the Gulf appeared to move inexorably toward war. While a Soviet delegation to Iraq in late December, headed by Igor Belousev, was able to make final arrangements for the withdrawal of Soviet advisers and the suspension of contracts while the Gulf crisis continued (at this point, with a possible war approaching, Saddam Hussein evidently felt he had to improve ties to Moscow), Belousev was unable to get any concessions on the Iraqi occupation of Kuwait.[91] When a belatedly arranged meeting of Baker and Tariq Aziz in Switzerland in early January failed to produce any diplomatic progress, and the U.S. Congress subsequently voted in favor of granting Bush the right to use armed force against Iraq, the outbreak of war, once the UN deadline of January 15 passed, seemed inevitable.

As the final countdown approached, the Soviet diplomatic position in the Middle East and in the world at large appeared strengthened. Despite the chill in U.S.-Soviet relations that had set in after Shevardnadze's resignation, Moscow's close cooperation with the United States during the crisis had earned it both words of praise from President Bush and economic benefits in the form of federally guaranteed loans. Similarly, with the establishment of diplomatic relations with Saudi Arabia and Bahrain, Moscow's political position in the Gulf strengthened, and the agreement of three GCC states to provide $4 billion in loans to the USSR was seen as a great boon for the hard-pressed Soviet economy. While strengthening ties with the United States and the GCC, Moscow had not burned its bridges to Iraq and could be seen to have some residual influence in that country. Although the issue of Soviet advisers had become a major irritant in Soviet-Iraqi relations, Gorbachev, by refusing to send troops to join the multinational force in the Gulf, had kept open Moscow's role as the only credible mediator between Iraq and the United States. Once the war erupted, Moscow was to use its mediating role to try to save both Iraq and the Iraqi regime of Saddam Hussein from destruction.

SOVIET POLICY DURING THE WAR

Moscow's position during the six-week war in the Gulf was in many ways similar to its policy in the prewar period of August 1, 1990–January 16, 1991. Thus at key junctures it cooperated with the United States while at the same time it tried to mediate the conflict and preserve its position in Iraq. The key difference between the two periods was the escalation of anti-U.S. rhetoric in the Soviet press, possibly a reflection of the increased influence of right-wing forces in Soviet society.

Thus when the UN ultimatum expired and the last-minute visit by UN Secretary General Pérez de Cuéllar to Baghdad failed, Churkin issued a statement condemning Iraq:[92]

> The goodwill pause that has lasted a month and a half has been packed full of various political and diplomatic peace efforts aimed at removing the threat of an explosion of immense destructive force created by the Iraqi aggression against Kuwait. With regret, it has to be stated that they have all been smashed by Baghdad's stubborn refusal to take into consideration norms of international law , civilized contact and the will of the international community voiced in 12 U.N. Security Council resolutions. By its behavior the Iraqi leadership is, in effect, pushing its own country and the region into the abyss of a military clash with catastrophic consequences.

Nevertheless, a military explosion in the Persian Gulf zone can still be averted. The Soviet Union supports any constructive steps leading to this end. But for such steps to be successful the Iraqi leadership should stop all attempts at balancing on the edge of war and make the only correct decision, that which the whole world expects of it.

At the same time, however, Soviet Deputy Foreign Minister Alexander Belonogov reassured Iraq that "the Soviet Union has no intention of taking part, even symbolically, in military action in the Gulf."[93] As if to emphasize this point once the war began, Moscow withdrew its two warships from the Gulf and as a precautionary move, also put its troops in its southern regions on limited alert.[94]

When the fighting began with a massive U.S. air strike against Iraqi military facilities in Baghdad and elsewhere in Iraq on January 16, Gorbachev himself, on Moscow Central TV, condemned Iraq:[95]

The tragic turn of events was provoked by the Iraqi leadership's refusal to fulfill the demands of the world community and to withdraw its troops from Kuwait. From the very outset of the Iraqi aggression, the Soviet Union has done everything incumbent upon it to resolve this acute international conflict by peaceful means. Until the very last minute we undertook vigorous efforts with the object of preventing war and restoring independence to Kuwait by political means.

Having received a report about the decision that had been made by U.S. Secretary of State Baker approximately one hour before the commencement of military hostilities, I immediately proposed to President Bush that additional steps be taken through direct contact with Saddam Hussein to achieve an immediate announcement by him of the withdrawal of his troops from Kuwait. . . . I once again emphasize that we have done everything possible to settle the conflict by non-military means.

When Iraq responded to the Allied attack by bombarding Israel with SCUD missiles, the Soviet Foreign Ministry—worried about the implications of an expanded war, especially the dilemma the USSR would face if Syria switched sides and aided Iraq—condemned Iraq and urged Israel to show restraint:[96]

On the night of January 17 Iraq staged missile attacks on the suburbs of Tel Aviv, Haifa and some other populated localities of Israel.

Obviously the purpose of that action was to transform the Kuwaiti problem into a regional conflict and to kindle military conflagration throughout the Middle East.

The Soviet Union has firmly opposed this development of events and expressed this view during contacts with the Iraqi leadership. We believe that it is not desirable to resolve one problem by creating another.

The Soviet Union hopes that the Israeli government will also display the needed restraint and will not take the path leading to further heightening of tension in the Middle East.

Then, less than one week into the war, Churkin made public a January 18 appeal from Gorbachev to Iraq, offering to try to get the United States to halt military action if Iraq announced the withdrawal of troops from Kuwait and the fulfilling of all appropriate Security Council resolutions.[97] Churkin also suggested that in the process, the Security Council could guarantee Iraq's sovereignty and territorial integrity.

The first major change in the official Soviet position on the war came on January 22 when Gorbachev, in a press conference, warned of the "dangerous" tendency toward further escalation of the conflict that was going beyond the Security Council's mandate to liberate Kuwait.[98] (Right-wing newspapers like *Sovetskaya Rossiya* had been condemning the U.S. position on the Gulf well before the war broke out,[99] and once it erupted *Sovetskaya Rossiya* and, to a lesser extent, *Krasnaya Zvezda* became mouthpieces for Iraqi propaganda.) Here emerged a major difference between the United States and USSR, because U.S. military commanders had decided that they were not going to launch a ground assault to free Kuwait until Iraq's military infrastructure and its ability to resupply its troops in Kuwait had been gravely weakened. This entailed widespread bombing of Iraq with the collateral damage or civilian casualties inevitable in such military actions.

In a reinforcement of Gorbachev's press conference statement, the newly appointed Soviet Foreign Minister, Alexander Bessmertnykh, on departing Moscow in late January for his first official visit to Washington, warned:[100]

The Persian Gulf requires a very careful comparison of positions. *On the whole we support the U.N. Security Council resolutions.* There are fears, however, that we are entering upon a second grave phase of the conflict, where, in addition to a resolution of the task stipulated by the Security Council resolutions—namely, the liberation of Kuwait—the fear is beginning to mount that Iraq is being subjected to very serious destruction, and there is a mounting danger for the country's peaceful population. Naturally, we are concerned about this. So, while adhering to the Security Council resolutions, we must at the same time show concern that the actions occurring in this zone do not go beyond the bounds stipulated in this resolution. Naturally, besides the Persian Gulf conflict itself, *it is necessary to take a look at the balance of forces in the Middle East* and think about the prospects for what will occur there. Thus the task is very great. (emphasis added)

Bessmertnykh's statement disclosed a difference in emphasis from that of his predecessor. While Shevardnadze had enthusiastically supported the Security Council resolutions, Bessmertnykh was much more reserved, and his comment about the "balance of forces" seemed more of a reflection of the old than of the new thinking. In any case, during his visit to Washington, Bessmertnykh persuaded Baker to sign a joint statement that stressed that the U.S. goal was the liberation of Kuwait and not the destruction of Iraq.[101] Baker also agreed to end military action against Iraq—if Iraq made an unambiguous pledge to leave Kuwait and followed it by specific steps leading to the complete fulfillment of the Security Council resolutions. Finally, Baker angered Israel and its U.S. supporters by agreeing to link the Gulf crisis more closely than ever before to the Arab-Israeli conflict. The joint statement noted that after the war, "Dealing with the causes of conflict, including the Arab-Israeli conflict, will be especially important." Bessmertnykh hailed the joint statement with its emphasis on the Palestinian problem as "probably for the first time since 1976 two ministers have spoken jointly on the Middle East."[102]

All was not rosy, however, in the U.S.-Soviet relationship at this time as the two countries agreed to postpone the planned February 1991 Bush-Gorbachev summit.[103] While Bush gave as reasons for the postponement the Gulf War and the still unfinished arms talks, the shadow of Gorbachev's crackdown in the Baltics also appeared to be an important factor.

Meanwhile, two weeks into the war, Soviet generals were beginning to prophesy its outcome. In an interview in the liberal *Komsomolskaya Pravda*, the conservative editor of the *Military Historical Journal*, Major General Filatov (who had previously run excerpts from *Mein Kampf* and was preparing to publish the *Protocols of the Elders of Zion*, an anti-Semitic forgery, in his journal), predicted that the war would end in a major U.S. defeat, a second Vietnam "which will be somewhat worse for it than the first."[104] He also stated that in the unlikely case that Iraq were to be defeated, other Arab countries will enter the war against the so-called international force. One week later, writing in *Izvestia*, Major General N. Kostin, a department chief at the Soviet General Staff Academy, perhaps in an attempt to counterbalance criticism of the poor performance of Soviet weaponry in the hands of the Iraqis, and of the Soviet specialists who trained them, asserted, "Iraqi units are manifestly superior to their enemies in desert warfare skills. They hold defensive positions that are well equipped in the engineering respect, and it will not be easy to take them even given air superiority. Soviet-made T-62 and T-72 tanks are better adapted for desert operations than the U.S. M-1 Abrams."[105]

While the Soviet generals were making these fallacious predictions, the pace of diplomatic activity speeded up. In early February, following the visit of an Iraqi envoy to Iran, President Rafsanjani of Iran offered to mediate between the United States and Iraq. Then Soviet Deputy Foreign Minister Belogonov himself went to Iran to coordinate policy as Moscow continued to maintain close diplomatic ties with the Rafsanjani regime. Before leaving for Tehran, Belogonov emphasized the central Soviet policy theme that the war was "getting out of control and doing irreparable harm to the Iraqi people."[106] While Iran and the USSR were coordinating policy, the United States was planning for the postwar structure of the Middle East. Secretary of State Baker, testifying before the House Foreign Affairs Committee on February 6, praised Iran's neutral position in the war, although he did not hold out any hope for Rafsanjani's mediation efforts. Baker also outlined five challenges that would demand U.S. attention in the postwar Middle East: Gulf security structures in which he intimated the United States would have a role to play; arms control; economic reconstruction; improved U.S. energy conservation, and a reconciliation among the Arab states, Israel, and the Palestinians.[107] As the secretary of state was laying out the areas of postwar U.S. concern, Gorbachev was moving to assert the Soviet position in the postwar world. In a major statement on February 9, in which he implicitly criticized Iraq both for threatening the use of weapons of mass destruction and for trying to draw Israel into the war, he again called on Saddam Hussein to "display realism which would make it possible to take the path of a reliable and just peaceful settlement." As far as the postwar security structure of the region was concerned, Gorbachev emphasized that "the countries of the region should play a decisive role in this process" and "Iraq should hold a worthy place in the postwar settlement." Gorbachev also announced that he was again sending Primakov to meet with the Iraqi leadership to try to bring about a peace settlement because developments in the Gulf zone were "taking an ever more alarming and dramatic turn."[108]

Primakov's visit to Baghdad coincided with an intensification of the U.S. bombing of Iraq.[109] While the Iraqi description of the Hussein-Primakov talks criticized the USSR for giving cover to the "U.S. and Allied crimes" against Iraq because Moscow supported Security Council Resolution 678, it also asserted that Iraq was "prepared to extend cooperation to the USSR and other nations and agencies in the interest of finding a peaceful, political, equitable, and honorable solution" to the Middle East's central issues, including the situation in the Gulf.[110] While Iraq, in this statement, seemed to cling to its old linkage position, Primakov stated that he saw "glimmers of hope" as a result of his visit to Baghdad.[111]

It was at this point that the United States bombed a shelter in Baghdad which the U.S. military command claimed was a military shelter but which housed a number of Iraqi civilians who became casualties. This incident threatened to inflame the Security Council discussion of the war that was set to begin, and the United States urged that the session be kept private so as to avoid the appearance of divisions in the council. This would have been an opportunity for the USSR to embarrass the United States by pressing for an open session, but instead Moscow again cooperated with the United States and voted with it to keep the session closed. Yuly Vorontsov, the Soviet ambassador to the United Nations, stated that a public debate in the Security Council could be misinterpreted in Baghdad and thus complicate efforts by the USSR and other countries to bring about a peace settlement.[112]

By mid-February, one month into the war, it appeared that Iraq was suffering so much destruction that Saddam Hussein began to search for a way out and sought to use the Soviet Union as the mechanism for extracting Iraq from the war with minimal political or diplomatic damage. Thus on February 15 Iraq announced its peace plan for a pull-out from Kuwait but linked the plan to so many conditions—including Allied payment of reparations to Iraq for the damages its bombing had caused, the repeal of all UN resolutions beyond Resolution 660, Israel's withdrawal from the occupied territories and the withdrawal of all Allied forces and weapons, including the U.S. Patriot missiles that had been sent to Israel to combat the SCUDS—that President Bush rejected the Iraqi offer as a "cruel hoax."[113] Moscow, however, which finally saw itself in the mediating position it had long coveted, took a much more positive view. Bessmertnykh, in words reminiscent of Shevardnadze's comments about Iraq's mid-August linkage plan, stated that the Iraqi announcement "opens up a new stage in the development of the conflict. This is an important development. We shall study this document attentively."[114] Then, with Aziz on his way to Moscow for talks, Gorbachev, in a letter to Bush, reportedly asked the U.S. president to hold off the planned ground offensive until the completion of talks between Aziz and the Soviet leadership in Moscow.[115] One of the results of the Aziz visit was a Soviet plan for peace which Aziz was given to take back to Baghdad. The Iraqi foreign minister was upbeat about the talks, stating that "the atmosphere between us and the Soviet friends was cordial and objective."[116]

There then began a diplomatic process that can best be likened to a defense lawyer seeking to work out a "plea bargain" with a district attorney. Over the next six days Moscow would be in contact both with Baghdad and Washington, trying to sell Bush on the concessions that Saddam Hussein was willing to make while at the same time trying to convince Saddam that he would have to make more concessions if he wished to avoid an Allied ground offensive. Meanwhile, while delaying the ground attack a few days in deference to Gorbachev, Bush refused the Soviet leader's offers, although always with great respect, as the U.S. president continued to seek to maintain Gorbachev's dignity if not Saddam's. Thus, after seeing the secret first version of Gorbachev's plan, Bush expressed appreciation for Gorbachev's sending the plan to the United States but said that it fell "far short of what would be required."[117] Meanwhile, in a possible effort to pressure the United States to accept Gorbachev's mediating efforts, Bessmertnykh warned that an Allied ground attack would "tremendously complicate" negotiations toward an Iraqi pullout,[118] while former Chief of Staff Marshall Sergei Akhromeyev stated in an Interfax interview that Allied strikes against the Iraqi economy and people 'can no longer be tolerated."[119] The commander in chief of the soon to be dissolved Warsaw Pact, General Vladimir Lobov, went farther in his criticism, asserting "no one should be allowed to use Security Council resolutions as a smokescreen to camouflage the massacre on Iraqi territory."[120]

While the growing influence of the military and other hard-line groups in the USSR may have encouraged these officers to speak out (*Sovetskaya Rossiya* went even farther, claiming that Iraq was "the main bastion and base against U.S. and Israeli domination of the region"),[121] Gorbachev nonetheless stuck to his diplomacy. When Iraqi obstinence over such issues as the paying of reparations to Kuwait and the speed of its military withdrawal from that country led to Bush's issuing an ultimatum and then beginning the ground war on February 24, Moscow essentially acquiesced in the decision, again cooperating with the United States at the United Nations, although a Soviet government statement was to complain that "the instinct to rely on a military solution prevailed, despite Iraq's declared readiness to pull all of its forces out of Kuwait unconditionally."[122] Primakov, interviewed on Moscow television the day before the ground war started, sought to put Moscow on the diplomatic high ground no matter what happened. "If this war starts today, it will start and the whole world will see that it has been started in circumstances where the USSR has indeed accomplished a tremendous achievement in the efforts to find a political settlement. . . . if at this moment it is frustrated by war, then those who have started it will take upon themselves the responsibility."[123] *Pravda* went even farther and on February 25 launched a blistering attack against the United States saying its decision to start the ground war was "based on its drive for sole leadership in the world."[124] Even Gorbachev was caught up in the rhetoric, noting in a speech in Minsk on February 26 that was also devoted to an attack on "so-called democrats" who "want to restore capitalism and favor the collapse of the union" that the progress in relations between the United States and USSR was "still fragile," and he called for responsible behavior "so that what has been achieved is not destroyed."[125]

Rhetoric aside, Moscow cooperated with the United States in convincing Saddam finally to accept the terms of the temporary cease-fire,[126] which it did on February 28, and then in strongly supporting the United States in working out the terms for a stringent permanent cease-fire. Essentially Moscow accepted the inevitability of the rapid collapse of its erstwhile ally, choosing to work with the regional victors (Syria, Egypt, and Saudi Arabia) as well as the United States rather than prolonging its efforts on behalf of a lost cause. Indeed, Moscow, after the war, was to change its tune on U.S.-Soviet relations as well. When asked at a press conference after the cease-fire about Gorbachev's statement that U.S.-Soviet relations were "fragile," Bessmertnykh replied that U.S.-Soviet relations had "withstood the test" during the Iraq-Kuwait conflict.[127]

MOSCOW AND THE MIDDLE EAST FROM THE CEASE-FIRE TO THE ABORTIVE COUP

The Arab-Israeli Peace Process

When the war came to an end, Moscow had one central concern—that the United States, because of its military victory over Iraq in cooperation with Saudi Arabia, Egypt, and Syria, would dominate the Middle East politically. The primary problem for Moscow was the possibility that the United States would follow through on its wartime planning and establish a major base system in the Persian Gulf region with both troops and planes to augment the large naval presence it had maintained in the region for more than a decade.

Another problem for Moscow lay in the U.S. effort to bring about an Arab-Israeli settlement. Moscow had long sought such a settlement and in the Gorbachev era had warmed its relations with Israel in an effort to try to bring one about. But given the weakening of the PLO's diplomatic position due to Arafat's support of Saddam Hussein, and given possible efforts by King Hussein of Jordan to get back into the good graces of the United States after bitter clashes during the war, the Soviet leader seemed concerned that the United States might orchestrate an arrangement whereby a delegation of West Bank and Gaza Palestinians together with King Hussein might negotiate a peace settlement with Israel, thereby freezing out not only the PLO from the process but also the Soviet Union.

Since Moscow was beset by increasingly severe economic problems during the postwar period and now was openly asking the United States and Western Europe for massive economic aid, it obviously could not directly oppose U.S. efforts in the Middle East. Nonetheless, it could quietly reinforce those countries in the Middle East opposed to a postwar U.S. hegemony, and leading the list of such countries was Syria.

Syria, for its part, had emerged from the Gulf War with improved economic and political positions. More than $2 billion in economic aid from the GCC states had enabled Assad to stabilize the Syrian

economy partially while at the same time making it possible for him
to purchase twenty-four SCUD missiles from North Korea[128] (and, possibly, M-9 missiles from China as well). In addition, for the first time
in many years Syria was playing a mainstream role in Arab politics, a
development that gave it enhanced political prestige both in the Arab
world and in the West, where Syria's role as an ally in the conflict
with Iraq was greatly appreciated. Further, Syria used the opportunity
presented by the Gulf War to oust General Aoun from power in Lebanon and reinforce the position of the pro-Syrian Lebanese government.
Finally, Assad's main Arab rival, Saddam Hussein, had suffered a crushing defeat in the war, and Assad may have hoped, particularly right after the war, that Saddam would be ousted from power and replaced by
a pro-Syrian regime.

While the position of Syria had greatly improved as a result of the
war, so too had that of its main enemy, Israel. By not retaliating
against Iraqi SCUD missile attacks, thus helping to preserve the Allied
coalition, Israel had gained great good will in the United States and
Western Europe, as well as economic and military assistance, including
anti-chemical warfare equipment from Germany and the Patriot anti-
missile system from the United States. Since Syria's main deterrent (or
means of attack) against Israel was chemical-tipped missiles, it could
not be pleased by this development, nor by the fact that with almost
all of Iraq's offensive power eliminated by the Allied attack Israel
could concentrate its forces against Syria.

As Syria began to engage in postwar diplomacy, Assad sought to
strengthen his diplomatic position vis-à-vis both the United States
and Israel by holding out an olive branch to the now weakened PLO,
and again coordinating his policy with King Hussein. He released hundreds of Arafat's followers from jail on the eve of Baker's visit to
Damascus in mid-March, an action that elicited from Arafat the comment "this positive initiative will help end the strain between us and
our brothers in Syria."[129] Two weeks later, he played host to King
Hussein of Jordan, the first visit of the Jordanian monarch in more
than a year.[130] Next he met President Hosni Mubarak in Cairo, and the
two Arab leaders formed a plan for an international conference to resolve the Arab-Israeli conflict that included a major role for the five
permanent Security Council members.[131] He also met with Iranian
President Rafsanjani to coordinate policy. With his diplomatic position
now stronger, Assad sent his foreign minister, Farouk al-Shara, to
Moscow for talks with Gorbachev in which both the Persian Gulf sit-

uation and the Arab-Israeli conflict were discussed. During the meeting, Gorbachev praised Assad and "expressed his belief that Syria's initiative-taking policy can do a great deal both to restore Arab unity and to resolve the Arab-Israeli conflict—in a spirit of realism and with an eye to the various interests that come together there." Gorbachev also promised to develop relations of "friendly cooperation" with Syria "in all areas, including the defense sphere—with due consideration, of course, for the new international situation and capabilities that are limited by the current state of the Soviet economy."[132] Although Moscow was clearly expressing the limits of its willingness to offer Syria military aid (indeed, Moscow's unwillingness to give advanced surface-to-surface missiles to Syria may have been the reason Assad turned to North Korea and China for such weapons), nonetheless a diplomatic link to Moscow was useful to Assad as he moved ahead in the diplomatic negotiations with Israel and the United States over the peace process.

His next move was an offer from the Syrian-backed National Salvation Front for a reconciliation with Arafat;[133] it was followed up in late May by a high-ranking PLO delegation of Arafat supporters who went to Damascus to negotiate a *modus vivendi* with Assad.[134] At the same time, Syria signed a treaty with Lebanon, consolidating its influence there. As Syria's diplomatic position strengthened, Assad took a hard-line position on the ground rules for talks with Israel in a ten-hour meeting with Baker during the secretary of state's visit to Damascus on April 23. In particular, Syria called for any peace conference to have a permanent structure to which parties could go back for help in breaking deadlocks, a "significant role" for the United Nations in the talks, and an advance commitment by Israel to abide by UN resolutions on land for peace.[135] Since Israel was taking an almost diametrically opposed position (no role for the United Nations, no advanced commitment on land for peace, and only a symbolic, one-day "regional" peace conference that would lead to direct talks between Israel and her Arab neighbors), Baker's shuttle diplomacy soon reached an impasse.

At this point, Baker, who had been in Moscow in mid-March, again went to the Soviet Union, this time meeting Foreign Minister Bessmertnykh in the Soviet Caucuses. He received a commitment from Bessmertnykh to cosponsor the Middle East peace conference—something Moscow had long wanted.[136] Bessmertnykh also told Baker he would visit the Middle East in May, and Baker may have hoped Bessmertnykh would use Moscow's influence with Syria to get Assad to

moderate his position on the modalities for holding a peace conference. Yet, while Moscow was ever mindful of its need for economic
assistance from the United States, Gorbachev did not share the U.S.
interest in pressuring Assad. Moscow itself had long wanted an active
and "effective" international conference to work out an Arab-Israeli
peace conference,[137] and the one-shot ceremonial conference proposed
by Israel did not meet Soviet needs. An extensive international peace
conference, cosponsored by the Soviet Union, would give Moscow the
opportunity to demonstrate its continued significance in the Middle
East. In addition, Moscow, under Gorbachev, had seen the United Nations as an effective tool both for covering the retreat of the USSR
from Third World conflict areas such as Angola and Cambodia and for
limiting unilateral U.S. actions, as in the Gulf War. Consequently, a
major role for the United Nations on an Arab-Israeli settlement was
very much in the Soviet interest.[138] Thus on both the issues of an active international conference and a UN role in the conference, Soviet
and Syrian interests coincided, and there was no indication of any Soviet pressure on Syria during Bessmertnykh's visits to Damascus during his mid-May trip to the Middle East. Indeed, according to Foreign
Minister Farouk al-Shara, the USSR and Syria had identical viewpoints
on the peace process "especially regarding the structure of the international peace conference, the participation of the United Nations and
the European Community, and the continuity of the conference."[139]
Whether or not the Syrian foreign minister was accurate in portraying
the Soviet position (Bessmertnykh himself was reserved in his comments on these issues), Syria's position clearly toughened as Baker was
to realize when he visited Damascus in mid-May, several days after
Bessmertnykh, and after meeting with the Soviet foreign minister in
Cairo.[140] The failure of the Baker visit to Damascus may well have
prompted the unplanned return of Bessmertnykh to the Syrian capital
as the Soviet foreign minister sought to demonstrate to the United
States that Moscow was doing everything possible to facilitate the
peace process.

On balance, the Bessmertnykh visit to the Middle East seemed
primarily aimed at "showing the flag," fact finding, and improving
Moscow's bilateral relations with the countries visited (Syria, Jordan,
Israel, Egypt, and Saudi Arabia, and also Switzerland, where Bessmertnykh met Arafat, thereby aiding in the Palestinian leader's postwar
political rehabilitation). A columnist in *Izvestia* summed up the
Bessmertnykh visit: "Baker's fourth tour of the region this year and

Bessmertnykh's first were marked by collaboration between the two powers. This was shown not only by the consultations between the two ministers in Kislovodsk and Cairo, but also by the fact that it was the United States which advocated that the USSR be co-chairman of the peace conference . . . the United States realizes that despite the victory for U.S. weaponry, it will not be able to carry the burden in isolation without Soviet participation. After all, even given the fact that our power has been weakened by domestic strife, the Arabs continue to see us as a counterweight to the U.S.-Israeli alliance."[141]

Meanwhile, as part of Moscow's efforts to demonstrate its continued relevance in the Middle East, Gorbachev had agreed to a meeting in mid-April between Prime Minister Pavlov and Prime Minister Shamir when both were in London for the inauguration of the Western Development Bank.[142] Shamir used the meeting to restate the Israeli position that there could be no Soviet participation in an international conference until the Soviet Union reestablished full diplomatic relations with Israel. For his part, Pavlov reportedly said that the USSR would consider the Israeli position on a Middle East peace settlement.[143] The Tass report of the discussion noted only that "the participants in the conversation displayed understanding of the necessity to coordinate the efforts of the Soviet Union and Israel in the matter of a Middle East settlement" and that "an exchange of opinions also took place on a number of bilateral Soviet-Israeli relations including the political, economic and cultural spheres."[144]

Israel was to be one of the stops on Bessmertnykh's visit to the Middle East in May. As in the past, the question arose of Israel's building of settlements in the occupied territories and the possibility that Soviet Jewish immigrants might settle there, and it became an important issue for Bessmertnykh. Angering both the Arab states and the United States, which was in a major drive to bring about the peace conference, Ariel Sharon announced the construction of 13,000 housing units in the West Bank and Gaza, out of a total of 250,000 to be constructed by Israel over the next two years. In an effort to reassure Moscow, however, Sharon stated, "We are building for Israelis. We are not providing housing for immigrants because we don't want to endanger Soviet emigration."[145] Nonetheless, neither Secretary Baker, who condemned the settlement construction, nor the Arab states were reassured by Sharon's statement, and Bessmertnykh, on his trip to the Middle East, was confronted by Arab opposition to the settlement building. Perhaps feeling that the United States, which had also condemned the Israeli settlements, would not oppose a hard-line Soviet statement on the settlements—even one that again threatened emigration—and seeing that this was an issue on which Moscow might achieve a political gain for its weakened Middle East position, Bessmertnykh took the opportunity to condemn the settlements strongly and threaten a possible cutoff of emigration. In a statement in Amman he asserted, "I cannot foresee, conceive, or accept a situation when a peace conference is in session while the settlements are going to be built. The Soviet Union and other countries who are interested in arranging such a conference are going to deal with that problem straightforwardly and directly as one of the things to be solved before the conference starts."[146] Then, when asked whether the Soviet Union planned to restrict Soviet Jewish immigration because of the settlements, Bessmertnykh said, "I do not exclude anything when we talk about the necessity to stop the construction of these settlements."[147]

Nonetheless, just as the year before when Gorbachev's threat to stop emigration because of the settlements had been followed by Shevardnadze's reassurance that this would not happen, so too Bessmertnykh's threat in Jordan was followed by Soviet reassurances on the emigration issue—this time by Bessmertnykh himself during his next stop, Israel. In talks with Shamir and David Levy, Bessmertnykh stated, "We have agreed that one country will not try to exert artificial pressure on another. Regarding immigration, this process is a result of [the] democratization of our society, of the new thinking in foreign and domestic affairs."[148] Shamir thanked Bessmertnykh for his comments and said that the policy of free emigration was another major Soviet contribution to Israel, after Kremlin recognition of the State of Israel.[149] For his part, Levy was upbeat, stating, "I must say the atmosphere was more than correct—it was friendly. There were no hints, no pressure, no threats, nothing like that."[150] A Tass report was more restrained, but still positive — and made no mention of the settlement issue.

> Foreign Minister Alexander Bessmertnykh made on Friday a brief working visit to Israel. He had a substantive conversation with Israeli Prime Minister Yitzhak Shamir and conducted negotiations with Israeli Foreign Minister David Levy.
>
> The minister's visit had the purpose of establishing how realistic is a step towards settling the Middle East conflict, taking into account the specific features of the present situation and statements of the Israeli leadership about Israel's striving for peace.

The conversation took place *in a businesslike and benevolent atmosphere. The sides exchanged views about possible steps to ease the situation and factors that still interfere with this.*

The Israeli side welcomed the Soviet Union's activity in the Middle East region and joint actions of the USSR and the U.S. towards a Middle East settlement.

The Israeli side expressed interest in closer contacts with the Soviet side, also at the level of foreign ministers. The Soviet minister expressed readiness for this.

During the conversations the Israeli side voiced serious concern about the danger of the arms race in the Middle East. The Soviet side noted that this problem could seriously [be] aggravate[d] if the present opportunity to begin the peace process slipped [away] and that this problem merits close attention.

Both sides expressed satisfaction with the fact that Soviet-Israeli relations began to enter [a] normal route in recent years and became very ramified.

The Soviet foreign minister's visit is the first such event in the history of relations between the Soviet Union and Israel. *It is apparently an important milestone in the natural development of Soviet-Israeli relations which will become full-scale diplomatic relations with the passage of time.*

At a joint news conference given on Friday at Tel Aviv airport prior to the departure of the Soviet Minister to Cairo, Bessmertnykh and Levy gave a positive assessment to the dialogue they had.[151] (emphasis added)

Two months after the Bessmertnykh visit to the Middle East, Syria, perhaps reacting to the enhanced Middle East position of the United States, changed its position and accepted the U.S. terms for the conference. Assad said that the U.S. plan was "an acceptable basis for achieving a comprehensive solution and a peace process in the region, especially since these proposals are based on UN Resolutions 242 and 338 which apply to all fronts and secure legitimate Palestinian rights."[152] Since the United States had acceded to Israeli wishes about having essentially symbolic roles for the United Nations and European Community at the conference, the Syrian president appeared to have decided that the future interests of his country—in the short term at least—lay in following the U.S. lead, and he gave in on these two points. Nonetheless Syrian television quoted Assad as saying that he highly valued "President Bush's pledge that the United States and the USSR will be a catalyst for peace and that they will have a special responsibility to make the conference succeed in its objectives as defined by the relevant U.N. resolutions."[153]

Once Assad had decided to attend the conference, Moscow praised the Syrian leader's decision and urged the Palestinians to follow his example.[154] Given the Soviet Union's reduced influence not only in Syria but in the region as a whole, Gorbachev clearly could not push the Syrian leader to hold out for a major UN role—much as he might have wanted to do so. Instead, Gorbachev capitalized on the joint U.S.-Soviet sponsorship of the conference, and in an interview on the rapidly evolving Middle East situation a Soviet Foreign Ministry official emphasized Moscow's role as a joint sponsor of the conference.[155] The Soviet Union continued this theme in late July as Bush journeyed to Moscow for a summit meeting with Gorbachev. There, on July 31, the two world leaders jointly announced plans to issue formal invitations to a Middle East peace conference in October:[156] "While recognizing that peace cannot be imposed and that it can only result from direct negotiations between the parties, the United States and the Soviet Union pledge to do their utmost to promote and sustain the peacemaking process. To that end, the United States and the Soviet Union, acting as co-sponsors, will work to convene in October a peace conference designed to launch bilateral and multilateral negotiations. Invitations to the conference will be issued at least ten days before the conference is to convene. In the interim, Secretary Baker and Foreign Minister Bessmertnykh will continue to work with the parties to prepare for the conference."[157]

At the same time, Bessmertnykh announced that the USSR was ready to establish full diplomatic relations with Israel if the Jewish state attended the Middle East peace conference,[158] and several days after the Moscow summit Israel in fact agreed to attend the conference, albeit on condition that any Palestinians attending could not live in Jerusalem, be members of the PLO, or live outside of the West Bank and Gaza.[159]

Moscow's renewed role in the Middle East peace process was played up by the Soviet media, as an Arabic language radio broadcast on August 2 noted:

> For the first time the U.S. side has referred to a just and durable Middle East peace—this is Soviet terminology—the essence of which is that peace in the region can only be established when it is just.

Also important is the fact that the Gorbachev-Bush statement was issued in Moscow. *Our commentator believes that this refutes allegations in the Arab world that the Soviet Union plays a weak role in the Middle East settlement. Once again, it was stressed that a durable peace in the region is impossible without the Soviet Union's participation.*[160] (emphasis added)

Seventeen days later, Gorbachev was temporarily overthrown in a coup which was to lead ultimately to the collapse of the Soviet Union. Prior to examining the impact of the coup on Soviet policy toward the Middle East, an analysis will be made of Soviet policy toward the Persian Gulf from the end of the Gulf War to the abortive coup.

Soviet Policy toward the Persian Gulf

Once the Gulf War ended, in a major military victory for the United States and its allies, Moscow urged that the nations of the Persian Gulf region themselves (including Iran) take primary responsibility for their security, that the United Nations play an important role in the process, and that foreign forces be no larger than they had been on August 1, 1990, the day before the Iraqi invasion of Kuwait.[161] Moscow was heartened when the GCC states, meeting with Syria and Egypt in Damascus in early March 1991, announced their reliance on Egypt and Syria to be the "nucleus for an Arab force which would guarantee the security and peace of Arab countries in the Gulf region"[162] and promised Egypt and Syria billions of dollars in economic aid. Given Syria's role in the alignment and the Gulf states' call for improved relations with Iran (Saudi Arabia and Iran restored diplomatic relations in mid-March), Moscow may have hoped that with Iran actively opposing a major U.S. military presence in the Gulf, the United States could be prevented from establishing its military hegemony in the region. Unfortunately for Moscow, however, a rift between Saudi Arabia, on the one hand, and Egypt and Syria, on the other, led to the pullout of the forces of the non-Gulf states,[163] and the GCC nations remained highly suspicious of Iran. Consequently, it appeared as if the United States, after all, would play a major military role in the region. Despite the statement of a Saudi general, Prince Khaled ibn Sultan (who had commanded the Arab and Islamic forces in the anti-Iraq coalition), that he did not think Saudi Arabia would need or want a larger U.S. military presence than it had before the war,[164] Moscow was clearly concerned as Secretary of Defense Cheney toured the Gulf in early May 1991 seeking to expand the U.S. military presence in the region.[165] Indeed, over the summer, in addition to arranging further arms sales to Arab allies, the United States continued to negotiate military arrangements, and in early September, shortly after the abortive coup in Moscow, a military agreement was signed with Kuwait. One month later the United States also signed a military agreement with Bahrain.[166]

The continuing concern over Iraq and fear of the potential threat from Iran were the main causes of the agreements negotiated by the two Gulf states with the United States and of the continued security discussions between the United States and Saudi Arabia. Moscow, while supporting the U.S. effort to achieve a stringent cease-fire resolution, continued to protect the Saddam Hussein regime. Although the massacres of Iraqi Shia and Kurds who had engaged in a postwar uprising were widely reported in the Soviet press,[167] Moscow not only opposed any war crimes trial for Saddam[168] but also strongly cautioned the United Nations against any intervention on behalf of the Kurds that might infringe on Iraq's sovereignty.[169] While this attitude may have reflected Soviet concern about a possible similar UN intervention on behalf of increasingly restive Soviet national minorities like the Lithuanians, it seemed also aimed at protecting Saddam. Thus while such Soviet liberals as Georgi Mirsky openly called for the termination of the Soviet-Iraqi treaty because of Saddam's genocide,[170] Gorbachev's Middle East adviser, Yevgeny Primakov, said he believed Saddam "has sufficient potential to give us hope for a positive development of relations with him."[171] Although the U.S. humanitarian effort on behalf of the Kurds was praised, Moscow also displayed concern that it would provide a pretext for U.S. forces to remain in northern Iraq.[172] Consequently Moscow warmly supported the beginning of negotiations between Saddam and Kurdish leaders, hoping this would expedite the departure of U.S. troops.[173]

When it was revealed that Iraq was hiding nuclear weapons research materials, Moscow took a tougher line toward its erstwhile ally.[174] Having already joined with the United States (and the other members of the Security Council) on June 17 in a resolution compelling Iraq to pay the full costs of destroying its chemical and biological weapons, its ballistic missiles, and its nuclear material and requiring that all states report to the secretary-general the steps they had taken to ensure that their citizens and corporations did not supply Iraq with military material or the technology and machinery to produce it,[175] a

Soviet Foreign Ministry official, in an Interfax interview on July 3, pointedly stated, "Should Baghdad's suspected involvement in nuclear weapons development be confirmed, the USSR would proceed not from the interests of the early reestablishment of its cooperation with Iraq, but rather from the will of the international community which is urging Baghdad to create all the necessary conditions for a peaceful settlement in the Gulf."[176]

Nonetheless, when the United States began to hint that a military strike to destroy Iraq's nuclear installations was being considered following an incident on June 28 when Iraqi soldiers fired over the heads of UN inspectors who were filming the hasty withdrawal of equipment from an Iraqi military base,[177] the Soviet ambassador to the United Nations, Yuly Vorontsov, who had cooperated closely with the U.S. representative to the United Nations on Iraqi issues, cautioned against the use of force: "Neither the United States nor anyone else has said one word within the walls of the United Nations about a resort to military options. We are talking strictly in terms of diplomatic solutions." The Soviet UN ambassador did, however, issue a strong warning to Iraq: "This is a very serious matter and the letter we received today (from Iraq) is not a satisfactory answer to all the questions in this business. Until these things are cleared up, there is no chance that the Security Council will address such questions as relieving the economic sanctions against Iraq. Iraq must understand that it is in its interest to resolve this."[178]

As U.S. pressure on Iraq mounted, the right-wing Soviet newspaper *Krasnaya Zvezda*, which had supported Iraq during the Gulf War, warned, "We have had enough of military operations. Common sense should prevail on both sides. The world can quite well do without a second round of 'Desert Storm.'"[179] In a similar vein, Soviet Foreign Ministry spokesman Vitaly Churkin, speaking on CNN, cautioned against the use of force, warning that it would have "negative consequences . . . larger than maybe the intended goal of those actions."[180] However, Moscow was willing to endorse another strong UN condemnation of Iraq, and on August 15 it joined the United States and other members of the Security Council in condemning Iraq's "serious violation of its obligation" to cooperate fully with the International Atomic Energy Agency and the special UN commission established to oversee elimination of its weapons of mass destruction. The resolution also demanded that Iraq "provide full, final and complete disclosure . . . of all aspects of its programs to develop weapons of mass destruction and ballistic missiles with a range greater than 93 miles," "cease immediately any attempt to conceal" research work on nuclear, chemical, biological, or ballistic missile programs, and give UN inspectors complete access to all parts of the country. It was also warned not to interfere with overflights by surveillance planes or helicopters and to provide Iraqi facilities to assist the inspections.[181]

In sum, while Moscow sought to retain influence in Iraq by protecting Saddam Hussein, in the two months before the Soviet coup, once Iraqi nuclear ambitions became clear, Soviet criticism of Iraq mounted (although Moscow continued to urge the United States not to use military force a second time against Iraq). When news of the coup reached Iraq, Saddam Hussein was overjoyed, and Iraq issued a statement praising the new Soviet government: "It is natural for us to welcome this change, as do the countries that were hurt by the policies of the former regime. . . . We hope that this change will contribute toward restoring the correct international balance to prevent hegemony and aggression. . . . Iraq will positively respond to every initiative of friendship from the Soviet Union in its new age."[182]

Unfortunately for Saddam, the coup proved abortive. Gorbachev, upon his return to Moscow, condemned Saddam, and Soviet-Iraqi relations sharply deteriorated, as the USSR began to cooperate more closely with the United States in its Middle East policies.

Soviet Policy toward the Middle East from the Collapse of the Coup to the Collapse of the USSR

In the aftermath of the abortive coup, major changes took place in the USSR. The individual republics, led by Russia under Boris Yeltsin became increasingly assertive, the Baltic states were given permission to leave the USSR, and Gorbachev found himself in a far weaker political position. The Soviet leader, over the next few months, would strive to arrange a new union agreement, which would preserve his position as the country's leader, but he was to run into increasing opposition from both Yeltsin and the leader of the Ukraine, Leonid Kravchuk. Under the circumstances, in his struggle for political survival, Gorbachev had little time for foreign policy initiatives other than to request more economic aid from the West. He also tried to draw closer to the United States and to exploit President Bush's warm personal regard for him as a political asset in maintaining his position in the fast-disintegrating Soviet Union. For this reason and because the conservatives who had blocked his policies had been removed from power as a result of the failed coup, Gorbachev moved to align Soviet policy closely with the United States all over the world and especially in the Middle East (although certain of the old thinkers in the Soviet foreign policy establishment, such as Yevgeny Primakov, continued to strive for a more independent Soviet position).

Perhaps the most important change in Soviet policy following the coup occurred with respect to Israel. In the two-year period before the coup, while Soviet-Israeli relations had developed extensively in the cultural, economic, and political spheres and Moscow had decided to allow free emigration of Soviet Jews to Israel[183] (300,000 had arrived between October 1989 and August 1991), there were still three main problems affecting bilateral relations: Moscow's unwillingness to join the United States in repudiating the General Assembly's "Zionism Is Racism" resolution; Moscow's unwillingness, despite urging by the United States and Israel, to allow direct flight of emigrants from Soviet cities to Israel; and, most important, Moscow's reluctance to establish full diplomatic relations with Israel. In the two-month period following the coup, Moscow fulfilled all three Israeli expectations.

Speaking at the United Nations on September 25, 1991, the new Soviet foreign minister, Boris Pankin (Bessmertnykh had been replaced for not opposing the abortive coup), stated, "The philosophy of new international solidarity signifies, as confirmed in practice, the de-ideologizing of the U.N. Our organization has been renewed and it is imperative that once and for all it rejects the legacy of the 'Ice Age' in which Zionism was compared with racism in an odious resolution."[184] Three weeks later, Aeroflot signed an agreement with Israel's quasi-governmental Jewish Agency and with Israel's El Al airlines to establish direct immigrant flights from Moscow and St. Petersburg to Tel Aviv.[185]

While neither move was popular either in Arab circles or among Soviet conservatives (Pravda complained on October 10 that "the Arab Foreign Ministers now have to rebuff not only the United States but also the USSR on this question [the "Zionism Is Racism" resolution] in the United Nations"),[186] the most controversial issue was the reestablishment of full diplomatic relations. Liberal circles in the USSR had long been campaigning for it; conservatives strongly opposed the move. Pravda, on October 15, asserted in an article highly critical of Israel, "On territorial questions, the United States is much closer to

the aggressor than to its victims."[187] By contrast an *Izvestia* editorial
reflecting the liberal point of view, pointedly noted on September 25:

> After M.S. Gorbachev, swayed by his ambitious advisers, tried un-
> successfully to snatch the initiative in ending the war in the Per-
> sian Gulf, the invitation extended to the USSR to take part in an
> Arab-Jewish reconciliation looked more like an act of kindness on
> the part of the White House rather than a calculation. U.S. Secre-
> tary of State Baker's series of tours of the countries of the region
> wove the fabric of the peace process. Former USSR Foreign Minister
> Bessmertnykh literally following in the footsteps of his U.S. col-
> league, saw for himself that they were able to manage very well
> without us, and therefore sensibly did not bother to launch any
> initiatives. . . .
>
> We will not end up in the absurd role of a dummy co-chairman
> [of the peace talks] if we remain honest and fair and that means we
> cannot go to the conference retaining full diplomatic relations with
> despotic Iraq while refusing to restore such relations with the dem-
> ocratic state of Israel.[188]

Given the cross-pressures, Gorbachev delayed the reestablishment
of full diplomatic relations with Israel—Israel's price for agreeing to
Moscow's co-chairmanship of the peace talks—until literally the last
minute. Nonetheless, after two rounds of talks between Pankin and
Foreign Minister David Levy, in Jerusalem, Moscow agreed on October 18 to reestablish full diplomatic relations. Immediately thereafter, in a joint statement issued in Jerusalem, Pankin and Baker invited
Israel, the Arab states, and the Palestinians to attend the Middle East
peace conference which was to convene in Madrid less than two
weeks later, on October 30, 1991.[189] It should be noted that at the time
of Gorbachev's decision to resume full diplomatic relations, former Israeli prime minister Shimon Peres, together with a large delegation of
Israeli businessmen, were in Moscow to discuss expanded trade relations. An *Izvestia* article on October 14 noted that there were already
200 Soviet-Israeli joint ventures at work, and the "impressive group of
representatives from the Association of Israeli Industrialists represented 1,100 Israeli enterprises that provided 80 percent of Israeli industrial production."[190] A Tass report of the Gorbachev-Peres meeting
stated that Peres "has close links with business circles in his country
that are interested in expanding cooperation with the Soviet Union."
Another Tass report of Gorbachev's earlier meeting with Shoshana

Cardin, director of the National Conference on Soviet Jewry (an organization once an anathema in the USSR), in which the issue of diplomatic relations with Israel had been raised, noted that her organization "enjoys wide support of state figures and business circles."[191] It would thus appear that the Soviet media reports dealing with the decision to resume diplomatic relations with Israel were aimed, at least in part, at convincing otherwise reluctant members of the Soviet elite and population that the resumption of relations would serve to aid the USSR's increasingly faltering economy as well as satisfy the United States, which had long called for the reestablishment of full diplomatic relations between Israel and the USSR.

A second area of U.S.-Soviet cooperation was Afghanistan. While Moscow had pulled its troops out of the country by February 1989, the United States had wanted Moscow to cease sending arms to the Najibullah regime as well, and Baker had negotiated on this issue with both Shevardnadze and Bessmertnykh. On September 12 the two countries reached an agreement to stop supplying arms to the rival groups in Afghanistan beginning on January 1, 1992, and not to increase the supply of arms until then.[192] Given the sensitivity of the Soviet prisoner of war issue to Moscow, Baker also promised to help resolve the issue of Soviet POWs. The two countries also urged other states "to follow the United States and USSR in limiting their assistance to Afghanistan to 'humanitarian assistance only'" and stated "we expect that our joint steps will facilitate launching an intra-Afghan negotiating process and should lead to a pause followed by a complete cessation of hostilities." The joint statement went on to note that both the United States and USSR wanted an independent and non-aligned Afghanistan and pledged to support a "free electoral process that is not subject to manipulation or interference by anyone." The two countries also requested that the United Nations, "with the support of the concerned governments, including those of Islamic countries, work with the Afghans to convene a credible and impartial transition mechanism."[193] Gorbachev, in signing the arms cutoff agreement with the United States, may have hoped to end the problem of Soviet military involvement in Afghanistan once and for all and improve U.S.-Soviet relations in the process. But given the heavy involvement of Iran, Saudi Arabia, and Pakistan in supplying arms to the rival Mujahadeen factions, it remained to be seen if the U.S.-Soviet arms cutoff would affect the level of fighting, much less lead to elections and the formation of a truly independent and nonaligned Afghanistan.

Nonetheless, Moscow later praised Iran for its willingness to cut off arms shipments to the Shi'a Mujahadeen it supported, and *Krasnaya Zvezda* on September 24 reported that UN Secretary General Pérez de Cuéllar had persuaded both Iran and Saudi Arabia to cease arming the Afghan guerrillas.[194] Pakistan, however, remained the major problem in terms of arms supplies, and many in Moscow continued to see Pakistan's goal as a federation with Afghanistan to create a more powerful state with which to confront Pakistan's longtime rival, India.[195]

A third area of U.S.-Soviet cooperation in the Middle East after the coup—albeit a much more limited one—came in the area of arms control. While Moscow and Washington had long discussed the problem of the proliferation of nuclear weapons to the Middle East, it was not until July 1991 that, at the United Nations, together with the other permanent members of the Security Council, they agreed to support a "zone free of weapons of mass destruction in the Middle East."[196] It was not until mid-October that a specific agreement on controlling arms sales to the Middle East was reached. The guidelines, agreed to in a London meeting by all five permanent Security Council members, stipulated that they would "avoid arms sales that would aggravate an existing conflict, increase tension or destabilize a region, break international embargoes, encourage terrorism, or be used other than for legitimate defense." They also agreed to avoid exports that would "seriously undermine the recipient state's economy" and to inform each other about the sales of tanks, armored combat vehicles, artillery, military aircraft and helicopters, naval vessels, and certain missile systems to the Middle East.[197] With the drop in oil production, arms sales were the major source of hard currency for Moscow, so any limit on its ability to sell weapons (even one as limited as this) posed a real problem. Indeed, in an interview with an Abu Dhabi newspaper prior to the agreement, a Soviet weapons official had noted that "in the absence of an agreement with the United States banning arms sales to the Middle East, Soviet arms exports to the region will be continued, and all the advanced weapons that are still in good shape were up for sale." He noted, however, that the USSR remained bound by all UN resolutions, especially those banning the sale of military hardware to the Iraqi regime.[198] An *Izvestia* correspondent, however, also writing before the limited UN agreement, urged that the United Nations work out a register of arms shipments and sales and that developed states agree to stop the shipments of high tech weapons of which they had a monopoly.[199] In Cairo, following the agreement, Soviet Foreign Minister Pankin stated in a burst of optimism that the USSR favored gradual cuts in arms supplies to the Middle East and that, if the forthcoming Madrid conference produced positive results, these supplies might be discontinued.[200] In any case, while Gorbachev may have been willing to sign such an agreement to placate the United States, the USSR would disintegrate soon after the agreement was signed and it remains to be seen whether the successor states of the Soviet Union, all of them starved for hard currency, will agree even to the limited check on their arms sales stipulated by the October 18 agreement.

The fourth major area of cooperation was in the Arab-Israeli peace process. Following the coup and the beginning of the disintegration of the USSR (the Baltic states were to get their full independence in early September), cosponsoring such a major world event as an Arab-Israeli peace conference was of particular importance to Gorbachev both for his own prestige and for his argument that keeping the union together enabled the country to play an important role in world affairs. Consequently, he dispatched a number of missions to the Middle East from early September until the convening of the Madrid Peace Conference on October 30 in what appeared to be Moscow's most serious effort to date to help bring about an Arab-Israeli settlement.

The first, led by his Middle East adviser Yevgeny Primakov, had a number of other goals as well. The leaders of the countries he visited—Egypt, Saudi Arabia, the United Arab Emirates, Kuwait, Iran, and Turkey—had all supported Gorbachev during the coup, and Primakov was sent both to give them Gorbachev's personal thanks for their support and to assure them Gorbachev was now firmly in control. A second goal was to discuss bilateral relations between the USSR and the country visited. Perhaps most important, however Primakov actively sought their financial aid for the faltering Soviet economy, and the special envoy had a number of Soviet economic specialists among his delegation to facilitate this task.[201] In Abu Dhabi, the capital of the United Arab Emirates, Primakov announced that the Soviet Union "has a new idea for building relations with the Arab states, which is based on developing and deepening economic links.[202] Upon returning from his trip, Primakov stated that "in a number of countries we were given serious financial support, credits for purchasing food and consumer goods."[203] He also noted that all the countries he visited wanted to develop economic relations with the USSR because of its large market, the opportunities available because

of the conversion of the Soviet military industry, and the USSR's
scientific production potential.[204]

Primakov also used the trip to make a number of political statements on Soviet policy, such as the one in Turkey in which he stated
that the USSR was against any new intervention by the Allied forces
in Iraq but that Iraq had to strictly comply with the Security Council's resolutions.[205] In evaluating his trip Primakov stated that all of
the countries he visited "clearly did not want the disintegration of the
USSR" and saw the need to preserve its united economic and strategic
area. He also pointedly noted, "The leaders I have met want a USSR
presence in the Near and Middle East because this would preserve the
balance of power. Nobody wants some power to maintain a monopoly
position there."[206]

While Primakov was upbeat about the political achievements of his
visit, a *Krasnaya Zvezda* correspondent cynically noted that the chief
aim of Primakov's trip was "to persuade rich Arab sheikhs to help us
with 'live' money." The correspondent went on to state that "if we are
able to give the Americans assistance in the Near East, maybe we will
accelerate the receipt of aid from the U.S. and the West."[207] Some of
this assistance was to be provided during the visit to Arafat in Tunis
undertaken by Soviet Deputy Foreign Minister Alexander Belogonov
on the eve of the Palestine National Council debate in late September
over whether or not to participate in the peace conference under Israel's conditions. Soviet-PLO relations were rather sensitive at this
time because Farouk Kaddoumi, a high-ranking PLO leader, and a
number of other prominent PLO figures had supported the coup (although once the coup had failed, Arafat sent a telegram of support to
Gorbachev). The PLO ambassador to Moscow, Nabil 'Amr, when asked
by *Komsomalskaya Pravda* on September 7 about the Palestinian reaction to the coup, replied, "I will be frank and say that the statements
of these Palestinian figures were too hasty and shocked Y. Arafat to
some extent." He noted, however, that "such remarks cannot adversely
influence the development of relations between our states, especially
as the official PLO viewpoint set out by the President of Palestine was
totally different."[208]

Belogonov had no fewer than three meetings with Arafat, holding
discussions that he termed "frank and businesslike." Also, possibly in
an effort to repair the Soviet-PLO breach and rebuild Soviet influence
in the PLO, he gave Arafat a message of gratitude for his support from
Gorbachev.[209] The Soviet deputy foreign minister was at least par-

tially successful in his efforts to act as a peace process facilitator between the United States and the PLO, as Arafat allowed Palestinian spokeswoman Hanan Ashrawi to meet Baker in Amman on September 20,[210] and a week later the Palestine National Council voted to attend the Middle East peace talks. It would be incorrect to attribute too much influence to the Soviet mediation effort, however. The PLO, which had supported Saddam Hussein during the Gulf War, had little choice about entering the peace talks, even under Israeli conditions, lest its diplomatic position further erode at a time when the Intifada was waning and Egypt and Saudi Arabia were pressing Arafat hard for a positive response to the talks. Nonetheless, Moscow hailed the PNC decision[211] and in the period leading up to the peace conference kept in close contact with the PLO, as two high-ranking members of the organization, Abu Mazin and Yasser Abd Rabboo, journeyed to Moscow for a meeting with Pankin on October 10.

A third major trip to the Middle East was undertaken by Pankin himself in mid-October, to Israel, Egypt, Syria, and Jordan, and then to meet Arafat in Paris. While the most important aspect of his trip was the agreement to resume full diplomatic relations with Israel (and thereby ensure the convening of the Middle East peace conference under Soviet cosponsorship), Pankin also noted that he had "very friendly and sincere" conversations with Assad[212] and useful talks with King Hussein and Arafat as well. Like Primakov, he claimed that none of the leaders he visited wanted the Soviet Union "to retire from the political arena. . . . All understand perfectly well that our troubles and all our problems are problems of maturing. The Union of Sovereign States [Gorbachev's new name for the USSR] remains and will continue to be a great power. The world needs it."

Gorbachev was also to undertake a trip related to the Middle East, although it was to the Madrid Conference, not to the region itself. The Soviet leader apparently had two goals during his visit: to meet President Bush again and, hopefully, obtain more U.S. aid to help the Soviet economy, and to demonstrate to his domestic opponents, above all to Yeltsin whose power was increasing while his own was decreasing, that as a world leader Gorbachev still commanded respect and that for their country to play a major world role it had to remain intact. Nonetheless, testifying to the growing independence of the Soviet republics, Gorbachev had to take along as part of his delegation Vladimir Lukin, the chairman of the Russian Parliament's Foreign Affairs Committee (later to be Russia's ambassador to the United States) and the foreign minister of the Republic of Tajikistan. When asked whether Gorbachev could speak for the Soviet Union, Lukin replied, "Of course, but the question is what is the Soviet Union?"[213]

If Gorbachev had hoped that Bush would offer him additional economic assistance during their preconference meeting, he was to be disappointed, although the U.S. president was lavish in his rhetorical praise for the Soviet leader as he stated that there was "no difference, certainly from my standpoint, in the respect level for President Gorbachev."[214] Bush also used the opportunity to thank Gorbachev "for the very constructive role that the Soviet Union had played in the actions leading up to this conference. We're grateful to him for that."[215]

Rhetoric aside, it was clear that the United States totally dominated the peace conference. A "senior European diplomat" told *New York Times* correspondent Thomas Friedman that when he asked a Soviet official who was supposedly working jointly with the United States on the conference a question about seating arrangements, the Soviet official just shrugged and said, "You have to ask the Americans. We don't know anything. The Americans are handling everything."[216] Similarly, an Arab delegate to the talks noted, "Let's face the facts. The United States is running the show. The Soviet Union cannot even feed its people and asks the world for food."[217]

Ironically, this was precisely what Gorbachev was to do during his address to the peace conference. After praising U.S.-Soviet cooperation for making the conference possible, and urging the delegates not to miss the opportunity for peace, Gorbachev went on to appeal to the entire world community to aid the Soviet Union because "what is happening in the Soviet Union has a larger bearing than any regional conflict on the vital interests of the greater part of today's world."[218]

Less than two months after the opening of the Madrid Peace Conference the Soviet Union collapsed, to be replaced by the Commonwealth of Independent States (CIS), and Gorbachev lost his job. During this period, at the same time that the republics of the former Soviet Union become independent, a major transformation of Middle East politics took place—one whose outcome is far from clear. Not only was the Soviet Union no longer a unified entity influencing the states of the Middle East, but the states of that region, particularly Turkey, Iran, Saudi Arabia, Pakistan, and even Israel became engaged in a competition for influence in the Moslem Republics of what became the CIS. There was also growing concern that Soviet nuclear scientists and possibly even nuclear weapons could slip away to the

Middle East. In any case, the Madrid Conference, which revealed the weakness of the Soviet Union's position to the world, is a useful point of departure for analyzing the thrust of Soviet policy toward the Middle East since the invasion of Kuwait.

Conclusions

The Gulf War, coming at a time when the Soviet Union was facing increasingly severe economic and political crises, was a major turning point in the erosion of the Soviet position in the Middle East. The brevity of the war, coupled with Gorbachev's unwillingness to support the U.S.-led coalition actively, marginalized the Soviet role in the region at the close of the war. Initially, following the war, Gorbachev sought to shore up the Soviet position and prevent the United States from dominating both the Gulf and the Arab-Israeli peace process. He did so by adopting positions that on the surface were supportive of U.S. aims—after all Moscow now needed more and more Western assistance—but still subtly reinforced anti-U.S. forces in the region. In the Gulf, Moscow both supported Iran's call for Gulf security to be a matter for the regional states themselves and continued to try to protect Saddam Hussein's regime from further U.S. military intervention. In the Arab-Israeli peace process Moscow first gave tacit support to the hard-line position of Hafiz Assad; but when Assad opted for the U.S. peace plan in mid-July, Moscow quickly sought to make the best of the situation by emphasizing the fact that the U.S. initiative called for joint U.S.-Soviet sponsorship of the peace conference. Following the abortive coup and the removal of a number of hard-liners from the leadership, Gorbachev, now in a desperate political situation, moved to shore up his position by even closer cooperation with the United States, whose leader held him in far greater respect than did his Soviet countrymen. Thus he removed the last obstacles in the Soviet-Israeli relationship by agreeing to join the United States in denouncing the General Assembly's resolution equating Zionism with racism, by agreeing to allow direct flights of emigrants between the USSR and Israel, and by establishing full diplomatic relations with the Jewish state. He also signed an agreement with the United States cutting off arms to Afghanistan and agreed, albeit in a limited way, to curtail arms shipments to the Middle East. Finally, he aided, although only marginally, the convening of the Madrid Peace Conference in the expectation that he could use the occasion to elicit more economic aid from the West and to demonstrate domestically that he was still a major actor on the world scene.

Unfortunately for Gorbachev all of his efforts to use Middle East events to shore up his domestic political position proved futile, and less than two months after the Madrid Peace Conference the Soviet Union fell apart. The policies of the successor states of the Soviet Union toward the Middle East remain open questions.[219]

Notes

1. There is now an extensive bibliography on Soviet "new thinking." See Mikhail Gorbachev, *Perestroika: New Thinking for Our Country and the World* (New York: Harper & Row, 1987), esp. chaps. 3 and 5. See also G.A. Trofimenko, "Novye Real'nosti i Novoe Myshlenie" [New Realities and New Thinking] *Ssha* no. 2 (1987): 3–15; Yevgeny Aleksandrov, "New Political Thinking: Genesis, Factors, Prospects," *International Affairs* 12 (1987): 87–95; Rodimir Bogdanov, "From the Balance of Forces to a Balance of Interests," *International Affairs* 4 (1988): 81–87 and Aleksander Kislov, "Novoe Politicheskoe Myshlenie i Regional'nye Konflicty" [New Political Thinking and Regional Conflicts] *MEIMO* 8 (1988): 39–47. Given Yevgeny Primakov's role in the crisis under study, the interested reader should also see Primakov, V. Martnynov, and G. Duligenskii, "Nekotorye Problemy Novogo Myshleniia" [Some Problems of the New Thinking], *MEIMO* 6 (1989): 5–18.

2. For an analysis of the change in Soviet-Egyptian relations, see Robert O. Freedman, *Moscow and the Middle East: Soviet Policy since the Invasion of Afghanistan* (Cambridge: Cambridge University Press, 1991), pp. 278–279, 299–301.

3. The sharp improvement in Soviet-Israeli relations is discussed in Robert O. Freedman, *Soviet-Israeli Relations under Gorbachev* (New York: Praeger, 1991).

4. For an examination of the decline in the Soviet-Syrian relationship, see Freedman, *Moscow and the Middle East.*

5. Ibid., pp. 293–94.

6. Ibid., pp. 302–4.

7. Soviet policy toward Iran under Gorbachev is discussed in Robert O. Freedman, "Gorbachev, Iran, and the Iran-Iraq War," in *Neither East nor West: Iran, the Soviet Union and the United States,* ed. Nikki R. Keddie and Mark J. Gasiorowski (New Haven: Yale University Press, 1990). For a more positive view of Soviet policy during the Iran-Iraq War, see Gary Sick, "Slouching toward Settlement: The Internationalization of the Iran-Iraq War, 1987–1988," in the same volume.

8. Moscow Radio Peace and Progress, broadcasting to Iran in Persian on December 24, 1990 discussed the sale of MIG-29s in the larger context of

Soviet-Iranian relations (*Foreign Broadcast Information Service Daily Report: Soviet Union* [hereafter *FBIS:USSR*], December 26, 1990, pp. 6–7). Tass had officially announced Iran's commissioning of a squadron of MIG-29s on October 8, 1990 (*FBIS:USSR*, October 11, 1990, p. 25).

9. During unrest on the border between Soviet Azerbaizhan and Iran in January 1990, Rafsanjani was in fact a calming influence in the face of attempts by Islamic hard-liners in Tehran to exploit the crisis.

10. According to testimony by Deputy Foreign Minister Belonogov before the Supreme Soviet's International Affairs Committee on August 30, 1990, Moscow reexported Iraqi oil to India, Bulgaria, Rumania, and other countries: Tass, August 30, 1990 (*FBIS:USSR*, August 31, 1990, p. 10).

11. Tass, December 28, 1990 (*FBIS:USSR*, December 28, 1990, p. 9).

12. Yevgeny Primakov interview, *Time Magazine*, March 4, 1991, p. 42.

13. In May 1990, Kuwait had agreed to give Moscow a two-stage $1 billion loan (*Izvestia*, citing the Kuwaiti Ambassador to the USSR, December 24, 1990).

14. Cf. Freedman, *Moscow and the Middle East.*

15. Interview with Konstantin Katushev, Soviet minister of foreign economic relations, *Sovetskaya Rossiya*, August 26, 1990 (*FBIS:USSR*, August 27, 1990, p. 27).

16. Most Soviet officials, including Gorbachev, cited the lower figure. In an *Izvestia* interview on August 16, 1990, Lt. General V. Nikityuk, first deputy chief of the Main Directorate of the Soviet Armed Forces General Staff, differentiated between "specialists" who "give assistance in mastering and operating military hardware supplied under contract" and "advisers" who "are called upon to resolve questions of building the armed forces" (*FBIS:USSR*, August 20, 1990, pp. 17–19). Interviews by the author with Soviet scholars and government officials in Moscow and Washington, however, elicited the higher figure. One of the points made by Nikityuk in the interview was that as a result of the work of the Soviet miliary advisers, the USSR had obtained "considerable amounts of foreign currency".

17. Interview, Moscow, October 1990. Such service enabled Soviet specialists to accumulate hard currency for the purchase of cars, VCRs, and other commodities hard to get in the USSR.

18. *Krasnaya Zvezda, Sovetskaya Rossiya,* and *Pravda* were the forums for their position. By contrast, *Moscow News* and *Komsomolskaya Pravda* reflected liberal viewpoints, calling for the USSR to help the international community punish Saddam Hussein. *Izvestia*, the government newspaper, took a midpoint in this debate, but many of its commentators, especially Alexander Bovin, supported the liberal position. For an analysis of the debate in the Supreme Soviet on Soviet intentions in the conflict, see Suzanne Crow, "Legislative Considerations and the Gulf Crisis," *Radio Liberty Report*, 2, no. 50(1990): 2–3.

19. Cf. *Pravda*, August 17, 1990.

20. Interviews, Moscow, October 1990.

21. Tass, August 2, 1990 (*FBIS:USSR*, August 3, 1990, p. 23).

22. Ibid., p. 24. One still-unanswered question about whether Moscow fully stopped sending military equipment to Iraq concerns the Soviet supply ship *Dmitry Furmanov*, which was intercepted on its way to Jordan with military equipment that did not fit the Jordanian table of organization and equipment but could have been used by Iraq. Given the fact that Jordan was a major transshipment point to Iraq during the Iran-Iraq War, there was suspicion that Moscow was secretly supplying Iraq. At this point it is not clear whether it was a Soviet governmental effort to strengthen ties with Iraq, an independent move by the Soviet military (this was the view of Viktor Levin, speaking on Moscow TV on January 13, 1991 [*FBIS:USSR*, January 16, 1991, pp. 13–14]), or an attempt by several Soviet officials to make some quick money. A Soviet colleague, who specializes in the Middle East, also indicated to me that it could have been a bureaucratic blunder.

23. *Washington Post*, February 23, 1991, Summary of UN Resolutions on the Gulf Crisis (hereafter *Washington Post Summary*).

24. *Izvestia*, August 5, 1990 (*FBIS:USSR*, August 8, 1990, p. 18).

25. Ibid.

26. *Washington Post Summary*.

27. Ibid.

28. *Izvestia*, August 10, 1991, translated in *Current Digest of the Soviet Press* (hereafter *CDSP*) 42, no. 32, p. 5.

29. Tass, August 17, 1990 (*FBIS:USSR*, August 17, 1990, p. 18).

30. *Washington Post Summary*.

31. Tass, August 20, 1990 (*FBIS:USSR*, August 21, 1990, p. 3).

32. *Pravda*, August 21, 1990. Moscow Radio, broadcasting in English on August 22, 1990, emphasized that the talks were being undertaken not to "appease the aggressor" but to "avoid a large scale military collision with unpredictable consequences" (*FBIS:USSR*, August 23, 1990, p. 25).

33. This was the view of *Izvestia* Commentator M. Yusin in an article on August 23, 1990.

34. *Izvestia*, August 24, 1990.

35. *Washington Post Summary*.

36. Tass, August 22, 1990 (*FBIS:USSR*, August 23, 1990, p. 25).

37. Tass, August 23, 1990 (*FBIS:USSR*, August 23, 1990, pp. 18–19).

38. Alexander Bovin, writing in *Izvestia* on September 5, 1990, noted "condemning Iraq as an aggressor, while at the same time leaving in Iraq 193 officers who can assist in handling Soviet weapons and equipment is dubious logic." (*FBIS:USSR*, September 6, 1990, p. 23).

39. Tass, August 30, 1990 (*FBIS:USSR*, August 31, 1990, p. 12).

40. For the text of the joint declaration, see *Izvestia*, September 10, 1990, (translated in *CDSP* 42, no. 37, p. 13).

41. Ibid., pp. 11–15.

42. Soviet officials differed among themselves as to the degree of the economic loss. Deputy Foreign Minister Alexander Belonogov, speaking to the Parliamentary Committee on International Affairs of the Supreme Soviet on August 30, 1990, said, "Soviet compliance with the economic sanctions would cost the USSR over $800 million: $520 million as a result of oil not supplied by Iraq for reexport to India, Bulgaria, Rumania, and other countries, and $290 million in the form of goods and services not supplied to the USSR. [In addition] a total of $115 million worth of goods, and financial resources from Kuwait of $700 million" (Tass, August 30, 1990 [FBIS:USSR, August 31, 1990, p. 10]). Because of declining oil production, Moscow could not take real advantage of the temporary increase in oil prices caused by the war, but Kuwait had sufficient financial resources not under Iraqi control that it could go ahead with its promised loan (see below).

43. Izvestia, September 19, 1990 (CSDP 42, no. 38, p. 20). Technically, the two countries were restoring relations which had been broken off in the 1930s. For a historical survey of Soviet-Saudi ties in the 1930s and the reason for their rupture, see Igor Belayev's article in Literaturnaya Gazeta, September 26, 1990.

44. Izvestia, September 30, 1990.

45. Izvestia, September 26, 1990 (CDSP 42, no. 39, pp. 15–16).

46. Izvestia, on October 2, 1990, repeated Shevardnadze's statement on the U.S. television program "Meet the Press" that "the USSR will unconditionally fulfill the UN decision even if it involves the need to use Soviet military forces" (FBIS:USSR, October 2, 1990, pp. 12–13). A Soviet public opinion poll, taken by the All-Union Center for the Study of Public Opinion in the USSR, revealed that the Soviet public opposed by 64 percent to 15 percent any decision to send Soviet naval ships to the Gulf to participate in the blockade of Iraq. Basically, conservatives opposed any action against Saddam Hussein's Iraq because it was a treaty ally and a "fighter against imperialism," while liberals like Alexander Bovin saw the USSR as still too enmeshed in its Afghan syndrome to send troops (Moscow TV, October 6, 1990). Some Soviet commentators like Igor Belyayev and newspapers like Moscow News favored sending Soviet forces to the Gulf to aid the war effort. For a discussion about the debate in the Foreign Affairs Committee of the Supreme Soviet on this issue, see New Times, 38 (1990): 5–6.

47. By early October the status of Soviet advisers in Iraq had become an issue in the Soviet press. See the article by A. Levchenko and L. Negra in Izvestia, October 4, 1990 (CDSP 42, no. 40 [1990]: pp. 18–19), and Argumenty i Fakty 39 (1990) (FBIS:USSR, October 2, 1990, p. 12). Reportedly, 400 Soviet specialists appealed to their government for help in getting out of Iraq.

48. See Primakov interview.

49. Izvestia, October 13, 1990.

50. Primakov interview.

51. Novosti report, *Rabochaya Tribuna*, October 14, 1990 (*CDSP* 42, no. 41, pp. 11–12).

52. Ibid.

53. See the report by Thomas Friedman, *New York Times*, October 17, 1990.

54. *Izvestia*, October 31, 1990.

55. *Izvestia*, October 16, 1990 (*CDSP* 42, no. 42, p. 20).

56. Tass, October 9, 1990 (*FBIS:USSR*, October 9, 1990, p. 21).

57. For the text of Bush's announcement, which came after the 1990 U.S. midterm congressional elections, see the *New York Times*, November 9, 1990.

58. See the articles by Paul Lewis in the *New York Times* on November 10, 16, 1990.

59. Cited in report by David Hoffman, *Washington Post*, November 9, 1990.

60. Cited in report by Michael Dobbs, ibid.

61. Cited in report by Paul Lewis, *New York Times*, November 16, 1990.

62. See the article by R. W. Apple, ibid.

63. *Izvestia*, November 22, 1990. The Moroccan proposal was made on November 11, 1990. See the report by Judith Miller, *New York Times*, November 12, 1990.

64. See the report by Andrew Rosenthal, *New York Times*, November 20, 1990.

65. Cited in report by Andrew Rosenthal, *New York Times*, November 21, 1990.

66. Cited in report by Ann Devroy and Michael Dobbs, *Washington Post*, November 21, 1990.

67. Tass, November 26, 1990 (*FBIS:USSR*, November 26, 1990, p. 14).

68. Cited in *Pravda*, November 27, 1990 (*FBIS:USSR*, November 27, 1990, p. 15).

69. Tass, November 27, 1990 (*FBIS:USSR*, November 27, 1990, p. 15).

70. Ibid.

71. Moscow Radio in Arabic, November 27, 1990 (*FBIS:USSR*, November 28, 1990, p. 17). Gorbachev's broadcast coincided with the visit of Saudi Foreign Minister Saud al-Faisal to Moscow.

72. For the text of Shevardnadze's U.N. speech, see Tass, November 30, 1990 (*FBIS:USSR*, December 3, 1990, pp. 12–14).

73. *Washington Post*, November 30, 1990.

74. *Izvestia*, December 4, 1990 (*CDSP* 42, no. 49, p. 17).

75. *Izvestia*, December 5, 1990, citing a Reuters interview with an Iraqi leader who said, "Any Soviet specialist wishing to leave Iraq is free to depart our country at any time, beginning Wednesday. However, the Soviet side must take full responsibility for violation of the contracts the Soviet specialists have signed" (*CDSP* 42, no. 49, p. 18).

76. Cited in report by Bill Keller, *New York Times*, December 1, 1990.

77. Ibid.

78. *Izvestia*, December 24, 1990 (*FBIS:USSR*, December 28, 1990, p. 10).

79. Cited in report by Andrew Rosenthal, *New York Times*, December 13, 1990.

80. Ibid.

81. Cited in report by David Hoffman, *Washington Post*, December 11, 1990.

82. Cf. Freedman, *Moscow and the Middle East.*

83. Cited in report by Thomas Friedman, *New York Times*, December 15, 1990.

84. Cited in report by Paul Taylor, *Washington Post*, December 16, 1990.

85. For the text of Shevardnadze's resignation speech, see the *New York Times*, December 21, 1990.

86. See the report by David Hoffman, *Washington Post*, December 21, 1990.

87. *Izvestia*, December 22, 1990 (*FBIS:USSR*, December 24, 1990, p. 1).

88. Cited in Associated Press report, *Washington Post*, December 25, 1990.

89. Ibid.

90. Ibid.

91. Tass, December 29, 1990 (*FBIS:USSR*, December 31, 1990, p. 11).

92. Tass, January 15, 1991 (*FBIS:USSR*, January 16, 1991, p. 6).

93. Cited in Agence France Presse (AFP) report, *Hong Kong Standard*, January 17, 1991.

94. *Asian Wall Street Journal*, January 18–19, 1991. AFP citing the Soviet Military command, January 18, 1991 (*FBIS:USSR*, January 22, 1991, p. 17).

95. Moscow Central Television, January 17, 1991 (*FBIS:USSR*, January 17, 1991 (pp. 9–10).

96. Tass, January 18, 1991 (*FBIS:USSR*, January 18, 1991, p. 5).

97. Tass, January 21, 1991 (*FBIS:USSR*, January 22, 1991, p. 5).

98. Moscow Domestic Service in Russian, January 22, 1991 (*FBIS:USSR*, January 23, 1991, p. 4).

99. For example, on August 22, *Sovetskaya Rossiya* had asserted that all the United States wanted to do in sending troops to Saudi Arabia was to control the region's oil.

100. Moscow Domestic Service, January 26, 1991 (*FBIS:USSR*, January 28, 1991, p. 4).

101. Tass, January 30, 1991 (*FBIS:USSR*, January 30, 1991, pp. 9–10).

102. Here Bessmertnykh erred in his chronology. He probably meant the joint U.S.-Soviet statement on the Middle East of October 1, 1977. See Robert O. Freedman, *Soviet Policy toward the Middle East since 1970* (New York: Praeger, 1982), pp. 308–9.

103. See the report by Don Oberdorfer, *Washington Post*, January 30, 1991.

104. *Komsomolskaya Pravda*, February 1, 1991 (*FBIS:USSR*, February 4, 1991, pp. 14–15). See also the article about Filatov by Bill Keller, *New York Times/International Herald Tribune*, January 8, 1991.

105. *Izvestia*, February 8, 1991 (*FBIS:USSR*, February 11, 1991, pp. 20–21). A similar evaluation was given by Major General Bogdanov in *Krasnaya Zvezda*, Janury 31, 1991 (*FBIS:USSR*, February 1991, pp. 6–8).

106. Tass, February 5, 1991 (*FBIS:USSR*, February 5, 1991, p. 9).

107. See the articles by David Hoffman, *Washington Post*, February 7, 1991, and Thomas Friedman, *New York Times*, February 7, 1991.

108. Tass, February 9, 1991 (*FBIS:USSR*, February 11, 1991, p. 18). Given the propinquity of Iraq to the USSR, some Soviet citizens were voicing their concern about "fallout" from weapons of mass destruction.

109. See report by Rick Atkinson, *Washington Post*, February 13, 1991.

110. For the text of the Iraqi statement, see *New York Times*, February 13, 1991.

111. Cited in article by Serge Schmemann, *New York Times*, February 14, 1991.

112. Tass, February 14, 1991 (*FBIS:USSR*, February 14, 1991, pp. 3–4).

113. For the text of the Iraqi offer, see *New York Times*, February 16, 1991.

114. See the report by Serge Schmemann, ibid.

115. Cited in report by Patrick Tyler, ibid.

116. Cited in report by Michael Dobbs, *Washington Post*, February 19, 1991.

117. Cited in report by Rick Atkinson, *Washington Post*, February 20, 1991.

118. Cited in report by Andrew Rosenthal, *New York Times*, February 20, 1991.

119. AFP report, February 18, 1991 (*FBIS:USSR*, February 20, 1991, p. 15).

120. Ibid.

121. *Sovetskaya Rossiya*, February 16, 1991 (ibid., p. 19).

122. Tass, February 24, 1991 (*FBIS:USSR*, February 25, 1991, p. 9).

123. Moscow Central Television, February 23, 1991 (*FBIS:USSR*, February 25, 1991, p. 13).

124. Cited in report by Trevor Rowe, *Washington Post*, February 26, 1991.

125. See the report by David Remnick, *Washington Post*, February 27, 1991, and the Reuters report, *Washington Post*, ibid.

126. See the reports by Paul Lewis, *New York Times*, February 27, 28, March 1, 1991.

127. Tass, February 28, 1991 (*FBIS:USSR*, March 1, 1991, p. 12).

128. See the report by Thomas Friedman, *New York Times*, March 15, 1991.

129. Cited in report by Thomas Friedman, *New York Times*, March 14, 1991.

130. Cited in report by Sarah Gach, *Washington Times*, March 26, 1991.

131. Cited in report by Youssef Ibrahim, *New York Times*, April 2, 1991.

132. Tass report, *Pravda*, April 5, 1991 (translated in *CDSP* 43, no. 14, p. 23).

133. Cited in report by Alan Cowell, *New York Times*, April 9, 1991.

134. For an evaluation of the motives of Assad and Arafat in renewing their cooperation, see Lanus Andeni, "The PLO and Syria: A Tricky Relationship," *Middle East International* 401 (May 31, 1991): 11–12. See also the comments by a PLO delegate to the Damascus meeting, Yasser Abd Rabboo, who said that the PLO, Jordan, and Syria have identical views on the role of the peace conference in the Middle East (Tunis Radio, May 29, 1991; *FBIS:NESA*, May 30, 1991, p. 3).

135. Cited in report by Thomas Friedman, *New York Times*, April 24, 1991.

136. Cited in report by John Goshko, *Washington Post*, April 26, 1991.

137. See Freedman, *Moscow and The Middle East.*

138. See the interview by Bessmertnykh on the eve of his trip to the Middle East in *Nues Deuchland*, April 29, 1991 (*FBIS:USSR*, May 1, 1991, p. 13).

139. Damascus Domestic Service, May 9, 1991 (*FBIS:NESA*, May 9, 1991, p. 27).

140. For a report of Baker's unsuccessful visit, in which Syria reportedly rejected Baker's compromise plan for a UN observer, see the article by Thomas Friedman, *New York Times*, May 13, 1991.

141. Article by V. Skosyrev, *Izvestia*, May 16, 1991 (*FBIS:USSR*, May 16, 1991, pp. 24–25).

142. See Reuters report, *Washington Post*, April 17, 1991.

143. Ibid.

144. Tass, April 16, 1991 (*FBIS:USSR*, April 17, 1991, p. 3).

145. Cited in *Jerusalem Post*, April 9, 1991.

146. Reuters report, cited by Dan Izenberg, *Jerusalem Post*, May 10, 1991. However, a weakened Moscow was to accept such a situation in October.

147. Ibid.

148. Cited in report by Dan Izenberg, *Jerusalem Post*, May 12, 1991.

149. Ibid.

150. Ibid.

151. Tass, May 11, 1991 (*FBIS:USSR*, May 13, 1991), p. 19.

152. Cited in report by Thomas Friedman, *New York Times*, July 15, 1991.

153. Ibid. See also the article by Caryle Murphy, *Washington Post*, August 20, 1991.

154. Cf. Radio Moscow, in Arabic, July 15, 1991 (*FBIS:USSR*, July 17, 1991, p. 19), Interfax interview with Soviet Foreign Ministry official, July 24, 1991 (*FBIS:USSR*, July 25, 1991, p. 18), and USSR Vice-President Gennady Yanaev's comments to a visiting Palestine National Council delegation as reported by Tass, July 24, 1991 (*FBIS:USSR*, July 26, 1991, p. 18).

155. Cf. Interfax interview, July 24, 1991 (*FBIS:USSR*, July 25, 1991, p. 17).

156. Cited in report by Ann Devroy and Michael Dobbs, *Washington Post*, August 1, 1991.

157. Cited in *Jerusalem Post*, August 1, 1991.

158. Cited in report by David Hoffman, *Washington Post*, August 1, 1991. See also report by Walter Ruby, *Jerusalem Post*, August 1, 1991.

159. Cited in report by Serge Schmemann, *New York Times*, August 2, 1991.

160. *FBIS:USSR*, August 5, 1991, p. 17.

161. *Izvestia*, March 20, 1991. For the official Soviet plan for Gulf security see Tass, March 16, 1991 (*FBIS:USSR*, March 18, 1991, pp. 14–16).

162. Cited in report by Caryle Murphy, *Washington Post*, May 11, 1991.

163. For a report on the background for this development, see ibid.

164. Cited in report by Judith Miller, *New York Times*, April 29, 1991.

165. See the Radio Moscow English language broadcast by Vladislav Kozyakov, May 6, 1991 (*FBIS:USSR*, May 8, 1991, p. 7).

166. *Washington Post*, October 28, 1991.

167. Tass, April 5, 1991 (*FBIS:USSR*, April 8, 1991, pp. 16–17).

168. Soviet Foreign Ministry spokesman Yury Gremitskikh, as cited by Tass, April 18, 1991 (*FBIS:USSR*, April 19, 1991, p. 2).

169. Cf. comments by Foreign Minister Bessmertnykh,, in a letter to the U.N. Secretary General as cited by Tass, April 10, 1991 (*FBIS:USSR*, April 11, 1991, p. 2).

170. *Izvestia*, April 24, 1991.

171. Paris, Europe Number One in French, April 28, 1991 (*FBIS:USSR*, April 30, 1991, p. 10).

172. Soviet Foreign Ministry spokesman Yury Gremitskikh, as cited by Tass, April 18, 1991 (*FBIS:USSR*, April 19, 1991, p. 2).

173. Ministry of Foreign Affairs chief spokesman, Vitaly Churkin, as cited by Tass, April 29, 1991 (*FBIS:USSR*, April 30, 1991, p. 3).

174. Cited in report by R. Jeffrey Smith and Trevor Rowe, *Washington Post*, June 27, 1991.

175. Cited in report by Paul Lewis, *New York Times*, June 18, 1991.

176. *FBIS:USSR*, July 3, 1991, p. 19.

177. Cited in John Goshko, *Washington Post*, July 6, 1991.

178. Cited ibid.

179. *Krasnaya Zvezda*, July 19, 1991, p. 30.

180. Cited in report by Gary Lee, *Washington Post*, July 29, 1991.

181. Cited in report by John Goshko, *Washington Post*, August 16, 1991.

182. Cited in report by Caryle Murphy, *Washington Post*, August 20, 1991.

183. Cf. Freedman, *Soviet Policy Toward Israel under Gorbachev*.

184. Interfax, September 30, 1991 (*FBIS:USSR*, October 2, 1991, p. 19), and *New York Times*, September 25, 1991.

185. *Izvestia*, October 15, 1991 (*FBIS:USSR*, October 16, 1991, p. 21).

186. *Pravda*, October 10, 1991 (*FBIS:USSR*, October 11, 1991, p. 8).

187. *Pravda*, October 15, 1991 (*FBIS:USSR*, October 18, 1991, p. 13).

188. *Izvestia*, September 25, 1991 (*FBIS:USSR*, October 2, 1991, p. 19).

189. Tass, October 18, 1991 (*FBIS:USSR*, October 21, 1991, p. 22). See also the articles by Thomas Friedman, *New York Times*, October 19, 1991, and Jackson Diehl, *Washington Post*, October 19, 1991. (At a news conference following the announcement of the restoration of full diplomatic relations, Pankin said, "In the past, the Soviet Union tended to sort of side with the Palestinians and the Arab states, while the United States sided with Israel, and this did not bring any tangible fruit. The new approach is certainly not to have any protégés.")

190. *Izvestia*, October 14, 1991 (*FBIS:USSR*, October 18, 1991, p. 12).

191. Tass, October 2, 1991 (*FBIS:USSR*, October 3, 1991, p. 4).

192. Interfax, September 13, 1991 (*FBIS:USSR*, September 13, 1991, p. 21). See also the report by David Hoffman, *Washington Post*, September 14, 1991.

193. Cited in report by Thomas Friedman, *New York Times*, September 14, 1991.

194. *Krasnaya Zvezda*, September 24, 1991 (*FBIS:USSR*, September 24, 1991, p. 13).

195. *Izvestia*, September 18, 1991 (ibid., p. 14).

196. Cited in report by Sharon Waxman, *Washington Post*, July 10, 1991.

197. Cited in *Washington Times*, October 19, 1991.

198. *Al-Ittihad al-Usbu'i* (Abu Dhabi), September 19, 1991 (*FBIS:USSR*, September 23, 1991, p. 13).

199. *Izvestia*, September 23, 1991 (*FBIS:USSR*, September 25, 1991, pp. 8–9).

200. Tass, October 22, 1991 (*FBIS:USSR*, October 23, 1991, p. 8).

201. Cf. Tass, in English, September 14, 1991 (*FBIS:USSR*, September 16, 1991, p. 15). See also Robert M. Danin, "Moscow and the Middle East Peace Conference after the Coup," *Middle East Insight* 8, no. 2 (September–October 1991): 4–8.

202. *Pravda*, September 16, 1991 (*FBIS:USSR*, September 17, 1991, p. 12).

203. Tass, September 21, 1991 (*FBIS:USSR*, September 23, 1991, pp. 10–11).

204. Tass, September 20, 1991 (ibid., p. 11).

205. Moscow Radio World Service, September 21, 1991 (ibid., p. 10).

206. Tass, September 20, 1991 (ibid., p. 11).

207. *Krasnaya Zvezda*, September 26, 1991 (*FBIS:USSR*, October 8, 1991, pp. 14–15).

208. *Komsomalskaya Pravda*, September 7, 1991 (*FBIS:USSR*, September 10, 1991, p. 9).

209. Tass, September 20, 1991 (*FBIS:USSR*, September 23, 1991, pp. 11–12).

210. Cited in report by David Hoffman, *Washington Post*, September 21, 1991.

211. Cf. comments of a Soviet Foreign Ministry official to Tass, October 2, 1991 (*FBIS:USSR*, October 3, 1991, p. 8).

212. Tass, October 20, 1991 (*FBIS:USSR*, October 21, 1991, pp. 23–24).

213. Cited in report by Fred Hiatt, *Washington Post*, October 29, 1991.

214. Cited in report by John Yang and Fred Hiatt, *Washington Post*, October 30, 1991.

215. Cited by Andrew Rosenthal, *New York Times*, October 30, 1991.

216. Cited in report by Thomas Friedman, ibid.

217. Associated Press report, *Baltimore Sun*, October 31, 1991.

218. Tass, October 30, 1991 (*FBIS:USSR*, October 30, 1991, p. 13).

219. For a view of the Middle East policies of the USSR's successor states in their first year of independence, see Robert O. Freedman, "Israel and the Successor States of the Soviet Union," *Mediterranean Quarterly* forthcoming.

4

FIRE ON THE OTHER SIDE
OF THE RIVER: JAPAN AND
THE PERSIAN GULF WAR

Eugene Brown

For Japan the Persian Gulf crisis of 1990–91 proved to be an acutely painful episode in its nascent effort to define its proper international role and responsibility. Throughout the seven months from Iraq's invasion of Kuwait on August 2, 1990, to the decisive U.S.-led defeat of Iraq in February 1991, Japanese political and intellectual life was convulsed by an intense debate over the nation's appropriate role in the crisis. The debate bore various guises; it was by turns analytical and emotional, high-minded and parochial, forward-looking and tradition-bound. At bottom, it was a debate about Japan's identity as a member of international society. It would, therefore, continue well beyond the cessation of the distant violence that had prompted it.

Certainly the Gulf crisis proved to be a watershed in terms of what the world expected of Japan. Throughout the four decades of the cold war it had been generally sufficient for Japan to cooperate with the U.S.-led effort to contain the Soviets and otherwise to maintain a determinedly apolitical low profile on divisive world issues. Now, and with apparent suddenness, the world was looking to Tokyo for decisive action in a distant conflict that could not be comprehended through the familiar prism of the cold war.[1] Worse, there was little in Japan's modern experience to prepare it for the expansive world role now expected of it.

For four decades after its defeat in World War II and the subsequent occupation, Japan's international position was circumscribed by its patron-client relationship with the United States. Shielded by the U.S. security guarantee, inhibited by fears of revived militarism both at home and among its Asian neighbors, and obliged to defer to U.S. political and strategic leadership under the rigors of the cold war, successive Japanese leaders clung to the essential elements of the so-called Yoshida Doctrine. Named for Shigeru Yoshida, twice prime minister between 1946 and 1954, the strategy called for Japan to keep a low profile on contentious international issues and focus the nation's prodigious energies instead on economic pursuits. If political and military engagements were equated with conflict, suffering, and humiliation, economic undertakings seemed to provide a legitimate and peaceful channel for Japanese talents. Postwar necessity thus became enshrined as national self-concept. For two generations of Japanese, foreign policy has been virtually synonymous with foreign economic policy.

By the late 1980s, however, the convergence of three trends—the demise of the cold war, Japan's dramatic emergence as an economic superpower, and the perceived relative decline of the United States—produced a mounting sense that Japan would have to rethink its truncated international role. Recent years have thus witnessed a mounting debate among Japan's opinion leaders and policy elites over what the nation's global role should be.[2] Reminiscent in some ways of earlier U.S. "Great Debates" on the eve of World War II, at the outset of the cold war, and during the Vietnam War, Japan's recent public dialogues are indicative of a nation confronting momentous change in its international role.

Left undisturbed by external crisis, Japan's broad rethinking would have proceeded at an exceedingly slow and deliberate pace because of two traits of Japanese society: the ingrained desire for broad consensus reached through comprehensive participation and the traditional absence of commanding public leadership inclined to promote an architectonic vision from the top down. However, the eruption of the Persian Gulf crisis in August 1990 found Japan still in the early stages of consensus-building through its newly begun national debate and without constitutional or statutory mechanisms for dispatching its uniformed personnel to foreign hot spots.

Lacking an agreed concept of national purpose in the post–cold war environment and hampered by the exceptionally weak leadership of Prime Minister Toshiki Kaifu,[3] Japan entered a seven-month ordeal of tepid measures, false starts, and arcane debate that did little to enhance its image as a major power.

Kaifu began firmly enough, halting oil imports from Iraq and Kuwait and suspending all commercial relations with Iraq on August 5.[4] In late August the government pledged that 100 to 200 medical personnel would be sent to the Gulf as the first step of a more comprehensive Japanese contribution.[5] A week later $1 billion was pledged to support the multinational coalition and front-line states, an amount raised to $4 billion in late September.[6]

Evaluated against the amoral pragmatics of its previous Middle East policy, the Japanese rightly regarded their initial steps as demonstrating firm solidarity with the anti-Iraq coalition. Unequivocal denunciations of Iraq's aggression and official declarations of alignment with the West were indeed departures from Japan's Middle East policy of the past twenty years. Japanese interest in the Middle East has traditionally been a virtual one-dimensional preoccupation with access to the region's oil. Even today, despite a growing number of cultural exchanges and area-studies programs, Japanese attention to Middle East issues remains filtered through the nation's quest for dependable petroleum supplies. No other major industrial nation is so starkly dependent upon external energy sources as is Japan. Over 80 percent of its energy supply comes from imports. Virtually 100 percent of its oil is imported, and of that a whopping 70 percent comes from the Persian Gulf.[7]

To be sure, Japan did establish diplomatic relations with Israel after regaining its sovereignty in 1952. Following the U.S. lead, those relations would remain generally cordial, if of mutually peripheral significance, for the next two decades. With the 1973 oil shock, however, Japan moved sharply away from its pro-Israel policy. Henceforth, Japanese diplomacy in the Middle East would amount to little more than a calculated "resource diplomacy."

Japan's fears that OPEC would deal it a crippling economic blow if it did not shift away from supporting U.S. and Israeli positions were confirmed by the dictum of Saudi Oil Minister Ahmed Yamani: "If you are hostile (i.e., continue to support Israel) to us, you get no oil. If you are neutral, you get oil, but not as much as before. If you are friendly (i.e., support Arab diplomatic/economic sanctions against Israel), you get the same oil as before."[8]

Similarly, Japan's response to a second oil shock in 1979–80 was grounded in a pragmatic calculus of its immediate economic self-interest. Despite intense U.S. pressure to participate in an embargo against Iranian oil in retaliation for Teheran's seizure of U.S. diplomats, Japan refused to do so. It sought instead to distance itself from the Western coalition in order to placate Iran and the Arab oil producers. Throughout the remainder of the 1980s Japan's Middle East policy was decidedly pro-Arab in order to cultivate favor with the principal OPEC producers.

While its pro-Arab posture had not changed by 1990, its vulnerability to oil interruptions had been much reduced, for four reasons. First, Japan's stringent energy conservation measures were so successful that its economy today produces twice the output for the same energy input as in 1973.[9] Second, it has systematically shifted away from energy-intensive manufacturing, such as aluminum production, in favor of information- and capital-intensive services and products.[10] Third, Japan has aggressively developed its nuclear energy capacity. Over one-fourth of its electricity now comes from nuclear reactors, a national proportion exceeded only by France.[11] Finally, Japan's ambitious petroleum stockpiling program had by August 1990 accumulated a 142-day reserve.[12] While there is thus some merit in Tokyo's concept that its early actions in the Gulf crisis demonstrated a new willingness to take a principled stand on intra-Arab aggression in solidarity with its Western partners, it is also the case that by 1990 Japan could afford to do so with minimal risk to its economic self-interest.

For Japan's leaders, opinion elites, and general public, matters would become more complex and divisive as the nation tried to move beyond its initial measures and attempt to formulate a more robust presence in the U.S.-led coalition. At the end of September, Kaifu unveiled his proposed UN Peace Cooperation Corps, a mechanism for Japanese personnel to participate in the coalition in noncombat support roles. In succeeding weeks deliberations became mired in arcane disputes over the legal permissibility of including elements of the Self Defense Forces (SDF) in the proposed corps.[13] Symptomatic of the debate were protracted discussions of whether overseas deployment of unarmed SDF forces would constitute merely the sending of personnel (haken) or the constitutionally suspect dispatch of troops (hahei). Similarly, Kaifu himself weighed in with the argument that while the dispatch of SDF forces in the name of collective defense (shudan boei) would indeed be unconstitutional, their participation in collective security arrangements (shudanteki anzen hosho) would be constitutionally permissible. By early November, Kaifu was forced to withdraw the UN Peace Cooperation Bill in the face of certain Diet rejection.[14] In late January 1991, with the war to liberate Kuwait well under way, the government pledged to secure Diet approval of an additional $9 billion for the Allied effort.[15]

Not until late April 1991, more than two months after the conclusion of the Allied drive to expel Iraq from Kuwait, did Japan dispatch four minesweepers to the Persian Gulf. The dispatch was by this point largely of symbolic import, an effort by the government of Japan to appear to be an active participant in the international coalition and thus to avoid the potential international isolation and rejection that is a source of chronic Japanese anxiety.[16]

The government's handling of the issue was not inspiring. Japan's conspicuous place on the sidelines prompted broad international criticism. "Where's the New 'Superpower?'" taunted *Newsweek* in its August 27 issue, expressing a widely held sentiment. Largely unrecognized amid the apparent public relations debacle, however, was the fact that the Gulf crisis intensified the broader national debate already under way on Japan's future international role. Competing paradigms advanced by Japan's opinion leaders were brought into sharp relief during the Gulf debate.

The remainder of this study examines five contending schools of thought that were prominent in Japan's debate over its role in the Gulf: the minimalists, who urged Japanese autonomy from the United States and minimal participation in the U.S.-led effort; the realists, who argued that the Gulf crisis required Japan to wield greater international clout due to the imperatives of the state system; the moralists, who advocated a policy of activism grounded in ideological precepts; the utilitarians, who saw the crisis as an occasion for Japan to enhance its international stature; and the bilateralists, who urged robust Japanese efforts in order to strengthen the key relationship with the United States. Each school illustrated in figure 4.1 is defined by its distinct theme, but it must be stressed that they are not entirely mutually exclusive.

The principal voices in the dialogue were the nation's opinion leaders. Drawn from think tanks, the media, business circles, universities, political parties, and legislative and bureaucratic elites, they compete to mold the projected new national consensus. Their efforts merit close study, since ideas are often the engines of action in foreign policy. It follows that the ultimate outcome of the competition among

Fig. 4.1. The Debate over Japan's International Role

SCHOOLS OF THOUGHT	POLICY PRESCRIPTION	DOMESTIC STRENGTH
MINIMALIST	Minimize Japan's participation in anti-Iraq coalition; maximize autonomy from United States	Strong; mass public opinion because of growing criticism of United States and widespread mass pacifism. Occurs in all five parties, but concentrated in Japan Socialist Party and Japan Communist Party.
REALIST	Participate vigorously in anti-Iraq coalition in order to maintain international balance-of-power system.	Moderate-to weak; influential advocates at elite level but little mass support for the politics of realpolitik. Occurs principally in ruling Liberal Democratic Party.
MORALIST	Participate vigorously in anti-Iraq coalition because the invasion and annexation of a sovereign member of the United Nations constitutes a clear case of right versus wrong.	Weak; several prominent elite spokesmen, but Japan's political culture offers little support to policies grounded in moral abstractions. No clear party affiliation
UTILITARIAN	Participate vigorously in anti-Iraq coalition as a means of enhancing Japan's international political stature.	Moderate; considerable strength among opinion elites, but introversionist public sentiment limits freedom of action of this school's advocates. Occurs principally in LDP, Democratic Socialist Party, and Komeito.
BILATERALIST	Participate vigorously in anti-Iraq coalition in order to shore up Japan's central relationship with the United States.	Moderate-to-strong; broad support among centrist and conservative opinion elites, but growing national self-confidence coupled with skepticism of U.S. leadership creates a less hospitable public climate for proponents of this traditional outlook.

Japan's opinion leaders will do much to answer an often-posed question: now that it is a true economic superpower, how will Japan wield the broader political influence ordinarily conferred by wealth?

The Minimalists

The minimalist school of thought in the Gulf debate stressed the need for Japan to minimize its participation in the U.S.-led effort and to distance itself generally from U.S. policies. Though sharing a common theme of criticizing U.S. leadership, members of this school of thought are an otherwise exceedingly heterogeneous lot—leftists, pacifists, isolationists, right-wing nationalists, and advocates of what might be called "realeconomic," or preoccupation with Japan's economic self-interest.

Early in the crisis former Chief Cabinet Secretary Masaharu Gotoda united this otherwise fragmented array of views by arguing in August that "Japan must not act simply for the reason that the United States tells us to."[17] Others soon echoed the theme. Euji Suzuki, chairman of the influential Japan Federation of Employers Associations (Nikkeiren), urged greater Japanese autonomy "rather than meekly following the leadership of the United States."[18] Political commentator Saburo Kugai agreed, arguing that "the interests of Japan and the United States are different. . . . [Japan should] set its own policies."[19]

Japan's Gulf diplomacy was similarly criticized by the Tokyo Shimbun for its "excessive leaning toward the United States."[20] As the crisis dragged on, Professor Takeshi Sasaki of Tokyo University observed that "more and more respectability is being given to opinions against the United States. A very strong counteraction has started in leading journals that are always sensitive to shifts in public opinion."[21]

Calls by the political left for minimal Japanese involvement in the U.S.-led coalition focused almost exclusively on the fear that any relaxation of the strict policy of nondeployment of the armed forces would undermine Japanese pacifism and Article 9 of the Constitution. This in turn would raise "the fear once again of repeating . . . the nightmare" of Japanese militarism, in the words of Socialist Party Secretary General Tsuruo Yamaguchi.[22]

Some commentators couched their criticisms of the United States in the broader argument that Japan enjoys generally good relations with the nations of the Middle East and is looked upon as a nation with clean hands in the region. It is thus well positioned, they argue, to play an independent broker role in the region's disputes.[23] This view is advocated by Tokyo University's Professor Yuzo Itagaki, a specialist on Arab issues. "Japan should do its own thinking and come up with its own policies," he argues.[24] Likewise, Shigeki Koyama, president of the Japanese Institute of Middle East Economics, asserted in December 1990 that "the American method of taking short cuts . . . and pushing for direct reaction is making more and more people worry."[25]

Some who advocated an independent role that would purportedly be less offensive to the Arab world did so from a belief that Japan's economic interests would be threatened by a war that could alienate Arabs from the industrial nations for many years to come. Kazuo Kukuzawa, managing director of Keidanren, the most important business trade group, put it this way: "The sentiment of business leaders is that the United States shouldn't be holding a gun to the head of Saddam Hussein."[26] As to the oft-voiced argument that Japan, which relies on the Middle East for 70 percent of its oil, is the nation with the most at stake in restoring stability in the region, it "is not a rational argument but an argument based on emotion," asserted Tomoharu Washio, a research fellow at the International Institute for Global Peace, a think tank founded by the former prime minister, Yasuhiro Nakasone.[27] Many business leaders and commentators believed that it was not in Japan's interest to join the U.S.-led effort because its own economy was not nearly as vulnerable as was widely believed due to advances in energy efficiency, because the overall strength of Japan's economy compared to those of its competitors, and because they believed Kuwaiti oil would soon flow regardless of who controlled the oil fields. To many Japanese predisposed toward political insularity and an economic-centered view of international affairs, the conflict in the Middle East looked like an instance of *taigan no kaji,* "a fire on the other side of the river."[28]

When the offensive to dislodge Iraq from Kuwait began in mid-January, it was clear that many of Japan's opinion leaders—and solid majorities of the mass public—opposed the military effort. Subsequent commentary often reflected an undercurrent of anti-U.S. sentiment. Hiroshi Kume, a popular television news anchorman, told his viewers, "We didn't ask for war. Japan said differences should be settled through diplomatic means, but Bush didn't listen. We should tell him that America started this war and it's up to America to finish it."[29]

This anti-U.S. undercurrent reflects the bilateral strains of recent years generated by bruising trade battles and the resentment felt among some Japanese over perceived U.S. pressure and high-handedness. After forty-five years as the decidedly junior partner in a patron-client relationship and amid growing national self-confidence and pride in Japan's economic ascendancy, it is inevitable that many Japanese feel the need to assert their nation's identity and independence from the United States. What remains to be seen is whether Japan's new-found pride and desire for foreign policy independence will lead to neo-isolationism on noneconomic issues, will find expression in cooperative forms of international interdependence,[30] or instead will be channeled into the nationalistic unilateralism espoused most prominently by the right-wing Liberal Democratic Party legislator Shintaro Ishihara, coauthor of the controversial *The Japan that Can Say No*. Several months before Iraq invaded Kuwait, Ishihara repeated his familiar complaint that Japan "has become a country which moves as the United States wishes" on matters of defense and diplomacy.[31]

It is certainly the case that opinion polls have captured a distinct Japanese cooling toward the United States in recent years. For example, a November 1989 poll conducted by Louis Harris for *Business Week* magazine asked Japanese respondents, "How much admiration and fondness do you have for each of the following—a great deal, a fair amount, not very much, or not at all?" By wide margins the most frequent reaction to both "America as a nation" and "the American people" was "not very much."[32] Reporting new evidence of elite and mass Japanese disenchantment with the United States, *Newsweek*'s April 2, 1990, cover depicted a U.S. infant with the headline "What Japan Thinks of Us: A Nation of Crybabies?"

The polls suggest that opinion leaders who urge greater Japanese autonomy in its international dealings are preaching to a mass public broadly predisposed to share their prescription. The *Yomiuri Shimbun* conducted two nearly identical surveys during the debate on Gulf policy, the first in September 1990 and again in December. When asked "if this Gulf crisis is to be used as a lesson, on what fields ought our country place emphasis?" the most popular response on both occasions was the establishment of "Japan's own autonomous diplomacy line so as to become able to contribute to the world in non-military fields" (43.3 percent in September, 44.2 percent in December).[33] In both surveys, the least popular response was "to revise the constitution and to make the overseas dispatch of the SDF possible" (8 percent in September, 8.9 percent in December).[34]

Yet it would be unwise to read a virulent anti-U.S. sentiment into the available evidence of a broad desire for greater autonomy from U.S. political leadership. Famously self-preoccupied with their presumed cultural uniqueness (there are over 1,000 titles in print in Japan on what it means to be Japanese, or *nihonjin-ron*)[35] and acutely self-conscious of their separateness from the rest of the world, the Japanese, in the words of the late Edwin Reischauer, "find it hard to join the human race."[36] Most Japanese still regard the United States more highly than they do any other nation. It is nonetheless true that economic success has bred a new national self-confidence that for some leads to a desire to step back from the forty-five-year-long U.S. embrace which they fear threatens to smother Japan's cherished uniqueness and separateness.

The Realists

Though clearly a minority outlook, realpolitik, or realism, appeared in the Gulf debate as the rationale for a policy of robust engagement. Opinion leaders in this category proceed from an analysis of the dynamics of the international system grounded in the familiar concepts of state sovereignty, systemic anarchy, the security dilemma, and the need for the states to practice the impersonal calculus of balance of power policies. Members of this school of thought give little weight to matters of national preference or moral ideals. Rather, they pursue a line of reasoning grounded in the belief that the decentralized state system generates its own logic and requirements and that prudent national policy lies in understanding the steps required to maintain the system and uphold international norms upon which the state's own well-being depends. Though realpolitik represents the thinking of a small minority of Japan's opinion leaders, its arguments are worth noting because they appear in prominent and prestigious forums.

Perhaps Japan's leading exponent of the realist school of thought is Seizaburo Sato, professor at Tokyo University, research director at the International Institute for Global Peace, and confidante of the former prime minister, Nakasone. From an interview conducted with him and an analysis of his writings, one can summarize the intellectual premises and policy prescriptions that lie at the core of Sato's worldview.

He begins with the axiom that "the sovereign nation-state system persists."[37] A decentralized system of sovereign states means an inherent structural anarchy. Derived from this is his second premise: that an inherently anarchic world will be a "world . . . full of dangers."[38] Third, a chronically dangerous world requires of its members "action to maintain order to prevent aggression anywhere in the world."[39] Peace and stability do not just happen. They must be made to happen through prudent statecraft grounded in the necessity of maintaining an overall balance within the system.

A fourth premise involves Sato's frank recognition of "how important military strength is to protect peace at this starting point of the post–cold war period."[40] Sato is in no sense a militarist. To the contrary, he agrees with those who stress the growing significance of economic and political instruments of power in an increasingly interdependent world.[41] To Sato noncoercive forms of power supplement traditional military might, but they emphatically do not supplant it as the ultima ratio of international conflicts.

From this it is a short step to Sato's fifth premise, his belief that Japan must assume greater responsibilities, including a role—if necessarily a noncombat one—for its armed forces, in order to help sustain a stable and peaceful world order.[42] To Sato, the Gulf crisis presented Japan with an inherent logic and set of requirements that it dare ignore only at its own peril. "The talk of constitutional constraints and demons of the past is all one big alibi," he argued. "We mustn't miss a golden opportunity to prove we recognize our responsibilities."[43] To Sato, the impersonal demands of realism require Japan to overcome its parochialism, its international timidity, and its preoccupation with economic pursuits to the exclusion of prudent attention to security needs.

Sato's brand of realpolitik is shared in varying degrees by other opinion leaders and foreign policy elites in Japan, though it must be stressed that not all agree with his conclusion about the need to dispatch the SDF abroad. A representative media view was the *Sankei*'s editorial assertion that "the times and the world situation have completely changed and . . . many things are sought of Japan . . . for the peace and stability of the world."[44] Michio Watanabe, an influential figure in LDP circles, offered this determinedly nonromantic analysis: "The Middle East is the foundation of Japan's prosperity. . . . We have the responsibility to do what we can do."[45] Komeito chairman Ishida's support for a time-limited law that would permit the dispatch of unarmed SDF personnel to the Gulf region to perform nonmilitary tasks was predicated on the conviction that Iraq's invasion of a weak neighbor was "a serious defiance against peace which appeared after the dissolution of the cold war structure."[46] Ishida argues that although it may wish to remain aloof from contentious international matters, Japan is simply required to participate in the construction and maintenance of a post–cold war global structure upon which its own well-being depends.

Ishida's analysis of the crisis was echoed by Satsuki Eda of Shaminren (Social Democratic Federation), who argued that Iraq must be stopped and that Japan had a responsibility to participate in the U.S.-led effort to do so.[47] Symptomatic of the attenuated realpolitik of a number of Japan's opinion leaders, though, is Eda's unwillingness to see Japan participate through any form of military contribution. He differs from other realists less in his analysis of the threats to Japan's security, posed by unchecked aggression and international disorder, than in his prescription of the instruments of power that Japan can properly contribute to the maintenance of world order.

As these examples show, there is an identifiable realist school of thought among Japan's opinion leaders. At this point its line of reasoning is not one that is particularly congenial to Japanese thought. Opinion polls show that the themes of realpolitik have minimal support among the mass public. For example, the *Yomiuri Shimbun*'s September 1990 poll of public perceptions of the Gulf crisis asked respondents to identify "a matter of concern to you about the Gulf crisis." The most frequent response by far was a humanitarian and emotional concern for "the problem of hostages" (64.9 percent) while only 16.3 percent indicated concern over the fact that Iraq's invasion threatened to reverse the general decline of tensions in the international system.[48]

However, the prominence and prestige of publicists such as Seizaburo Sato suggests that realism is an outlook likely to gain support in the future, at least among policy elites and opinion leaders. Such a development would, over time, affect the premises and conduct of Japanese foreign policy. Realpolitik connotes a dispassionate attentiveness to global political currents, a realization that Japan's interests are inextricably bound up with distant forces, and a willingness to take decisive action to maintain the broader political and security structure upon which Japan's safety and well-being depend. A Japanese diplomacy grounded in realpolitik would probably be one of greater independence from the United States and would certainly require, if pursued fully, the will to utilize the nation's armed forces in a greater capacity than defense-of-the-home-islands. A rise in realist sentiment is unlikely to lead to a revival of Japanese militarism per se. Japan's immense stake in avoiding the isolation and rejection that renewed militarism would surely provoke will serve to temper the nation's reliance on military power for the foreseeable future. On balance, however, the growth of realist sentiment will help Japan step up to the broad array of global responsibilities ordinarily borne by major nations.

The Moralists

Joseph Nye argues that in an increasingly interdependent world, so-called "hard" instruments of power such as military or economic coercion are of declining utility while "soft" power, such as a nation's cultural and ideological appeal, takes on greater significance.[49] He notes, "Many Japanese are concerned about their . . . failure to project a broader message" internationally.[50] This failure is rooted in Japan's traditional aversion to abstract formulations of overarching purpose. Japanese culture, with its philosophical relativism and group-defined situational ethics, has placed less weight on moral absolutes and abstract concepts than has been the case in Western societies.[51] Lacking fixed principles of right and wrong grounded in religious or secular tradition, Japan's culture conditions its members to focus on shifting requirements of their immediate group. Right behavior springs from an individual's appreciation of his position within the group and his desire to be perceived as a team player who goes along with the group's consensual views. Wrong behavior arises from individualistic impulses to follow one's own beliefs when they diverge from group-defined norms. The key point is that among the major nations, Japan stands apart in its relative absence of transcendent principles of right and wrong.

In foreign policy, this trait has given Japanese leaders broad latitude in making decisions pragmatically on a case-by-case basis, but to critics it is seen as evidence of Japan's unprincipled opportunism and incapability of acting on behalf of transcendent values. Certainly the nation's lack of ideological appeal, along with its insular culture, have put Japan at a disadvantage in projecting a clear vision of its national purpose.

It is thus interesting to note that in the debate over the Gulf crisis, this third school of opinion leaders who urged Japan to take vigorous action did so on frankly ideological grounds. Japan's foreign policy, they argued, must be grounded in a set of explicit principles with wide international appeal. Those principles, in turn, will require of Japan greater international participation and responsibility than has previously been the case.

Among the most outspoken proponents of this view is Yukio Okamoto. Prior to his recent resignation, Okamoto was a career diplomat who headed the First North America Division in the Ministry of Foreign Affairs. To Okamoto, too many Japanese suffer from what he calls "a disease of relativism" that leaves them without a standard for judging right and wrong in world affairs and leaves the nation vulnerable to the charge of cynical opportunism. "There are no examples in our history of Japan standing up for one value against another," he says.[52] He is openly appalled that too few of his countrymen viewed the invasion, annexation, and destruction of a sovereign member of the United Nations as a clear affront to the norms of international society. "I lecture on this all the time," he said in December 1990. "The business people say, 'you know, so what if Saddam Hussein gets hold of the oil fields? He has to sell his oil somewhere.'"[53]

Okamoto is also concerned about Japan's depiction by U.S. critics as a nation with a "faceless diplomacy." He argues that there is a need to articulate a "diplomatic ideology . . . so others will understand Japan's foreign policy."[54] To Okamoto, "the words or concepts most favored by Japanese are 'cooperation,' 'coordination,' 'harmony,' 'dialogue,'—all of which are pleasing to the ears but do not contain a value in themselves. These are ethical standards of social behavior; they are not . . . moral goals."[55] He believes that Japan's diplomatic ideology must include, at a minimum, the values of freedom, democracy, free markets, and nonaggression.[56]

Other opinion leaders share Okamoto's belief that the Gulf crisis presented an opportunity for Japan to take a principled stand in a clear case of right against wrong. Ichiro Ozawa, the outspoken secretary general of the Liberal Democratic Party, expressed concern over the broad perception of Japan as "a country without a face."[57] His call for vigorous Japanese participation in the anti-Iraq coalition was couched in explicitly ideological terms: "It is only when there is peace and freedom in the world that Japan can enjoy peace and affluence as at present."[58] Another opinion leader who urged Japan to take a stand on behalf of ideological principles was a former deputy prime minister, Kiichi Miyazawa, who argued that the Japanese people are so steeped in postwar pacifism that "we have hardly come to ask ourselves . . . if we will not bleed for freedom, either."[59]

Agreeing with Miyazawa that Japan should dispatch personnel along with its financial contribution to the Gulf effort, Chairman Ouchi of the Democratic Socialist Party warned against what he called "an unprincipled course of steadily pouring in Japan's blood taxes."[60] In a similar vein, the newspaper *Nihon Keizai* sharply criticized what it saw as a "lack of fixed principles" among Japan's leaders in international dealings.[61]

Though still a minority, a growing number of Japanese opinion leaders are sensitive to the perception of Japan as a selfish, unprincipled, opportunistic nation committed to nothing higher than its own economic interest. The vigorous debate over Japan's role in the Gulf crisis gave them added visibility and presented frequent opportunities to inject their views into the broader stream of public thought about Japan's relationship with the outside world. The available polling data offer no clear evidence of the general public's receptivity to their argument, but in all probability appeals to foreign policy activism grounded in ideological concepts still find only moderate support among Japan's public.

In the longer term, however, it seems likely that the ranks of opinion leaders who advocate a principled basis for foreign policy actions will grow, both in numbers and in visibility. It seems equally likely that their appeals to moral values such as freedom and democracy will become increasingly popular as a younger generation attains maturity and influence. Less content than the postwar generation with the amoral pragmatics of economic growth and more attuned to global values through travel and communication, today's youth may one day fulfill Yukio Okamoto's vision of a Japan taking its diplomatic bearings from the moral criteria of universal precepts.

The Utilitarians

Perhaps the most prominent school of thought among Japan's opinion leaders was the view that Japan should respond positively and vigorously in the Gulf crisis as a means of strengthening the nation's

standing and credibility as an independent global power. Advocates of
this approach tended to place little emphasis on Japan's stake in the
Middle East per se or on Japan's responsibilities in constructing a stable international order, nor did they speak of moral imperatives or
ideological vision. Rather, their analyses and commentaries dwelt almost exclusively on matters of Japan's international role and reputation. Their prescriptions were heavily colored by utilitarian assessments of how Japan would be perceived if it did not take firm steps in
the Gulf and how those perceptions would hamper Japan's ability to
gain acceptance as a genuine international power. Put another way, if
adherents of the realist school believe that the crisis *required* Japan to
wield influence in the name of systemic imperatives, adherents of the
utilitarian school believe that the crisis *permitted* Japan to wield influence in order to enhance its role as a recognized power.

This school of thought generally shares the view of David Rapkin
that Japan's international leadership has been limited by what he calls
a "legitimacy deficit" which arises from "the legacy of militarism and
colonialism, a mercantilistic reputation, and disbelief that Japan can
articulate universalizable norms, values, and principles."[62] Proponents
of this school of thought ardently wish to see Japan overcome its "legitimacy deficit" and gain international acceptance as what Hideo
Sato has termed a "core member" in an emerging "system of plural
leadership by major economic powers."[63]

Contained within this overall school of thought advocating firm action in order to enhance Japan's stature as a major power are two distinct subthemes: an acute concern about what other nations think of
Japan and the argument that Japan's contribution must go beyond
money alone in order to be credible to the world community.

Reflecting characteristic sensitivity to how other nations view Japan, the first theme emphasizes the need for Japan to play a major role
in the Gulf crisis because its image would suffer if it failed to do so.
This was a ubiquitous message in the major newspapers. At the
outset of the crisis the *Asahi* feared that Japan would be seen as "lag-
ging behind"[64] while the *Tokyo Shimbun* warned that Japan's conduct
will be closely watched and its "responsibility . . . will be questioned."[65] *Sankei* argued that without firm steps, "it will be difficult to
obtain the understanding of other countries."[66] A few days later the
paper stressed that "Japan is now being criticized as the 'Japan which
does not take risks.'"[67] Still later *Sankei's* editors warned that Japan
"appeared to be buying time while pretending to check into contribu-

tion measures; its reputation in numerous foreign countries is extremely bad."[68]

A number of prominent opinion leaders echoed the media's preoccupation with Japan's international reputation. Former ambassador to the United States Nobuo Matsunaga believed that "the eyes of the world are on Japan" in the Gulf crisis[69] while LDP Secretary General Ozawa feared that Japan would become "isolated in the world . . . expecting that others will defend peace and security for us [while] we will do nothing for the peace and security of others."[70] He warned that "such a selfish way of living cannot pass muster in the world."[71]

Echoing Ozawa's fear of an isolated, ostracized Japan was Jiro Aiko, Japan's former ambassador to Kuwait, who worried that Japan and Kuwait were alike in three ways: each was wealthy, militarily weak, and unpopular. Would Japan experience the same fate as Kuwait, he wondered?[72] The anxiety of international disapproval was shared by no less a figure than Prime Minister Kaifu, who argued in January that Japan faced "international isolation" if it did not contribute personnel and more money to the coalition effort.[73] Similarly, Michio Watanabe, a key LDP leader, warned that Japan would become an international orphan if it failed to participate fully in the Gulf.[74]

This concern with international image and acceptance grew more acute when the U.S.-led coalition succeeded in liberating Kuwait while Japan remained mired in seemingly interminable debate over its proper role. The *Yomiuri Shimbun*, though closely linked to the ruling Liberal Democratic Party, nonetheless offered this harsh postmortem: "Japan's poor skills in diplomacy surfaced during the seven-month crisis. Underlying the nation's political immaturity was its intellectual inadequacy in tackling the realities of a changing world."[75]

Among those advocating a vigorous Gulf role as a means of shoring up Japan's stature in the world, many shared the second theme: that Japan's contribution must go beyond money alone. Several major newspapers developed this theme early in the crisis. In August the *Yomiuri* noted that many countries view Japan as a country that "will not dirty its hands, though it is the country which benefits most from the Middle East oil."[76] Similarly, the *Tokyo Shimbun* argued against relying solely on "a lavish scattering around of aid" and asserted that "Japan will have to sweat" as well.[77] Tadahiko Nasa of the paper's editorial committee expressed the prematurely optimistic view that Kaifu's August 29 measures "will probably help eliminate the international image of Japan . . . that supplies money but does not sweat."[78]

Opinion leaders echoing the same sentiment included Komeito Secretary General Yuichi Ichikawa[79] and Takashi Yonezawa, secretary general of the Democratic Socialist Party, who argued in October that "up
to now we have contributed money and materials alone, but if we do
not carry out personnel support, Japan cannot fulfill its role."[80] In official circles Japan's top career diplomat bluntly asserted that "the time
has passed for us to cooperate with money alone. . . . The government's view . . . was . . . to create a structure where the Japanese
people will sweat with their participation."[81]

The long and complex debate over the permissibility of utilizing elements of the SDF in noncombat support of the U.S.-led coalition, along
with the embarrassing response to Kaifu's pledge to send at least 100
medical personnel to the Gulf region—only twenty-four agreed to go,
and they returned home after a brief stint—demonstrates the great
amount of work that remains to be done in developing modalities for
Japan's citizens to take part in cooperative efforts to solve international
crises. It is nonetheless significant that the need for Japan to do just
that has become a central theme among some of Japan's key opinion
leaders.

The Bilaterists

A final school of thought among Japan's opinion leaders
viewed the crisis in the Middle East principally in terms of the bilateral U.S.-Japan relationship. These opinion leaders proceeded from a
straightforward thesis: Japan should participate as fully as possible in
the multinational coalition because failure to do so would jeopardize
its critical relationship with the United States. Like the opinion leaders whose policy prescriptions were grounded in utilitarian assessments of what was expected of Japan if it is to be fully accepted as a
major international power, members of this school of thought placed
almost no emphasis on the importance of the Middle East to Japan or
on Japan's responsibilities in the maintenance of world order. Rather,
the U.S. connection is, for these opinion leaders, the sine quo non of
Japan's international position, and it is from this axiom that Japan's
proper conduct in the Gulf should be deduced.

Given the centrality of the United States to Japan for the past forty-
five years, it is scarcely surprising that many Japanese elites respond
to specific foreign policy issues through the intellectual prism of the
U.S.-Japan relationship. Interviews with numerous opinion leaders in

Tokyo just weeks before Iraq invaded Kuwait underscored the importance that many opinion elites place on the maintenance of a sound
partnership with the United States. This was true, for example, in
media circles. Yoshio Murakami, foreign editor of the *Asahi Shimbun*,
argued that most Japanese realize that there is much to lose if U.S.-
Japan relations break down: "They want to go with the winning
horse," as he put it.[82] Similarly, Mikio Haruna, deputy editor on the
foreign news desk of the Kyodo News Service, believes it is essential
to keep the United States militarily engaged in Asia, less to curb the
Soviets than as a "guarantor of regional stability."[83]

A number of policy intellectuals voice similar sentiments, including Nushi Yamamoto of Tokyo University, Tomohisa Sakanaka of
Aoyama Gakuin University, and Shigekatsu Kondo of the National
Institute for Defense Studies.[84] All stressed the need to maintain and
strengthen the bilateral tie, both in security and economic links.

Officials in the Ministry of Foreign Affairs and the Japan Defense
Agency echoed the sentiment. For example, Toshinori Shigeie, then
director of the National Security Affairs Division in the Foreign Ministry, stated emphatically that "the United States must stay in the Pa-
cific. Nobody can replace it. Japan must educate its people and support
the United States and the basic structure in Asia, whose main pillar is
the U.S. presence."[85] Shigeie's sentiments were seconded by Jiro Hagi,
counsellor of the Japan Defense Agency, who stated flatly that "the
U.S. presence is indispensable for peace and stability in Asia."[86]

More than any other single opinion leader, it is Motoo Shiina who
has stressed the centrality of the U.S. relationship longest and most
consistently. For many years the LDP's acknowledged leader on security issues in the Diet, Shiina continues to promote his views as a private citizen. A central imperative for Japan, he argues, is to keep the
United States engaged in the security of Asia, and to do that it "must
help the United States feel comfortable staying in Japan."[87] In August
1990, Shiina urged a robust Japanese effort in the Gulf largely as a
means of maintaining "the Japan-U.S. Security Treaty structure."[88]
Shiina added that "if public opinion in the United States were to view
that the Soviet Union, which they had thought to be an enemy until
now, did more to help, it will be considerably troublesome. Japan
ought to do as much as it can."[89]

Shiina's central premise was repeated in a November 1990 editorial
in the daily *Nihon Keizai*, "Do Not Drive U.S. to Road of Isolationism."
The paper's editors urged Japanese support of the U.S.-led effort out of

fear that the U.S. might otherwise withdraw into isolationism.[90] From this premise of the criticality of continued U.S. engagement in the world and in Asian security especially, it follows that Japan must be closely attuned to U.S. perceptions of Japanese cooperation. In August and again in November 1990, the daily *Sankei* reported on U.S. "dissatisfaction 'with a Japan which does not bear risks'"[91] and noted its fear that "Japan's awkward or belated measures toward the Middle East crisis" could lead to a breakdown in U.S.-Japan relations.[92] Sharing this anxiety over U.S. opinion were Yukio Okamoto of the Foreign Ministry, who feared that U.S. mistrust of Japan's policy reluctance had created the most severe crisis in the bilateral relationship in years,[93] and Masashi Nishihara of the National Defense Academy, who told reporters that "if I were an American, I would see Japan as not reliable as a friend."[94]

From these premises, it follows—according to this school of thought—that Japan's responses to international crises must be framed with the requirements of the United States clearly in mind. Writing in the prestigious foreign affairs magazine *Gaiko Forum*, Foreign Ministry official Shigeo Takenaka framed the issue this way: "The policy which Japan ought to take must be a policy which will foster sound U.S. internationalism. It must be a policy which will give self-confidence to the American people that the United States can manage with internationalism, because there is the cooperation of Japan and other countries, even at a time like the present when the United States has fallen into financial difficulties."[95]

It is in this context that we must view Prime Minister Kaifu's September proposal to contribute both money and unarmed elements of the SDF to the coalition effort. As the *New York Times* put it, Kaifu was attempting "to counter what Japanese officials fear is a tide of [U.S.] resentment over Japan's role in the Persian Gulf."[96] In the same vein, Motoo Shiina argued in the November 1990 issue of *Chuo Koron* magazine that Japan's failure to act appropriately in the crisis—which, to Shiina, meant dispatching SDF personnel—might well trigger a move in the United States to review the overall U.S.-Japan relationship, a prospect he viewed with grave concern.[97]

It remains to be seen if Japan's seven months of torturous indecision did indeed create the very bilateral crisis that opinion leaders of this school of thought wanted all along to avoid. There is some fragmentary evidence that Japan's reputation has in fact declined in U.S. eyes. A senior State Department official spoke in December 1990 of "a very distinct cooling" in U.S.-Japan relations.[98] At the mass level, a January 1991 poll found evidence of growing U.S. resentment of Japan for its indecision and aloofness in the war: 42 percent of voters responded that they had lost respect for Japan during the crisis, while only 10 percent said their respect for Japan had increased.[99] It is against this background that the *Economist* reported in February 1991 that "the Japanese now make no pretense of doing anything over the Gulf except repairing relations with the United States. Foreign policy has given way to damage control."[100]

Certainly no one would claim that the Gulf crisis represented Japan's finest hour. As the U.S. rejoiced in the striking success it engineered and discovered a new measure of international respect and popularity, the celebration was without Japanese participation (as was, precisely, the effort to liberate Kuwait). But as time passes and the United States addresses new issues, it is likely to view its relationship with Japan in a balanced context. Though Japanese behavior in the crisis did little to endear it to the United States, as opinion leaders such as Motoo Shiina had warned all along, it remains uncertain whether U.S. disillusionment will lead to the unraveling of a relationship that is of such manifest importance to both sides.

Conclusions

Japan's awkward efforts to craft an appropriate role for itself in the Persian Gulf crisis yielded two principal effects. First, as this analysis has shown, the Gulf War greatly intensified Japan's broader debate over its proper international role. The vitality, richness, and diversity of the debate are readily apparent. Evaluated by the standards of thoughtfulness, intelligence, and the evident energy with which it has been pursued, the contemporary debate among Japanese opinion leaders merits high marks indeed. One must assume that this will be so as long as the central question—Japan's proper world role—remains unresolved.

Recall that four of the five schools of thought called for Japan to accept substantially greater international burdens. Only one, the minimalists, prefer a continued peripheral political role for Japan. Thus it is not surprising that Japan's opinion leaders had only modest short-term impact on national policy makers and the mass public.

Polls routinely reflect a mass public whose international views are characteristically parochial, emotional, and modestly informed. Deeply rooted habits of mind, including those of insularity, ethnocentrism, and an aversion to firm national stands on contentious international issues present a challenging public environment for the kind of sophisticated analyses and informed policy preferences advanced by most opinion leaders.

Similarly, Japanese political leaders have traditionally paid relatively little attention to foreign policy issues, focusing instead on the personalist and pork barrel character of factional politics within the Diet. Despite its intellectual merits, then, the vigorous foreign policy debate conducted by Japan's opinion elites had little evident effect during the Gulf crisis itself.

The second effect of the crisis, however, is a postwar effort to address some of the principal critiques and prescriptions so ably articulated by the opinion leaders' debate. Efforts are currently under way to remedy long-standing concerns about both Japan's foreign policy process and its much-criticized image as a check-writing conscientious objector in the maintenance of international order.

In the aftermath of the crisis, there was renewed interest in reforming and strengthening the foreign policy decision-making structure. The problem is two-pronged: an overworked, understaffed Foreign Ministry and the absence of effective interagency mechanisms.

Japan's Foreign Ministry is by far the smallest of any of the major industrialized nations. Its 4,300 officers contrast sharply with Britain's 8,200 or the U.S. State Department's 16,000 foreign service officers.[101] Japan's career diplomats are simply unable to keep pace with the mounting volume and complexity of their work load. "The Ministry is in chaos," argues Nihon University's Motofumi Asai, himself a former career diplomat. "The offices are concerned with day-to-day routine, spending little time to collect and analyze intelligence, to engage in research and to work in long-term planning."[102] While some of the attention now being paid to bureaucratic deficiencies smacks of political scapegoating, the most likely result will be increased investment in the ministry's budget and professional personnel.

The problem of interagency gridlock was apparent throughout the crisis. Japan's National Security Council, composed of cabinet ministers and chaired by the prime minister, lacks the institutionalized staff expertise of its U.S. counterpart and, in any case, was never convened until actual hostilities were under way in the Gulf.

The cabinet secretary at the time, Misoji Sakamoto, is the prime minister's liaison with the individual ministries and is expected to fa-

cilitate interagency coordination, but his influence is only as strong
as that of the prime minister he serves. The much-noted political
frailties of Prime Minister Kaifu thus undercut Sakamoto's ability to
forge interagency consensus on Japan's Gulf policy.

The government's weak performance has stimulated efforts to reform the overall foreign policy process. A government council on administrative reform has recommended a strengthening of the prime
minister's interagency apparatus and the creation of a unified command center for crisis management.[103]

Beyond matters of process, Japan is rethinking its forty-five-year-
long aloofness from international peacekeeping and conflict-resolution
efforts. The most tangible expression of that rethinking is the proposal before the Diet to permit up to 2,000 members of the Self Defense Forces to be dispatched overseas for UN peacekeeping operations.
The September 9, 1991, agreement by the opposition Komeito and
Democratic Socialist parties to back the ruling Liberal Democratic
Party proposal virtually ensures the eventual adoption of the measure
in some form.[104]

There can be no doubt that this momentous shift is a direct result
of the broad criticism of Japan for its failure to participate with personnel in the anti-Iraq coalition. Japan's $13 billion contribution to
the Allied cause—$11 billion to support the military coalition and $2
billion to aid states near the fighting—made Japan the Allies' fourth
largest financial supporter, ranking behind only the United States,
Saudi Arabia, and Kuwait. Its large contribution was financed with the
help of a $5 billion tax hike adopted by the government. Yet the hes-
itant character of its support and its refusal to send personnel to assist the multinational effort against Iraq led to broad international
criticism.

Surely never before has a nation contributed so much and received
so little credit in return. In March 1991 two events further clarified
Japan's unpopularity among its allies. A *Washington Post*-ABC News
poll showed that 30 percent of U.S. citizens said they had lost respect
for Japan because of the Gulf crisis, while only 19 percent said their
respect for Japan had increased. When the Kuwaiti government published a full-page advertisement in the *New York Times* to thank
members of the UN coalition, Japan was conspicuously absent from
the list of countries named.[105]

The first major crisis of the post–cold war era left Japan smarting
over what it saw as the world's lack of understanding of its efforts. To

a nation chronically anxious about what the rest of the world thinks of it, the experience was a singularly painful and bitter one. For better or worse, the Gulf crisis marks a profound turning point in Japan's relations with the outside world. It will soon become clear if the crisis created in Japan the political will to play a more active and assertive role in world affairs. The post–World War II order, and with it Japanese deference to U.S. leadership on contentious international issues, has ended. A new era of Japanese political activism may have begun.

Notes

1. Seizaburo Sato, "The Unfolding Gulf Crisis and Japan's New Responsibility," *Japan Times Weekly*, September 10–16, 1990.

2. See Richard Drifte, *Japan's Foreign Policy* (New York: Council on Foreign Relations, 1990), p. 3; Masaru Tamamoto, "The Japan that Can Say Yes," *World Policy Journal* (Summer 1990): 493–520.

3. Representative editorial assessments of Kaifu are "Stand Up, Mr. Kaifu," *Sankei*, September 29, 1990 (U.S. Embassy, Tokyo, "Daily Summary of the Japanese Press" [hereafter DSJP], October 10–11, 1990), and the characterization of Kaifu by *Yukan Fuji*, a popular Tokyo newspaper, as "politically tone deaf" (quoted in *New York Times*, September 16, 1990).

4. "Japan Follows U.S., Cuts Trade with Iraq," *Washington Post*, August 6, 1990.

5. "Japan Restricted in Ways to Help, Will Send Medical Aid to Middle East," *Washington Post*, August 24, 1990.

6. "Japan Pledges $1 Billion in Aid for Use in the Gulf," *New York Times*, August 31, 1990; "Nation Ups the Ante: $4 Billion in Gulf Aid," *Japan Times Weekly*, September 24–30, 1990.

7. Ronald A. Morse, *Turning Crisis to Advantage: The Politics of Japan's Gulf Energy Strategy* (New York: The Asia Society, 1990), p. 4; see also *Japan Times Weekly*, August 13–19, 1990, p. 1.

8. Quoted in Richard W. Sims, *Japanese Resource Dependency* (Monterey, Calif.: Naval Postgraduate School, 1982), p. 82.

9. Kenneth Courtis, "Oil Shortage to Challenge Japan's Policy," *Japan Times Weekly*, August 27–September 2, 1990.

10. Ibid.

11. "A Crack in Japan's Nuclear Sangfroid," *New York Times*, February 17, 1991.

12. "Japan Follows U.S., Cuts Trade with Iraq," *Washington Post*, August 6, 1990.

13. "Kaifu Outlines His Proposal for Unarmed Japanese in Gulf," *New York Times*, September 28, 1990.

14. "The Mouse that Was Stillborn," *Economist*, November 10, 1990, pp. 36–38.

15. "Japan Stares Down the Barrel of a Gun," *Economist*, February 2, 1991, pp. 31–32.

16. "Breaking Tradition, Japan Sends Flotilla to Gulf," *New York Times*, April 25, 1991.

17. "Considering Japanese Diplomacy," *ASAHI*, August 23, 1990 (DSJP, August 30, 1990).

18. "Nation Told to Stop Being a Bystander," *Japan Times Weekly*, January 14–20, 1991.

19. "Middle East Turmoil Causes Tension to Rise in Japan," *Japan Times Weekly*, September 10–16, 1990.

20. "Gulf Crisis," *Tokyo Shimbun*, December 10, 1990 (DSJP, December 18, 1990).

21. "Japanese Leaders See Support for U.S. Stand in Gulf Ebbing," *New York Times*, December 11, 1990.

22. "Interview with JSP Secretary General Tsuruo Yamaguchi on Dispatch of SDF," *Mainichi*, October 18, 1990 (DSJP, October 25, 1990). See also "1990 Middle East Diet Session; Interviews with Party Heads: JSP Chairperson Doi," *ASAHI*, October 5, 1990 (DSJP, October 16, 1990); "Interview with JSP Chairperson Takako Doi," *Nihon Keizai*, October 28, 1990 (DSJP, November 3–5, 1990); "Interview with JCP Chairman Tetsuzo Fuwa on Middle East Diet," *Tokyo Shimbun*, October 29, 1990 (DSJP, November 3–5, 1990).

23. "Gulf Crisis," *Tokyo Shimbun*, December 10, 1990 (DSJP, December 18, 1990).

24. "Middle East Turmoil Causes Tension to Rise in Japan," *Japan Times Weekly*, September 10–16, 1990.

25. "Japanese Leaders See Support for U.S. Stand in Gulf Ebbing," *New York Times*, December 11, 1990.

26. Ibid.

27. "Fire on the Other Side," *Newsweek*, January 21, 1991.

28. "Tokyo's 'Full Support' for U.S. in Gulf Is Limited by Japanese Public's Apathy," *Wall Street Journal*, January 17, 1991.

29. "Test for Japan's Leader," *New York Times*, February 8, 1991.

30. See, for example, the thoughtful analysis of Takashi Inoguchi, "Japan's Politics of Interdependence," *Government and Opposition* (Autumn 1990): 419–37.

31. "Is the U.S. Necessary for Japan?" *Shokun* (May 1990) (U.S. Embassy, Tokyo, "Selected Summaries of Japanese Magazines," [hereafter SSJM], August 1990).

32. "Japan's Hardening View of America," *Business Week*, December 18, 1989, p. 63.

33. "Results of Nation-Wide Public Opinion Survey on Gulf Crisis," *Yomiuri*, September 30, 1990 (DSJP, October 6–9, 1990); "Results of Public Opinion

Survey on Gulf Crisis and International Contribution," *Yomiuri*, December 26, 1990 (DSJP, December 29–31, 1990).

34. Ibid.

35. Ellen Frost, *For Richer, for Poorer: The New U.S.-Japan Relationship* (New York: Council on Foreign Relations, 1987), p. 78.

36. Edwin O. Reischauer, *The Japanese Today* (Cambridge: Harvard University Press, 1989), p. 409.

37. Author's interview with Seizaburo Sato, Tokyo, July 16, 1990.

38. Seizaburo Sato, "The Unfolding Gulf Crisis and Japan's New Responsibility," *Japan Times Weekly*, September 10–16, 1990.

39. Ibid.

40. Seizaburo Sato, "The U.S.-Japan Alliance under Changing International Relations," *Washington Quarterly* (Summer 1990): 71–75.

41. Ibid.

42. Seizaburo Sato, "Strategy at This Time," *Chuo Koron* (October 1990) (SSJM, October 1990) and "This Is the Time for Eliminating the Inertia of Postwar Outlook," *Chuo Koron* (November 1990) (SSJM, November 1990).

43. Quoted in Strobe Talbott, "Japan and the Vision Thing," *Time*, October 1, 1990, p. 58.

44. "Government's View Ought to Be Revised," *Sankei*, September 13, 1990 (DSJP, September 21, 1990).

45. "Interview with Former LDP Policy Board Chairman Michio Watanabe on International Responsibility," *Yomiuri*, October 6, 1990 (DSJP, October 18, 1990).

46. "1990 Middle East Diet Session; Interviews with Party Heads: Komeito Chairman Ishida," *Asahi*, October 6, 1990 (DSJP, October 17, 1990).

47. "Iraqi Invasion and Japan," *Sankei*, September 1, 1990 (DSJP, September 18, 1990).

48. "Results of Nation-wide Public Opinion Survey on Gulf Crisis," *Yomiuri*, September 30, 1990 (DSJP, October 6–9, 1990).

49. Joseph S. Nye, Jr., "Soft Power," *Foreign Policy* (Fall 1990): 153–71.

50. Ibid.

51. Kazuo Kawai, *Japan's American Interlude* (Chicago: University of Chicago Press, Midway Reprint, 1979), pp. 4 ff.

52. Quoted in "Japanese Leaders See Support for U.S. Stand in Gulf Ebbing," *New York Times*, December 11, 1990.

53. Ibid.

54. Author's interview with Yukio Okamoto, Tokyo, July 18, 1990.

55. "In Japan, the Politics of Hesitation," *Washington Post*, February 17, 1991.

56. Author's interview with Yukio Okamoto.

57. "Interview with LDP Secretary General Ichiro Ozawa," *Nihon Keizai*, October 24, 1990 (DSJP, November 1, 1990).

58. "Cooperation with International Society," *Sankei*, October 24, 1990 (DSJP, October 27–29, 1990).

59. "Interview with Former Deputy Prime Minister Kiichi Miyazawa," *Nihon Keizai*, October 27, 1990 (DSJP, November 1, 1990).

60. "Interview with DSP Chairman Ouchi," *Yomiuri*, October 11, 1990 (DSJP, October 19, 1990).

61. "Japanese Politicians Who Are Weak at Diplomacy," *Nihon Keizai*, October 15, 1990 (DSJP, October 23, 1990).

62. David Rapkin, "Japan and World Leadership," in *World Leadership and Hegemony*, ed. D. Rapkin (Boulder, CO: Lynne Rienner, 1990), pp. 196–99.

63. Hideo Sato, "Japan's Role in the Post-Cold War World," *Current History* (April 1991): 145.

64. "Feared Being Late in Making Decision," *ASAHI*, August 6, 1990 (DSJP, August 11–13, 1990).

65. "Make Sanctions against Iraq Have Satisfactory Results," *Tokyo Shimbun*, August 7, 1990 (DSJP, August 15, 1990).

66. "Dispatch of Personnel to Become Focal Point," *Sankei*, August 17, 1990 (DSJP, August 22, 1990).

67. "We Urge Opposition Parties to Take International Contribution Measures in a Positive Manner," *Sankei*, August 23, 1990 (DSJP, August 29, 1990).

68. "Use of Armed Force by UN and Dispatch of SDF," *Sankei*, August 28, 1990 (DSJP, September 7, 1990).

69. "Urges Action from Viewpoint of Cooperation with UN," *ASAHI*, September 20, 1990 (DSJP, October 2, 1990).

70. "Interview with LDP Secretary General Ozawa on Middle East Diet," *Tokyo Shimbun*, November 1, 1990 (DSJP, November 7, 1990).

71. Ibid.

72. Jiro Aiko, "Nation Which Has Continued to be Aimed At," *Bungei Shunju*, October 1990 (SSJM, October, 1990).

73. "Tokyo Chief, Facing New Debate, Appeals for Support for War Aid," *New York Times*, January 26, 1991.

74. "Japan Counts the Costs of Gulf Action—Or Inaction," *New York Times*, January 27, 1991.

75. "Japan Says It Hid Americans in Kuwaiti Embassy," *New York Times*, March 7, 1991.

76. "Distance from Middle East Brought into Relief," *Yomiuri*, August 13, 1990 (DSJP, August 17, 1990).

77. "Foreign Minister Nakayama Ends Middle East Visit," *Tokyo Shimbun*, August 24, 1990 (DSJP, September 31, 1990).

78. "Will Step Out of Hitherto-Maintained Scope," *Tokyo Shimbun*, August 30, 1990 (DSJP, September 6, 1990).

79. "Interview With Komeito Secretary General Yuichi Ichikawa on Middle East Diet," *Tokyo Shimbun*, October 27, 1990 (DSJP, November 1, 1990).

80. "Interview with DSP Secretary General Takashi Yonezawa on Middle East Diet," *Tokyo Shimbun*, October 30, 1990 (DSJP, November 6, 1990).

81. "Interview with Administrative Vice Foreign Minister Kuriyama," *Tokyo Shimbun*, October 26, 1990 (DSJP, October 31, 1990).

82. Author's interview with Yoshio Murakami, Tokyo, July 9, 1990.

83. Author's interview with Mikio Haruna, Tokyo, July 9, 1990.

84. Author's interviews with Nushi Yamamoto, Tokyo, July 16, 1990; Tomohisa Sakanaka, Tokyo, July 19, 1990; Shigekatsu Kondo, Tokyo, July 17, 1990.

85. Author's interview with Toshinori Shigeie, Tokyo, July 18, 1990.

86. Author's interview with Jiro Hagi, Tokyo, July 13, 1990.

87. Author's interview with Motoo Shiina, Tokyo, July 19, 1990.

88. "Thoughts on Japanese Diplomacy; Interview with Former LDP International Bureau Chief Motoo Shiina," *ASAHI*, August 25, 1990 (DSJP, September 5, 1990).

89. Ibid.

90. "Do Not Drive U.S. to Road of Isolationism," *Nihon Keizai*, November 22, 1990 (DSJP, December 1–3, 1990).

91. "American People Irritated with Japan Which Does Not Bear Risk," *Sankei*, August 17, 1990 (DSJP, August 22, 1990).

92. "Japan and U.S. Should Become Power to Stabilize World," *Sankei*, November 16, 1990 (DSJP, November 27, 1990).

93. "Japan Sending Off-Road Vehicles for Military Effort in the Gulf," *New York Times*, September 3, 1990.

94. "Japan Counts the Costs of Gulf Action—Or Inaction," *New York Times*, January 27, 1991.

95. Quoted in "In Japan, the Politics of Hesitation," *Washington Post*, February 17, 1991.

96. "Kaifu Outlines His Proposal for Unarmed Japanese in Gulf," *New York Times*, September 28, 1990.

97. Motoo Shiina, "UN Policy or Japan-U.S. Alliance?" *Chuo Koron*, November 1990 (SSJM, November 1990).

98. "What Japan's 'Checkbook Diplomacy' Isn't Buying," *Business Week*, December 10, 1990.

99. *Wall Street Journal*, January 25, 1991.

100. "The Japanese Casualties of Shrapnel from the Gulf," *The Economist*, February 16, 1991, p. 29.

101. "Government Stymied in Times of Crisis," *Japan Times Weekly*, May 13–19, 1991.

102. "Lack of Vision in Diplomacy Hurts Ministry," *Japan Times Weekly*, August 5–11, 1991.

103. Ibid.

104. "SDF Readies for Role with United Nations," *Japan Times Weekly*, September 16–22, 1991.

105. "Japan's New Frustration," *Washington Post*, March 17, 1991.

Three

THE GULF REGION

5

IRAQ AFTER ITS
INVASION OF KUWAIT

Laurie Mylroie

Saddam Hussein had no intention of complying with the UN Security Council's deadline of January 15, 1991, for Iraq to withdraw from Kuwait because he believed that he could prevail in a war with the U.S.-led coalition—if a war came. Such a miscalculation ranks among the worst blunders in military history.[1] Yet long after the cessation of hostilities, initiated by the unilateral U.S. decision to cease fire, Saddam Hussein and his regime remain in power. Mistakes of lesser magnitude led to the immediate and ignominious collapse of regimes elsewhere (the fate of the Argentinian generals after the Falkland Islands War being a recent and comparable example), at least in terms of the recklessness of the decision for war and the speedy, unequivocal defeat that followed. I will examine here the situation in Iraq after the second Gulf war, with a focus on two factors: the erosion of the regime's control over the peripheral areas of the country in the north and south, concomitant with Saddam Hussein's ability to retain and consolidate control in the center of the country, around Baghdad.

Political Developments in Iraq: After the Iran-Iraq Cease-fire

The immediate precipitants of Saddam Hussein's decision to invade Kuwait are widely understood to lie in the growing political and economic problems inside Iraq after the August 1988 cease-fire in the Iran-Iraq War.[2] Although the regime portrayed the war with Iran as a great victory, much of the population did not share that view. Eight years of bloody conflict had succeeded merely in restoring the status quo ante. The cost had been immense—nearly 400,000 casualties, over 2 percent of the Iraqi population—the per capita equivalent of 4.5 million U.S. citizens.

The popular response to the August 8, 1988, cease-fire was tremendous elation that the fighting, which had seemed as though it would never end, had finally come to a halt. The celebrations continued for fifteen days, and the regime was powerless to stop them. Little did the population imagine that they would soon be at war again.

The Iraqis looked forward to enjoying life after eight years of terrible war. They expected prosperity, without much reflection on the $80 billion debt that Baghdad had incurred during the war years. They also looked forward to the quick signing of a peace treaty with Iran and the return of some 65,000 Iraqi prisoners of war held there. Finally, they looked forward to more democracy, and an easing of the regime's war-time repression.

None of these expectations could be met easily. Peace itself proved elusive. By November, the UN-sponsored peace negotiations were stalemated and the exchange of POWs suspended. The ostensible reason for the deadlock was Baghdad's demand for sovereignty over the entire Shatt-al-Arab, which had been divided between Iran and Iraq in a 1975 treaty. But even if Baghdad had been more forthcoming, it is questionable whether any formal peace could have been reached between the two countries as long as Ayatollah Khomeini lived. When Khomeini accepted the cease-fire he had affirmed that it "was more lethal for me than poison."

Nor did the cease-fire bring prosperity. Instead, a two-track economy had developed. A small private sector, which had emerged during the war, became immensely rich. The public sector, which employed the bulk of the labor force, remained poor, and increasingly so. Inflation ran over 40 percent annually, while public sector workers had received no pay increases during the eight years of war.

Nor could Saddam easily meet expectations of more democracy. In November 1988, as the Iraq-Iran peace talks faltered, Saddam Hussein suddenly announced a new program of democracy for Iraq, including freedom of speech, constitutional reform, and pluralism, permitting the formation of political parties besides the Ba'ath. Three high-level committees were established to study these three issues. Each foreign embassy in Baghdad was asked for a copy of its country's constitution, and "democracy in Iraq" became a prominent theme in government propaganda.

Minor changes followed. All the newspapers introduced a page for readers' letters of complaint, with a statement by Saddam Hussein at the top of the page: "Write what you like without fear." Almost all such letters, however, were limited to complaints of administrative problems and police abuse. With one exception known to the author, the Iraqi press avoided making fundamental criticisms of the regime.[3]

The results of Iraq's National Assembly elections in April 1989 similarly held initial promise. Although candidates were well screened for their loyalty to Saddam, a fairly honest process followed. Ba'ath party members won only 40 percent of the assembly seats, considerably fewer than the 75 percent they had won in the last elections in 1984. The expectation even existed, briefly, that the newly elected National Assembly would approve a new constitution before its spring session closed at the end of May, then dissolve itself to pave the way for new elections under a liberalized regime.

But as with the press, nothing much changed. No new constitution appeared, and no new elections were scheduled. In fact that long-promised constitution was not promulgated until July 30, 1990—three days before the invasion of Kuwait. Among its provisions, Chapter 1, Article 15, affirmed that Iraq adhered to the principle of "settling conflicts through peaceful means on the basis of equality, mutual interests, and reciprocal dealing." Chapter 3, Article 46, stated that "the individual's sanctity, dignity and honor shall be safeguarded," while Article 64 affirmed, "All state organs . . . must protect the environment from pollution and nature from damage that destroys its beauty and function."[4]

Of course, as events were to demonstrate, none of this had any relation to reality, and the new constitution was suspended immediately after the invasion of Kuwait. What the draft articles of the new constitution reflected was the people's longing for a more normal existence in which the arbitrary abuse of authority was checked and some scope provided for the expression of their own sentiments.

By June 1990, Israeli intelligence had learned that Iraq was practically bankrupt. Baghdad had almost no hard currency.[5] Yet that spring, the Israelis also learned that Iraq's centrifuge program—then Iraq's only known covert nuclear program—had been accelerated. European firms making centrifuge parts were offered twice the original contract price to complete their work by September.[6]

There seems little doubt that Iraq's political and economic problems following the cease-fire with Iran determined the timing of the invasion of Kuwait, precipitating the attack. But they were not the cause. The cause was Saddam's ambition and his aim was to control the oil on the Arab side of the Persian Gulf. Perhaps he originally intended to wait until he was better prepared for that project, above all until he had a nuclear device. After the war, UN inspectors concluded that Iraq was perhaps only eighteen months from a bomb. But even without one, Saddam convinced himself that he could prevail.

The Coup that Never Came

While the United States prepared for war with Iraq, Washington expected that if war came, the United States would deliver Iraq such a decisive defeat that the Iraqi military would blame Saddam for the loss and the humiliation that his policies had brought upon them and oust him. The Arab members of the coalition shared the same assumption. Even the Syrian president, Hafiz al-Assad, ruling the only other Ba'athist state and presumably understanding better than most the foundations of power in such a regime, assured the United States as late as April 1991, a month after the cease-fire, that Saddam Hussein would not last more than a few months.[7] Partly because of the conviction that the Iraqi army would overthrow Saddam, the United States took almost no measures to become familiar with and promote an Iraqi opposition to Saddam in the period after August 2, 1990. In fact, Bush administration officials at the policy level were explicitly prohibited from meeting with any of Saddam Hussein's Iraqi opponents until late March 1991, when the war was over and Saddam had pretty well crushed the revolts that broke out after the cessation of hostilities.

To the extent that efforts were made to secure a particular postwar outcome in Iraq by working with Saddam's Iraqi opponents, these efforts were left to Saudi Arabia. A tacit understanding was reached between Washington and Riyadh. The Saudis had not been happy with U.S. insistence that General Norman Schwarzkopf exercise overall control of military operations, but they came to accept that arrangement, while the United States acquiesced to the Saudis' desire to dominate dealings with the Iraqi opposition to secure the establishment of a friendly regime in Baghdad.[8]

The Saudis sought to promote a military coup, but they fixed on a problematic figure, Salah Omar Ali al-Takriti, a member of the Iraqi Ba'ath's Regional Command in 1968, when the Ba'ath seized power in Iraq. Salah Omar Ali soon broke with Saddam but in subsequent years reached a reconciliation with him, serving as Iraq's UN ambassador in the early 1980s. He broke with Saddam again in 1982, after Iraq was forced on the defensive in its war with Iran and looked like losing that conflict. A year before Iraq invaded Kuwait, Salah Omar Ali had once again reconciled with Saddam and was given the lucrative position as head of the London-based Iraqi Freight Services Limited, the cargo division of Iraqi Airways. Iraqi Freight was among those businesses named as Iraqi-front companies by the U.S. Treasury Department, and it helped smuggle military contraband into Baghdad. When Iraq invaded Kuwait, Salah Omar Ali again went into opposition, and Saudi efforts to promote a coup came to center on him.

Salah Omar Ali claimed that he was uniquely placed to oust Saddam while preserving the old power structure and minimizing disorder within the country, because he was a Sunni and a Ba'athist and was from Takrit. As was widely reported in opposition circles in London, Salah Omar Ali told the Saudis that he could arrange a coup through a cousin who was chief of Army Aviation (the helicopter squadrons), Lt. Gen. al-Hakam Hassan 'Ali.[9] Yet no coup ever came and the helicopter gunships, which fired a variety of noxious substances, including napalm and phosphorous, played an important role in suppressing the postwar revolts particularly in the north, where the Kurds, unlike the Shi'a, had some military organization and enjoyed the advantages of rough terrain but possessed no defense against Saddam's helicopters.[10] Al-Hakam Hassan 'Ali was twice awarded medals by Saddam Hussein after the war for Kuwait, once on the second anniversary of the cease-fire of the Iran-Iraq War for his role "in the glorious al-Qadisiyah of Saddam" and two months later for his role in the "Mother of Battles."[11] Given that Salah Omar Ali's promises to the Saudis were well known among the Iraqi opposition, they were likely also known to Saddam Hussein. Al-Hakam Hassan 'Ali's continued favor with Baghdad suggests either that Salah Omar Ali was an incompetent braggart who had no commitment from his cousin or that one or both men were double agents. Nonetheless, he was the Saudis' primary candidate to carry out a coup.

The Attitude of the Iraqi Population toward Saddam Hussein

The popular revolts against Saddam Hussein that followed the February 28, 1991, cease-fire—the most widespread in Iraq's modern history, even more broadly based than the 1920 uprising that followed the announcement of British mandatory rule in Baghdad—decisively refuted prominent misconceptions about Ba'athist rule in Iraq. As late as the day before the cease-fire, the *New York Times* reported, "The working assumption in Washington is that if Mr. Hussein is toppled, he would likely be replaced by another senior member of his Ba'ath party, probably in conjunction with some element of the Iraqi army. The Ba'ath party still provides a coherent structure to control Iraq."[12] The misperception in Washington about the viability of Saddam's regime was matched, and perhaps fed, by misleading reporting during the crisis by the U.S. media in Iraq, which suggested that Saddam Hussein had far more backing from the population than he actually did. As one of the BBC's top journalists later complained, "The clear evidence in Baghdad that there was no great support there for Saddam Hussein was mostly ignored. . . . Some [news organizations] were still talking in terms of supporters until the end. That was what viewers and readers expected, so that was what they got. For the most part politicians, soldiers and civilians alike found it impossible to believe that someone who spoke as fiercely as Saddam might not have a united people behind him."[13]

Indeed, one of the arguments for relative U.S. passivity toward a future Iraqi government was the notion that an overt U.S. move to overthrow Saddam, or even U.S. pressure on his regime, would backfire by causing Iraqis to rally around the regime.[14] This was, for example, part of the argument against lending U.S. backing to the European Community's call in April 1991 for war crimes trials against the Iraqi regime.[15] Such an argument, however, presumed that the regime in Baghdad enjoyed the population's fundamental support. That was not the case, as reflected by the population's attitude after the war's end. The principal complaint of the Iraqi population was not about the devastation that the United States had wreaked on the country but that Washington had not finished the job by ousting Saddam. Among many such anecdotes reported by the Western media was the advice of one Iraqi to a U.S. reporter in November 1991: "Tell Mr. Bush that there is a silent majority in Iraq that is against this regime, but we can't do anything about it and we are holding him responsible."[16]

Political Developments in Iraq:
After the Second Gulf War

The constitution promulgated on the eve of the invasion of Kuwait resurfaced in March 1991, as the population rose in revolt against the regime. The announcement of the new constitution was accompanied by the appointment of a new cabinet, headed by Sadun

Hammadi, a U.S.-educated figure, who was a Shi'a and a longtime Ba'athist. Hammadi represented the more sophisticated, less thuggish elements within the Iraqi regime. Those who visited Baghdad then reported that a quite different atmosphere prevailed from that even a few weeks earlier, before the cease-fire and the popular uprisings. As one journalist explained, "The old terror of speaking frankly [seemed] to have evaporated and the assessment was that political forces had been loosed in Baghdad which Saddam Hussein would be unlikely to be able to control."[17]

Yet the view that events had created a situation in which Saddam Hussein would be forced to follow his proclaimed policy of liberalization were not borne out by events. Even as earlier promises of reform were renewed, senior Iraqi officials were advised by Saddam privately that "the move toward democracy was merely a ploy."[18] This is what proved to be the case.

Indeed, such signs were already evident. On March 6, soon after the uprisings began, the most brutal figure in the regime, a cousin of Saddam's, Ali Hassan al-Majid, the man most responsible for the ruthless suppression of the Kurdish uprising during the Iran-Iraq War, was promoted from minister of local government to minister of the interior, while his brother, Hisham, whom Saddam had previously dismissed from an administrative position in Babylon province for blatant corruption, was rehabilitated and made governor of Kurdistan.

In subsequent months, Saddam made further moves to strip authority from those possessing the least modicum of independence, while promoting figures closely connected to him, sharing his background (members of the Sunni Arab tribes from the region north of Baghdad, with minimal education or social standing, often with close ties to the security services, and figures noted for their brutality). In September 1991 Sadun Hammadi was suddenly ousted as prime minister and replaced by Muhammad Hamza Zubaydi. Although Zubaydi was also a Shi'a, he was far more Saddam's creature. Zubaydi's education stopped at high school, but he was appointed to the party's Regional Command in 1982 as Iraq began to face a mortal threat from Iran and Saddam acted to remove potential rivals and replace them with figures close to him. Nor was there any doubt about Zubaydi's brutality. Film clips seized after the uprising and smuggled out of Iraq, later to be broadcast on U.S. television, showed pictures of Zubaydi and Ali Hassan al-Majid kicking Shi'a prisoners who were kneeling on the ground, their hands bound.

The ostensible reason for replacing Sadun Hammadi in September

1991 was the result of the tenth Ba'ath Party Congress. According to the Iraqi press the meeting lasted twenty-eight continuous hours, its length perhaps meant as testimony to the regime's claim of its new democratic practices. Elections were held for a new Regional Command. Consistent with Saddam's promises of the spring, greater obeisance was made to the appearance of democracy. For the first time the results of intraparty elections were announced publicly. Yet the outcome seemed to be what Saddam Hussein himself would have dictated.

The Arabic press reported that Hammadi had argued forcefully during the congress that it was vital for the regime to open up internally, implementing political and economic reforms while complying with the UN resolutions in order to end economic sanctions. Saddam, however, was seen to abandon Hammadi during the discussions,[19] and out of a field of forty-two candidates Hammadi ran thirty-ninth, receiving only twenty-eight votes.[20]

It would seem that despite the regime's claims that the elections for party leadership were held by secret ballot, Saddam had the means to secure the results he wanted. He was reelected unanimously to lead the party, while his longtime deputy Izzat Ibrahim al-Duri received four votes less than Saddam and the notorious Ali Hassan al-Majid followed. Kamil Yassin Rashid, head of security in Baghdad, another cousin of Saddam's and brother of his bodyguard, Arshad, came in fourth in the party poll. Of the seven new members elected to party leadership, all had joined the party as young men, several as young as fourteen years old. Six were Sunni Arabs from the regions to the north and west of Baghdad, while five had backgrounds in the military academy. (One of the regime's techniques for ensuring its continued hold on power after 1968 was to conduct quick courses in the military schools and promote its friends speedily.)[21]

The next month, in October, changes were made in the composition of the regime's highest governing body, the Revolutionary Command Council. Among the three new members was the infamous Ali Hassan al-Majid. In November, Ali Hassan was shifted to the Defense Ministry, while a half brother, Watban Ibrahim, who had headed the security services until 1983, was made interior minister. Thus, soon after the "Mother of All Defeats," and despite promises of more democracy engendered by the war, the second most important man in Iraq was the figure most notorious for his brutality, while Saddam had managed to consolidate control in Baghdad by promoting and relying upon an increasingly tighter and narrower circle of associates.

Yet Saddam's departure was not necessarily made more imminent because of personnel changes. Following the dismissal of Saddam's cousin and son-in-law, Hussein Kamil, as defense minister in November 1991, much was made of cleavages within the regime, portending Saddam's possible ouster. Yet in early 1992, Hussein Kamil returned as a top presidential adviser in no apparent disgrace. Increasingly it appeared that the elite accepted a situation in which Saddam shuffled them around. Saddam's regime is a Stalinist government. Such regimes, where all live in mortal fear, are not ousted by the manipulation of economic sticks and carrots.

Yet even as Saddam Hussein managed to consolidate his control in Baghdad, the regime's authority over the south and north grew weaker. In the south, a low-level guerrilla war against the regime continued, conducted by Iranian-backed Shi'a elements. In the north, the international protection afforded the Kurdish population removed the heavy hand of the Iraqi security forces and limited Saddam's ability to reestablish Baghdad's control there.

The Iraqi Army after the Cease-fire

Although the United States and its Arab allies looked to a coup to remove Saddam, important aspects of the war had not been conducted in such a way as to promote one. If a coup were to come from any quarter, it would come from the army rather than the Republican Guard. But the war left the guard relatively stronger than the army, partly because of the character of the Iraqi deployment, which put the army at greater risk than the Republican Guard, and partly because of faulty U.S. intelligence which overestimated the damage inflicted on the Republican Guard by the heavy aerial bombing campaign during the war.

Concerned about leaving Iraq strong enough to maintain a balance of power between Iran and Iraq, but basing his decision on faulty intelligence, President George Bush ordered a unilateral cease-fire after only 100 hours of the ground war. British officials disagreed at the time with Bush's decision, as did General Schwarzkopf. Bush's decision saved significant elements of the Iraqi military most loyal to Saddam. Seventy percent of the Republican Guards' Hammurabi division, the best division Iraq had, escaped with its equipment across the Euphrates River and later played a critical role in suppressing the rebellions.

Yet Saddam's relations with his military were never easy and his disastrous war with the U.S.-led coalition generated strains. Both the wartime defense minister, General Sa'di Tu'ma 'Abbas al-Jabburi, and the wartime chief of staff, Hussein Rashid Muhammad al-Windawi al-Takriti, were removed from their positions after the conflict. However, they remained in sufficient favor to receive medals for their role in the "Mother of Battles." However, Nizar 'Abd al-Karim al-Khazraji, chief of staff at the time of the invasion of Kuwait, and replaced in October 1990, remained unaccounted for, amid rumors that he had been arrested and executed. The chief of Iraqi military intelligence was thought to have been arrested in June 1991, along with Brigadier General Nushwan Dhanun, liaison with the U.S. forces in northern Iraq.[22] In addition, there were frequent reports of officers plotting against Saddam and Saddam moving against them.[23] Probably some of those reports had foundation. The cycle of plotting by the military and contrary measures by Saddam was not new to Iraq, even if it accelerated after Desert Storm.

Signs of Saddam Hussein's concern about the army were evident, and he used his accustomed method of a little carrot and a big stick to control potential opposition. Military officers received unwonted attention as they were twice honored for their performance in Iraq's recent wars, first with an awards ceremony in August marking the third anniversary of the cease-fire of the war with Iran and again in October and subsequent months to mark Iraq's so-called victory in the "Mother of Battles." The public recognition accorded individual officers was highly unusual. Perhaps it served to give them some satisfaction and reward. More important, it was Saddam's way of demonstrating that he retained significant authority over the army, even if he did not have support from the officers. After all, the appointment of Ali Hassan al-Majid as defense minister—a man without military experience—was meant to intimidate them.

The Economic Situation in Iraq

When the Gulf War did not produce the overthrow of Saddam Hussein that the Allies had anticipated, they at first seemed to reconcile themselves to living with a presumably chastened Saddam and looked to continuing economic sanctions to provide the leverage necessary to ensure Iraqi compliance with Security Council Resolution 687, the complex cease-fire to the war, which provided for stripping Iraq of its weapons of mass destruction. However, Saddam Hussein was not chastened by defeat. He called it victory, and as intelligence reports began to filter back that he had begun to rebuild his armed forces, the Bush administration began to shift its policy, looking to sanctions as a way to prod the army to overthrow Saddam. In May 1991, Washington began to state explicitly that it would not agree to lift sanctions as long as Saddam Hussein remained in power. That inclination was soon reinforced as information from Iraqi defectors revealed that Western intelligence agencies had grossly underestimated the mammoth size of Iraq's nuclear program and in fact had entirely and unwittingly missed the most critical of Iraq's nuclear efforts.

While intended to affect Saddam's base of power, the economic sanctions imposed on Iraq caused the population great suffering. The problem was not an absolute shortage of food but the high prices of that food available to supplement inadequate government rations, which provided only 30 percent of individual food needs. UN relief workers estimated the rate of inflation at 150 percent a month. A sack of flour that cost six Iraqi dinars (ID) before the invasion of Kuwait cost 550 ID afterwards. With state-run industries idled, much of the work force was without jobs, and the purchasing power of an Iraqi family was estimated to be less than 10 percent of its prewar value.

An international public health team visited Iraq in the autumn of 1991 and reported widespread disease, malnutrition, and unsanitary conditions as a consequence of the war and sanctions. They estimated the mortality rate of children under the age of five to be 380 percent greater than before the war, with the mortality rate of children in the Shi'a south to be three and one half times that in the central Sunni areas, north of Baghdad, where mortality rates had risen only slightly as a consequence of the war. Water was commonly polluted with sewage, causing epidemic levels of such diseases as typhoid and cholera. Outbreaks of preventable childhood diseases such as polio, measles and tetanus occurred because of the lack of vaccines.[24] Yet these facts could hardly be said to move the regime in Baghdad. It sought to block the efforts of international relief workers to alleviate the hardship of the population and prevented the release from warehouses of some $4 million worth of food aid, including infant formula and high-protein food packages designed for young children.[25]

The international sanctions in fact scarcely touched the ruling elite. Their main impact was to decimate the middle class which was forced to sell its property to buy food, while the elite benefited from the widespread economic dislocation. Visitors to Baghdad reported that the economic structure increasingly favored the rich. For example, spare parts for Toyotas were in short supply but not for Mercedes. The lists of imported wines in first-class restaurants grew longer than before the war, while luxuries like caviar were readily available.[26]

Baghdad was, of course, anxious to end the sanctions, and one way to achieve that goal was to let the population suffer to the point that Western governments would feel obliged to relent. For that reason Iraq initially rejected Security Council Resolution 706, which, by providing for the supervised sale of Iraqi oil and the supervised distribution of food within the country, would have alleviated many of the hardships on the population but would also have made sanctions more viable over the long run.

It was also with the object of forcing the lifting of sanctions that the regime convened an "Arab Popular Congress" in Baghdad in October 1991. Delegates to the three-day conference were transported to Iraq and hosted at the regime's expense, testimony to the extent of its still-untapped financial reserves. The message of the Iraqi leaders who addressed the conference was that the Arab regimes who supported the war and continued to endorse sanctions on Iraq—if only by their silence and inaction—were traitors. "The [Saudi] hireling rulers paid $160 billion so that the U.S. could hit Iraq," affirmed Vice-President Taha Yassin Ramadan as he warned that "Umm al-Maarik will not be the last against the U.S. and its allies." Saddam Hussein advised, "The slogan that the blockade on Iraq must be lifted should first be raised inside Arab and Islamic countries. . . . It should be directed at Arab rulers," even as he vowed that "Iraq can live under the blockade for twenty years."[27]

Conclusion: Lessons Learned in Baghdad

From the experience of the past decade, it would seem that few lessons were learned in Baghdad. Saddam Hussein should have learned from his protracted conflict with Iran that war is a risky enterprise, the outcome of which, once begun, is often unpredictable. Yet the regime chose to view that war, "Saddam's Qadisiyah," as a victory for Iraq. By the same processes, "Umm al-Maarik," the "Mother of Battles," was portrayed as another victory. No doubt Saddam was shocked initially by what happened in his war with the United States and the revolts that followed. But as the war ended and the revolts were suppressed, he began to recover and likely saw that he would survive another day. The regime began the reconstruction of much of Iraq's destroyed infrastructure, proving immensely more successful than the victorious Allies had anticipated at the war's end. As that process continued, the prospect grew that Iraq could even recover militarily and that after all, what had been achieved—the steadfastness and reconstruction in the face of the U.S.-led coalition—was more significant than what had been lost.

The sycophancy around Saddam, born of terror, ambition, ignorance and isolation, no doubt contributed to reinforce his image of himself and his situation. Long after the war's outcome became something of an embarrassment in Washington, Iraqi generals and senior officials of the regime were still being decorated for their role in the "Mother of Battles." A series of "Mother of Battles" sports tournaments were held, with participants from other Arab countries. Others within and without Iraq were prepared to endorse Saddam's view that after all the war was, in important respects, a victory.

As Saddam Hussein recovered, he reverted to the same tactics that he had used during the period between August 2 and January 15. Saddam calculated then that if there were a war, Western and Arab opinion would not tolerate the sight of large-scale civilian casualties in Iraq—hence the regime's willingness, if not eagerness, to keep CNN in Baghdad during the conflict. After the war, Saddam expected, or at least hoped, that international opinion would not tolerate indefinitely the suffering of the Iraqi population, and therefore Baghdad should not exert itself to alleviate that suffering.

The regime habitually overestimated the internal vulnerabilities of its foes. It viewed Margaret Thatcher's resignation in the autumn of 1990 as a major triumph, believing that the departure of one of its strongest and most articulate foes would decisively weaken the coalition. It is possible that Baghdad viewed the setback to Turgot Ozal's Motherland party in the Turkish elections in the fall of 1991 as the first step in the eventual erosion of Turkey's position. No doubt Saddam looks to the domestic positions of his other democratic opponents and continues to see weaknesses that will redeem him.

Finally, and perhaps most immediately, the regime looked to force a split between the West and the Middle Eastern members of the coalition by appealing to indigenous populations, while intimidating local governments, and otherwise hoping to break up and undermine the anti-Iraq coalition. The Marxist Kurdish organization in Turkey, the PKK, began receiving large-scale Iraqi aid after the war, to the point that it threatened to become, in the words of a Western diplomat, "a viable guerrilla army."[28] Not only did supporting the PKK serve as Iraq's revenge for Turkey's role in the war, but it could be hoped that it might also serve as leverage to force Ankara to reopen Iraq's oil pipeline.

The UN sanctions on the import of goods were soon practically defunct, as the Jordanian border became a sieve. Tender offers for supplies, the import of which were prohibited by UN resolutions, were openly advertised in the Iraqi press soon after the war's end. And in March 1992 Syria even opened its border with Iraq, providing hope of another avenue for Baghdad to undo the coalition against it.

The great German military thinker, Karl von Clausewitz wrote that "in war the results are rarely final." Although on February 28, 1991, it seemed that his observation could scarcely apply to Desert Storm, the more time passed, the more it seemed that it was relevant to this conflict as well.

Notes

1. Arguably, Saddam Hussein made the worst blunder in military history. The author can think of no other case in which the following conditions obtained: a belligerent chose to risk war against such seemingly overwhelming odds while it had an easy and obvious way to avoid war, and then suffered such a massive defeat.

2. See Laurie Mylroie and Judith Miller, *Saddam Hussein and the Crisis in the Gulf* (New York: Random House, 1990), chap. 7. Efraim Karsh and Inari Rautsi, ("Why Saddam Hussein Invaded Kuwait," *Survival* [January/February 1991]) make the same argument, although they stress the notion that Saddam sought only survival to the point where it distorts events.

3. A journalist, Sabah al-Lami, wrote an article in *Al-Iraq*, March 7, 1989, entitled "How the People Are Made Quiet about the Crimes of Public Corruption in the Name of Fear of Troubles." He asked a series of allegorical questions about prominent personalities close to the regime, beginning, "Did you hear of the *zarzour* (pesky bird) whose ancestors were *zarzours*, who, between night and day, became a falcon living in the palace of *Kawarnak* (a rich man or ruler's dwelling)? My colleagues answered, probably they were merchants. But I replied that a merchant is a clever man. I can't remember a 'clod' becoming a millionaire." The article continued in this vein, the first question most readily suggesting a reference to Saddam and his family.

4. *Al-Jumhurriyah*, July 30, 1990, in *Foreign Broadcast Information Service-Near East/South Asia* (hereafter *FBIS-NESA*), August 10, 1990.

5. Israeli official to author, 1991.

6. Ibid.

7. U.S. official to author, September 1991.

8. Ibid.; a Gulf journalist provided the author a similar account of the U.S.-Saudi understanding about the Iraqi opposition, while John Simpson reported that King Fahd had initially proposed that he be overall commander of the Gulf forces, with General Schwarzkopf as one of his deputies and the Saudi defense minister as the other. See Simpson, *From the House of War* (London: Arrow Books, 1991), p. 205.

9. The U.S. failure to enforce the terms of the provisional cease-fire concluded by General Schwarzkopf and his Iraqi counterparts after the war—particularly limiting Iraq's use of helicopters to transportation purposes only—raises the question whether the United States was aware of the Saudi plans and perhaps hoped to facilitate them by its passivity.

10. The *New York Times*, March 26, 1991, quoted unnamed administration officials as saying that the insurgents "just can't deal with helicopter gunships."

11. *Al-Qadisiyah*, August 9, 1991 in *FBIS-NESA*, August 15, 1991; Iraq News Agency, October 22, 1991 in *FBIS-NESA*, October 23, 1991.

12. Thomas L. Friedman, "The Rout Bush Wants," *New York Times*, February 27, 1991.

13. John Simpson, *The Observer*, April 20, 1991, p. 336.

14. Gerald Seib, "How Miscalculations Spawned U.S. Policy toward Postwar Iraq," *Wall Street Journal*, May 3, 1991.

15. As the assistant secretary of state for international organization affairs testified before Congress then, "the risks of a trial in absentia are such that it might preserve [Saddam] in power." David Hoffman, "U.S.: No Plans to Try Saddam in Absentia," *Washington Post*, April 24, 1991.

16. Patrick E. Tyler, "Iraqi Suffering Deepens as the Economy Rots," *New York Times*, November 10, 1991.

17. John Simpson, *The Observer*, April 20, 1991, p. 336.

18. Ibid.

19. *Middle East Mirror*, September 16, 1991.

20. As a reflection of the arbitrary nature of the change, Iraq's ambassador to the United Nations claimed that Sadun Hammadi "had not been feeling well" and "had probably asked to be replaced." Jordan Television, September 14, 1991 in *FBIS-NESA*, September 16, 1991.

21. John Simpson met one of the new figures promoted by Saddam to the Regional Command. Abdul-Rahman al-Duri, a Sunni Arab from the north and director of Public Security from 1988 until 1991, was made governor of Najaf immediately after the war. According to Simpson, "He was thoroughly unprepossessing; oleaginous, soft-footed, his hair a miracle of the trichologist's art, combed and plastered sideways and forwards to cover his bald patch. There

was too much flesh on his face and it lay in folds along the line of his chin. He praised Saddam Hussein so intensively and so long . . . that it became necessary to interrupt in order to ask him some questions" (*From the House of War*, p. 364).

22. *Washington Post*, June 16, 1991.

23. For example, Agence France Presse reported October 4, 1991 that seventy-six officers had been executed after a failed coup attempt.

24. The report as summarized in *Mideast Mirror*, October 22, 1991.

25. Patrick E. Tyler, "Iraq Is Blocking Aid Distribution," *New York Times*, November 3, 1991.

26. Reuters' Bernard Debusman to author, February 1992.

27. *FBIS-NESA*, October 15, 1991.

28. Chris Hedges, "Iraqis Are Arming the Rebel Kurds in Turkey's South," *New York Times*, October 20, 1991.

6

IRAN FROM THE AUGUST 1988 CEASE-FIRE TO THE APRIL 1992 MAJLIS ELECTIONS

Shireen T. Hunter

The period following the establishment of the UN-sponsored cease-fire in the Iran-Iraq War on August 20, 1988, was an important and eventful time for Iran, both in terms of the evolution of its domestic politics and in respect to its external relations.

Domestically, less than a year after the cease-fire, the death of the Ayatollah Ruhollah Khomeini focused Iran's attention on the question of his succession. The Iranian leadership hand led the succession issue with dispatch and effectiveness. But before they could savor this smooth transition of power, which led to the emergence of the dual leadership of the Ayatollahs Ali Khamenei and Ali Akbar Hashemi Rafsanjani, Iran was hit by a devastating earthquake in June 1990. This incident, in addition to being a human tragedy of vast dimensions, posed significant domestic problems and difficult foreign policy choices for the new leadership in Iran. The long-term developmental problems created by the earthquake will take a long time to be resolved. But the government was able to deal with its immediate aftermath relatively successfully. It also managed to prevent any serious damage to its position, either domestically or internationally. Indeed, this tragic event may have contributed to the strengthening of more moderate and pragmatic trends in Iranian foreign policy.

However, regional and international developments soon posed new challenges for the Iranian leadership. The aftermath of these events is also likely to pose serious problems and dilemmas for Iran for years to come. These events included Iraq's invasion of Kuwait on August 2, 1990, that led to the massive introduction of U.S. and other Western military forces into the region and the outbreak of war between Iraq

and a U.S.-led international coalition. Of even greater long-term consequence has been the dissolution of the Soviet empire and the emergence of eight new republics in Iran's close proximity. These developments have drastically altered Iran's geostrategic environment and
have already affected the character of its relations with some of its
neighbors. Given Iran's long history of association with these areas and
the overlapping of ethnic groups in these republics and in some Iranian
provinces, these events will also have serious implications for Iran's
internal affairs (though at this stage their ultimate impact on Iran's
domestic scene and its position within the region are not yet clear).

The time that has elapsed since the establishment of the cease-fire
in 1988 and the completion of this study has been relatively short.
Nevertheless, within this time frame, three distinct periods can be
identified in terms of the evolution of Iran's domestic situation and
the direction of its foreign policy. What follows is an analysis of
events in each of these periods and their long-term ramifications.

From the August 1988 Cease-fire to
Ayatollah Khomeini's Death in June 1989

Internally, the two most salient characteristics of this period
were a dramatic intensification of national debate on the mistakes
and shortcomings of the revolutionary government, including its
handling of the war with Iraq, and intense jockeying for power in the
post-Khomeini era among various groups and individuals. Externally,
this period was characterized by a dramatic improvement in Soviet-
Iranian ties; a slow but steady amelioration of relations with the Persian Gulf Arab states; and a sharp fluctuation in ties with the West.
Ties between Iran and the West reached a new low in the winter and
spring of 1989 following the advent of the so-called Rushdie Affair,
which was to be one of the most serious political challenges faced by
the regime since coming to power in 1979.

After eight years of war, many parts of Iran were left physically devastated, its economy and military were in shambles, and the country
was internationally isolated. Meanwhile, Iraq was claiming victory
and was occupying large chunks of Iranian territory. It is, therefore, no
wonder that popular criticism of the government's handling of the war
and its mismanagement of the nation's domestic and external affairs
was mounting. Nor was this criticism limited to the regime's opponents. On the contrary, even certain individuals within the regime

were criticizing its record. For example, none other than the speaker of the Iranian Parliament, the Ayatollah Rafsanjani, addressing Iran's handling of its foreign relations, said that Iran had unnecessarily antagonized its neighbors and had created enemies for itself. Moreover, the fact that the cease-fire had come about after U.S. military intervention and U.S. destruction of one-third of Iran's naval forces had further undermined the government's standing in the public's eyes.

However, this national mood of criticism and the changing regional and international configuration of power had one positive result, namely the total discrediting of the hard-liners' vision and the slow but steady validation of the moderate pragmatic perspective on domestic and international issues.

Nevertheless, despite discredit brought on their policies, the hardliners did not abandon their efforts to sabotage the pragmatists' efforts to reform domestic policies and to improve Iran's international ties. On the contrary, they used every opportunity to prevent reformist trends from gaining momentum. One such opportunity presented itself when Salman Rushdie, an Indian-born Moslem and a citizen of the United Kingdom, published *Satanic Verses* in 1988. The book created an uproar in the Moslem world; it was declared blasphemous by Moslem religious leaders, and played a similar—though shorter— role to that of the U.S. hostage crisis in the period 1979–81.

All Western countries, particularly Great Britain, reacted strongly against Iran and against the Ayatollah Khomeini's edict of death to Rushdie. Even such West European countries as the Federal Republic of Germany, which had throughout difficult times in the 1980s maintained good relations with Iran, adopted an unyielding and harsh attitude. In fact, the German government was instrumental in developing a strong and unified European position against Iran within the European Community.[1] To emphasize their displeasure, the members of the European Community recalled their ambassadors from Tehran. Iran's pragmatic leaders tried to defuse the situation by trying to portray the edict as a purely religious matter and not representative of the government's views.

Technically this interpretation has some validity. However, the Ayatollah Khomeini was no ordinary Moslem jurist or theologian. For all practical purposes he was head of the Iranian state (even though his position as supreme leader was considered above politics). But this argument did not convince the Europeans, who demanded the rescinding of the edict. Given the ascendancy of the radicals at that moment,

Iran could not comply with this demand, and its ties with the West suffered. Iran's relations with the United Kingdom deteriorated so much and political passions rose so high in Iran that the radical-dominated Iranian Parliament pressured the government to break diplomatic relations with the United Kingdom. This was done on Iran's initiative. The resumption of relations had to wait until after the Ayatollah Khomeini's death and Saddam Hussein's invasion of Kuwait.

The Rushdie affair put the pragmatist elements in a difficult position—they could not disagree with or, worse, denounce the Ayatollah Khomeini's edict. But to go along with it meant the undoing of all their efforts to improve ties with the West. By the summer of 1989, however, the moderates began to recoup some of their losses, and there was no widespread and systematic effort to implement the Ayatollah Khomeini's edict. As a result, a slow thaw developed in Iran's relations with Europe and the European Community ambassadors gradually began returning to Tehran.

In this period, the most significant development in Iran's foreign relations was the meeting between the Soviet Union's foreign minister, Eduard Shevardnadze, and the Ayatollah Khomeini in February 1989. The grounds for this meeting were prepared by the visit of the Ayatollah's special envoy to Moscow, the Ayatollah Javad Amoli, in January 1989, during which he delivered a message from the Ayatollah Khomeini to President Mikhail Gorbachev.[2] These Soviet-Iranian exchanges, especially the Khomeini-Shevardnadze meeting, were highly significant for the future of Soviet-Iranian relations because they indicated the Ayatollah Khomeini's blessing for close ties between the two. It was also a victory for the Iranian radicals who had always favored closer economic and political ties with the Soviet Union and the Communist bloc countries. However, with rapid changes in the Soviet Union and its gradual disintegration, their success proved ephemeral, although Iran was to receive MIG-29 and SU-24 military aircraft from the USSR as part of a major agreement signed in June 1989.

Domestically, during the period between the outbreak of the Rushdie affair and the Ayatollah Khomeini's death, Iran's political scene was dominated by debate over the reform of the constitution and the nation's future economic policy, especially the respective roles of the private sector and the government in the economy. Another hotly debated economic issue was the extent to which Iran should be seeking external financing in the form of loans and foreign investment. As expected, the radicals still favored a larger role for the government in the economy and opposed foreign borrowing. However, given Iran's enormous needs and inadequate financial resources, they had to soften their position somewhat and agree to the necessity of external financing in certain cases.[3]

From Ayatollah Khomeini's Death to Iraq's Invasion of Kuwait

The Ayatollah Khomeini died on June 5, 1989. From his death until Iraq's invasion of Kuwait on August 1, 1990, Iran's political scene was dominated by succession to the Ayatollah Khomeini and the reform of the constitution of 1979; the presidential elections; and the preparation of a five-year development plan and its passage through the parliament.

SMOOTH TRANSITION OF POWER

Since the creation of the Islamic regime, many foreign and Iranian observers had predicted that the regime could not outlast its founder. This prognosis was based on the assumption that factional divisions within the regime, including within the military, would lead to conflict, possibly even to some form of civil war, and eventually to the regime's self-destruction.

After dismissing the Ayatollah Montazeri as the future supreme leader, the Ayatollah Khomeini had not appointed anyone else as his successor, further clouding the prospects for a smooth transition of power in post-Khomeini Iran.

In choosing the Ayatollah Khomeini's successor the Iranian leadership faced two sets of problems: constitutional/theological and political. The first problems related to the lack of any well-established process of determining those characteristics and qualifications required for the supreme leader by the constitution of 1979, or of assessing whether a given religious leader possessed them, in the Shi'a tradition. According to the Islamic constitution of 1979, the supreme religious leader should be a "Marja-e-Taglid," a source of emulation— in other words, a figure whom others emulate in religious matters. This in itself is not an insurmountable problem, yet it posed a difficult dilemma for the regime. The problem lies in the fact that in the Shi'a tradition there are no clear-cut criteria or procedures to determine who is a source of emulation. Traditionally, Shi'a sources of emulation emerge through an unstructured and informal process, and as

a result of the development of an incremental consensus within the
clerical establishment. Thus, traditionally, religious leaders have either
been recognized as sources of emulation or not by their peers and
their followers. However, by the time of the Ayatollah Khomeini's
death, none of the major figures within the Iranian leadership were so
recognized. Even the Ayatollah Montazeri, who was initially selected
as the next supreme leader, was not one. He himself recognized this
fact and stated that in religious matters he himself emulated the Ayatollah Khomeini. Among the existing sources of emulation, such as
the Najaf-based Ayatollah Khoie, none was of an age or had either the
inclination or the physical strength to assume the charge and responsibility of being the next supreme religious leader. The problem of
this leader goes even further than the lack of clear procedures for the
selection of sources of emulation. The concept of the custodianship
of the supreme religious leader (Velayat-e-Faqih) is an innovation in
Shi'a theory of government and political legitimacy. Indeed, this institution was created to provide a constitutional basis for the uncon-
tested leadership of the Ayatollah Khomeini.[4]

The political difficulties in choosing the next leader derived from
intraregime differences and the problem of agreeing on a consensus
figure. However, in a remarkable show of their capacity to put aside
factional bickering when the regime's future survival was at stake, the
Iranian leadership chose the Ayatollah Khamenei as the country's
new leader.

In order to overcome the problem of the Ayatollah Khamenei not
being a source of emulation, the 1979 constitution was amended. The
new version stipulates that the person or persons who possess the
qualities needed to be a source of emulation but were not recognized
as such could be considered to be the new leader. This amendment,
however, was a clear political act. While it did facilitate the selection
of the Ayatollah Khamenei as the new leader, it did not resolve the
problem of selecting future leaders. (As noted, there are no clearly defined criteria for identifying sources of emulation, although it is generally recognized that they include a high degree of learning, scholar-
ship, and high moral character.) Thus, all arrangements and councils
for settling this issue on the basis of political expediency will be vulnerable to challenge on the basis of longer established Shi'a traditions.

In effect, the impact of this amendment was to emphasize the political character of the position of the supreme leader and downgrade its
religious aspects. In fact, during the debate on the needed qualifica-

tions for the leader, many prominent religious figures closely associated with the regime emphasized the point that religious qualifications are not enough to allow one to be the supreme leader. Rather, the supreme leader should also have strong political and managerial skills. However, the constitutional amendment and the separation of the functions of "leadership" (Rahbariat) from those of a "source of emulation" were criticized by many as the beginning of the separation of religion and politics in Iran and the subordination of religion to politics.[5]

Whether this amendment is, as the critics claim, the beginning of the separation of church and state in Iran is hard to say. However, it is clear that the elimination of the requirement that the leader be a source of emulation has widened the gap between traditional Shi'a theory and the current regime's institutions and structures. It has also widened the gap between traditional Shi'a clerics and those members of the clerical establishment who are actively involved in government and politics. In addition, it has emphasized the basically political basis of the current regime's legitimacy and power rather than some long-established religious notions or the Shi'a theory of government and political legitimacy. It has also further accelerated the process of the subordination of religious principles to political necessity and the requirements of state and regime survival. This process had already begun under the Ayatollah Khomeini. The creation of the so-called Council of Expediency, which under certain circumstances can suspend the application of religious rules because of other necessities, was the result of this trend. Indeed, this new process of selecting the supreme leader and the constitutional amendment related to it are a reflection of the phenomenon of the "rise of statism" in Iran. In other words, increasingly, state interests are being given priority over other considerations, even if they are still rationalized in religious terms.

The other major problem which made constitutional reform necessary was the nature of the executive power and the tensions inherent in an executive branch whose authority is divided between the president and the prime minister. To understand the problem, it is important to mention here the respective functions and responsibilities of the president and the prime minister, as stipulated by the Constitution of 1979. According to Article 113, the president was not a mere ceremonial figurehead but rather "the highest official in the country" after the supreme leader. He was "responsible for implementing the constitution, ordering relations among the three powers, [president, Parliament, Guardian Council] and heading the executive power except in matters pertaining directly to the leadership." In addition, the president appointed the prime minister and could accept or reject the ministers chosen by him. Meanwhile, according to Article 134, the prime minister was primarily responsible for determining "the program and policies of the government."

In fact, the 1979 Constitution had created a two-headed executive in Iran, and that entails potential problems for effective government. Indeed, such a system can function effectively only if there is perfect harmony and convergence of views between the president and the prime minister. Given the significant difference of opinion in the Iranian leadership, such harmony was never achieved. Indeed, this duality of the executive power, combined with other difficulties deriving from disagreements between the Parliament and the Guardian Council, which has the task of ensuring that legislation is compatible with Islamic law, had resulted throughout most of the 1980s in near governmental paralysis and inability to tackle controversial issues.

During the constitutional debate, which officially began on April 24, 1989, two principal views on the character of the executive power were in competition. One advocated the adoption of a parliamentary-style executive, another favored a presidential-style. In the former case, the office of the prime minister would have become the principal focus of executive power, and the president's position would have been reduced to that of a figurehead. The latter group advocated the elimination of the post of prime minister and the concentration of executive power in the presidency. The critics of a presidential-style executive believed that the concentration of power in the presidency could lead to a dictatorship and argued in favor of keeping the division of the executive power between the president and the prime minister as prescribed by the 1979 Constitution. Failing that, they argued for strict parliamentary-style supervision over the president.

Indeed, the nature of the relationship between the president and Parliament was one of the more controversial issues discussed during the constitutional debate. The opponents of a strong presidency argued that such a move would eliminate not only the post of prime minister but also Parliament's control over the executive. As one commentator put it, "It would no longer allow the Majlis to give its vote of confidence to the president's choice for premiership."[6] But this is a false argument because presidential appointments could always be made subject to parliamentary approval. In fact, the executive that emerged after the constitutional amendments is indeed more rational and streamlined, with the presidency as its core. But it is far from an imperial presidency. Under the amended constitution, Parliament not only has to approve the president's appointments; it can question the president himself. If Parliament finds the president's explanations inadequate, it can appeal to the supreme leader to dismiss the president in the interests of the country, even though he was elected by popular vote. In addition, the president is not the commander in chief of the armed forces; this honor belongs to the supreme leader. Given the vital political role of the military, this situation further tips the balance of power against the president, constitutionally if not in practice.

In short, even after the above-noted constitutional amendments, Iran's political system leaves much to be desired as a system of effective management of the country's affairs. While the problems deriving from the division of executive power between the president and the prime minister have been eliminated, there remains the underlying duality of power centers in Iran's political structure built around the president and the supreme leader. Such a system can function effectively if these two are in agreement. Otherwise, indecision and confusion will be the order of the day. Nevertheless, these amendments and the system that has emerged as a result are improvements over past practices. The new arrangements imply a more collegial system of governance for Iran with stronger emphasis on consensus building. Such a system may not be efficient from a managerial point of view, especially at a time when dealing with many of Iran's problems requires quick and decisive actions, but it has the advantage that whatever decisions are reached have a broader base of support and stand a better chance of being implemented.

Another important constitutional amendment is related to the creation of a Supreme National Security Council. The council is designed to facilitate the process of decision making and to serve as a forum where different options are discussed and a consensus developed. Other minor amendments, including some related to the judiciary system, were also adopted.[7]

The Rafsanjani Presidency and the Continued Radical-Moderate Split

Constitutional reforms did not solve those problems that derived from philosophical differences among the leadership with regard to the radical-moderate split. Indeed, debate about the constitution and the positions of various groups on the nature of the executive power reflected these divisions.

For example, the radicals, who dominated the Parliament, advocated a weak presidency and a strong Parliament. Moreover, the radicals' support for those contesting the presidency depended largely on their expectations regarding the outcome of the constitutional debate. As long as the radicals expected the presidency to be weak, they supported the candidacy of the speaker of Parliament, Ayatollah Rafsanjani. But after it became clear that the presidency would be more than just a ceremonial office, they tried to persuade the Ayatollah Khomeini's son, the Hodjat-al-Islam Ahmad Khomeini, to contest the presidency. The radicals lost this contest, too, but for the first year of the Ayatollah Rafsanjani's presidency they continued to pressure him by manipulating their position in Parliament. A first confrontation between the new president and Parliament took place during the presentation of the Rafsanjani cabinet to Parliament in August 1989. Parliament finally ratified Rafsanjani's cabinet but only after harsh criticism of the fact that many of his ministers had been educated in U.S. or European universities.

Moreover, radical influence in Parliament, as well as in other parts of Iran's political structure, forced Rafsanjani to include a number of hard-liners in his cabinet. Indeed, after Parliament approved the cabinet, its new speaker, the Ayatollah Mehdi Karubi, himself a hard-liner, warned that this approval should not be interpreted as indicating that in the future Parliament would be only a rubber stamp.

After successfully passing over the hurdle of getting Parliament's approval, the Rafsanjani administration's next challenge was to gain the delegates' approval of its five-year economic development plan. By the time the Ayatollah Rafsanjani assumed the presidency, a decade of war, mismanagement, and ideological rigidity had left Iran's economy in shambles. Further, after this long period of hardship and deprivation, the people were impatient for rapid economic improvement. The underlying economic philosophy of the Rafsanjani administration was to encourage the privatization of the economy, to reform and rationalize its exchange rate system, and to attract Iranian and foreign capital by reintegrating Iran into the international economy. However, given the far-reaching implications of such economic reforms for Iran's social and political structure and the character of its foreign relations, there were strong reservations, if not all-out hostility, to this program of the radicals. The radicals were particularly concerned about the consequences of foreign borrowing and foreign investment. Another concern, which the moderates also shared, was the short-term negative impact of economic and financial reforms on the living standards of the poorest Iranians and those sectors with fixed incomes, such as retirees and civil servants. Despite these concerns, however, Parliament finally approved the Rafsanjani administration's development plan.

Since then, the government has taken a number of measures in the direction of privatization, exchange rate rationalization, and enticement of Iranian and foreign capital to return to Iran. However, progress on all these fronts has been limited, and it is not yet clear whether the government will be able to meet all of the plan's targets. There are several major barriers to its successful implementation, including a foreign exchange shortage, the problem of law and order, bureaucratic inertia and resistance, and concern over the political fallout of harsh economic reforms.

The problems deriving from the state of law and order and bureaucratic inefficiency are perhaps the most serious impediment to the flow of capital into Iran. In fact, without the establishment of law and order, which is absolutely essential for the restoration of the people's and the business community's confidence in the continuity of government policy, it is unlikely that many Iranians or foreigners would be prepared to invest heavily in Iran's economy. The government has taken a number of measures, including the amalgamation of various security forces, to improve the law and order situation in the country. But Iran is still a long way from the ideal state of the rule of law, and many of those revolutionary elements that had benefited from the state of near lawlessness in the country are still resisting the government's reform efforts.

The same situation more or less prevails in the bureaucracy, which since 1982 has been filled with people short in professional skills but long on revolutionary zeal. The government of President Rafsanjani realizes the importance of bureaucratic reform and improving the level of its professionalism, but again it is difficult to translate good intentions into results. In short, because of the resistance of those elements who feel that their privileges are being endangered, the pace of reform in Iran has been slow. Nevertheless, the government does seem determined to carry through with its reform agenda, even if it does take longer than Iran's conditions require. The government's strategy has been to try to convince the recalcitrant elements of the necessity of reform rather than merely forcing it upon them. This attitude is dictated in part by the balance of power within the Iranian body politic, where the hard-liners still have influence and are at least capable of sabotaging reform efforts. At some point the reformists may have to confront directly those elements that are beyond the reach of rational argument and eliminate them from positions where they could do damage. Failure to do so might deepen Iran's economic and political malaise, enhance the feeling of a government adrift, and intensify popular dissatisfaction, ultimately eroding the regime's power.[8]

RAFSANJANI'S FOREIGN POLICY CHALLENGES

In addition to facing a daunting and pressing domestic agenda, and even before formally assuming the office of the presidency, the Ayatollah Rafsanjani was handed his first foreign policy challenge: events in Lebanon. On July 28, 1989, Israel abducted a Lebanese Shi'a cleric named Sheikh Abdul Karim Obeid, one of the leaders of the Hezbollah, to gain the freedom of the Hezbollah-held Israeli airman Ron Arad. In retaliation for these Israeli actions, Hezbollah reportedly executed the U.S. hostage Colonel Higgins and threatened to kill Joseph Cicippio, another U.S. hostage, if Israel did not release Sheikh Obeid. The United States reacted to this threat by declaring that it would hold Iran directly responsible if any harm were to come to Cicippio, producing an extremely serious dilemma for President Rafsanjani. On the one hand, after the devastation of the war with Iraq and the military confrontation with the United States in the spring and autumn of 1988, he could not risk another such confrontation. On the other hand, he could not be too conciliatory toward the United States without providing new opportunities for the Iranian hard-liners to undermine his position by accusing him of having betrayed the Ayatollah Khomeini's legacy so soon after his death. His problem was to be conciliatory without giving the impression that he was intimidated by U.S. threats.[9] President Rafsanjani met this first test successfully. Through Iran's efforts Joseph Cicippio's life was spared, and the danger of a U.S. military strike against Iran was averted. However, despite some expectation that this crisis could lead to the freeing of U.S. hostages and an improvement in U.S.-Iran relations, there was no immediate breakthrough in that area.

Several reasons accounted for this lack of progress. One was the continuing power struggle in Iran, despite the relative ascendancy of the moderate, pragmatic elements, and the manipulation of the issue of U.S. hostages in Iran's domestic politics. Indeed, the hard-liners may have allowed President Rafsanjani to defuse the Sheikh Obeid–Cicippio crisis, provided there would be no further talk of hostage releases. The second reason was the reflection of Iran's internal divisions within the Lebanese Shi'a groups holding the hostages. Those Lebanese groups affiliated with the Iranian hard-liners adopted a wait-and-see policy until the fate of Iran's power struggle became clear.

The third reason was Syria's desire to obtain certain advantages for itself through the resolution of the hostage problem. Immediately following Iraq's invasion of Kuwait, Iran and the United Kingdom established diplomatic relations. Iran, eager to improve ties with the United Kingdom, tried to gain hostage Terry Waite's release in September 1990. At that time Syria and the United Kingdom did not have diplomatic relations, and the British were also preventing an improvement in Syria's relations with the European Community. Therefore, Syria's foreign minister, Farouk Al Shara'a, stated that if the United Kingdom wanted the release of Terry Waite, it must resolve its differences with Syria because improving relations with Iran would not be enough.[10] Naturally, this did nothing to improve U.S.-Iranian relations.

The fourth reason no progress occurred was U.S. unwillingness to offer any incentives to Iran that could have strengthened the moderates' bargaining position. This approach, however, was in line with the overall U.S. policy toward Iran and its new president. The basic premise of U.S. policy adopted since 1988 was that in light of international changes, notably the end of the cold war, Iran was no longer very important to the United States. Thus the United States could wait until Iran was ready to accept U.S. conditions and take the first step for better relations. The United States also felt that it did not need to help Rafsanjani and that it would deal with him only after he had demonstrated his actual control over Iran and his ability to marginalize the radicals, and after he met U.S. terms.[11] This basic U.S. policy would change, but only temporarily, after Iraq's invasion of Kuwait.

Having survived its first foreign policy crisis, the Rafsanjani administration faced another dilemma following the massive and devastating earthquake that struck Iran's northern regions in June 1990. In view of the magnitude of the devastation, it soon became clear that Iran would need external help. Yet asking for that help involved two problems for President Rafsanjani. First, if Iran asked for external help but the response turned out to be disappointing, it could jeopardize the government's strategy of opening Iran to the outside world. The second problem was the resistance of the radicals who feared that the moderates might use this opportunity to open up the country to the outside world completely, especially to the West.

Despite these uncertainties and difficulties, the government did declare that it would accept external assistance, even from the United States. The international response was relatively positive. However, international aid to the victims of the Iranian earthquake did not reach the levels achieved in similar cases such as the Armenian earthquake of 1988. Among Western countries, Germany and France provided the bulk of the aid. Assistance from the United States was not significant and was slow in coming.

Despite the relatively modest level of Western aid, earlier fears of a possible backlash did not materialize. On the contrary, President Rafsanjani and his pragmatic colleagues used the positive international response to convince the people, especially certain hard-line elements, of the benefits of having good relations with other countries. But neither did this episode lead to a breakthrough in Iran's relations with the West. Despite Iran's efforts, progress in improving ties with the West and the Persian Gulf states remained slow, partly because of inflexible Western attitudes. For instance, Britain continued to insist that the Iranian government rescind the Ayatollah Khomeini's edict on Salman Rushdie before any improvement in relations could be possible, knowing full well that given Iran's political atmosphere no one could afford the risk of repudiating a religious edict of the Ayatollah Khomeini. The British also prevented any significant improvements in Iran's relations with the European Community, although relations between Iran and some EC members took a turn for the better.[12]

Iran had more success in improving ties with the Arab states of the Persian Gulf. But here, too, progress was slow on the most difficult issues, such as resuming diplomatic relations with Saudi Arabia and resolving the problem of Iranian pilgrims to Mecca. There were, however, some positive developments in Iran's relations with Iraq, raising Iran's hopes of finally getting Iraqi troops out of its territory and moving toward the signing of a peace treaty which would recognize Iran's rights over the Shatt-al-Arab. The issue of securing the withdrawal of Iraqi troops and asserting its rights over the Shatt-al-Arab was politically important for the Iranian government. The Iranian people were already angry about the war's heavy costs and meager results. Popular criticism of the Islamic leadership's unwillingness, or inability, to sign a favorable peace treaty in 1982 was widespread. Thus, to lose territory or rights over the Shatt-al-Arab would have been politically costly to the regime. It would have elicited unfavorable comparisons with the previous government, which had succeeded in forcing Iraq to recognize Iran's sovereignty over half of the Shatt-al-Arab in the context of the 1975 Algiers agreement.

By May 1990, when Saddam Hussein indicated in a letter to President Rafsanjani a new Iraqi flexibility, Iran had also lost any hope of securing its rights through UN intervention and by the full application of Security Council Resolution 598. Indeed, the attitude of the Security Council's permanent members, especially the United States, which throughout 1987–88 had been adamant that Iran accept Resolution 598 without a single change, adopted a position that a state of no war, no peace in the Persian Gulf would best serve their interests. Saudi Arabia and most of the Persian Gulf Arab states shared this view. Only Oman was active in trying to mediate peace between Iran and Iraq. Indeed, during the spring of 1990 there was speculation that President Rafsanjani and Saddam Hussein would meet in Oman. But before any of these trends could crystallize into concrete actions, Iraq's invasion of Kuwait set in motion a dynamic that dramatically altered the region's political setting and posed new challenges but also new opportunities for Iran.

The Persian Gulf War: Dilemmas for Iran

Iraq's invasion of Kuwait confronted Iran with serious dilemmas. Prior to the invasion Iran's position, both regionally and internationally, had improved. By spring of 1990, Iraq's belligerence and Saddam Hussein's threatening language against Israel had shown the naïveté of those who throughout the 1980s had maintained that after defeating Iran, Saddam Hussein would become a Western ally and might even be persuaded to make peace with Israel. Many in the West, and even in the United States, had begun to admit that the Western policy of weakening Iran beyond what was necessary for its containment had been wrong. There was also a grudging admission that Iran should be rehabilitated as the only viable counterweight to Iraq.

At the same time, Iraq, which wanted to pursue other goals in the Persian Gulf and the Arab world, was showing increasing signs of flexibility in regard to the resolution of outstanding issues with Iran, notably the withdrawal of its troops from Iranian territory. When Iraq attacked Kuwait, none of the available responses was very attractive to Iran. Clearly, Iran could not condone Iraq's invasion of Kuwait, given its own bitter experience with Iraqi aggression. Nor could Iran be comfortable with the prospect of seeing Saddam Hussein emerge as the hegemon of the Persian Gulf, then perhaps once more turn his aggression toward Iran.

President Rafsanjani expressed Iran's fears when, in response to those arguing for Iran to join hands with Iraq in an Islamic union against the "Western imperialist onslaught," he asked rhetorically, "Do you want Saddam Hussein this time to really turn the Persian Gulf into the [Arabian] Gulf?" But neither could Iran be comfortable with the overwhelming U.S. military presence in the region. In fact, in view of U.S.-Iranian hostility, the Islamic regime could not be confident that the United States might not use the opportunity offered by the crisis to unseat the Iranian government also. Under these circumstances, there were basically three options available to Iran, two of them highly problematic.

First, Iran could have joined the U.S.-led coalition against Iraq and agreed to keep Iraqi troops occupied on its frontier. Indeed, this is what the West expected Iran to do, and when it did not occur, Iran was accused of duplicity. However, those Westerners who accused Iran ignored two fundamental points: Iran's domestic politics would not have allowed such a posture; and the West's preference for a state of no war, no peace between Iran and Iraq, coupled with Western unwillingness to implement fully Security Council Resolution 598, had left Iran with no choice but to accept Iraq's offer of withdrawing its troops from its territory. Indeed, had the West adopted a different attitude on Resolution 598, Iran's behavior might have been different.

Second, Iran could have aligned itself with Iraq. But that would have been highly dangerous and damaging to Iranian security.

Third, Iran could have remained neutral, but with a tilt in favor of the coalition. This is, indeed, what Iran did, and given the conditions described above, it was the most reasonable and prudent choice. Iran did not join the anti-Iraq coalition, but it vigorously condemned Iraq's invasion of Kuwait, fully abided by the Security Council resolutions, and scrupulously observed the international embargo on Iraq. More significantly, Iran clearly repudiated Saddam's claim that his war was waged by forces of Islam against forces of blasphemy. This aspect of Iran's policy has not been fully appreciated in the West. Had Iran joined Iraq and turned the Persian Gulf War into an Islamic Jihad, many Moslem countries whose population's pro-Iraq sympathies were strong may not have been able to join the anti-Iraq coalition. Unlike Saddam Hussein, whose late conversion to Islam was suspect in the eyes of many Moslems, Iran still enjoyed considerable Islamic credentials. Thus, a call from Iran for a Jihad is likely to have had a stronger impact and, at the least, would have deterred some countries, such as Pakistan, from joining the coalition.

Iran pursued a similarly cautious policy in the aftermath of the war. For instance, it did not take advantage of Iraq's internal problems, and even when Saddam Hussein destroyed the holiest places of the Shi'a, Iran essentially remained on the sidelines. It also bore the brunt of supporting Iraqi Kurdish and Shi'a refugees without receiving a tenth of the help that poured into Turkey.[13]

Because of the necessity of confronting Iraq, there was some improvement in Iran's relations with Western countries, especially with the Europeans. But no major concessions were made to Iran by either the United States or the European countries. Indeed, no sooner was the war over than Iran resumed its place in Western eyes as the most significant threat to their interests in the Persian Gulf, this time under the title of "resurgent Iran."

As a sign of continued Western suspicion of Iran, the early postwar plans for Persian Gulf security excluded Iran. Turkey and Egypt were billed as the new pillars of Western security in the region. However, because of considerations related to Arab-Israeli peacemaking, Syria later had to be added to the list. For reasons whose discussion is beyond the scope of this study, none of these schemes was implemented.[14] The security system that finally emerged in the Persian Gulf region was based on a U.S. military umbrella and the establishment of a series of bilateral security pacts between the United States and individual Persian Gulf Arab states. Iran understandably was not happy about these developments, and the Iranian media continued to attack and oppose the U.S. military presence in the area. But in reality Iran has accepted that a greater U.S. presence in the Persian Gulf is an inevitable fact of life.

In exchange, the Persian Gulf states have admitted that Iran cannot be kept out of security arrangements for the region, although no one envisages a military role for Iran. In the last two years there have been high-level meetings between Iran and the six members of the Gulf Cooperation Council (GCC). Some members, weary of Saudi overlordship, have shown greater eagerness to expand ties with Iran. The staying power of Saddam Hussein has also acted as a further impetus for the GCC states to improve relations with Iran.

THE NEW WORLD ORDER AND IRAN

The Persian Gulf War and its aftermath brought home to Iran in a dramatic way the revolutionary changes that had occurred in the international political system and the necessity for Iran to adapt its policies to these changes.

Already by mid-1987 changes in the Soviet Union and the introduction of the so-called new thinking in Soviet foreign policy had undermined Iran's bargaining position, especially vis-à-vis the United States. These trends intensified in the following years as U.S.-Soviet relations changed from confrontation to cooperation, a trend best exemplified during the Persian Gulf crisis. The U.S. victory over Iraq led to a reassertion of its dominance in the Middle East. Coupled with Soviet withdrawal from the region, this left the United States—at least for the foreseeable future—as the only superpower with a presence there. Moreover, the collapse of the Soviet Union and its socialist allies meant that Iran had no alternative to the West as a source of technology and financing for its economic reconstruction. Even more significantly, the collapse of the Soviet Union created new security challenges for Iran on its northern and eastern borders as a result of the emergence of six new Moslem republics in the vicinity.

These fundamental systemic changes and their regional consequences further enhanced the necessity for Iran to get rid of the excessive revolutionary baggage of the 1980s. A special priority was to end the problem of Western hostages and gradually to extricate itself from the Lebanese morass. This has, indeed, been the direction that Iran has taken, although its progress has been somewhat erratic and slow. To achieve an end to the hostage problem, Iran finally enlisted the services of the UN secretary-general, which proved to be a wise move. His intervention changed the process from a U.S.-Iran deal into an international effort and thus allowed the Iranian moderates some political cover. After a long and difficult process of bargaining, by the end of 1991 Iran succeeded in gaining the freedom of all remaining Western hostages, with the exception of two German nationals. The fate of these two Germans had become entangled with that of two Lebanese nationals—the Hammadi brothers—held in prison in Germany on charges of terrorism.

Iran also continued to improve its relations with the Arab states beyond the Persian Gulf region. It reestablished diplomatic relations with Morocco, and there was some reaching out to Egypt. Relations with the European countries continued to improve. For instance, after the release of the two British hostages in late 1991, relations between the United Kingdom and Iran relations took a turn for the better with growing expectations that the two countries would soon exchange ambassadors. However, disagreements over the fate of the Ayatollah Khomeini's death edict on Rushdie and other aspects of Iran's foreign policy seemed to dash hopes for a dramatic improvement in ties. In general, the influence of past patterns of thinking and behavior, including the negative impact of the hard-liners, could still be observed in Iran's foreign policy in 1991. Three events particularly stand out.

The first was the assassination in Paris in August 1991 of the shah's last prime minister, Shapur Bakhtiar, and the alleged involvement of members of the Iranian government or individuals closely associated with them in his murder. This incident cost Iran heavily and eroded some of the positive impact generated by its behavior during the Persian Gulf War and its role in the release of some of the Western hostages.

To begin with, it delayed indefinitely the official visit of French President François Mitterrand to Iran, which was expected to take place in November 1991. This trip was to seal the expansion of Franco-Iranian relations, but its symbolic importance went even farther. The trip was to be the most important sign of Iran's newly found international respectability. It was also to open the way for the official visit of German Chancellor Helmut Kohl to Tehran. These visits were then to be followed by return visits by President Rafsanjani. But as long as there were any doubts that the Iranian government, especially anyone associated with Rafsanjani and his close collaborators, was involved in the Bakhtiar assassination, neither France nor Germany would, or could, run the political risk of seeming to confer prestige and respectability on Iran.

Nevertheless, the French government, while pursuing the investigation into the assassination of Prime Minister Bakhtiar, did not allow this incident to derail Franco-Iranian relations totally. The negative consequences of the Bakhtiar affair were later felt in Swiss-Iranian relations when, in response to a request by the French authorities investigating the Bakhtiar affair, the Swiss government decided to extradite an Iranian national working at the Iranian Embassy in

Berne, who was accused of being an accessory to Bakhtiar's assassination. The Iranians refused and suggested that French authorities should question him on embassy grounds. In the meantime, the Swiss government claimed that its embassy staff in Tehran had come under pressure and their movements were restrained. The Swiss authorities further added that fearing for the safety of their diplomats, they would close their embassy in Tehran. This problem was finally resolved and the Swiss embassy remained open, but relations between the two countries remained tense over the problems flowing from investigations of the murder of Bakhtiar.

The assassination and its ramifications have raised troubling questions about the state of Iranian politics, especially the balance of power and influence within the Iranian leadership: if the assassination of Bakhtiar was the work of Iranian hard-liners, to what extent are the more moderate pragmatic elements in control of the government? Even more disturbing would be clear evidence that the assassination had the blessing of the moderates. This question cannot be fully answered until the results of the investigation are known. But, most likely, the act was the work of hard-liners wanting to undermine Iran's opening to the West and the position of President Rafsanjani. There was no conceivable benefit, and considerable damage was done to the pragmatists' policies by this act. Nevertheless, even this is quite disturbing as it proves that despite their discrediting in the public eye, the radicals continue to have strongholds in Iran's political and military institutions, especially the revolutionary guards and security services, and that the pragmatists do not seem capable of eliminating their influence.

A second aspect of Iran's foreign policy that opposed the pragmatic realist trend was the convening of a conference on the Palestinian question in Tehran on October 19, 1991, a few days before the opening of the U.S.-sponsored Middle East peace talks in Madrid. This conference assembled Palestinian and Arab groups opposed to the peace talks. It, too, reflected the hard-liners' influence and the moderates' unwillingness to press them beyond their tolerance, especially with parliamentary elections scheduled for April 1992. This event, however, also reflected Iran's anger at being ignored after the Persian Gulf War and at not receiving—unlike other countries, notably Turkey— any financial compensation, although it did bear the brunt of Iraqi refugees, both Kurdish and Shi'a.

In contrast to these blunders, the third event—Iran's handling of Soviet developments, in particular the failed coup attempt of August 1991—showed a good deal of diplomatic sophistication. During the few days that the coup lasted, Iran remained cautiously silent, indicating that it considered this event an internal Soviet affair. When the coup failed, however, Iran heartily congratulated Mikhail Gorbachev on his return to power. Iran's approach to the question of the dissolution of the Soviet empire was also cautious. The basic Iranian approach was that Iran would accept whatever decisions the constituent members of the Soviet Union decided on. But once it became clear that the process of the Soviet Union's disintegration was irreversible, Iran moved quickly to recognize the independent states that emerged from the ashes of the Soviet empire and to establish economic and political ties with them.

Conclusion: The Record of the Past and Coming Challenges

The balance of developments in Iran since the establishment of the cease-fire of August 1988 has been mixed, although the overall trend is encouraging. The Islamic regime's ability to effect a smooth transition of power and to introduce necessary constitutional reforms was impressive. However, the regime has been less successful in resolving its internal divisions and the underlying contradictions of its ideological foundations. The result has been a painfully slow process of reform that has delayed Iran's economic reconstruction and its social and political stabilization.

The deleterious impact of the regime's inability to reach a broad consensus among its most influential members has been felt particularly in foreign policy. Thus, although Iran's foreign policy has basically evolved in a moderate, pragmatic, and nonconfrontational direction as illustrated by its policy in the Persian Gulf and in handling Soviet events, the radicals' influence has prevented Iran from reaping the fruits of its positive behavior.

Thus, actions such as the murder of Shapur Bakhtiar and the rejectionist approach with regard to the Middle East peace talks have largely blunted the impact of more positive trends. This situation has also been costly in terms of Iran's economic prospects as it has slowed the flow of much-needed capital and technology that must come from the West.

Even more seriously, Iran is left open to the manipulation of Middle

Eastern states and other powers who find it in their interest to retain Iran's status as a pariah state. Turkey, Pakistan, Afghanistan, and even Israel, who have seen their strategic value to the United States being eroded as a result of the end of the cold war and the collapse of the Soviet Union are using the so-called threat of Iran to recapture some of their lost importance and are offering themselves to the United States as bulwarks against the Iranian-Islamic threat. Others, including some in the United States, for their own reasons, find it expedient to exaggerate an actual or potential Iranian threat. In the meantime, the Iranian leadership's inability to control the hard-line elements completely and make the necessary adjustments in its rhetoric and behavior provides ammunition to those who want to exploit Iran's mistakes and prevent its reconstruction and rehabilitation.

In the future, the price that Iran must pay for foreign policy mistakes could be costlier than the losses it has suffered in the past and could indeed put Iran's territorial integrity at risk. The disintegration of the Soviet Union and the emergence of six new Moslem states, some of whose peoples overlap with Iran's own ethnic minorities, and the disruptive dynamics involved in the process of nation building, including the upsurge in ethnic irredentism, pose new challenges for Iran on its borders with the successor states of the Soviet Union. In addition, the rise of ultranationalist and irredentist trends such as pan-Turkism can also become a threat to Iran's territorial integrity. Turkish and Iranian relations have already become strained as Turkey is aggressively pursuing a policy of influence in the new Moslem republics, while also marketing itself as the West's favored partner and a barrier to the spread of Islamic fundamentalism. In short, because of new international conditions and geopolitical realities the Iranian leadership faces perhaps its gravest foreign policy test. If Iran fails the test, not only its economic prosperity and political stability but also its territorial integrity could be seriously compromised.

An encouraging development, however, was the result of Iran's parliamentary elections, which were held on April 10, 1992, and in which the moderates scored a clear victory. Even more important than the moderates' victory was the strong support extended by the spiritual leader, Ayatollah Khamenei, to President Rafsanjani and the Guardian Council. This support showed that the two principal figures in the Iranian leadership are cooperating closely. The victory of the moderates also raised hopes that the pace of reform in Iran will accelerate.

A note of caution, however, is in order; the elimination of the radicals' influence from the Parliament does not mean that they have lost their capacity for affecting Iran's policies. Quite the contrary, they still have influence in the bureaucracy, the Revolutionary guards, the press, and the universities. In fact, some fear that the radicals may resort to subversive activities against the regime. Also, President Rafsanjani's ability to move rapidly with reforms depends to some extent on the reaction of the outside world and the extent to which other countries, especially those in the West, would be willing to help Iran in its economic reconstruction effort.

Notes

1. There were two major reasons for the German government's behavior. The first, unrelated to Iran, was to ward off growing U.S. and European criticism of German companies' links with Libya, which allegedly had helped Kaddafi develop chemical weapons. Germany wanted to dispel the perception that it was soft on radical states. The second was what the Germans perceived as a breach of a promise by Iran to release an Iranian dissident who had long been a resident of Germany and was imprisoned after returning to Iran. For more details on this point, see Shireen T. Hunter, *Iran and the World: Continuity in a Revolutionary Decade*, (Bloomington: Indiana University Press, 1990), pp. 156–57.

2. This message has now become a historical document following the collapse and disintegration of the Soviet empire. In his letter the Ayatollah Khomeini said that communism belonged to the dustbin of history and recommended that the Soviets study Islam and return to spirituality.

3. For a detailed study of these issues, see Shireen T. Hunter, *Iran after Khomeini* (New York: Praeger/CSIS, 1992), pp. 76–78.

4. Traditional Shi'a theory maintains that there can be no just and legitimate government until the return of the twelfth Imam, the Mahdi.

5. On the implications of this amendment for the relationship between religion and politics, see the discussions in *Resalat*, reproduced in *Foreign Broadcast Information Service-Near East/South Asia* (hereafter *FBIS/NESA*), July 27, 1989, p. 49.

6. On the relationship between the president and the Parliament, see the text of the *Tehran Times* article reproduced in *FBIS:NESA*, May 25, 1989, pp. 37–38.

7. Other amendments dealt with the following issues: the reform of the judiciary, the management of the Voice and Vision (Iranian radio and television), a reassessment of the number of Parliament deputies, the workings of the Council of Discerning What Is Good, and changing the name of National Consultative Assembly to *Islamic* Consultative Assembly.

8. On Iran's economic problems, see *Iran after Khomeini*, pp. 57–91.

9. For an analysis of this period and U.S.-Iranian difficulties, see Shireen T. Hunter, "Post-Khomeini Iran," *Foreign Affairs*, 68, no. 5, (Winter 1989–90).

10. On Syria's position, see "Al Shara'a Links British Hostages, Diplomatic Ties," *FBIS-NESA*, October 19, 1990, pp. 42–43.

11. On the U.S. attitude toward Iran see "U.S.: Diplomatic Ball Is in Tehran's Court," *Christian Science Monitor*, June 13, 1989, pp. 1–2.

12. Interview with a European Community official.

13. Indeed, Iran has the largest refugee population in the entire world, over 4 million.

14. See Shireen T. Hunter, "Persian Gulf Security: Lessons of the Past and Need for New Thinking," *SAIS Review* 12, no. 1 (Spring 1992).

7

SAUDI ARABIA:

DESERT STORM AND AFTER

F. Gregory Gause, III

Desert Storm brought change to Saudi Arabia, but not nearly as much as outside observers had expected during the height of the coalition war against Iraq. The results of the crisis altered the distribution of regional power and opened up the possibility of new security alignments for Saudi Arabia. The Saudi regime's need to respond to domestic pressures generated by Saddam's challenge to Saudi legitimacy and the presence of hundreds of thousands of U.S. troops opened a brief window on the politics of the country for outside observers, and led to some significant domestic responses by the regime. While not gainsaying the importance of the Gulf War for the region, what strikes the observer more in regard to Saudi Arabia is how little has changed in the basic Saudi approach to regional security and its relations with the United States. The changes in the domestic political realm have the potential, depending upon how they develop, to be of much more enduring importance.

The Iraqi Invasion and the Saudi Response

In the two years between the end of the Iran-Iraq War (July 1988) and the Iraqi invasion of Kuwait, Saudi Arabia was unable to resume its preferred geopolitical position of equal distance between the two major Gulf powers. It had broken diplomatic relations with Iran in 1987 and in effect prohibited Iranians from making the pilgrimage to Mecca, as a result both of the continued propaganda assaults on the Saudi regime from Tehran and of Iranian attacks on Kuwaiti and Saudi shipping.[1] The end of the Iran-Iraq War did not produce any immediate improvement in Saudi-Iranian relations. Ideological differ-

ences between the states on the definition of legitimate Islamic politics continued, and Riyadh still feared efforts by Tehran to export its
brand of islamic revolution across the Gulf. The Saudis thus maintained their tilt toward Iraq, though not without reservations. Saudi
financial support for Baghdad, so important during the Iran-Iraq War,
was certainly curtailed if not completely stopped after the war, and
Saudi relations with both Egypt and Syria improved as a counterweight to Iraqi power in the Arab world. However, in the Gulf, Riyadh
still lined up with Iraq against the perceived Iranian threat. That continued alignment was expressed tangibly in the March 1989 nonaggression pact signed by Iraq and Saudi Arabia.

Given this set of interests, Saudi Arabia's initial response when Iraq
began to raise demands against Kuwait in the summer of 1990 was to
seek a negotiated settlement that would give the Iraqis some tangible
gains. The Saudis were noticeably silent when Baghdad threatened
Kuwait on the issue of Kuwaiti oil production, in some measure because they themselves wanted to see Kuwait abide by its OPEC production quota. At the OPEC meeting of July 25–27, 1990, Kuwait
agreed to cut its production to the quota level. When Iraq continued
to pressure Kuwait, the Saudis and Egypt's president, Hosni Mubarak,
joined in a mediation effort in late July that resulted in the Kuwaiti-
Iraqi meeting of August 1 in the Saudi city of Jidda, just one day before the invasion.

Circumstantial evidence indicates that, while there was no detailed
Saudi-Egyptian plan put forward to the parties at Jidda, the thrust behind their mediation effort was to extract some concessions from
Kuwait to mollify Saddam. President Mubarak revealed after the invasion that he had told the Kuwaitis that they should make an offer including border modifications and financial aid to Iraq.[2] Saudi decision
makers have not been as revealing about their stance in those days,
but there are indications that Riyadh had about the same idea. The
Saudis had pressured Kuwait before the invasion to reduce their oil
production to their OPEC quota, as Saddam had demanded.[3] Crown
Prince Hassan of Jordan told an interviewer that King Fahd had asked
King Hussein of Jordan on August 2 to get the Iraqis "to withdraw to
the disputed area" on the border, not completely out of Kuwait.[4]
Yemeni President 'Ali 'Abdallah Salih said that King Fahd had told
him on August 5 that Kuwait had been mistaken in its hard-line policy toward Iraq.[5]

Comments by Saudi Defense Minister Prince Sultan ibn 'Abd al-

'Aziz in late October 1990 also gave some hint as to the Saudi stand. Prince Sultan, after asserting that Saudi Arabia would not accept any solution short of unconditional Iraqi withdrawal from Kuwait and the return of the Kuwaiti government, referred to the general Saudi position on how to settle inter-Arab problems. He said that "any Arab who has a right vis-à-vis his brother Arab must assert it, but not by means of using force. This is an undesirable thing." He indicated that Saudi Arabia "is among those who call for Arab national security, including brotherly concessions from Arab to Arab, whether such a right is established or more doubtful." He went on to say that "it is not a bad thing for any Arab country to give a brother Arab country land, or money, or access to the sea."[6] The Western press saw Sultan's remarks as a signal of Saudi willingness to compromise with Iraq.[7] However, given that the quote came directly after Sultan's direct refusal to accept anything but an unconditional Iraqi withdrawal from Kuwait, it might be more accurate to interpret his remarks as an indication of what Saudi policy was before the invasion, defending Saudi efforts at avoiding this crisis and indirectly criticizing the Kuwaitis for refusal to compromise.

It is against this backdrop of the Saudi willingness to accommodate Saddam Hussein that their reaction to the invasion must be analyzed. Their sense of shock and betrayal reflected not only the unprecedented nature of the Iraqi action but also the feeling that Saddam had reneged on a tentative agreement that the Saudis had constructed for his benefit.[8] Their perception of Saddam's ultimate intentions must have been colored by this specific sense that the Iraqi leader could not be trusted to keep his commitments. Little else can explain the relatively quick decision by the Saudis to abandon their historical position of keeping their U.S. military connection "over the horizon" and at arms' length. While much is made of the two-day delay in taking this decision, and of the hints of differences of opinion within the Saudi royal family over it, what is more striking to the author is the relative ease with which the Saudis reversed their past aversion to an open U.S. military presence in the kingdom and the lack of substantial opposition within the ruling elite to that policy. Even if some members of the royal family were unhappy with the decision, they did not make a public or even a quasi-public issue out of their feelings. The religious establishment, which might also have been expected to oppose the deployment of the U.S. troops, officially approved the policy line in a *fatwa* (religious judgment) by Sheikh 'Abdallah bin 'Abd al-'Aziz bin Baz, chairman of the Supreme Council of Islamic Research, Ruling, Call, and Guidance and the leading religious official in the kingdom.[9]

Once they accepted the U.S. military presence, the Saudis were in effect committed to the U.S. strategy of confrontation with Saddam. Between mid-August 1990 and late February 1991 Saudi Arabia took a back seat to U.S. political and military leaders in the crisis. During this period the regime used its propaganda organs, diplomatic weight, and financial clout to garner support within the Arab and Moslem worlds for its policy. While attracting considerable political and some military support from other governments in the region, it largely failed in efforts to convince public opinions of the legitimacy of the Saudi decision to invite what the Saudi media always referred to as "the Arab, Moslem and friendly armed forces" to the kingdom. The Saudis were particularly disappointed that popular Islamic organizations, like the Moslem Brotherhood in Egypt and Jordan, the Islamic Tendency Movement in Tunisia, and the Islamic Salvation Front in Algeria, with which they had had good informal relations, came out against Saudi policy in the crisis.

Postwar Security and Saudi Foreign Policy

Saudi Arabia is confronting three sets of interrelated issues in devising a security strategy for the post–Gulf War period: the size and structure of its own armed forces and the forces of other members of the Gulf Cooperation Council (GCC); the extent and visibility of its enhanced security coordination with the United States; and the nature of its security relations with its Arab coalition partners Egypt and Syria. Overreliance on any one element could entail serious problems for the Saudis, which will be discussed below. Therefore, Riyadh is attempting to balance the three elements to minimize the negative aspects of each. However, there are tensions in this balancing act that could disrupt Saudi plans.

The first natural impulse of any state that has experienced a serious threat to its security is to increase the size and improve the capabilities of its own armed forces. Saudi officials have been discussing a program that will more than double the size of their total armed forces, to about 200,000, over the next five to seven years and to equip that force to be able to fight a large-scale, mobile war like Operation

Desert Storm.[10] Riyadh has also been consulting with its GCC allies (Kuwait, Bahrain, Qatar, United Arab Emirates, and Oman) on an Omani proposal for a joint GCC force of 100,000 to replace the largely symbolic Peninsula Shield force that was stationed at the Saudi base at Hafr al-Batin. At the GCC chiefs of staff meeting in late August 1991, the member states agreed in principle to form such a force, though implementation has been left for working groups to study. Questions remain about the distribution of costs and contributions among the members and about command structure.[11] Subsequent meetings have produced no tangible plans for forming such a force.

The Saudi and GCC emphasis on self-reliance raises a number of questions and problems that preclude a completely independent security strategy. Even if these states were able to meet their ambitious goals, it is doubtful that their combined forces could be a serious deterrent to the much larger armies of potential threats like Iraq and Iran, whose populations are substantially larger than the combined GCC populations and whose armies number in the hundreds of thousands. Increasing the number of men under arms in Saudi Arabia (not to mention the smaller GCC states) will itself be difficult. The Saudi population is relatively small, there is no history of compulsory military service, and the financial and career opportunities outside the military are more inviting to most young Saudi men than a military career. Instituting a draft or a national service requirement would be a substantial change for a regime which has asked little of its citizens save political quiescence and given them substantial material benefits but little input into political decision making. (I will return to the domestic repercussions of Saudi security choices below.)

Equipping and training a Saudi force or a joint GCC force for the kind of offensive, mobile warfare that characterized Operation Desert Storm would entail a large-scale commitment from the United States. For Washington to make such a commitment, particularly for Congress to approve the arms sales that would be part of that commitment, Saudi Arabia would have to be more willing than it has been in the past to enter into an open, public, and formal long-term security arrangement with the United States. U.S. military officials have already floated plans to pre-position a huge stockpile of U.S. armor and equipment in the kingdom, enough to outfit 150,000 troops, and a large logistical organization to support them.[12]

Despite the presence of hundreds of thousands of U.S. troops in the kingdom during the Gulf War, Saudi Arabia still wants to limit the

public profile of its U.S. security connection. Given the history of foreign military bases in the Middle East, anything that resembles an
outside power's permanent military facility in the region raises questions about the independence of the host country. Being seen as a de
facto colony of the United States is risky for the Saudis both domestically and regionally. There were undercurrents of opposition in Saudi
Arabia to the presence of the U.S. forces during the Gulf crisis, particularly in religious circles, even though such opposition did not become a public issue.[13] A petition to King Fahd signed by hundreds of
prominent Saudis identified with Islamic political currents after the
Gulf War requested, among other things, that the kingdom avoid foreign alliances that contradict Islamic legitimacy.[14] At the regional
level, a high-profile U.S. presence in the kingdom runs the risk of
alienating Iran, with which relations have improved considerably
since the end of the Gulf War, and of legitimating Saddam Hussein's
effective propaganda charge during the crisis that the United States
was using the war to occupy Saudi oil fields.

Saudi leaders are acutely sensitive to the problems that the U.S.
connection raises. King Fahd, in a speech to the country in late November 1990, denied that Saudi Arabia had made any agreements for
the permanent stationing of foreign forces in the kingdom.[15] In a
statement to the press after the war, Saudi Defense Minister Prince
Sultan referred to a commitment on the part of the United States to
withdraw its forces from the kingdom once their mission was completed.[16] The quick drawdown of U.S. ground forces in the region after
the war indirectly confirms the Saudi leadership's desire not to be
seen as hosting a long-term U.S. presence.[17] It is interesting to contrast Saudi hesitancy on this score with the eagerness of Kuwait,
which actually suffered defeat and occupation by a regional neighbor,
to have a U.S. military base on its territory.

While appreciating the risks involved, the Saudis also realize that
their U.S. connection is the ultimate safeguard of their country's security against foreign attack. They want U.S. weapons and training, as
well as the political and deterrent power the U.S. commitment to
Saudi security gives them. While unwilling to play host to a permanent U.S. ground force presence in the kingdom, the Saudis do seem
willing to pre-position some U.S. equipment, increase the frequency
and size of joint training missions, and provide more formal access arrangements for U.S. naval forces in Saudi ports. They are also more
accepting of a higher-profile U.S. presence in other GCC states. Before

the Iraqi invasion of Kuwait, Riyadh preferred that U.S. ground and naval forces remain based outside the Gulf. Now it appears not to object to the formal U.S.-Kuwaiti security agreement of September 1991 to large-scale U.S. pre-positioning in GCC states or to proposals to move a forward element of the U.S. Central Command headquarters to Oman or the United Arab Emirates.[18] In fact, the enhanced U.S. presence in the smaller states could bring the security benefits the Saudis want while limiting the domestic and regional repercussions for the kingdom. While the tensions and differences between Riyadh and Washington on the details of their postwar security arrangements are real, the general outlines of what the Saudis are and are not willing to accept are clear.

The third aspect of postwar Saudi security policy is the kingdom's relations with Egypt and Syria, its Arab coalition partners in Desert Storm. Immediately after the war, it appeared that Cairo and Damascus were poised to play a significant, permanent role in Gulf security issues. On March 6, 1991, at a meeting in Damascus, the foreign ministers of Egypt, Syria, and the GCC states agreed on what appeared at the time to be far-reaching security cooperation. The Damascus Declaration, as the agreement came to be known, seemed to many to be the basis for a permanent Egyptian and Syrian military presence in the Gulf. One Saudi newspaper said at the time that the declaration considered the Egyptian and Syrian forces as "the nucleus of an Arab peacekeeping force for guaranteeing the security and safety of the Arab states in the Gulf region."[19] Four days later, the eight foreign ministers met in Riyadh with Secretary of State James Baker. They endorsed President Bush's broad framework for Middle East security enunciated in his speech before Congress immediately after the Gulf War, and Baker in turn expressed U.S. support for the Damascus Declaration and for an Egyptian and Syrian military role in the Gulf.[20] The foundation had apparently been laid for a real Egyptian-Syrian-GCC military alliance, with an umbrella of U.S. support.

Almost immediately, however, Saudi Arabia and other Gulf states began to back away from these far-reaching readings of the Damascus Declaration. Saudi decision makers began to reassess the consequences of having Egyptian and Syrian troops in the kingdom on a permanent basis. At a time when the Saudi treasury was stretched to its limits by the financial commitments undertaken during the Gulf War, the idea of taking on a greater, open-ended aid commitment to Egypt and Syria, which would be the quid pro quo for their troop deployments, was not seen to be in the Saudis' interest. Moreover, there were fears that the existing good relations with the Assad and Mubarak governments might change over the long term, either because of domestic political changes in Syria and Egypt or because of regional realignments. In that case, the presence of the troops in Saudi Arabia would become at minimum an irritant, perhaps even a threat, to the Saudis.[21]

Another reason for this reassessment was the negative Iranian reaction to the Damascus Declaration. Iranian officials condemned what they saw as efforts to isolate their country in the Gulf and reiterated their view that Gulf security was the sole responsibility of the states of the Gulf themselves.[22] In June 1991 Iranian and Egyptian officials engaged in a public war of words over the Iranian insistence that Egypt could not play a major role in Gulf security affairs.[23] Saudi Arabia saw the end of the Gulf War as an opportunity to improve relations with Iran. In the Saudi view Iran had acted responsibly during the crisis over Kuwait. Moreover, since the death of Ayatollah Khomeini, the Islamic Republic had downplayed its desire to spread its ideological message across the Gulf by propaganda and subversion, which had been its main threat from the Saudi perspective.[24] The Saudis therefore sought to build on this basis by reassuring Tehran about their security plans.

Saudi Foreign Minister Prince Saud al-Faisal visited Tehran in early June 1991, assuring his hosts that Riyadh had no intention of hosting a permanent foreign military presence and that the Damascus Declaration was not aimed against Iran. The two sides agreed on a framework for cooperation on Gulf, Islamic, and economic issues and on continuing the GCC-Iranian dialogue on security matters.[25] Saudi Arabia also agreed to allow an Iranian delegation of over 100,000 to attend that year's hajj, in June 1991. Since the Islamic Revolution came to power, the hajj came to be a barometer of Saudi-Iranian relations. In 1991, the hajj was quiet, with the Iranian delegation refraining from the provocative political demonstrations that have characterized past years. The head of the Iranian pilgrimage delegation praised the Saudi government's efforts to provide for the needs of the Iranian pilgrims, and Iranian Foreign Minister Velayati, who accompanied them, said that Saudi-Iranian relations were "developing and going in a very positive direction."[26]

The improvements in Saudi-Iranian relations opened the door for the previously tentative process of GCC-Iranian contacts to proceed at a new level. Iranian Foreign Minister Velayati said in an August

1991 interview that the GCC states "have invited us to reassess the status of the members of the Council. . . . They have somehow come to the conclusion that they must seek Iran's cooperation, or else it will be impossible to defend regional security."[27] The GCC foreign ministers and GCC Secretary General 'Abdallah Bishara met with Velayati in New York in late September 1991, during the UN General Assembly meetings. They issued a statement which set out seven principles upon which their relations would be based: sovereignty of the parties; "unity of regional territories," implying that Gulf issues, including security, must be dealt with by the Gulf countries themselves; inviolability of recognized international boundaries; peaceful settlement of disputes; no resort to force or the threat of force in relations; noninterference in the domestic affairs of others; and encouragement of dialogue and mutual understanding.[28] Differences remain with Iran, especially over the nature and extent of the GCC states' ties with the United States, but it is clear that relations, particularly with Saudi Arabia, have improved considerably since the Gulf War.

The price of those improved relations with Iran was a distancing from the close security relationship that Egypt and Syria inferred from the Damascus Declaration. As early as May 1991 the dissatisfaction of Cairo and, to a lesser extent, Damascus with the reluctance of their Gulf partners to follow through with practical implementation of the Damascus Declaration became apparent. Egypt announced plans on May 8 to begin withdrawing its troops from Saudi Arabia, troops which just two months before it had seen as the "nucleus of an Arab peacekeeping force" in the Gulf. Syria announced its intention to withdraw in early June 1991 and completed that operation by the end of July.[29] By the end of June there were reports from the Gulf that the GCC states wanted to add amendments to the Damascus Declaration regarding security issues, dropping plans for a permanent Arab force and replacing them with a system of coordination and consultation on security issues.[30] After much wrangling and one official postponement, the scheduled meeting of the Damascus Declaration foreign ministers was held in Kuwait on July 15–16, 1991. The final version of the Damascus Declaration agreed on at that meeting contained no mention of a permanent Egyptian-Syrian military presence in the Gulf.[31]

By the summer of 1991, it had become clear to all the parties that original ambitious interpretations of the Damascus Declaration were dead and that security cooperation rather than an actual military alliance was what the Gulf states wanted. At their summit meeting of July 18, 1991, Egypt's President Mubarak and Syria's President Assad both denied that they wanted a permanent military presence in the Gulf and spoke in terms of general security cooperation with the Gulf states. Mubarak said, "A permanent presence is not requested, and we will not impose ourselves, but we are ready to participate in defensive operations if that is requested of us at any time."[32] Egyptian policy began to shift from the Damascus Declaration framework to bilateral arrangements with individual GCC countries, particularly the smaller ones.[33] There seems to be general, though not formal, agreement among the Damascus Declaration states that a symbolic Egyptian and Syrian presence of about 3,000 troops each will remain in Kuwait as part of a larger force made up of troops from the GCC states.[34] No Egyptian or Syrian forces will be stationed in Saudi Arabia. Rather, the Saudis see the Damascus Declaration as a framework for future security consultations with Egypt and Syria and, if events call for it, a basis for inviting Egyptian and Syrian forces into the kingdom as was done after the invasion of Kuwait. This is a different, looser alignment than Egypt and Syria were seeking and reduces the claim they can make on Saudi economic aid as the quid pro quo for help on the security front. But Saudi Arabia is not willing to go farther, and Egypt and Syria have little choice but to make the best of the situation.[35]

Saudi security policy in the postwar period remains somewhat in flux. As of March 1992, formal security agreements and implementation arrangements have yet to be finalized either with the United States or with Riyadh's Arab coalition partners, Syria and Egypt. Agreement on a set of principles to govern relations has been reached with Iran, but those principles are of the most general sort and do not include practical steps on security cooperation. That flux is the result of Riyadh's desire to maintain a balance among a number of relationships , some of which create their own internal tensions, and not to rely on any one pillar to guarantee Saudi security. Self-reliance is seen as preferable to foreign military presences but not sufficient for real defense. The U.S. connection is important and must be enhanced but still kept at arms' length so as not to create too many domestic or regional problems. Iranian and Egyptian-Syrian influences should be used to check each other, with Saudi Arabia maintaining good relations with each side but not choosing one over the other. Keeping options open, avoiding permanent commitments, keeping the U.S. connection at some public distance, and maneuvering among larger regional actors were all characteristic of the Saudi foreign policy modus operandi before the Gulf War. With some important changes in tone, they remain so after the war.

Other Regional Issues:
Iraq and Its Allies and the Arab-Israeli Conflict

While Iraq remains a major factor on any Gulf or regional security scenario, Iraq under Saddam Hussein's leadership can play no role in formal or informal security arrangements with its neighbors. He remains persona non grata with his neighbors, including Saudi Arabia. The removal of Saddam from power was a clear, if unstated, goal of Saudi policy during the Gulf crisis. During the crisis the Saudis began publicly to support a group of Iraqi anti-regime exiles who formed a grouping called the Free Iraq Council.[36] Even more significant, Riyadh began to reach out to the Iranian-supported Iraqi Shi'a opposition.[37] During his visit to Tehran, on June 6, 1991, Saudi Foreign Minister Prince Saud al-Faisal met publicly with Muhammad Baqir al-Hakim, the head of the Supreme Assembly of the Islamic Revolution in Iraq, the Shi'a Islamist government-in-exile supported by Iran during its war with Iraq.[38] It was fear that such groups would gain preponderant influence in Iraq that, in part, led Saudi Arabia to support Saddam Hussein during his war with Iran.

The Saudis, along with Syria and Iran, actively encouraged their various Iraqi clients to put aside their substantial differences and agree to a common program for opposing Saddam and organizing for the post-Saddam transition period. Twenty-three Iraqi opposition groups, ranging from Shi'a Islamists and Kurdish nationalists to liberals, dissident Ba'thists, tribal leaders, and communists met in Beirut on March 11–13, 1991. They issued a lowest common denominator statement of their intention to cooperate on the ouster of Saddam and to form a new regime based on freedom of expression and political organization leading to free elections. Kurdish and other minority rights were also affirmed.[39] Whether this disparate group could hold together and manage a post-Saddam transition is an open question. Kurdish negotiations with the Ba'thist regime for autonomy have already divided the opposition front. However, what is important from the Saudi perspective was Riyadh's willingness to support former opponents in the Iraqi domestic scene, to tolerate calls for free elections from their clients, and to consider Iraqi domestic politics as an issue for cooperation and joint management with its neighbors, not as an arena for unilateral advantage. All these points demonstrate how far Saudi Arabia was willing to go to get rid of Saddam Hussein.

The Saudi support for Iraqi popular forces opposed to Saddam was called into question during the uprisings against the Iraqi regime centered in Shi'a and Kurdish areas in March and April 1991, immediately following the Gulf War. The Saudis seemed hesitant about openly supporting the rebels, probably for fear that Iran would reap the most benefits from the chaos in Iraq. Western news sources implied on occasion that Saudi fears led the United States to withhold support for the rebels.[40]

The evidence that has come to light up to 1993 paints a far more ambiguous picture of the Saudi role during those months. It seems that, while Riyadh was certainly nervous about the prospects of increased Iranian influence in Iraq, it was the Bush administration that took the lead in backing away from the Iraqi rebels.[41] In order to respond to U.S. public opinion, which questioned why, after portraying Saddam Hussein as the equivalent of Hitler, the United States was refusing to support Saddam's people as they rose up against him, administration spokespersons tried to shift the blame to the Saudis. However, a senior member of the staff of the Senate Foreign Relations Committee asserted in a published committee report that Saudi leaders told him that they were willing to support the Iraqi uprisings but that the United States would not.[42] Since that time the Saudis have continued to support the Iraqi opposition coalition, and even sponsored a subsequent (largely unsuccessful) meeting of that group in Riyadh in February 1992.[43] It seems that, given their actions before and after the Iraqi uprisings immediately following the war, the Saudis would have followed a U.S. lead in supporting the Iraqi rebels in order to remove Saddam Hussein from power.

While maintaining its absolute refusal to have any truck with Saddam Hussein, Saudi Arabia has begun, reluctantly and under U.S. pressure, to mend fences with some of the pro-Saddam elements in the Arab world. From the Iraqi invasion of Kuwait through the Gulf War and after, the Saudi media conducted a vitriolic campaign against Jordan's King Hussein and PLO leader Yasser Arafat for what the Saudis saw as their unabashed support for Saddam. Saudi aid to Jordan and the PLO was substantially reduced, if not completely cut off.[44] Saudi Arabia closed its border to Jordanian products and trucks, damaging the Jordanian agricultural and transit sectors which rely heavily on exports to the Gulf. After the war, Saudi Foreign Minister Saud al-

Faisal met in Damascus with Palestinian leaders opposed to Arafat, and the Middle East rumor mill was full of talk that Riyadh wanted to sponsor an alternative Palestinian leadership.[45]

However, as both Jordan and the PLO began to play central roles in the U.S. effort to convene an Arab-Israeli peace conference after the Gulf War, Saudi Arabia slowly began to reestablish ties. On October 17, 1991, Riyadh reopened its border with Jordan, allowing Jordanian products and trucks into the Kingdom again.[46] Prince Saud al-Faisal met on October 23–24 with the PLO's "foreign minister," Faruq al-Qaddumi, during a meeting in Damascus of all Arab foreign ministers involved in the peace process.[47] Though it is unlikely that the Saudis will ever be as enthusiastic in the support for either Arafat or King Hussein in the future, it appears that relations are on the mend.

The same cannot be said of Saudi relations with the one state on the Arabian Peninsula which did not line up on Riyadh's side in the Gulf War—Yemen. Saudi Arabia was caught by surprise when the two former Yemeni states, the Yemen Arab Republic and the People's Democratic Republic of Yemen, decided in May 1990 to merge into the Republic of Yemen. Yemeni unity had been a staple of the rhetoric of their politics for years, but past efforts to achieve it had never been carried through. Saudi Arabia played a role in keeping the two Yemeni states apart, fearing a challenge to its dominance of the peninsula from a united Yemen. The united Yemeni state has a larger citizen population than Saudi Arabia; it is the only republican regime on the Peninsula, and it has outstanding border disputes with Riyadh. No sooner had unity occurred than the Iraqi invasion of Kuwait divided the Arab states. Yemen, which had been allied with Iraq in the short-lived Arab Cooperation Council, refused to follow the Saudi line. Its independent position received much more world attention than would have been expected, as it held the Arab seat on the UN Security Council during that body's deliberations on the crisis.

Saudi Arabia reacted harshly to the Yemeni position. Beginning in late September 1990, the Saudi government enacted new labor regulations governing the Yemeni migrants in the Kingdom. Previously they had been able to enter the country without a visa and to work without an official Saudi sponsor, privileges shared by no other nationality, Arab or foreign. With the new regulations, Yemenis were subject to the same regulations as other workers. As a result, a massive number of Yemenis, returned to their homes, a number estimated to be between 250,000 at the low end and 750,000 at the high end.[48] The economic and social consequences of such a large number of return-

ees have been substantial. Moreover, the Saudi media gave prominent
coverage to Yemeni exiles and tribal groupings in the country who
opposed Yemen's President Ali Abdallah Salih's policy on the Gulf
crisis and his regime more generally, in an effort to weaken his position domestically.[49] Salih attempted to reach out to Riyadh after the
crisis, offering to begin negotiations to settle the outstanding Saudi-
Yemeni border issues, but Riyadh did not respond.[50]

One area where major changes were expected in Saudi policy by
many U.S. observers after the Gulf War was on Arab-Israeli questions.
Previously, the kingdom had been supportive of U.S. initiatives in that
conflict but always behind the scenes. Not only was Riyadh reluctant
to take the lead publicly on peace issues (the Fahd Plan of 1981 was
one exception), but also in public it maintained a strong anti-Israeli
position, expressed tangibly in its adherence to the Arab League boycott of companies doing business with Israel and in its support for the
Palestinian cause. Many Saudis and other Arabs considered the Saudi
oil embargo on the United States during the 1973 Arab-Israeli war the
country's finest hour, and the regime had no desire to put its domestic
and regional legitimacy at risk by making initiatives toward Israel.

Since the war, the Saudis have demonstrated a new willingness to
deal with Israel as a reality in the region. Rumors circulated of Saudi
willingness to drop the economic boycott of Israel in exchange for a
halt to Israeli settlement building in the occupied territories. The
kingdom's ambassador to the United States, Prince Bandar ibn Sultan
ibn Abd al-Aziz Al Saud, was a conspicuous public presence at the
opening session of the Madrid peace talks. Saudi Foreign Minister
Prince Saud al-Faisal represented the kingdom at the multilateral
talks in Moscow in January 1992, despite the Syrian and Palestinian
boycott. Real changes have occurred in the Saudi position. However,
Riyadh has not fulfilled the unrealistic demands of some in the
United States by taking a high profile in the Arab world on the Arab-
Israeli issue or by making unilateral gestures toward Israel. Once
again, Riyadh is playing a role behind the scenes to encourage other
Arab states and the Palestinians to accept U.S. plans on the Arab-
Israeli issue. At the same time, it is avoiding, to the greatest extent
possible, putting itself in the limelight on this issue.

The Financial Picture

At first glance, the Gulf crisis would appear to have been a financial windfall for Saudi Arabia. Making up for the shortfall created

by the removal of Kuwaiti and Iraqi oil from the world market, Saudi oil production increased from 5.6 million barrels per day (BPD) on the day of the Iraqi invasion to 8.7 million BPD by November 1990. Saudi production remained around that level through 1991. Oil prices spiked up sharply at times during the crisis but eventually settled down by 1991 to $20–$23 per barrel, which was still above the level of around $18 per barrel, before the invasion. By 1992, prices had returned to the $18–$20 range. So the Saudis enjoyed both greater production and, for a time, higher prices.

That first impression, however, is deceiving. It does not take into account the costs assumed by Saudi Arabia as a result of the war. Brookings Institution political scientist Yahya Sadowski, who "followed the money" during the Gulf crisis, reports that the Saudis probably experienced a net shortfall of around $10 billion in 1990. The kingdom not only underwrote the in-country costs of the coalition military forces but also made aid commitments to Arab and other regional coalition partners. By August 1991, Sadowski estimates, the kingdom had spent $64 billion on the war and associated costs, including arms purchases commitments, about $36 billion of that in 1991. Saudi planners were hoping that continued high production and stable prices through 1991 would allow them to make up the 1990 deficit and meet 1991 expenses.[51] If we assume that Saudi domestic consumption, including in-country coalition forces use, averaged about 1 million BPD, that prices averaged $21 per barrel through 1991, and that production and shipping costs for the Saudis were about $3 per barrel, Saudi oil revenue for 1991 would have been approximately $50.6 billion.[52] If the regular Saudi government budget for 1991 is approximately the same as that for 1990, about $38 billion, that leaves only around $12 billion for the extra expenses of the war, including the $10 billion shortfall from 1990. In fact, the Saudis went to the international capital markets in February 1991 for the first time since the late 1950s, raising $3.5 billion in loans.[53]

Domestic fiscal stringency does not mean that Saudi Arabia has become a poor country. In fact, the domestic economy will probably be less strained than it was in the mid-1980s, when oil prices fell to $10 per barrel and the kingdom substantially depleted its foreign reserves to maintain the domestic economy and fund the Iraqi war effort against Iran. It does bode ill for prospective foreign aid recipients in the region and for ambitious U.S. plans for the Saudis to fund a regional development bank. In the twelve months following the invasion, the Saudi government reported to the UN secretary-general that it had distributed over $5 billion in aid to countries and refugees as a result of the Gulf War, including $1.79 billion to Egypt, $1.05 billion to Syria, and $1.16 billion to Turkey.[54] The Saudis forgave the debt Egypt owed it, though it is questionable whether any of that would have been repaid. The kingdom also committed $1.5 billion in loans and $1 billion in humanitarian aid to the former Soviet Union, both in thanks for Soviet support in the Gulf crisis and as part of a deal allowing the Saudis to increase their religious and financial presence in the Moslem areas of Soviet Central Asia.[55] These commitments, given the domestic demands on the Saudis, seem to be more on the order of one-time emergency payments rather than pledges of long-term aid. Saudi aid to key Arab allies like Egypt and Syria will continue but probably not at these levels and certainly not at the levels that Cairo and Damascus anticipated at the signing of the Damascus Declaration.

Domestic Issues

King Fahd announced, on March 1, 1992, a series of significant changes in the Saudi domestic political system. For the first time, a set of general guidelines outlining the powers of and limits on the government and the rights and obligations of citizens was issued. This "Basic System of Government" (al-nizam al-'asasi lil-hukm) explicitly reaffirmed that the Qur'an and the Sunna of the Prophet Muhammad remain the "constitution" of the kingdom (Articles 1 and 7), the public position of the royal family for decades. It also reaffirmed shari'a, Islamic law, as the basis for the kingdom's judicial system (Articles 23 and 26). However, the document is clearly intended to serve as a constitution-like source of authority for the state. It establishes that executive authority will reside in the sons and grandsons of the founder of the modern kingdom, King Abd al-Aziz ibn Saud (Article 5); sets out the relationship among the king, the crown price, and the council of ministers (Articles 5, 56–58); and codifies in a general way the role of the judiciary (Articles 44–54).[56]

The Saudi and international press highlighted the guarantees provided in the Basic System for the sanctity of private homes and private communications against intervention or inspection by state authorities, except by due process of law (Articles 37 and 40).[57] The Basic System of Government also guarantees health care to every citizen (Article 31) and the right to private property (Articles 17–18). Equality of citizens under the shari'a (Article 8) and freedom from arbitrary arrest and punishment (Article 38) were mandated. The *majlis* (public meeting) of the king and the crown prince is declared open to any citizen, who can petition there for redress of grievance against the government (Article 43).

The Basic System of Government, like most constitutions, leaves a number of important questions open to interpretation. Nothing is said of the extent of judicial power to review actions of the government. Human rights are guaranteed "according to the Islamic *shari'a*" (Article 26), but it is not clear which executive or judicial body or bodies will authoritatively interpret that clause. No mention is made of any special legal status for members of the royal family, but no explicit statement that the royal family members will be subject to the same legal and judicial processes as commoners was included either. It is clear from the Basic System that the press in the kingdom will remain an organ of the government, subject to its guidance and control (Article 39). How the provisions of the Basic System come to be interpreted and implemented is in many ways more important than their content.

The king also announced a plan to establish a Consultative Council (*majlis al-shura*), to be made up of sixty individuals to be appointed by the monarch. That body will have the right to propose laws and amendments to laws to the cabinet, to review budgets and international agreements, and to question ministers and government officials on policy. Each ministry will have to submit a yearly report to the council, which has the right to review it and make recommendations; likewise the king or his representative will give an annual policy statement to the council. The council will have a four-year term, though the king has the right to dissolve it at any time and appoint another (Article 68 of the Basic System). No member of the government can sit in the council, though it is not clear from the founding document whether membership in the council will be open to royal family members or limited (tacitly or by statute) to commoners.

The council is clearly not a representative legislative body. Its members are appointed. It has no constitutional veto power over government policy. It can only recommend laws and amendments to the government. However, it is an important step in two senses. It guarantees greater transparency in government decision making, as reports must be made to the council and the council can question ministers. It also provides an institutionalized forum for some amount of non-royal family participation in the decision-making process. How the council's relationship to the government and to Saudi society develops will depend upon a number of factors, including the social, regional, and ideological profile of its membership, how they work together, and the precedents set by the government in the next few years in dealing with it. It could develop into a rubber-stamp body like so many Middle Eastern parliaments. It could be the first step toward significant changes in the Saudi political system.

The third of the royal decrees of March 1, 1992, established a system of regional government for the kingdom's fourteen provinces. This decree established greater autonomy for provincial governors (all of whom are currently royal family members) on spending and development priorities in their regions and authorized the establishment of provincial consultative councils on the model of the national Consultative Council.[58]

These three decrees, taken together, are the most important domestic reform program in the kingdom since then Crown Prince Faisal's ten-point modernization program of November 1962. Many of the ideas contained in them have been circulating in the kingdom for decades. On a number of occasions in the past the Saudi leadership had committed itself to developing a basic system of government and establishing a consultative council, only to postpone implementation for "further study." The question presents itself: Why were these changes introduced at this time?

A number of plausible reasons can be suggested. First, the Saudi regime has weathered a number of regional storms in the past thirteen years, giving it confidence in its own stability. The Islamic Revolution in Iran posed a direct challenge to Saudi legitimacy, as Ayatollah Khomeini declared monarchy to be an un-Islamic form of government and called upon Saudi citizens to rebel against their government. The security threats entailed by the Iran-Iraq War of 1980–88 headed the agenda of all the Gulf states during that period. Iraq's invasion of Kuwait was both a military and a political challenge to Saudi Arabia, as Saddam Hussein branded the Saudis traitors to Arabism and Islam and, like Khomeini before him, encouraged Saudis to overthrow the monarchy.

Through all these challenges the Saudis were able to maintain domestic order and at least the passive loyalty of their citizens. The regional order is now much less threatening to the Saudis. Saudi-Iranian relations are the best they have been since the revolution, and Tehran has eschewed its past policies of actively trying to export its revolution to Saudi Arabia. Saddam Hussein has been militarily and politically humbled. Conditions are auspicious for risk taking at the domestic level.

But the ability to ride out these regional storms could have equally convinced the Saudi leadership that no fundamental changes need be made in the political order. The second reason behind the March 1 reforms might then be found in the expressions of domestic discontent that bubbled to the surface in Saudi Arabia during the crisis in Kuwait. Political currents in Saudi society were able to organize more publicly at that time. Various petitions circulated in the kingdom, expressing two general strands of opinion—the liberal and the Islamist.[59] The groups differed on a number of issues, and even where they voiced similar concerns one can imagine that their ideas about implementation would differ markedly. However, it is interesting to note general points on which both currents of opinion agree. Such agreement might represent the best we can discern of a consensus among politically active and involved Saudis.

Both groups expressed their loyalty to the country and to the leadership of the Al Saud family during the crisis. There were no calls for fundamental change in the nature of the regime. However, both expressed support for the king's promise to convene a *Majlis al-shura* (made in an interview in November 1990).[60] The liberal petition called for the reviving of municipal councils, the establishment of provincial and district councils, and the right of corporate groups to organize on the model of the chambers of commerce in the major cities. Neither demanded that these representative institutions be staffed by means of popular election, but these requests do indicate a widespread desire for greater participation in the political process. Both petitions also reflected a desire to curb arbitrary practices in government, in asserting the central role of *shari'a* in the country, in calling for equality of opportunity and treatment of all citizens, regardless of geographical, tribal, or sectarian background, and in requesting a reform of the judiciary.

The decrees of March 1 went some distance, at least on paper, to address these concerns. In that sense, these reforms are a timely effort by the Saudi elite, dealing from a position of domestic strength and regional stability, to reassure its citizens that their loyalty to the regime is being repaid in tangible ways. As mentioned, how these reforms are implemented will be in many ways more important than their announced content in determining how far they have met the expectations of Saudi citizens.

These reforms, and the timing of their announcement, can also be seen as part of the domestic balancing act that the Saudi regime has pursued for the last three decades between two major components of their political constituency—more secular, Western-educated modernizers and those whose education, employment, and ideological orientation are tied up with the Saudi religious establishment and its strict interpretation of Islam. In the immediate aftermath of the crisis, the Saudi regime re-emphasized the Islamic roots of its legitimacy, returning to themes it had used for decades to justify the status quo in the kingdom. King Fahd, in an address to the country on March 5, 1991, soon after the liberation of Kuwait, asserted that the nature and duties of Saudi Arabia and its people are different from any other country, because of its role as protector of the holy places of Mecca and Medina. He went on to say:

> On this basis we will not adopt any principle of social organization
> except those which emerge as beneficial to Islam and to Moslems,
> on the condition that they do not differ from or oppose what God
> has made clear in his almighty Book, and what His gracious
> Prophet, His rightly-guided Caliphs, and the Imams of the Moslems
> have made clear. Therefore we are never interested in any way,
> shape or form with those who want to say that this country is a
> backward country. . . . Why are we backward or underdeveloped?
> Because we hold fast to the Book of God, and the Sunna of his
> Prophet? This is a strength and an honor. We take pride in it. . . . I
> promise before God that the Islamic faith is our basis, our foundation, our starting point. What contradicts it we are not interested in
> and will not follow. We are not concerned by those who want to
> talk about us, be they the great or the small.[61]

These words were given content by the regime's deference to the official Islamic establishment in the period following the crisis. They were permitted to define the terms of the debate on the women's driving issue (discussed below). Islamic political currents also came to dominate the intellectual agenda in the educational sector.[62] It was no surprise that the Saudis tilted in this direction. Despite some grumblings in the religious establishment about the presence of the foreign troops, the kingdom's Islamic authorities supported with *fatwas* both the decision to invite the troops and the decision to attack Iraq.[63] It is clear that these currents represent both a larger and a better organized segment of the Saudi population than the liberals. It is these constituencies that have served as an important basis of the regime since its founding.

However, this tendency to give the Islamic social tendencies freer rein after Desert Storm led to some excesses on the part of the more extreme elements. Sheikh Abd al-Aziz bin Baz, the kingdom's senior religious official, in December 1991, publicly criticized Islamic militants who were using university lectures and the distribution of cassettes to speak out against government policies on women's issues, on economics, and on foreign policy which they saw as un-Islamic. He termed their assertions "lies" and "conspiracies against Islam and Moslems."[64] One prayer leader in a Riyadh mosque was relieved of his duties after harshly condemning the activities of some women's benevolent organizations in the kingdom in which some royal family members were involved.[65] Opposition sources reported a number of arrests in January 1992 of Islamic militants opposed to Saudi policy on Arab-Israeli peace talks and the continuation of what they saw as a banking system based on "usury" (interest).[66] The king personally defended the soundness of the kingdom's policies before a group of senior religious scholars in late January 1992, warning more radical elements against pushing their criticisms too far. He told a meeting of the Saudi Council of Ministers at the same time: "I find [that] with those [with] whom I speak that we are still able to pursue peaceful and level-headed approaches in dealing with certain actions. But if matters exceed their limit, then every action has a response."[67]

The announcement of the Basic System of Government and the plan for the Consultative Council came therefore at a time when the regime was reining in the extremist elements of its Islamist constituency. That led some analysts to see the reforms as part of a decisive turn by the royal family against that constituency and toward more Westernized and secularist elements.[68] It is true that many of the elements of the king's March 1 reform package were meant to appeal to these liberal elements. However, it would be a mistake to see these moves as a decisive choice by the royal family for one section of its constituency over another. The king emphasized in his announcement of the plans that they were in accord with Islam and were animated by Islamic principles. He also stressed that the reforms were not changes in the Saudi political system but rather a codification of trends and practices that have been present for some time.[69] Judgments about the ultimate political effect of these reforms awaits further information on the composition of the Consultative Council and the implementation of the Basic System of Government.

A good example of how the royal family plays this balancing act among the elements of its constituency was the "women's driving issue," which became a cause célèbre in the Western press. In November 1990 forty Saudi women in Riyadh challenged the unwritten law prohibiting women from driving by publicly driving through the streets of the city.[70] Elements in the religious establishment vehemently protested the act. The women drivers lost their jobs (most were teachers in women's schools), had their passports confiscated, and experienced unofficial house arrest for months after the event. The Interior Ministry issued an official ban on driving by women, backed up with a *fatwa* from the kingdom's highest religious authorities to the same effect.[71] In late 1991 King Fahd rehabilitated the women, restoring their passports and their academic positions but without changing the policy.[72] The regime would not be pushed to enter a confrontation with its Islamist constituency over an issue that it did not see as central. Yet at the same time, and in a quiet way, the king eventually worked to shield the women involved in the protest from the wrath of the more extremist religious elements.

Another domestic issue that bears watching for hints of the future direction of politics in the kingdom is that of obligatory military service. As mentioned, a plan to double the size of the Saudi armed forces has been circulating among Saudi decision makers. Assuming that manpower for this plan could be raised only through universal conscription for all young Saudi men, this issue could raise more general questions about the rights and duties of citizens toward their government, the role of citizens in the political process, and the relation of the Saudi state to its society.

The strength of the Saudi regime over time has been remarkable. The analysts who have been forecasting its imminent demise since the 1950s have been proved wrong time and again. It has enormous material resources with which to vest social interests in its continuation and coerce those who oppose it. It has substantial, though not unchallenged, ideological resources in its claim to represent the ideal Islamic state and its role as the protector of the holy places of Islam. These ideological resources have come to be embodied in durable institutions linking the religious establishment to the state. It withstood the challenges of Abd al-Nasser and the Arab nationalists in the 1960s, of Ayatollah Khomeini and the Iranian Revolution in the 1980s, and of Saddam Hussein in 1990–91. The challenges of the 1990s, however, will arise domestically, not from transnational ideological appeals and military pressures from abroad. How the reforms of March 1, 1992, are implemented, and how the regime deals with difficult issues like women's rights and the obligations of citizens to the state, will set the terms of the domestic political debate.

Conclusions

Without denying the important regional consequences of the Gulf War, the overriding emphasis in Saudi foreign policy is one of continuity with the major policy outlines and style of action in place before Iraq invaded Kuwait. Saudi Arabia has not assumed a leading role in regional politics, nor engaged in high-risk policy initiatives. Relations with the United States are closer and more open but not on the level of explicit alliance and a large-scale U.S. presence as one sees in NATO, Japan, Thailand, Australia, or Panama. Rather than ally closely with one regional power or bloc, Riyadh is balancing between Iran and the Egyptian-Syrian alignment. While more willing to be identified with U.S.-sponsored peace initiatives, Saudi Arabia is playing more of a background than a public role, as was the case before. Changes on the domestic level have the potential to be of major import, though their ultimate effect can only be determined over time as it becomes clearer how the March 1, 1992, reforms are implemented.

Notes

1. The Islamic Conference Organization had accepted Saudi-sponsored limits on the size of national delegations to the pilgrimage which were aimed at severely curtailing the size of the Iranian contingent. Rather than accept these limits, the Iranian government chose to boycott the pilgrimage between 1987 and 1990. For an account of Gulf security issues leading up to the Iraq-Kuwait crisis, see F. Gregory Gause, "Gulf Regional Politics," in *Dynamics of Regional Politics: Four Systems on the Indian Ocean Rim*, ed. Howard Wriggins (New York: Columbia University Press, 1992).

2. *New York Times*, November 8, 1990, p. 14.

3. *New York Times*, July 18, 1990, pp. D1, D5; July 25, 1990, p. 8; July 27, 1990, p. 2.

4. *New York Times*, September 21, 1990, p. 1.

5. *New York Times*, October 26, 1990, p. 11.

6. *al-Hayat*, October 22, 1991, p. 1, 7.

7. *New York Times*, October 23, 1990, p. 1; October 27, 1990, p. 4.

8. In a speech to Saudis in early January 1991, King Fahd emphasized the sense of personal betrayal he felt when he heard that Saddam had invaded Kuwait. See the *New York Times*, January 7, 1991, p. 10.

9. The full text of the *fatwa* can be found in *al-Sharq al-Awsat*, August 21, 1990, p. 4.

10. *New York Times*, October 13, 1991, pp. 1, 18; October 25, 1991, p. A9.

11. *al-Hayat*, July 8, 1991, pp. 1, 4; August 28, 1991, pp. 1, 4; August 29, 1991, p. 4.

12. *New York Times*, October 13, 1991, pp. 1, 18.

13. See, for example, the account of remarks against the U.S. presence by Dr. Safar al-Hawali, dean of Islamic studies at 'Um al-Qura University in Mecca in the *New York Times*, November 24, 1990, p. 21. See also the *New York Times*, December 25, 1990, p. 6.

14. The author obtained a copy of this petition from sources in Saudi Arabia. It will be discussed at greater length in the section on domestic politics. An English translation of a version of this petition which was published in the Cairo newspaper *al-Sha'b* can be found in *Foreign Broadcast Information Service: Near East/South Asia* (hereafter *FBIS:NESA*), May 23, 1991, p. 21. Another English language version can be found in the "Makka News," no. 8, June 16, 1991, published by the Information Bureau of the Organization of the Islamic Revolution in the Arabian Peninsula. This group, headquartered in Iran, distributes material in the United States from a post office box in Bowling Green, Kentucky.

15. *al-Sharq al-'Awsat*, November 28, 1990, p. 3.

16. *al-Hayat*, March 14, 1991, p. 1.

17. According to the U.S. Central Command, by the end of October 1991 all but 13,000 U.S. troops had been withdrawn from Saudi Arabia and Kuwait. See the *New York Times*, November 8, 1991, p. A4.

18. *New York Times*, October 25, 1991, p. A9.

19. *al-Sharq al-'Awsat*, March 7, 1991, p. 1.

20. *New York Times*, March 11, 1991, pp. A1, A8.

21. Personal interviews with Saudi and GCC officials, Riyadh, May 1991.

22. See, for example, the statement by Iranian Foreign Minister 'Ali Akbar Velayati immediately after the Damascus Declaration in *al-Sharq al-'Awsat*, March 8, 1991, pp. 1, 4. Velayati traveled to Syria two days after the signing of the declaration to seek clarification of its content.

23. *al-Hayat*, June 26, 1991, pp. 1, 7; June 27, 1991, pp. 1, 7. See also comments on the subject made by Iranian Foreign Minister Velayati in *Kayhan International* (English edition), August 29, 1991, p. 4, and by Egyptian Foreign Minister 'Amr Musa in *al-Hayat*, September 26, 1991, p. 5.

24. 'Abdallah Bishara, the secretary general of the Gulf Cooperation Council, said during the Gulf War, "[Iran] has left behind the songs of revolution for the reality of life. . . . I trust that it [good relations] will be very easy to achieve with today's Iran, a country which understands reality, because we are now entering a period of 'new pragmatism' in the Gulf." See *al-Sharq al-'Awsat*, February 6, 1991, p. 6.

25. *al-Hayat*, June 8, 1991, p. 4.

26. *al-Hayat*, June 25, 1991, p. 4.

27. *Kayhan International* (English edition), August 29, 1991, p. 4.

28. *al-Hayat*, September 29, 1991, pp. 1, 4.

29. *al-Hayat*, June 4, 1991, pp. 1, 7; July 30, 1991, p. 5.

30. *al-Hayat*, June 25, 1991, pp. 1, 7.

31. Egyptian newspapers published this final version of the text in early August 1991. For an English translation, see *FBIS:NESA*, August 7, 1991, pp. 1–2.

32. *al-Hayat*, July 19, 1991, p. 5.

33. *al-Hayat*, June 25, 1991, pp. 1, 7. The final version of the Damascus Declaration states, "In this context, any GCC country has the right to employ the services of Egyptian and Syrian forces on its territories if it so desires": *FBIS:NESA*, August 7, 1991, p. 2.

34. *New York Times*, July 8, 1991, p. 2.

35. Egyptian Foreign Minister 'Amr Musa told an interviewer regarding the Damascus Declaration discussions, "As in any natural difference between any group and any other group of Arab states, I do not deny that there are various points of view, but the important thing is that there be an open discussion among the Damascus Declaration countries which will lead us to an agreed upon document for security, cooperation, coordination and consultation": *al-Hayat*, September 26, 1991, p. 5.

36. *New York Times*, February 22, 1991, p. 8.

37. The Saudi media signaled this switch by beginning to feature news on Iraqi Shi'a organizations. For example, see the following interviews and articles: interview with Muhammad Taqi Mudarrasi, spokesman for the Islamic Action Organization in Iraq, in *al-Sharq al-'Awsat*, March 13, 1991, p. 5; interview with Muwaffiq al-Rubayya', member of the politburo of al-Da'wa party, the oldest Islamic opposition group in Iraq, in *al-Sharq al-'Awsat*, March 6, 1991, p. 5; interview with Hussein al-Sadr, nephew of Ayatollah Muhammad Baqir al-Sadr, who was killed by the Iraqi government in 1980, in *al-Sharg al-'Awsat*, February 11, 1991, p. 6; and a flattering article on Muhammad Baqir al-Hakim, the leader of the Iranian-sponsored Supreme Assembly of the Islamic Revolution in Iraq, in *al-Sharq al-'Awsat*, March 5, 1991, p. 5. See also the *New York Times*, March 5, 1991, p. 11, for an account of Saudi support for the Iraqi Salvation Movement, a coalition of opposition forces including Shi'a groups.

38. *al-Hayat*, June 7, 1991, pp. 1, 7.

39. *al-Hayat*, March 14, 1991, pp. 1, 7; *New York Times*, March 14, 1991, p. A11. For an English translation of the conference's concluding document, see *FBIS:NESA*, March 14, 1991, pp. 1–2.

40. See, for example, the *New York Times*, March 21, 1991, p. 14; March 24, 1991, p. 18.

41. As the popular uprisings against Saddam were raging, *New York Times*

senior correspondent R.W. Apple said in a news analysis story from Riyadh, "Cognizant of Iraq's Shiite [sic] majority, and horrified by the prospect of fundamentalist governments in the two most populated countries bordering on the Gulf, the U.S. concluded, as one ranking official put it, that 'it's far easier to deal with a tame Saddam than with an unknown quantity.'" In the same article, Apple asserts that Saudi Arabia and Egypt wanted to continue the war until Saddam's downfall, but that the United States, Great Britain, and France did not. See the *New York Times*, March 10, 1991, p. 16; March 27, 1991, p. 1.

42. U.S. Senate, Committee on Foreign Relations, "Civil War in Iraq," Staff Report, 102d Cong. 1st sess., 1991, S.Prt. 102–27, pp. 16–17: "Saudi officials proposed that the United States and Saudi Arabia together militarily assist both Shi'a and Kurdish rebels. The Saudis indicated they had only recently developed contacts with the mainstream Iraqi opposition groups, but said they were prepared to support the Shi'a foes of Saddam as well as the Kurds. The Dawa [sic] party has sent Saudi Arabia a message assuring the Kingdom it has no intention of causing problems among the Shi'a in the strategically sensitive Eastern Province, and the Saudis expressly denied that concerns about the Shi'a would affect their plans to assist the rebellion. According to the Saudis, the United States had not even responded to their proposal by the end of March. If a response came later, it was too late to tip the balance in favor of the rebels."

43. *New York Times*, February 25, 1992, p. A6; February 28, 1992, p. A8.

44. As of the end of July 1991, Western diplomats in Jordan said that Saudi Arabia and the other Gulf countries had yet to resume financial aid to that country: *New York Times*, July 30, 1991, p. A8. For various accounts of the Saudi aid cutoff to Jordan and the PLO, see the following *New York Times* stories: September 21, 1990, p. 8; September 30, 1990, p. 21; October 18, 1990, p. 12; November 26, 1990, p. 12; January 13, 1991, p. 12; March 31, 1991, p. 8.

45. *New York Times*, March 8, 1991, p. 8.

46. *al-Hayat*, October 18, 1991, p. 1.

47. *al-Hayat*, October 25, 1991, pp. 1, 4.

48. The figure of 750,000 was cited in the *New York Times*, November 28, 1990, p. 14. An account of the changed Saudi regulations can be found in *al-Hayat*, September 21, 1990, p. 1.

49. See for example accounts of domestic Yemeni opposition to Salih published in the Saudi press: *al-Sharq al-'Awsat*, September 18, 1990, pp. 1, 4; September 21, 1990, p. 2; March 6, 1991, p. 5.

50. Salih's offer was reported in *al-Hayat*, September 18, 1991, p. 1, 4.

51. Yahya Sadowski, "Power, Poverty and Petrodollars: Arab Economies after the Gulf War," *Middle East Report* 170 (May/June 1991), 4–10. See also the *Washington Post*, April 3, 1991, pp. A25, A26.

52. This estimate is general and could be off by perhaps as much as $10 billion in either direction. Factors affecting it would include the distribution

of types of crude exported by the Saudis (higher quality crude fetches a higher price), actual production, domestic consumption and price figures for 1991 (which are not yet available), and long-term contract sales which might not reflect market prices. The estimate is simply an order of magnitude and needs to be checked against actual figures when they are made available.

53. *New York Times*, February 13, 1991, p. 15; Sadowski, "Power, Poverty and Petrodollars," p. 7.

54. *al-Hayat*, September 24, 1991, p. 5.

55. *New York Times*, December 1, 1990, p. 8; October 9, 1991, p. A9.

56. In a separate royal decree, King Fahd reconfirmed his half brother Amir Abdallah ibn Abd al-Aziz Al Saud as crown prince of the kingdom. It is not clear from the text of that decree whether Abdallah's right to immediate succession to the throne was reconfirmed. The Basic System of Government does not guarantee that the crown prince will succeed to the throne. For a text of this decree, see *al-Hayat*, March 2, 1992, pp. 1, 4. The account of the Saudi reforms in the *New York Times* (March 2, 1992, p. A1, A8) implies that Abdallah's right to succession was guaranteed.

57. See the accounts of the king's decrees in the *New York Times*, March 2, 1992, pp. A1, A8; *al Sharq al-'Awsat*, March 2, 1992, p. 1.

58. The text for the three royal decrees, upon which this summary was based, can be found in *al-Sharq al-'Awsat*, March 2, 1992, pp. 4–5. See also the news articles in that edition of the newspaper; *al-Hayat*, March 2, 1992, pp. 1, 4; and the *New York Times*, March 2, 1992, pp. A1, A8.

59. The author examined a number of versions of both the liberal and the Islamist petitions, in Arabic and in English translation. This analysis is based upon versions of the petitions provided by sources in Saudi Arabia. For sources of the Islamist petition, see note 14. An English language version of the liberal petition can be found in *FBIS:NESA*, April 29, 1991, pp. 9–10, and in "Makka News," No. 3, January 26, 1991. An English version of an accompanying amplification of the Islamist petition can be found in *FBIS:NESA*, August 22, 1991 pp. 22–26.

60. *al-Sharq al-'Awsat*, November 9, 1990, pp. 1, 3.

61. The text of the king's speech was published in *al-Sharq al-'Awsat*, March 7, 1991, p. 3. An English language version (different from my translation of this passage) can be found in *FBIS:NESA*, March 6, 1991, pp. 18–22.

62. Personal interviews, Riyadh, May 1991. See also the *New York Times*, November 11, 1991, p. A4.

63. The *New York Times*, January 20, 1991, p. 18, reports on a *fatwa* by Sheikh 'Abdallah bin 'Abd al-'Aziz bin Baz sactioning the offensive against Iraq and terming it a legitimate jihad.

64. *New York Times*, December 31, 1991, pp. A1, A10.

65. *al-Hayat*, January 29, 1992, 1, 4.

66. *Makka News*, vol. 2, no. 1 (February 18, 1992); *Arabia Monitor* (issued

by the International Committee for Human Rights in the Gulf and Arabian Peninsula, a Washington-based group), vol. 1, no. 1 (February 1992).

67. *al-Hayat*, January 28, 1992, p. 1; January 29, 1992, pp. 1, 4.

68. This is the core of the analysis put forward by *New York Times* correspondent Youssef Ibrahim in his reporting on the kingdom. See, for example, *New York Times*, January 1, 1992, p. 3; January 30, 1992, p. A3; February 25, 1992, p. A6; March 2, 1992, pp. A1, A8.

69. See text of the king's speech in *al-Hayat*, March 2, 1992, p. 6.

70. See the following *New York Times* articles: November 7, 1990, p. 1; November 13, 1990, p. 14; November 15, 1990, p. 19; November 18, 1990, p. 16.

71. Eleanor Abdella Doumato, "Women and the Stability of Saudi Arabia," *Middle East Report* 171 (July/August 1991): 34–37.

72. *New York Times*, November 11, 1991, p. A4.

Four

THE EASTERN
MEDITERRANEAN

8

ISRAEL, THE GULF WAR, AND ITS AFTERMATH

Marvin Feuerwerger

Following Israel's national elections in November 1988, the delicate balance between left and right which had marked the National Unity Government of 1984–88 slowly eroded and then disappeared. The religious concerns that drove the initial coalition negotiations assumed a lower profile than expected as Israelis focused their attention on foreign policy issues.

The remarkable transformation that shook the world in the late 1980s had extraordinary effects in Israel as well. The crumbling of the Soviet empire led directly to the highest immigration levels in Israeli history: over 300,000 Soviet Jews entered Israel in 1990–91. The implosion of the Soviet Union also revolutionized Israel's strategic environment. Soviet and East European support for Syria and for other radical states and groups diminished as newly emerging East European democracies halted military assistance and renewed relations with Israel. The changed Soviet approach to the Middle East facilitated U.S.-Soviet cooperation in the peace process, leading to the convening of the Madrid Peace Conference under joint U.S. and Soviet auspices in October 1991.

Of course, the most traumatic event during this period also came from abroad. In August 1990, Iraq conquered Kuwait and threatened order in the entire Middle East. An international coalition, led by the United States with UN Security Council support, defeated Iraqi aggression in a surprisingly short ground campaign following a five-month buildup of forces. But during the preliminary air campaign and in the full-scale war, Iraq launched 39 SCUD missiles at Israel— paralyzing the Israeli economy and reinforcing Israelis' feelings of vulnerability.

The United States deployed Patriot missiles and U.S. soldiers to

Israel, clearly enhancing the credibility of the U.S. commitment to Israel's survival and security. At the same time, U.S. exclusion of Israel from the international coalition opposed to Iraq reinforced the view that the U.S.-Israeli strategic relationship was at a crossroads. Israel's confidence in the United States was further eroded when President George Bush failed to grant Israel's request for $10 billion in loan guarantees for expenses resulting from the immigration of Soviet Jews—apparently linking U.S. aid for Jewish resettlement to Israeli performance in the peace process.

Developments at home failed to match the revolutionary transformation in the international arena. Israel failed to replicate the economic achievements seen under the 1984–88 National Unity Government; instead, the economy muddled through. The Palestinian Intifada accomplished nothing on the ground for the residents of the occupied territories, but neither did it end. Instead, while public demonstrations diminished, Palestinians increasingly used violence against Israelis and against other Palestinians.

The major development on the home front was the replacement of Israel's National Unity Government in 1990 with the most right-leaning government in Israeli history. The center-right Likud remained the main element of the new government, while the leftist Labor party moved to the opposition benches of Israel's Knesset. With the departure of any vestige of Israel's left from the coalition, the new government was forced to rely on virtually all of Israel's religious and far-right parties to govern. Non-Zionist ultraorthodox figures sat as ministers in the new government. They were joined by personalities from the far right of the political spectrum. Led by Prime Minister Yitzhak Shamir, this right-center coalition was entrusted with leading Israel through the political and economic mine fields that characterized the new international order. Despite its inherent fragility (with over ten factions providing a slim six-seat majority), the Shamir government maintained a relatively stable course under Likud leadership through the end of 1991, but Likud policy was to be increasingly questioned during the campaign for the June 23, 1992, Israeli elections.

This chapter will begin by exploring the domestic political context for Israeli policy as it evolved following the 1988 elections, through the formation of a National Unity Government and its collapse. It will then explore Israel's approach to the peace process, first under the National Unity Government and then under the center-right coalition. It will examine the impact of the Gulf War on Israel. Finally, it will discuss developments in U.S.-Israeli relations and some of the longer-term issues facing Israel in the last decade of the twentieth century.

Domestic Political Context

Israel's 1988 national elections produced a near deadlock between the Likud and Labor parties. But the loss of support suffered by the moribund Labor Alignment in 1988 (slipping by four seats in the Knesset)[1] meant that the Left could no longer block Prime Minister Yitzhak Shamir's Likud party from forming its own coalition with right-wing and religious parties.

This reality was not immediately clear in the aftermath of the elections. Despite the fact that Labor had trailed Likud in the polls (by some 24,000 votes), Labor party leader Shimon Peres made an extraordinary effort to block the Likud and bring Labor to power. He adopted a strategy of appealing to Israel's relatively dovish ultraorthodox parties, who had gained a surprising electoral success.[2] In early December 1988 the Labor party signed an agreement with negotiators from the ultraorthodox Agudat Israel party giving the Labor-led center-left coalition 60 seats in the 120-member Knesset—sufficient support to block the Likud from power.[3] As part of the deal, Peres promised within three months to bring the "Who Is a Jew?" legislation favored by Agudat Israel up for consideration by the Labor party.

Peres stood within a hair of enlisting the support of another ultraorthodox party, Degel Hatora, for his coalition and premiership. But Agudat Israel's central committee and Council of Torah Sages refused to ratify the pact with the secular Labor party, and within days both Agudat Israel and Degel Hatora signed coalition agreements with the Likud.[4] These agreements gave the Likud the ability to form a narrow center-right coalition.

But Shamir declined to form such a coalition, which he saw as potentially unstable. He also preferred Labor's Yitzhak Rabin as a potential defense minister to his own Likud party rival, Ariel Sharon. In addition, Shamir was concerned about depending on extremist religious parties who would push for religious legislation such as "Who Is a Jew?" that would isolate Israel from its supporters among world Jewry. Finally, both Likud and Labor were affected by President Ronald Reagan's decision to open a dialogue with the Palestine Liberation Organization (PLO) on December 19, 1988.

Thus, Likud and Labor agreed again to enter a National Unity Government. Each party gained ten cabinet ministries, but—unlike the National Unity Government of 1984—Yitzhak Shamir won the premiership for the full four-year term of the government. Yitzhak Rabin retained the position of defense minister, and Shimon Peres was relegated to the Treasury Ministry and to the largely symbolic position of alternate prime minister. The religious parties, which had seemed ready to seize key positions of influence, became minor partners in the new coalition. And religious legislation, which had dominated the debate within Israel over government formation, was basically set aside.[5]

The 1988 government was, in reality, a partnership between Yitzhak Shamir and Yitzhak Rabin, a marriage of convenience to pursue agreed policies to suppress the Intifada and promote the peace process. When this partnership broke down in 1990 (as discussed below), Shamir felt he had no choice but to anchor his government firmly on the right.

Shamir's decision to move to the right was consistent with the results of Israel's municipal elections of February 28, 1989. For the first time, Likud was able to translate the national success it realized in 1977 into dominance at the local level. The Likud swept Labor from power in such historic strongholds as Beersheba, Ashdod, Petah Tiqva, Holon, and Ramat Gan and scored significant gains in Jerusalem and Haifa. Labor party stalwart Teddy Kollek retained his mayoralty in Jerusalem but lost control of the city council. Haifa's Labor party mayor barely hung on to his seat in the "red" city.[6]

The Labor party did manage to retain control of the Histadrut in the November 1989 elections, a fact that provided encouragement to Labor's leaders.[7] But outside of the Histadrut, the Israeli public expressed support for the right and opposition to Labor in virtually all public opinion polls taken during this period. Had national elections been held during 1990 or 1991, poll data indicated that Labor would have had no chance of wresting power from the Likud unless there were a dramatic transformation in the orientation of the religious parties. While the Likud itself did not improve on its 1988 performance, it held its own and would have been well positioned to lead a new center-right coalition.[8]

It was against this backdrop that Prime Minister Shamir presented a new government to the Knesset in June 1990, following the collapse of the National Unity Government and Shimon Peres' failure to form a Labor-led coalition.[9] Shamir's government had fallen in March when a motion of no-confidence on the peace process passed by a five-vote margin with the support of the ultraorthodox Shas party. Israeli President Haim Herzog gave Shimon Peres the opportunity to form a new government, but Shamir carefully wooed the religious and right-wing parties to his side with promises on issues important to those constituencies.

Shamir's government was the most right-wing in Israeli history, including representatives from all of Israel's right-wing and religious parties—and eventually incorporating MK Rehavam Ze'evi (Gandhi)—who had run on a platform advocating the "transfer" of Arabs from the West Bank and Gaza. The new government's policy guidelines promised to strengthen settlement activity.[10] It was this government that faced the Gulf War and critical peace process issues in 1991.

The Shamir-Rabin Peace Plan

In the wake of the 1988 election campaign, Likud Prime Minister Yitzhak Shamir and Labor Defense Minister Yitzhak Rabin came to an understanding about the course that the new government should follow on the key issue of the peace process. During the election campaign, Rabin had suggested holding elections in the West Bank and Gaza to choose Palestinians to negotiate about the implementation of autonomy under the Camp David Accords. On October 17, 1988, Shimon Peres announced that, if elected, a Labor government would permit Palestinians to elect delegates to participate in talks with Israel.[11] During the campaign, Likud's platform focused on strict adherence to the Camp David Accords and suppression of the Intifada. But the seeds for an initiative had been planted by Rabin's suggestion.

In presenting the National Unity Government to the Knesset in December 1988, Prime Minister Shamir declared that

> In the political-security field, we primarily have to act to promote the peace process. We are not doing this out of weakness or out of fear of pressure. . . .
>
> This government is united in calling the Arab states to enter negotiations with us toward an honorable and viable peace settlement. There is no issue which unites all sectors and communities in our nation more than the desire for peace.[12]

While Shamir claimed to feel no pressure at the time, he had reason to believe that Washington would soon make its weight felt. The November 1988 elections in the United States had brought George Bush to the White House as president and James Baker to Foggy Bottom as secretary of state. Bush had a substantial background in Middle East issues from his previous service as U.S. ambassador to the United Nations, director of Central Intelligence, and vice president. He was also considered far less sympathetic to Israeli concerns than his predecessor, Ronald Reagan.

In an effort to seize the initiative on the peace process, Shamir presented a four-point plan to Bush when he visited the White House on April 6, 1989.[13] Shamir proposed improvement in Egyptian-Israeli relations; state-to-state negotiations for a comprehensive settlement of the Arab-Israeli problem; an international effort to resolve the refugee problem for persons living in Judea, Samaria, and Gaza; and free and democratic elections for representatives from the territories "to conduct negotiations for a transitional period of self-rule."

Shamir's proposal set forth the theme articulated by Rabin and Peres. Rather than waiting for an autonomy agreement before holding elections in the West Bank and Gaza (as had been proposed in the Camp David Accords), the proposal suggested near-term elections to choose those Palestinians who would negotiate the details of the autonomy accord. This approach was viewed favorably in Washington, and Yitzhak Rabin became the key interlocutor between the National Unity Government and the Bush administration on the issue.

However, the Shamir initiative soon ran aground in Washington. While the United States pushed hard to persuade Arabs about the value of pursuing elections in the Palestinian community, it could win no support in the Arab world for negotiations on the second track—of state-to-state negotiations—before progress was made between Israelis and Palestinians. Moreover, the ongoing Intifada led U.S. officials to believe that the most appropriate focus for negotiations was the Israeli-Palestinian track.

However, the Israeli-Palestinian track soon became mired in its own problems. It was clear that Israelis and Palestinians would have to negotiate about the modalities of the elections that would occur in the West Bank and Gaza, but the selection of Palestinians to participate in those preliminary negotiations was itself complex—as it would indicate the nature of "acceptable" Palestinians for subsequent negotiations. The fact that this subject was not only discussed with Israel but with the PLO—either directly in the context of the U.S.-PLO dialogue or indirectly through the Egyptian government—was viewed with alarm and displeasure by Prime Minister Shamir and soured the atmosphere of U.S.-Israeli discussions.

So, too, did the demands that the Palestinians made. It became clear early in the process that Palestinian support would depend on the presence of a deportee and a Jerusalemite on the Palestinian delegation. These demands were adopted by Secretary of State Baker in his approach to the Israeli government.[14] But they raised symbolic, final status issues for Shamir. Inclusion of an expatriate on the delegation would imply Israeli recognition of the Palestinian "right of return". Inclusion of a Jerusalemite would imply Israeli willingness to negotiate about Jerusalem.

Defense Minister Rabin tried to devise compromise positions that could have dodged issues of principle: Israel could, on its own, repatriate a deportee (which it had frequently done in the past), while it could permit a Palestinian with dual residence in Jerusalem and another West Bank city to join the delegation. But Shamir balked at the last minute in the wake of an ill-timed declaration by President Bush that Israeli neighborhoods in East Jerusalem constituted "settlements".[15]

Shamir's position led to the collapse of the National Unity Government, and to a hiatus in the peace process and a freeze in Shamir's relations with the Bush administration. Shamir's new government moved David Levy to the Foreign Ministry, and Levy scheduled a visit to Washington in early August 1990 to explore the chances for revitalizing the Shamir initiative. But just before Levy was to visit Washington, Iraq's Saddam Hussein threw a new wrench into Middle East diplomacy with his August 2 invasion of Kuwait.

The Gulf War

Although Israelis had traditionally stressed the danger posed by Iraq—particularly in the wake of Saddam Hussein's threat to incinerate half of Israel—the Gulf War took Israel by surprise. Most analysts expected that, in the wake of the Iran-Iraq War, Iraq would spend years rebuilding its economy before it could again consider a foreign adventure.

But Saddam Hussein viewed the situation differently. In the wake of the decline of Soviet power, he saw the opportunity to assert Iraq's position as a regional superpower. He marched into Kuwait virtually unopposed and declared it to be an integral part of Iraq.

Most Israelis believed that Saddam would not attack Israel, but the government was not willing to take chances. After a period of debate, the Israeli government distributed gas masks to the civilian population and implemented unparalleled civil defense procedures. Israeli leaders also repeatedly attempted to deter Iraq from attacking Israel by threatening retaliation. On August 9, 1990, Prime Minister Shamir stated that "anyone attempting an attack on Israel will be bringing upon himself a great disaster."[16] On December 28, Defense Minister Moshe Arens said that, "even one missile fired at Tel Aviv or any Iraqi attack on Israel would lead to an Israeli reaction."[17]

But these retaliatory threats did not deter Saddam Hussein from striking Israel. Iraq launched 39 SCUD missiles at Israel and undoubtedly would have fired many more had it not been for the U.S.-led coalition air force attacks on Iraqi missile launchers. At the same time, the United States urged Israel not to retaliate because its participation might shatter the carefully assembled international coalition against Iraq. Instead, the United States dispatched Patriot missiles and U.S. soldiers to help defend Israel against the Iraqi threat.

These developments had a profound effect on Israel. Israel's doctrine had always stressed the requirement for retaliation in dealing with threats to the state. Israel retaliated against Jordan in the years before 1956, against Syria in the years before 1967, and against Palestinians in Lebanon through the 1970s and 1980s. In addition to retaliation, another cardinal principle of Israeli military policy had been the need for self-reliance. Israelis have proudly pointed out over the years that they never asked for troops from foreign countries but were able to handle their military problems alone.

Both of these principles came under assault during the Gulf War. For the first time in its history, Israel was asked to exercise restraint in a situation in which Israeli civilians came under attack. To the surprise of many, Israel eschewed retaliation and relied instead on the United States to deal directly with the threat to Israeli security. Indeed, with respect to the Patriot missile deployment, for the first time in its history Israel relied on foreign soldiers to defend its population. This policy, again surprisingly, won widespread support among the Israeli public.

Understandably, the Gulf War changed the attitudes of many Israelis about security matters. Palestinian and Jordanian support for Saddam Hussein caused a hardening of Israeli attitudes toward Arabs. However, the war also furthered what Asher Arian characterized as the "creeping conciliation" that has been growing in Israel in recent years, leaving 58 percent of Israelis to favor territorial compromise.[18]

The war also heightened extreme changes in the international environment. Arab radicalism lay in ruins with Saddam Hussein's defeat.

The Soviet Union demonstrated both its new approach to international politics—begun in the late 1980s—by its support for the anti-Saddam coalition and its overall international weakness. The United States gained new credibility as the world's only remaining superpower.

These transformations had a number of dramatic effects on Israel. The most obvious was already evident with the changes in the former Communist bloc. East European states had begun to renew relations with Israel in the late 1980s, and the Soviet Union itself moved toward full diplomatic relations with Israel following the establishment of consular level relations in 1989. But the most important change was the opening of Jewish emigration from the Soviet Union that had begun in late 1989. Suddenly, Israel found hundreds of thousands of new, highly educated, skilled immigrants who promised both to solve Israel's demographic problems vis-à-vis the Palestinians within Eretz Yisrael and to revitalize the Israeli economy.

It is difficult to overemphasize the impact this immigration had on the average Israeli. It reemphasized the raison d'être of the state and provided renewed justification for the Zionist enterprise. It opened the possibility that Israel would not have to rely on Arab labor, which had become unreliable during the Intifada. Instead, Russian Jews poured into all sectors of Israeli industry—often replacing Arabs.[19] And it demonstrated the viability of a Jewish state, to which Soviet Jewry decided to immigrate. This morale reinforcement was only heightened by the rescue of the remnant of Ethiopian Jewry in an extraordinary airlift during May 1991.

Resuming the Peace Process

In the immediate aftermath of the Gulf War, President Bush signaled his determination to press forward toward a resolution of the Arab-Israeli dispute. In a joint address to the Congress on March 6, 1991, he stated that

we must work to create new opportunities for peace and stability in the Middle East. . . .

All of us know the depth of bitterness that has made the dispute between Israel and its neighbors so painful and intractable. Yet, in the conflict just concluded, Israel and many of the Arab states have for the first time found themselves confronting the same aggressor. By now, it should be plain to all parties that peacemaking in the

Middle East requires compromise. . . . We must do all that we can
to close the gap between Israel and the Arab states—and between
Israelis and Palestinians.

Bush quickly dispatched Secretary of State Baker to the Middle East
to commence a vigorous U.S. effort to promote a two-track negotiation between Israelis and Arabs. During the summer and fall of 1991
Baker made eight trips to the Middle East and held countless meetings with Middle East leaders in an effort to bring them to the negotiating table.

Israeli leaders were hardly at ease about the Bush-Baker approach.
In the first instance, Bush's strong affirmation that he would press for
an exchange of territory for peace was at odds with the Likud's basic
approach. Second, Baker clearly pointed a finger at Israel's policies in
the West Bank and Gaza when he told a Senate committee that there
was no greater obstacle to peace than Israel's settlements. In addition,
Shamir was less than happy about the projected role for the European
Community and the United Nations in the process.

At the same time, however, the Bush-Baker approach came much
closer to the contours of the original Shamir-Rabin plan than had U.S.
policy in 1989–90. The United States was now clearly pressing for
state-to-state negotiations between Israel and its Arab neighbors. Not
only was the administration pushing for negotiations with Syria, Lebanon and Jordan, but it was insisting that the Gulf Arab states join
multilateral discussions on issues such as arms control, water, refugees, economic cooperation and the environment.

Perhaps most important, the administration was insisting on concrete changes in the Palestinian procedural and substantive position
on negotiations. The standing of the PLO had suffered in the United
States almost from the outset of the stillborn U.S.-PLO dialogue,
which was suspended in June 1990 following an abortive terrorist raid
on Tel Aviv. In the aftermath, the PLO was widely perceived as supporting Saddam Hussein's aggression against Kuwait and suffered re-
versals not only with the United States but with the Arab states that
had joined the international coalition.

The Palestinians had to pay heavily in peace process terms for these
positions. First, the PLO could play no explicit role in the process. Second, the United States accepted Israel's position that no Jerusalemites
or deportees could be on a Palestinian delegation. Third, Baker returned to the Camp David timetable for negotiations on the Palestin-

ian issue—reversing a concession that Secretary of State George Shultz had made in speeding up the negotiations timetable.

Despite these Palestinian concessions, Prime Minister Shamir was ready to reject the U.S. approach until Syria surprisingly accepted it on July 14, 1991. The Syrian acceptance quickly led to a reconsideration in Israel. Israeli public opinion strongly supported attending the conference. Polls in July and August 1991 demonstrated public support at well over 70 percent.[20] And Shamir was able to win decisive support in his cabinet to attend at the Madrid Conference.

At the same time, Israel retained deep reservations about the U.S. position and the dangers posed by negotiations. President Bush's demand to delay the consideration of $10 billion in loan guarantees for the resettlement of Soviet Jews implicitly linked U.S. support for Jewish immigration with Israeli behavior in the peace process. The U.S. insistence on a settlement freeze as part of a negotiations process called into question basic Likud principles.

But despite all of these problems, the Madrid Conference marked a significant departure for Israel. For the first time, Israel sat as an equal at the negotiating table with all of its Arab neighbors. For the first time, Israel engaged in face-to-face political negotiations with Syria and the Palestinians. And for the first time, more distant Arab states from Saudi Arabia to Mauritania signaled their willingness to make peace with Israel if acceptable terms could be found.

Shamir responded to these developments in a cautious manner but without closing doors. His remarks in Madrid broke no new ground except in his direct appeal to the Palestinians to make peace. But he also did not foreclose any negotiating options. He did not characterize the Golan Heights as essential for Israeli security. He did not rule out concessions on settlements or on territorial compromise. And he did not even rule out discussions about Jerusalem. There was no reason to expect that Shamir had altered any of his own positions on these critical issues, but in the new environment created by Madrid a moderate tone seemed the wisest course.

Looking Ahead

Despite the positive developments created by the end of the cold war, the coalition victory in the Gulf War, and the Madrid Conference, Prime Minister Yitzhak Shamir faced difficult challenges in both international and domestic arenas at the end of 1991.

At home, Israel's economy suffered from increased unemployment, stagnating exports, a stifling bureaucracy, and inadequate investment. Soviet Jewish immigration, while welcome on the political and ideological level, threatened to create considerable short-term economic tension because of housing and job shortages. The requirements for reform of the Israeli economy were relatively well understood by most Israeli economists but were difficult to implement in practice.

Abroad, while the prospects for serious post-Madrid negotiations were good, there was little doubt that Israel would come under considerable pressure to modify its negotiating position in significant ways. The United States and Israel's Arab interlocutors demanded a settlements freeze, serious negotiations about the future of the Golan Heights, and far-reaching interim self-government for West Bank and Gazan Palestinians.

In February 1992, with defections of right-wing parties from his government because of their fears of Israeli compromises in the peace process, Shamir decided to advance the date of the scheduled elections from November 1992 to June 23. Assuming no major changes in the political landscape, it would have been reasonable to expect that the Likud and its allies would gain strength in the 1992 elections. This expectation was based on two demographic developments: the changing nature of Israel's population as older pro-Labor voters exited and younger pro-Likud voters entered, and the short-term impact of Soviet Jewish immigration.

In the former case, in every election since 1977 younger voters tended to favor the parties of the right to a larger extent than older voters did. This occurred at a rate of approximately two Knesset seats per election. With respect to Soviet immigrants, early poll data indicated that they tended to lean to the right and were likely to add to the strength of the Likud and its allies.[21] Assuming that more than half of the 350,000 immigrants who had arrived in Israel by the late summer of 1991 would vote in the 1992 Knesset elections, it was reasonable to expect that they would contribute as many as three seats to the Likud and its allies.

Moreover, poll data consistently showed that the Israeli public preferred the Likud party to lead the government in peace process negotiations. While a majority of the Israeli public supported positions much closer to those of the Labor party than Likud, they apparently believed that the Likud was more likely to negotiate an acceptable arrangement.

While all analysis at the end of 1991 indicated that Israel's right-wing government should gain in strength in 1992, no analysis could confidently account for the dramatic transformations that were brought about by a breakdown in negotiations attributable to the Shamir government or to an economic failure blamed on the Likud.

Moreover, Israel's government and public were poised for a crisis as U.S.-Israeli relations deteriorated over peace process issues. The U.S. exclusion of Israel from the international coalition during the Gulf War raised doubts in the minds of many Israelis about the importance of U.S.-Israeli strategic relations. The improved U.S. relations with Syria and other Arab states raised fears about prospective isolation of Israel. And President Bush's approach to the peace process collided directly with that of Prime Minister Shamir.

The 1992 Israeli Elections and Their Aftermath

Israel's electorate carried out a revolution by bringing Yitzhak Rabin and the Labor party back to power in elections held on June 23, 1992. Labor increased its representation in the 120-member Knesset to 44 seats (from 39 in 1988), enabling it to form a coalition government with the leftist Meretz party (12 seats) and the Sephardi ultraorthodox Shas party (6 seats). Labor also enjoyed the tacit support of small Arab-oriented parties and elements of the ultraorthodox Ahdut Hatorah (United Torah party). This combination put the Labor party on the verge of establishing a stable coalition.

While Labor and its allies gathered strength, the Likud virtually collapsed. It fell from 40 seats in 1988 to 32 seats, losing as much support to its right as to its left. The deep divisions in early 1992 within Likud (among David Levy, Yitzhak Shamir, Moshe Arens, and Ariel Sharon) gave the impression that the Likud was unable to solve its own problems, let alone those facing Israel. The public believed that the Likud had brought the country to economic crisis (12 percent unemployment), that it was squandering the opportunity to absorb immigrants from the former Soviet Union (immigration was down about 75 percent from 1991) and was growing increasingly corrupt after fifteen years in power. As a result, the Likud lost support across the spectrum, and particularly among the two groups—young voters and Soviet Jewish immigrants—that had been expected to provide a wide margin for the right. In the most dramatic turnabout, Jews from the former Soviet Union favored Labor over Likud by a margin of four to one.

Rabin interpreted Labor's success as his own personal victory and moved rapidly to consolidate his newfound control. He sped through coalition negotiations, forming his new government far ahead of the statutory deadline. He announced a reordering of Israel's priorities and quickly began to reverse the decade-long increase in Israeli settlement activity in the West Bank and Gaza. Rabin froze new Jewish settlements, canceled about half of the housing projects previously undertaken, and removed incentives that the Likud had created to encourage settlement activity.

Rabin also revealed dramatic changes in Israel's approach to the peace process. While retaining some of the Likud's negotiating team for a time, he promised to accelerate negotiations and offer the Palestinians far-reaching autonomy. He also named a new moderate negotiator, Tel Aviv University Professor Itamar Rabinovich, to head the Israeli negotiating team for bilateral talks with Syria.

Finally, Rabin moved decisively to improve relations with the United States. He welcomed Secretary of State Baker to Jerusalem just days after forming his government and then journeyed to Kennebunkport in August 1992—where President Bush announced support for $10 billion in loan guarantees to help Israel absorb new immigrants. Bush and Rabin also conducted an extensive dialogue on the peace process and U.S.-Israeli strategic cooperation, turning a new page in the U.S.-Israeli special relationship.

In the wake of Rabin's initial efforts, many Israelis expressed a renewed optimism that they had found a government that could begin to address some of Israel's basic problems. Hopes were high that Rabin could move Israel closer to peace with security while bringing about economic reforms. While prediction in the Middle East remains as difficult as ever, there seems little doubt that Rabin will try his utmost to change Israel's basic environment in fundamental ways.

Notes

1. In 1984, the alignment included Israel's Labor party (38) and Mapam (6). Ezer Weizman's Yahad party won 3 seats, and eventually joined the Labor party, making a total of 47. During the coalition negotiations, Mapam left the alignment and stood in the 1988 elections on its own. In 1988, the parties of the former alignment won 43 seats, distributed among Labor (39), Mapam (3), and the Arab Democratic Party (1).

2. For a study of Israel's religious parties in the election and its aftermath, see Robert O. Freedman, "Religion, Politics, and the Israeli Elections of 1988," *Middle East Journal* 43 (Summer 1989): 406–22.

3. Glenn Frankel, "Peres Forms Coalition to Block Bid by Shamir," *Washington Post*, December 2, 1988, p. A29.

4. "Agudat Israel Discusses Agreement with Labor," *Jerusalem Domestic Service in Hebrew*, 0500 GMT, December 2, 1988, cited in *Foreign Broadcast Information Service: Near East/South Asia* (hereafter *FBIS:NESA*) 88–232; "Council of Torah Sages, Degel Hatora Back Shamir," *Jerusalem Domestic Service in English*, 1800 GMT, December 4, 1988, cited in *FBIS:NESA* 88–233.

5. John Kifner, "Two Major Parties Agree in Israel to Form Coalition," *New York Times*, December 30, 1988, p. A1; Asher Arian, "Israel's National Unity Governments and Domestic Politics," in *The Elections in Israel—1988*, ed. Asher Arian and Michal Shamir (Boulder: Westview Press, 1990), pp. 205–22.

6. "Likud Expands Power Base in Local Elections," *Jerusalem Domestic Service*, in English, 0500 GMT, March 1, 1989, cited in *FBIS:NESA* 89-039; Ilan Shehori, "Likud's Second Upheaval," *Ha'aretz* (Hebrew), March 2, 1989, cited in *FBIS:NESA* 89-041.

7. "Labor Wins 55 Percent in Histadrut Elections," *Jerusalem Domestic Service*, in English, 0500 GMT, November 14, 1989, cited in *FBIS:NESA* 89-218.

8. For example, see Hanoch and Rafi Smith, "Likud and Right Riding Crest of Strong Support, Poll Finds," *Jerusalem Post*, July 7, 1991.

9. Jackson Diehl, "Shamir's Government Voted Out by Parliament," *Washington Post*, March 16, 1990, p. A1; Glenn Frankel, "Peres Concedes Apparent Defeat," *Washington Post*, April 26, 1990, p. A25.

10. "Document: The New Government's Policy Guidelines," *The Jerusalem Post*, June 25, 1990, p. 2.

11. See Peres' remarks in *FBIS/NESA*, October 18, 1990.

12. "Shamir Presents New Government to Knesset," *Jerusalem Domestic Service*, in Hebrew, 0836 GMT, December 22, 1988, cited in *FBIS:NESA* 88-246.

13. For an excellent discussion of the initiative, as well as its text, see Harvey Sicherman, "Palestinian Self-Government (Autonomy): Its Past and Its Future," *Policy Papers*, no. 27, (Washington: The Washington Institute for Near East Policy, November 1991).

14. David Makovsky, "Peace Moves: Likud Insists on Labor Vow Not to Bolt," *Jerusalem Post International Edition*, March 10, 1990, p. 1.

15. "Tension Mounting in East Jerusalem," *Jerusalem Post International Edition*, March 17, 1990, p. 1.

16. *Davar* (Hebrew), August 10, 1990.

17. "Arens on Internal Security, Gulf Crisis," *Yediot Aharonot*, December 21, 1990, p. 8, cited in *FBIS:NESA* 90-250.

18. Asher Arian, "Israeli Public Opinion on Security Issues and the Peace Process in the Aftermath of the Gulf War," The Jaffee Center for Strategic Studies, mimeo, April 14, 1991.

19. Sabra Chartrand, "Curfews Lifted, Arabs Find Jobs in Israel Taken," *New York Times*, February 17, 1991, p. A16.

20. "Majority for Positive Response to U.S. Initiative," *Ma'ariv* (Hebrew), July 26, 1991, pp. A1, 2, cited in *FBIS:NESA* 91-144; "86% support gov't decision to go to peace conference in October, according to phone poll in *Ma'ariv*," *Mideast Mirror*, August 9, 1991, p. 6.

21. Yaron London, "The Immigrants Lean to the Right," *Yediot Aharonot* (Hebrew), June 18, 1991, p. 10.

9

THE PALESTINIANS AND THE
IRAQI INVASION OF KUWAIT

Helena Cobban

The attitudes and actions of Palestinians toward the Gulf crisis of 1990–91, including the Gulf War, were heavily shaped by the experiences of their various communities over previous years. These included such developments as Fatah's long-term consecration as the locus of greatest power within the Palestinian Liberation Organization (PLO), the shift of the nationalist movement toward the constituency of Palestinians still resident in their historic homeland (the West Bank and Gaza), the 1987 outbreak and subsequent institutionalization of the Intifada in the occupied territories, the subsequent empowerment of a significant Islamic fundamentalist trend which challenged many of the most long-standing assumptions of the PLO's historic leadership, and the socioeconomic status of communities vulnerable to the downturn in oil prices of the 1980s. However, since most of these phenomena have been described in more detail elsewhere, this chapter will cover only the period from the nineteenth session of the PLO's quasi-parliamentary body, the Palestine National Council (PNC), in November 1988, through the end of 1991.

November 1988–August 1990

In November 1988, PLO Chairman Yasser Arafat convened the PNC to a session, the nineteenth since the PLO's founding twenty-four years earlier, which endorsed major changes in PLO/PNC policy. For the first time ever, the PLO now accepted the 1947 UN resolution calling for the partition of Mandate Palestine into two states, a Palestinian Arab state and a Palestinian Jewish state. In the "Declaration of Palestinian Statehood" adopted at this meeting, the PNC referred to the partition resolution as providing the basis in international law for

Palestinian statehood. Yasser Arafat was elected, by consensus accla-
mation on behalf of PNC members, as president of the putative state.
Accepting the partition resolution also, of course, implied an acceptance of Israeli statehood.[1] (The resolutions of the PNC were accepted
over opposition of the Popular Front for the Liberation of Palestine
[PFLP], but the PFLP's leaders decided not to block their implementation.)

After the PNC meeting, a flurry of indirect contacts between the
PLO leadership and the Reagan administration succeeded in persuad-
ing Yasser Arafat, the following month, to spell out clearly that the
PLO did accept Israel's legitimacy and that it renounced the use of
terrorism. In response to these declarations, the outgoing Reagan team
agreed to open up a formal dialogue with the PLO, in Tunis.

These far-reaching changes in PLO policy represented a victory for
those pro-PLO activists within the occupied areas who had been urging their exiled leaders to take such steps and thus unlock the
political-diplomatic process that might lead to relief from the occupation.[2] However, throughout 1989, it became clear that such diplomacy
as did ensue was far slower, and far less encouraging, than they had
hoped. In April 1989, Israeli Prime Minister Yitzhak Shamir came up
with a proposal for elections for a self-governing authority in the occupied territories. In response to it, and to a counterproposal from
Egyptian President Hosni Mubarak, the new U.S. Secretary of State
James Baker proposed his own plan in November 1989. It called for an
opening round of talks in Cairo between Israeli and Palestinian teams.
Neither the Israelis nor the Palestinians wanted to be the ones to refuse Baker's proposal, but significant differences remained between
these sides both over the makeup of the Palestinian team and over the
basis on which the proposed talks would be held. The prenegotiating
shuttle diplomacy that the United States felt it had to undertake between the two sides thus dragged on throughout 1989 without succeeding in bringing about the start of the hoped-for talks.

Meanwhile, the direct dialogue with the United States that the December 1988 decisions had made possible was proving far from satisfactory for many PLO supporters. The U.S. side, apparently wary of
the campaign against these contacts that continued to simmer in Israel and in the U.S. Congress, kept the whole conduct of the dialogue
well out of the Washington limelight and, despite Palestinian entrea-
ties, refused to raise it officially above the ambassadorial level.[3]
Neither side seemed to treat the dialogue with the seriousness that it

deserved, and most of the real negotiating over the details of the Baker plan was conducted through the mediation of the Egyptian government rather than through the new direct channel of the two sides' respective ambassadors in Tunis.

The outbreak and sustained nature of the Intifada had underlined to all within the Palestinian movement the new centrality of the resident Palestinians. Although the net political effect of the residents' influence on the national leadership was to push it toward making the political concessions embodied in the decisions of late 1988, the mood in the occupied areas became increasingly angry as 1989 dragged on with no immediate reward for these concessions coming into sight. Indeed, by July 1989, it was evident that many intellectuals and activists in the occupied territories had deep reservations about the PLO leadership's continued pursuit of political compromise with the United States.[4] Over the months that followed, it seemed that the net effect of the pressure from the resident Palestinians was to restrain rather than encourage the PLO leadership's shift toward moderation.[5]

Under the circumstances—continuation of Israel's harsh countermeasures against the Intifada and of the spread of settlements in the occupied areas—criticism of the PLO leadership grew fairly rapidly inside the territories. The groups best placed there to take advantage of this new shift in mood were the Islamic groups, primarily Hamas, which had opposed all along the move to signal recognition of Israel. Palestinians inside and outside the occupied territories meanwhile criticized Egypt's pressure on the PLO leadership to make the concessions required by the United States.

By the beginning of 1990, Yasser Arafat was spending an increasing amount of time in Baghdad. It is possible that his major motivation was an attempt to deflect the criticism that continued to mount that he was selling out the Palestinian cause by associating himself with an Arab leader who was voicing increasingly loud denunciations of Israeli and U.S. policy. It is also possible that his increasingly close tie to Iraq was an attempt to try to build up an Iraqi counter to the pressure that Palestinians saw being exerted by Cairo. It may also have simply been the pursuit of the financial support that the PLO needed so urgently, since traditional money flows from governments and Palestinian communities in the Gulf had dried to a trickle after four years of low oil prices. The PLO's now-veteran leader was likely motivated by a combination of such factors. But whatever his motivation, by the middle of March 1990 some of his closest associates in the PLO leadership had become highly critical of what they saw as an unresisted capture of Arafat by Iraqi President Saddam Hussein.[6]

The relationship between leaders of Fatah and of Hussein's Ba'thist party had long been conflictual. The Fatah mainstream in the PLO had first come out in favor of a two-state solution for the Palestinian problem in 1974, and Saddam Hussein and the whole of the pro-Baghdad Ba'th party and its international terror apparatus had opposed such a step. Throughout the rest of the 1970s, pro-Baghdad operatives, led by the shadowy Fatah renegade Abu Nidal, had battled the Fatah security apparatus led by Salah Khalaf in a worldwide "war of the spooks." Many long-time associates and allies of Arafat were brutally killed by Baghdad's operatives in these encounters; they included Said Hammami, Isam Sartawi, and many others around the world, most of them prominent advocates of a more moderate line in Palestinian politics.

After the start of his war against Iran in 1980, Saddam suspended his campaign against the Fatah mainstream and a reconciliation took place. But many who remained in the Fatah leadership could not erase the memory of their comrades who had been slain. Why, Khalaf and other Arafat associates were asking in March 1990, was Yasser Arafat now throwing his lot in with the Iraqi leader?

In May 1990, the frustration of the resident Palestinians increased significantly when a deranged Israeli man opened fire on a group of Palestinians from the West Bank who were waiting in an area near the Israeli town of Rishon LeZion to be hired for day labor. Seven Palestinians died in the slaughter, which sparked a militant outburst from Palestinians everywhere. (Editor's note: The Rishon LeZion incident followed a series of Palestinian Arab terrorist attacks on Israeli Jews.) PLO and Arab diplomats requested that Yasser Arafat be allowed to address an emergency meeting of the UN Security Council. The U.S. administration did not want him to come to New York for this purpose, so the Security Council moved to Geneva for a special session that he could address. When the British proposed a resolution to have the secretary-general send a mission to Israel and the territories to report on the situation, the U.S. ambassador to the United Nations vetoed it. Palestinian frustration with the United States deepened.

Further problems in U.S.-Palestinian relations arose when a group of sea-borne guerrillas was intercepted by the Israelis in coastal waters off Tel Aviv in May 1990. Under interrogation, the captured operatives revealed that they were members of the small, Baghdad-backed Palestinian group known as the Palestinian Liberation Front (PLF). The

PLF held one seat, occupied by its leader Mohammed Abbas (Abul Abbas), on the PLO's fifteen-member Executive Committee. The United States demanded that, if the PLO were to prove its adherence to the December 1988 renunciation of terrorism, then it should expel Abul Abbas from the executive. Arafat resisted these demands (though Khalaf and others urged him to find ways to be flexible). On June 20, 1990, the United States announced the suspension of the dialogue with the PLO.

The major response to this development inside the occupied territories seemed to be an outpouring of anger against the United States. The Unified National Leadership of the Uprising (UNLU), the major coordinating body for the secular nationalist groups inside the territories, had tried hard throughout preceding months to provide guidance that would keep the Intifada focused on the PLO's political goals. On July 5, 1990, however, UNLU's fifty-ninth communiqué ("Call") to its followers, as validated by a broadcast from the PLO's broadcasting station in Sanaa, Yemen, expressed its anger toward the U.S. administration:

> As for the United States' decision to suspend the dialogue with the PLO using the flimsy pretext of the seaborne operation and terrorism, the PLO views it as a consecration of the organic link with Israel which should be in the dock for engaging in the most sophisticated kind of terrorism against our children and elderly in our villages, camps, Nazi-like detention centers, and chambers of torture and interrogation. . . .
>
> The UNLI (UNLU) reconfirms the decision to boycott the emissaries and official envoys of the U.S. administration. It also calls on Palestinian importers to find alternative sources to American goods . . . and urges Arab masses across the Arab homeland to take the initiative and set up popular and parliamentary committees to promote the cause of boycotting all American products.[7]

Thus, by the fateful day in August on which Saddam sent his tanks into Kuwait, Arafat and his associates in the PLO leadership found themselves in a difficult situation. The political strategy into which they had poured so much effort since November 1988 had led virtually nowhere, and even the much desired dialogue with Washington had proved to be a dead end. Meanwhile, on the ground in the occupied territories, the Islamic forces—which had reportedly received considerable financial support from Saudi Arabia over the preceding years—continued to mount the most serious challenge the Fatah leadership had ever seen to its predominant position within the crucial constituency of resident Palestinians.

Palestinian Developments during the Gulf Crisis

In the spring of 1991, after it had become clear that Saddam had been defeated by the United States, Yasser Arafat tried to claim that he had never clearly aligned himself with the Iraqi leader. Rather, he claimed, his intention had been merely to keep open a channel of communication with Saddam in the hope that inter-Arab diplomacy could find a negotiated resolution of the Iraq-Kuwait-Saudi conflict and obviate the need for broader international intervention.

Events, however, moved much faster than the creaking machinery of inter-Arab diplomacy was able to deal with. Within two weeks of Iraq's invasion of Kuwait it was clear that the Saudis had put their trust not in inter-Arab diplomacy but in the strength of the U.S. military to reverse Saddam Hussein's aggression against Kuwait and remove the threat he posed to their militarily vulnerable kingdom. The Saudi authorities refused to let Arafat enter the kingdom in continued pursuit of his mediation effort. At this stage, it should have become clear to him that his stance as a mediator was no longer credible and that his continued visits to Baghdad would be seen by the Saudis and their Arab and international allies as a clear indication of PLO alignment with Baghdad.

The Iraqi invasion of Kuwait provided a severe test of Fatah's traditional policy of avoiding entanglement in inter-Arab disputes. A number of factors favored supporting Iraq. These included the tremendous waves of support that Saddam's militant anti-Israel and anti-West posture engendered in the crucial resident Palestinian constituency. (UNLU's sixty-first communiqué, broadcast from Sanaa on August 31, 1990, warned that "the aggression against our Arab land is taking a new turn these days at the hands of the American soldiers and their allies. The Arab peninsula is falling prey to U.S. invasion.")[8] Additional factors behind Palestinian support for Saddam included the repeated humiliations that Palestinians felt they had met in their attempts to shift toward a political strategy involving major compromises of long-held nationalist goals.

A countervailing set of factors, however, should have militated in favor of supporting Kuwait. These included the weight of the support that Kuwait had given the Palestinian movement since the 1950s—including, most important, its provision of a safe harbor from which

Arafat, Khaled al-Hassan, and others had first incubated the Fatah movement in 1958 and the continued importance of Kuwait's fairly well treated Palestinian community as key financial and ideological supporters of the broader national movement. More fundamental than these pragmatic considerations should have been a basic issue of principle. The PLO was basing its support for Security Council Resolution 242 on the clause in it that stressed "the inadmissibility of the acquisition of territory by force." How, therefore, could it not be at the forefront of the attempt to uphold the same principle with respect to Iraq's "acquisition" of the territory of Kuwait?

Given the strength of these opposing pulls on the PLO leaders' allegiances, it would seem that the traditional Fatah policy of nonentanglement might have provided a workable strategy for minimizing the PLO's losses in the difficult circumstances posed by Saddam's aggression. But such was not to be.

Meanwhile, the international crisis provoked by Saddam's action had eliminated all remaining momentum from U.S.-Palestinian diplomacy. As of late July 1990, many in Washington were awaiting with interest the imminent arrival of David Levy, who had been named Israel's foreign minister after Likud's victory in the March–June 1990 government shake-up had enabled Shamir to dispense with the burden of running a coalition with Labor. Many in Washington had expected that when Levy came to Washington, Secretary Baker might outline to him a U.S. position on the Palestinian issue with some firmness. But that never happened. After Saddam invaded Kuwait, Levy's visit was postponed; when he arrived in Washington in August, most of the discussion concerned Israel's posture in the Gulf crisis, with scant attention, if any, paid to the continuing plight of the Palestinians in the occupied territories. Thus, although it became a shibboleth of U.S. rhetoric after August 1990 that there was "no relationship at all" between the Gulf crisis and the Palestinian issue, in actual practice of U.S. diplomacy there was clear linkage from the beginning—negative linkage, that is.

In October, the Palestinian issue briefly burst again into world headlines when Israeli police opened fire on Palestinians in the Haram al-Sharif in Jerusalem's Old City. (The police claimed that they started shooting only after some of the Palestinians threw stones at Jewish worshippers in the area in front of the Wailing Wall, though this claim was challenged by an independent Israeli inquiry which was published sometime later.)

In January 1991, as the countdown to the expiration of the UN deadline for an Iraqi withdrawal from Kuwait approached, a further blow struck the national movement when Salah Khalaf (Abu Iyad) and Hayel Abdel-Hamid (Abu Hul) were gunned down in the latter's villa in Tunis. The perpetrator, who later gave himself up to the Tunisian authorities, was one of Abdel-Hamid's own bodyguards, thought to be acting under orders from the Iraqi-backed terror group headed by Sabry al-Banna (Abu Nidal).

Khalaf had been one of the first architects of the nationalist movement that was reborn after the Palestinians' first dispersal in 1948. In 1951, he worked alongside Arafat in forming a students' union for Palestinian students in Cairo, which broke important new ground by including within its ranks students from a variety of ideological tendencies. Throughout the 1950s, he continued to organize new cohorts of Palestinians from Gaza and the Gulf into the fledgling movement that gradually took organizational form as Fatah toward the end of the decade. After the Palestinian guerrillas were violently expelled from Jordan in 1970–71, Khalaf was one of the key organizers of the shadowy Black September organization that expressed Palestinian rage against Israeli, Jordanian, and Western targets throughout the world, including the killing of Israeli athletes at the 1972 Munich Olympics. But after the 1973 Arab-Israeli war, he provided critical high-level support to the movement to steer the PLO toward a more political, less violent strategy. Throughout the rest of the decade he and his operatives in the PLO's Unified Security apparatus were at the forefront of the effort to defend that decision against the criticisms and violent attacks of the Iraqi-backed Palestinian hard-liners.

During the PLO's post-1982 exile in Tunis, Khalaf was also at the forefront of efforts to steer the PLO even more firmly toward recognizing the reality of Israel's existence; he worked closely with Mahmoud Abbas (Abu Mazen) to build up links with a range of Israeli personalities and organizations. Throughout 1990, he had been one of the most open critics, within the historic leadership of Fatah, of Arafat's yearlong alignment with Baghdad. Thus, it was assumed by many Palestinians that the orders to kill him had come from the Iraqi leadership.[9]

March–September 1991

During the whole buildup to the Gulf War of 1991, and during the massive engagements of late January and February 1991, the vulnerability of the Palestinians' status as a stateless people (like that of the Kurds) was heavily underlined. They had none of the attributes that were in demand during a world crisis on this scale: no vote in the United Nations, no army that could offer or withhold cooperation, no territory under their control that might have a strategic value. Instead, during the Gulf crisis, two of the Palestinians' key constituencies were subject to new and debilitating hardships.

In August 1990, the Palestinian community in Kuwait was faced with making the difficult choice of whether to collaborate with the Iraqi occupation. A portion of the resident Palestinians did decide to collaborate, and a portion, probably similar in size, decided to work actively with the Kuwaiti nationals' nascent resistance movement. The bulk of the Kuwaiti Palestinians probably sought to avoid alignment either way; but in March 1991, following Kuwait's liberation, nearly all the Palestinians still in Kuwait were irredeemably tainted, in the eyes of the returning Kuwaitis, by their implied association with Arafat's pro-Iraqi stand. Thus, many segments of Kuwaiti society turned against the Palestinians in their midst. A once-proud anchor of Palestinian society in the diaspora was reduced to a fragment. Nearly destitute Palestinians streamed out of the principality, some of their own volition and others expelled by the Kuwaitis. Many of these individuals and families were forced to throw themselves on the charity of family members in Jordan, or even in the occupied territories, who had been the beneficiaries of generous intrafamily aid sent from Kuwait in earlier years.

The Palestinians living in the occupied territories had their own harrowing stories to tell after the war. Most of them had been subject to prolonged, round-the-clock curfews that had lasted the length of the war, with only brief reprieves. As the curfews were lifted, these Palestinians emerged to find that the Israeli authorities were placing tough new restrictions on the number of Palestinians who would be allowed to enter the Israeli labor market. They also found that, for the first time in six or seven years, the Israeli authorities were resuming the habit of expropriating not only some of the occupied areas' vast tracts of "state" lands but some Palestinians' privately owned lands as well.

Many residents of the occupied areas seemed, to many observers, to be shocked by the humiliation on the battlefield of the once-militant Saddam Hussein, but the PLO's national leadership in Tunis moved with remarkable speed to try to limit the damage caused to the national movement by the whole sequence of events during the war.

After the Gulf War the Bush administration also moved with un-

characteristic speed, to follow up its battlefield victory with a renewed focus on Arab-Israeli diplomacy. On March 6, President George
Bush addressed a joint session of Congress in what was undoubtedly,
from the point of view of the popularity polls, his finest hour. Fresh
from the military and political victory that his administration had
just orchestrated, the victor used the unprecedented strength of his
national podium to urge a broad-based attempt to bring about a comprehensive peace among Israel, the Palestinians, and the Arab states.

One significant addition to the Bush administration's earlier round
of Mideast diplomacy was a new insistence that the state-to-state
conflict between Israel and its Arab neighbors should be addressed
along with the Israeli-Palestinian conflict. But Bush's team still insisted that there should be a Palestinian-Israeli dimension to its diplomacy. Within days of Bush's address to Congress, Secretary of State
James Baker set off on what was to be the first of eight trips he would
make to the Middle East during as many months. On that first visit,
he made a point of seeking a meeting, while he was in Jerusalem, with
the generally acknowledged leader of the secular-nationalist Palestinian intellectuals there, Faisal al-Husseini.

If Baker's invitation to Husseini and Palestinian colleagues (including literature professor Hanan Ashrawi) came as a surprise to many in
Israel, then the response of these Jerusalem-based intellectuals came
as a surprise to those who had become accustomed to a degree of foot-
dragging and equivocation in the decision-making of the Palestinian
movement. Husseini and Ashrawi agreed, presumably after consultation with PLO headquarters in Tunis, to meet with Baker. That decision provided a clear contrast to the decision all the Jerusalem-based
intellectuals, including these two, had made in June 1990: They had
declared that, because the United States had vetoed the Security
Council resolution on the Rishon LeZion affair and had broken off
the dialogue with the PLO, they would refuse to meet with any U.S.
officials. Nine months later, with no U.S.-PLO dialogue anywhere in
sight, they agreed to meet with the U.S. secretary of state. The weakness of the Palestinian position in postwar diplomacy was thus clearly
illustrated.

Over the months that followed, Yasser Arafat seemed to have regained the sense of direction that many in the movement feared had
been lost during the regionwide turmoil of the Gulf crisis. During
their first meeting with Baker on March 12, Husseini and his colleagues presented him with a memorandum—doubtless drafted in

close collaboration with Tunis—that spelled out explicitly that "the PLO is our sole legitimate representative." The memorandum also affirmed that "we confirm our commitment to the Palestinian peace initiative and political program as articulated in the 19th PNC of November 1988. . . . Our objective remains to establish the independent Palestinian state on the national soil of Palestine, next to the State of Israel and within the framework of the two-state solution."[10]

As Baker continued his shuttle diplomacy throughout the summer of 1991, he came ever closer to formulating the ground rules for the Mideast-wide peace conference that he sought. Many of the issues that had previously caused contention, including the question of the auspices under which this conference would be held, were overcome when the PLO offered up major new concessions. The issue of how the Palestinians would be represented in the conference was resolved when all sides agreed that they should be folded into a joint Jordanian-Palestinian delegation. The fact that Jordan's King Hussein had also, along with Arafat, been closely identified with the militant Iraqi position during the Gulf crisis made the prospect of a return to his involvement in Palestinian affairs more palatable for the residents of the occupied territories than it had ever been before.

Another, fairly paradoxical outcome of the emotions generated in the occupied territories by the Gulf crisis was that Yasser Arafat's pro-Iraqi position had won him renewed support from resident Palestinians who throughout 1989–90 had been urging him toward greater militancy. The popularity of Hamas in the occupied areas had meanwhile lessened because of its long-standing association, in many minds, with a Saudi monarchy that to many Palestinians had compromised itself by its close alliance with the Western forces. Thus, while anti-Westernism continued to simmer in many parts of the occupied territories, Jerusalem intellectuals were able to continue their prenegotiation diplomacy because of the cover provided for them by Arafat's previous militancy.

In June, Secretary Baker firmed up the administration's plans for the coming negotiations by exchanging letters with each of the proposed participants separately. In these letters he spelled out secret guarantees of what the United States would support during the negotiations. Although the texts of these letters were not revealed during the months that followed, it soon became evident to all the Palestinians that, in at least two important respects, the U.S. position on how they would be represented in the talks was tougher than it had been during the 1989–90 round of U.S. diplomatic activism. In that earlier round of diplomacy the United States had sought to give the Palestinians some support for their long-held positions that their delegates to the opening-round talks should include Palestinians from Jerusalem and from the diaspora (to be achieved, essentially, by finessing the issue by finding delegates who could straddle the categories concerned). This time around, the U.S. position was tougher, and more pro-Likud, on both these issues: Washington insisted that the delegation not include Jerusalemites or diaspora Palestinians at all. This position meant that even such figures as Jerusalemite Faisal Husseini, a key interlocutor for Baker in meetings both in his family's historic hometown and in Washington, would not be permitted to take part in the opening talks with Israel.

In September 1991, when the prospect of the peace talks had been made even more imminent by announcement that the United States intended to start them before the end of October, the East Jerusalem periodical *Al-Bayadir al-Siyasi* conducted a poll of an apparently scientifically selected sample of 1,734 Palestinian residents of the occupied territories. Opinion on whether the Palestinian National Council, the PLO's quasi-parliamentary body, should agree to participate in the proposed peace conference was split almost exactly down the middle: 48.6 percent supported participation, 46.7 percent opposed it.[11] The poll also showed great distrust of the seriousness of the United States: 93.1 percent of respondents answered "no" to the question "Do you trust that [the] U.S. Administration endeavor for peace is serious?"

September–December 1991

During September, Yasser Arafat proceeded with an internal political strategy that seemed to many outsiders to be extremely risky: the convening of another meeting of the PNC—the first since its historic meeting of November 1988—in order to win a mandate for his proposed peace diplomacy. Showing once again the acuteness of his political instincts at the tactical level, Arafat succeeded in winning the mandate he sought. In the process, he strengthened the legitimacy of the negotiating team that the PLO was proposing to send to the talks. But the possibility of causing a serious political split within the Palestinian movement was, perhaps, only postponed, rather than eradicated; there was a 20 percent minority at the PNC which voted against Arafat's plan, and in the weeks that followed two of the PLO's historic constituent groups—the Popular Front for the Liberation of

Palestine and the Democratic Front for the Liberation of Palestine—both moved farther into open opposition against Arafat.

The setting of the twentieth PNC meeting was in Algeria, a country already wracked by Islamic fundamentalist discontent and seriously distracted from its traditional support of the Palestinian nationalist movement by disputes over the arrangements of its forthcoming elections. (To that extent, the situation in Algeria could have provided an unsettling metaphor for Arafat of what might lie ahead for his own secular-nationalist leadership.) In its concluding Political Communiqué, the PNC gave oblique endorsement to the decisions of the preceding PNC session. It judged, however, that the nineteenth PNC's peace initiative had been met with an "Israeli policy of stubbornness and pressure [that] led to the failure of all initiatives and peaceful efforts, bringing them down a dead-end street." The statement also noted, "The PLO has closely monitored the course of events in the world and their effect on the Palestinian question and the Arab-Israeli conflict. If the Palestinian people have had their homeland usurped as a result of the prejudices of the old world order, it is impermissible, according to any logic, that they be denied these rights in a phase witnessing the emergence of the new world order that raises slogans of democracy, human rights, and the sanctity of peoples' right to self-determination."[12]

The document was, as is common with PNC statements, a model of drafting dexterity. In it, there were two separate lists of six items. One was placed in the context that "the PLO . . . believes that the success of the efforts aimed at holding the peace conference requires the continuation of work with the other sides so as to achieve the following foundation. . . ." The other was described as the aims that the PLO seeks to establish.[13] It was notable that neither list was described as containing essential preconditions for the PLO's participation in the talks. Thus, though these two lists enshrined long-held PLO positions on a range of issues, they could not be used to constrain the PLO leadership from entering the talks on the basis they might judge appropriate.

The PNC statement charged the PLO Executive Committee with continuing current efforts to bring about the success of the peace process. But it instructed the committee to submit its decisions on the peace process to the PLO's intermediate level ruling body, the Central Council, "to make a final decision in light of the supreme national interest of our people."[14]

In the middle of October, the Central Council duly met, in Tunis, and some of the differences that had been papered over in Algiers immediately surfaced. Subsequent accounts of the decisions made at the meeting varied greatly. But on October 22, 1991, Nayef Hawatmeh, the secretary general of the DFLP, went public in an interview broadcast on Algerian television in which he accused Yasser Arafat of having acted contrary to decisions that the Central Council had reached on October 18. Hawatmeh claimed that the council had agreed that "the PLO would form and announce its delegation to the peace negotiations and that the negotiating delegation would be from the West Bank, the Gaza Strip, Jerusalem, and the diaspora and would be on equal footing with the other delegations." But, in his view, "the bitter thing that happened, unfortunately, was that this decision of the PLO Central Council has been obliterated. . . . The thing that happened, only three hours after this decision, was completely the opposite."[15] (On November 8, the DFLP was to announce its resignation from the delegation to the peace talks.)[16]

Regardless of the criticisms that their decisions engendered, Arafat and his colleagues in the mainstream Fatah-based leadership of the PLO went ahead with forming a delegation to the peace talks along the lines stipulated by the United States. It was headed by a veteran Gaza physician, Dr. Haidar Abdel-Shafei. Although this Palestinian delegation betrayed no public links with the PLO, many Palestinians noted that Dr. Abdel-Shafei had been on the first Executive Committee of the PLO when the organization had been founded in 1964. And although the PLO, diaspora Palestinians in general, and residents of Jerusalem were all excluded from the delegation, all were represented in the multiple layers of advisory committees that surrounded the official negotiating team.

In his opening statement to the Madrid conference, Dr. Abdel-Shafei underlined most Palestinians' deeply held attitudes toward the issue of national unity and the leadership role of the (excluded) PLO:

The Palestinian people are one, fused by centuries of history in Palestine, bound together by a collective memory of shared sorrows and joys, and sharing a unity of purpose and vision. . . . Yet, an invitation to discuss peace, the peace we all desire and need, comes to only a portion of our people. It ignores our national, historical, and organic unity. We come here wrenched from our sisters and brothers in exile to stand before you as the Palestinians under occupation, although we maintain that each of us represents the rights and interests of the whole.

We have been denied the right to publicly acknowledge our loyalty to our leadership and system of government. But allegiance and loyalty cannot be censored or severed. Our acknowledged leadership is . . . the symbol of our national unity and identity, the guardian of our past, the protector of our present, and the hope of our future. . . .

And Jerusalem, ladies and gentlemen, that city which is not only the soul of Palestine, but the cradle of three world religions, is tangible even in its claimed absence from our midst at this stage.

. . . Jerusalem, the city of peace, has been barred from a peace conference."[17]

Dr. Abdel-Shafei stressed that "the settlements must stop now." He also made a strong appeal directly to the Israelis:

In the name of the Palestinian people, we wish to directly address the Israeli people with whom we have had a prolonged exchange of pain: let us share hope, instead. We are willing to live side by side on the land and the promise of the future. Sharing, however, requires two partners, willing to share as equals. Mutuality and reciprocity must replace domination and hostility. . . . Your security and ours are mutually dependent, as entwined as the fears and nightmares of our children. . . .

We have seen you agonize over the transformation of your sons and daughters into instruments of a blind and violent occupation. And we are sure that at no time did you envisage such a role for the children whom you thought would forge your future. . . . Let us look forward in magnanimity and hope."[18]

The head of the Palestinian team concluded his speech by mentioning "Chairman Arafat" by name, and recalling the words Arafat had used when he addressed the UN General Assembly seventeen years earlier: "Let not the olive branch of peace fall from the hands of the Palestinian people."[19]

Six days later, Dr. Abdel-Shafei's erstwhile colleague in the healing profession, Dr. George Habash, announced that the PFLP, the organization he had headed since its foundation in 1967, would be suspending its representation in the PLO Executive Committee. Habash broadcast his statement on the clandestine "Al-Quds (Jerusalem) Palestinian Arab Radio," which since the beginning of the Intifada had been beamed into the occupied territories from a clandestine transmitter probably located in Syria. "Brothers," Habash told his listeners, "the most painful thing for us is the acceptance by the influential leadership of the PLO of the U.S. plan in full, and its acceptance to form the Palestinian delegation tailored to the condition or the conditions and standards set by the U.S. Administration." The PFLP leader spelled out that his organization, which had a significant following inside the occupied territories, would try to thwart U.S. plans "by escalating the Intifada and all other forms of struggle. On the other hand, we will maintain the PLO as an entity and protect it with all our might because it is our moral home."[20] Habash expressed his hope that the PLO leadership would rectify its position, which would allow the PFLP to rejoin the Executive Committee: "For example, if the bilateral talks continued without stopping the detrimental settlement process, we expect the Palestinian delegation to withdraw. I hope that a person like Dr. Abdel-Shafei will withdraw and stop this farce if the settlement building continues during the next three months."[21]

Habash and Hawatmeh's organizations had both been among the ten Palestinian organizations that had taken part in a meeting held in Tehran in late October. That meeting, which not surprisingly also included Hamas and other Islamic fundamentalist organizations from the Palestinian community, had marked a significant, high-level meeting of the two most hard-line trends in Palestinian society—the fundamentalists and the Christian-led secular pan-Arabists. On November 15, an interviewer for the prestigious Egyptian weekly *Al-Musawwar* asked Arafat whether he believed that the fundamentalists might "make a move in the next stage, as some expect." He replied, "I say they will indeed. They have a right to move when the negotiations and the peace endeavors fail. The United States, Europe, and the entire world must realize that should the peace steps fail, the region will explode. . . . I warn that unless the peace conference reaches a solution, the region will explode. We are not demanding the impossible. We are demanding the implementation of international legitimacy and UN resolutions."[22]

In the interview, Arafat was dismissive about the organizations that had taken part in the Tehran meeting. "There are ten organizations that met in Tehran," he said, "but the fact is they cannot be described as organizations in the true sense of the word. Some of them are just names or small groups, while others have nothing to do with Palestinian activities." (He hurried, however, to add a nod toward the value of internal Palestinian democracy.)[23] Meanwhile, the Palestinian leader was downplaying reports that political differences between Hamas and his supporters had led to clashes inside the occupied territories.

Throughout the late summer and early fall of 1991, tensions between advocates and opponents of the PLO leadership's policy had indeed continued to simmer in the West Bank and Gaza. The major coordinating body that sought to contain the effects of these differences—at least the differences within the secular nationalist camp—continued to be the Unified National Leadership of the Uprising (UNLU). In early October, UNLU's Call Number 75 had carefully avoided coming down definitively for or against the decisions of the September PNC session. Instead, the Call stated somewhat diplomatically that "The 20th session of the PNC has painted an honorable picture of democracy and national Palestinian unity, and a responsible adherence to the Palestinian peace strategy which was approved by the 19th session of the PNC in 1988. . . . The statement of the PNC's 20th session was the outcome of democratic discussions which reflected the various political endeavors regarding the legitimacy of our people, including their right to return, self-determination, and an independent state on their national soil with Jerusalem as its capital."[24]

Call Number 75, like many of its predecessors, made explicit reference to the dangers that this "picture of democracy" might result in a split between the different nationalist factions participating in the Intifada. "Masses of our people!" it warned, "the differences of views in the political process . . . require all the national forces to be committed to the ethics of the national action and the bases of the democratic process." The Call also tried to deal with recurrent problems of vigilante activities by some of the nationalists when it spelled out that "the unified national leadership reaffirms the need not to use masks while dealing with the masses, not to assault citizens or violate the sanctity of homes for whatever reason."[25]

The political tone of Call Number 76, issued on October 25, 1991, seemed closer to expressing criticism of the policies being pursued by the PLO leadership. Although the Madrid Peace Conference was only days away, this Call made no explicit reference to it at all. This fact alone signaled that among the four organizations that traditionally had to sign off on the texts of all the Calls (Fatah, the PFLP, the DFLP, and the PCP, the Palestinian Communist Party), differences remained so deep that the drafters could find no mutually satisfactory way to refer to the event. The Call noted the anniversary of the 1917 Balfour Declaration and asserted the existence of a link "which has existed for a long time, between imperialism and Zionism in Palestine. This link is still in place today and still binds the positions of imperialist powers, America in particular, together with all that is likely to entrench the role of Israel in the region."[26]

One month later, the political position expressed in Call Number 77 was even farther from that espoused by the PLO's exiled leadership: "We, as the Unified Command—the field arm of the PLO—are of the view that halting settlement, dismantling settlements, and placing the occupied territories under the temporary supervision of the U.N. in concert with the withdrawal of occupation in all its aspects and establishments, is the appropriate mechanism for the retrieving of our national rights and the embodiment of our independent state in which our people live in dignity and pride, like the rest of the peoples of the world. The conspiracies of slaughter cannot annihilate six million Palestinians full of the dreams of independence and firm patriotism."[27] This Call also offered explicit "greetings and congratulations to the PFLP on the occasion of the 24th anniversary of its establishment."[28]

Analysis of these three UNLU calls indicates that, despite the evident existence of major policy differences regarding the big diplomatic issues, UNLU continued to embody a working coalition inside the occupied territories between those of the secular nationalist organizations that supported Arafat's diplomacy—Fatah and the PCP—and those that opposed it. However, within that coalition, and throughout those weeks, the expressed opinion seemed to swing away from neutrality on the diplomatic question toward more criticism.

Arafat also came in for criticism for his diplomatic stance from within Fatah's major leading body, the Revolutionary Council. In early December, the council held a meeting that resulted in the broadcasting of a political statement that fell far short of the outright endorsement that Arafat must have sought from his own home base. The statement, as broadcast by the Voice of Palestine from Sanaa, noted in a couple of paragraphs that "Brother Abu-Ammar (Arafat) presented a political report on his decision-making concerning the Madrid conference" and "explained the dimensions of the U.S. connivance with Israel." A brief sentence described the report by Fatah Central Committee member Mahmoud Abbas, one of the major architects of the PLO's shift toward a peace strategy. The statement then reported that "during the general discussion of the political situation, a number of the [Revolutionary] Council members made detailed observations on the various aspects of the Palestinian struggle, emphasizing adherence to the firm national Palestinian principles, our people's unity inside and outside the occupied territories, and their unity of representation." The statement stressed, twice, that "the unity of the masses and the revolution, the unity of the people and the leadership, and the unity of struggling, fighting, and brave arms is our sharpest weapon." "Further, the Israeli enemy," the statement said at one point, "is being continuously encouraged and supported by Washington."[29]

Inside the occupied territories, a second opinion poll was taken in late November. Its results gave a remarkable echo of the views reflected in the September poll. In the new survey, respondents were asked whether they thought the Palestinian delegation should withdraw from the bilateral talks. This time, 48.6 percent replied "yes," 46.7 percent "no."[30] In both polls, it was notable how few of the respondents seemed undecided regarding this issue and also how evenly split the expressed opinions turned out to be. What did these results augur? They indicated that the deep criticism of the peace process that was being voiced by many political activists inside and outside the occupied territories, inside and outside Fatah, was not fully backed by popular opinion. But they also indicated that the few days of enthusiastic support with which the negotiators had been greeted immediately after the opening of the peace talks in Madrid were not reflective of a major trend in favor of the talks, either.

Conclusions

The three-year period from November 1988 through the end of 1991 brought many difficult challenges to the Palestinians. Throughout late 1988 and 1989, a number of factors combined to dampen the enthusiasm engendered by the euphoric early months of the Intifada. The shift toward acceptance of the Partition Plan and the recognition of Israel's right to exist that had occurred during November and December 1988 were viewed by Palestinians everywhere as representing major concessions, which were offered, as they saw it, as a generous down payment for a speedy and successful peace process. Instead of calling forth equivalent generosity from the United States and Israel, however, what happened in the view of many Palestinians was that these two latter parties merely pocketed the PLO's concessions and asked for more. Meanwhile, the start of the rapid migration of hundreds of thousands of Soviet Jews to Israel promised to shift the demographic balance west of the Jordan River against the Palestinians, and the acceleration of settlement building in the West Bank, Gaza, and Greater East Jerusalem threatened to take from under the Palestinians' feet any of the remaining part of their territory for which they hoped to negotiate. In addition, on the international scene, this period witnessed the total implosion of the one great power—the Soviet Union—that many Palestinians had hoped could provide a check to the power of a United States that was viewed as extremely skewed toward support of the government of Israel.

The frustration experienced by many Palestinians, inside and outside the occupied areas, doubtless helps to explain the deep swing in their community's mood during 1989 and early 1990, away from moderation, toward a pro-Saddam Hussein stance. To that extent, Yasser Arafat was probably correct when he claimed that, in aligning with Saddam, he was keeping in touch with grass-roots feeling—although one may justifiably ask a leader to lead rather than merely follow.

The whole experience of the Gulf crisis and the Gulf War brought new difficulties to the Palestinians, this time not only to those still resident in their homeland but also to the 300,000 in Kuwait, which had been one of the most secure bases of Palestinian economic and social activity. During the war, the core of veteran organizers who were the historic leadership of the main nationalist organization, Fatah, was dealt a blow with the killing of Abu Iyad and Abu Hul. Coming less than three years after the assassination of Abu Jihad, and in the context of a serious split between Arafat and Khaled al-Hassan (Abu Said), these killings left the leadership with no major presence capable of balancing the individualistic style of operating that had always been Arafat's hallmark.

Arafat made a serious break with Fatah traditions when he allowed himself to become dragged into the inter-Arab crisis in the Gulf on Iraq's side. Many Palestinians suffered because he did so. But he, and those around him, were lucky (and regained a high degree of good tactical judgment) in that they were able to save their own leadership position in the wake of the Gulf crisis, despite many attempts by the Arab victors to find an alternative Palestinian leadership.

The whole experience of the Gulf crisis did serve the PLO leadership's interests in one respect: it seriously damaged the influence of the Islamic fundamentalist organizations within the Palestinian communities. But even though their major external sources of funding in the Gulf were cut off during the crisis, there was no indication that the damage was permanent. And indeed, the rise of the fundamentalists in Algeria, where secular nationalist leaders had always been important role models for the PLO's secular leaders, could augur a resurgence of fundamentalist influence within Palestinian ranks as well.

In the aftermath of the crisis, the PLO's leadership maneuvered its way through the thickets of internal and external criticism and into the first successful public negotiation between avowedly nationalist Palestinian negotiators and the government of Israel. In early December, the perceptive Israeli strategic analyst Ze'ev Schiff wrote that "the answer to the question of what is the most important achievement of the Intifada to date can be seen in Washington: the beginning of a dialogue between the Palestinians and the representatives of the government led by the Likud and the extreme right-wing parties. . . . It is clear that the Intifada made Shamir et al. recognize the need to talk to the Palestinians. The method of negotiating the fate of the Palestinians with Egypt . . . or with Jordan had been abandoned. Today, the Likud representatives travel to Washington to meet the leaders of the Intifada from the territories, most of whom have served time in our prisons."[31]

The opening of the Palestinian-Israeli negotiations represented an achievement for the Intifada, and, as Schiff noted, the very fact that the Intifada continued after four years of attempts by the Israel Defense Forces to suppress it also constituted a considerable gain. But the opening of the talks also represented an achievement for the Arafat leadership of the PLO, which moved quickly and effectively, after the outcome of the Gulf War was apparent, to regain as much negotiating strength for the Palestinians as would have been humanly possible, under the circumstances.

The conditions under which the PLO entered the talks were not comfortable. For Arafat in particular, the effacement of his own role and of that of the PLO, as insisted on by the United States, left him without personal credit for the series of decisions he made that were an essential precondition for the negotiations to have taken place at all, and that he made at some risk to his own political standing.

Meanwhile, there were signs of considerable political maturity within the secular nationalist movement of which Arafat had long been the doyen. The ability of Fatah and the PFLP to continue to work together inside the occupied territories while they engaged in fierce political polemics at the leadership level in the diaspora stood in considerable contrast to the way these two groups, in particular, had behaved toward each other during periods of political disagreement before the Intifada.

Would the whole effort by the Arafat leadership to win tangible gains for the Palestinians by engaging in negotiations have any more hope of succeeding during the post–Gulf War round of diplomacy than it had during 1989–90? As of the end of 1991, the outlook was not particularly good. The Likud leadership was, as usual, dragging its feet as much as possible on the peace process; the settlements continued to proliferate in the occupied territories; and the Bush administration looked weakened and distracted on the international scene as it went into the presidential election year.

There were already signs by the end of 1991 that if Dr. Abdel-Shafei's team should continue to be incapable of realizing tangible gains for their people, opposition to their engagement in the process might increase as rapidly as it had during 1989. Under these circumstances, the secular-nationalist leadership that had played such a central role in rebuilding the Palestinians' sense of community and purpose over the decades following their tragedy of 1948 might itself become vulnerable to threats from the Islamicists.

Notes

1. Helena Cobban wrote this article in her personal capacity as a researcher. See Helena Cobban, "The Palestinians: From the Hussein-Arafat Agreement to the Intifada", in *The Middle East from the Iran-Contra Affair to the Intifada*, ed. Robert O. Freedman (Syracuse, NY: Syracuse University Press, 1991), pp. 255–59.

2. For more details, see Helena Cobban, "The PLO and the Intifada," in *The Intifada*, ed. Robert O. Freedman (Miami: Florida International University Press, 1991), pp. 70–106.

3. On a couple of occasions, the U.S. diplomat entrusted with the dialogue, Robert Pelletreau, ambassador to Tunisia, did hold informal meetings with Arafat's second-in-command, Salah Khalaf (Abu Iyad). But after these contacts were revealed in the *Washington Post* in July 1989, the administration agreed to accede to requests from Israel and from Congress that they not be continued.

4. This was evident from interviews conducted by the author over six weeks in the occupied areas during this period.

5. A comparison of responses received during July 1989 and March 1990 interviews and conversations in the occupied territories demonstrates this point.

6. Conversations with Salah Khalaf and others in Tunis, March 1990.

7. *Foreign Broadcast Information Service: Near East/South Asia* (hereafter *FBIS:NESA*) 90-130, July 6, 1990, pp. 4–5.

8. *FBIS:NESA* 90-174, September 7, 1990, p. 3.

9. See, for example, the interviews that Khalaf gave to various European and Arab media during the later months of 1990, in *FBIS:NESA* 90-220, November 14, 1990, p. 3; *FBIS:NESA* 90-222, November 16, 1990, p. 4; *FBIS:NESA* 90-249, December 27, 1990, p. 7; and *FBIS:NESA* 91-001, January 2, 1991, p. 4.

10. Text of the Palestinian memorandum as printed in *Mideast Mirror* (London), March 12, 1991, pp. 10–11.

11. See "Gaza, West Bank Poll on Peace Conference," in *FBIS:NESA* 91-196, October 9, 1991, pp. 3–6.

12. "Palestine National Council 20th Session Ends," in *FBIS:NESA* 91-189, September 30, 1991, p. 2.

13. Ibid., pp. 2, 3.

14. Ibid., p. 3.

15. "Hawatamah on PLO 'Participation,'" in *FBIS:NESA* 91-205, October 23, 1991, pp. 15–16.

16. See *FBIS:NESA* 91-217, November 8, 1991, p. 1.

17. "Palestinian delegation head," in *FBIS:NESA* 91-212, November 1, 1991, p. 1.

18. Ibid, p. 2.

19. Ibid, p. 4.

20. "Habash announces withdrawal from PLO body," in *FBIS:NESA* 91-216, November 7, 1991, pp. 10, 11.

21. Ibid, pp. 11–12.

22. "Arafat interviewed on outcome of Madrid talks," in *FBIS:NESA* 91-224, November 20, 1991, p. 5.

23. Ibid.

24. "Algiers VOP airs Intifadah Call No. 75," in *FBIS:NESA* 91-196, October 9, 1991, p. 7.

25. Ibid.

26. "Text of Intifada Call 76," in *FBIS:NESA* 91-209, October 29, 1991, p. 18.

27. "Text of Intifada Call No. 77," in *FBIS:NESA* 91-228, November 26, 1991, p. 4.

28. Ibid, p. 5.

29. "Fatah Revolutionary Council meets, issues statement," in *FBIS:NESA* 91-237, December 10, 1991, pp. 12, 19–20.

30. "West Bank, Gazans polled on talks," in *FBIS:NESA* 91-233, December 4, 1991, p. 10.

31. "Commentary examines Intifada achievements," in *FBIS:NESA* 91-239, December 11, 1991, pp. 49–50.

10

SYRIA SINCE 1988:
FROM CRISIS TO OPPORTUNITY

Alasdair Drysdale

Syria's Middle East policies since 1988 must be understood in the context of Hafiz al-Assad's strategic vision. During the twenty-three years that he has been in power, Assad has been almost entirely preoccupied with formulating an effective strategy for Syria in its struggle with Israel.[1] The fundamental and abiding premise of his foreign policy has been that Syria can neither fight a war with Israel nor negotiate a favorable peace agreement with it from a position of weakness—that is to say, on its own. Almost all of Assad's maneuvering within the region during the past two decades—not just the past two or three years—has been designed to counter Syria's intrinsic weakness by mobilizing whatever compensating external resources are available. More than most rulers in the Middle East, Assad has sought to increase Syria's leverage within the region through key alliances. To Assad, ideology has always been subordinate to pragmatic calculations about where Syria's best interests lay. He has been shrewd and aggressive in pursuing those interests: perhaps no other regime in the region has demonstrated such resolve in protecting its position and such adroitness at navigating its way to center stage to ensure that its interests are accommodated. Through a combination of ruthlessness and acumen in exploiting strategic opportunities, Assad has built Syria into the strongest weak state in the Middle East—a state whose military power and political influence far exceed its population and resource base. Syria's controversial decision to support the U.S.-led coalition against Iraq during the Gulf crisis, and all of its maneuvering since then, must be seen in this light.

The strategic principles anchoring Syria's foreign policy have been remarkably consistent through the years, despite all the tactical twists and turns.[2] First, Assad has always attached the highest priority to building an alliance with Egypt, the Arab world's most influential and powerful state, since such a link offers the most effective way to achieve his goals vis-à-vis Israel. Assad views Syria and Egypt as the twin pillars of the Arab world: when they are aligned, the Arabs are strong; when they are not, the Arabs are weak and vulnerable to outside plots. Immediately after he seized power in 1970, Assad rebuilt ties between the two countries in preparation for the 1973 war to liberate the territories Israel had occupied in 1967. Nonetheless, shortly after the war, relations deteriorated sharply as a result of Egypt's willingness to pursue a separate peace with Israel. Between the mid-1970s and the late 1980s, therefore, the paramount goal of Syria's regional policies was to isolate Egypt within the Arab world and prevent other Arab leaders from following Sadat's lead in cutting a separate deal, thereby leaving Syria isolated and exposed. As recently as June 1988, at an Arab summit in Algiers, Syria worked to postpone discussion of Egypt's readmission to the Arab League.

A second goal of Assad's foreign policy has been to counter Israel's power in the Levant by bringing Lebanon, Jordan, and the Palestinians into Damascus's orbit, either through intimidation or military intervention. This policy, only partly successful, has sometimes been characterized as an irredentist drive to create a "Greater Syria" and restore the Levant's natural unity, which the British and French had sundered.[3] In fact, Assad did not seek to annex Syria's neighbors; rather, he hoped to create a new regional power center that would have more leverage in the Arab world and could challenge Israel more effectively. This policy was pursued most energetically after Egypt and Iraq removed themselves from the military equation, the former by pursuing a separate peace, the latter by getting bogged down in a war against Iran. Assad believed that this left Syria standing alone against Israel. His fear was that Israel might strike Syria through Lebanon or Jordan or, with U.S. encouragement, pressure them to sign separate peace agreements, completing Syria's isolation and neutralization.

Third, Assad has always known that Syria, with its small population and meager resources, could never be a major player in the region without generous external financial help. Thus, he has depended heavily on the resources of the Arab oil-producing states, particularly Saudi Arabia, to bankroll his ambitious political and military goals. Unlike his Ba'thist predecessors, who openly called for the overthrow of the conservative monarchies of the Arabian peninsula, Assad, upon seizing power, immediately set about gaining access to the lavish financial aid he needed to build up Syria's military power and get the economy moving. In return, he stifled his criticism of regimes he actually held in contempt. The relationship was lucrative for Syria but also tenuous because of the immense ideological differences separating a quasi-socialist republic with close ties to the Communist bloc from traditional monarchies that aligned themselves with the capitalist West. Moreover, Saudi Arabia and the Gulf states were always uneasy about the growth of Syrian power and had serious misgivings about some of its policies, particularly in Lebanon and during the Iran-Iraq War.

Fourth, Assad has always recognized the need for superpower backing to overcome Syria's fundamental weakness, particularly in relation to Israel.[4] Until recently, he expertly exploited superpower tensions to Syria's benefit, depending heavily on Soviet military, economic, and diplomatic support to build Syria into a regional power. Without that assistance, Assad could not have built such an impressive military force, nor could he have pursued such an ambitious foreign policy. In return, the Soviet Union gained a key ally in the very heart of the Middle East and an opportunity to widen its influence in the region by demonstrating its political and military support for the Arab position. For almost twenty years, Syria remained one of the Soviet Union's principal points of access in the region.

The Failure of Assad's Regional Policies

By the late 1980s, Syria's regional policies had led it to a dead end, and it found itself almost totally isolated in the Middle East, as well as increasingly unsure of Soviet support. Egypt's ostracism in the Arab world, which Assad had tried to enforce for the best part of a decade, could not be sustained in view of its political and military power, cultural influence, and demographic weight. One by one, and for their own different reasons, the Palestinians, Jordanians, Iraqis, and Saudis reached out to Cairo. In November 1987 the Arab League formally adopted a resolution allowing member states to reestablish diplomatic ties with Egypt. In effect, Egypt's separate peace with Israel had been vindicated, and Syria, once again, found itself in a small minority. Syria's efforts to bring the Levant into its orbit were not much more successful than its campaign to isolate Egypt: Jordan built a durable alliance with Iraq, Syria's main Arab foe; Lebanon, unresponsive to Syrian wishes, descended farther into chaos; and the Palestinians stubbornly resisted Syrian efforts to control them. Syria's support for

Iran against Iraq in the Gulf War aroused the ire of Saudi Arabia and the other Gulf states, which sharply reduced the financial aid they had pledged to Syria as a frontline state following the signing of the Egyptian-Israeli peace treaty. When the aid agreement expired in 1988, the donors did not renew it, leaving Syria mumbling unconvincingly that reducing its dependence on foreign aid was much the best medicine anyway. Equally troubling, the Gulf War ended on terms that allowed Iraq to claim a victory of sorts. For almost a decade, Saddam Hussein, Assad's archrival, had been distracted by war and thus posed little threat to Syrian power in the region.[5] Now, the Iraqi leader emerged as a hero of the Arab masses. With its immense oil wealth, relatively advanced technological and human resources, and apparently formidable military power, Iraq also presented itself anew as the champion of the Arab cause against Israel. This, too, caused some unease in Syria, which claimed the same role for itself. Furthermore, to punish Assad for supporting Iran in the Gulf War, Saddam Hussein turned his attention westward to Lebanon, which Assad considered to be his sphere of influence, and offered support to Michel Aoun, the renegade Maronite officer who openly challenged the Syrian presence. The formation of the Arab Cooperation Council, which created an Egyptian–Jordanian–Iraqi–North Yemeni axis, heightened Syria's growing sense of isolation and peripheralization. By virtue of its location, Syria, the self-described "beating heart of Arabism," also found itself shut out of the Gulf Cooperation Council (GCC) and the Arab Maghreb Union, the two other Arab regional blocs. In fact, its only real allies in the region were Iran and Libya—hardly the best company. Iraq's ascendance within the region, and Syria's decline, were highlighted at the Arab League summit in Baghdad in May 1990, which Assad, alone in the Arab world, refused to attend. Elsewhere, Syria found itself with even fewer friends. Its alleged support for various terrorist organizations and involvement in an attempt to blow up an Israeli airliner earned it near pariah status in the West. Even more worrisome than all of this, however, was the upheaval in the Eastern bloc, which undercut Syria's position more sharply than any event in the previous two decades.

The Collapse of the Eastern Bloc

The Assad regime has been more adversely affected than any other regime in the Middle East by the end of the cold war, the collapse of communism, and the severe erosion of the former Soviet

Union's global power and preoccupation with its own debilitating problems. With good reason, Assad has felt deeply threatened by these changes. In a speech in May 1990, he warned darkly that "what is coming seems to be more dangerous and far more destructive. And those who do not prepare themselves to counter the approaching deadly monsters will be destroyed by these monsters. . . . There is something new in the world that we must not ignore or neglect."[6]

The profound shift in Soviet global and Middle East policies under President Mikhail Gorbachev seriously undermined Syria's credibility as a regional power. Although both Damascus and Moscow asserted that their friendship remained on solid ground, the Soviet Union made it abundantly clear that the relationship had changed fundamentally and that there were limits to its backing. In April 1987, Gorbachev told Assad during a visit to Moscow that he would not support Syria's quest for strategic parity with Israel, which could not succeed. He also openly urged Assad to seek a political solution to the conflict with Israel, remarking pointedly that "the reliance on military force in settling the Arab-Israeli conflict has completely lost its credibility."[7] This message was reinforced on many subsequent occasions. In February 1989, Eduard Shevardnadze, the Soviet foreign minister, delivered a key speech in Cairo in which he castigated the parties involved in the Middle East conflict for their "distorted ideas and hypertrophied emotions." Noting that the Middle East is a "museum of lost civilizations," he warned that without a peaceful solution to the conflict and an end to the arms race in the region, "future archaeologists will find yet another layer of buried civilization." The rest of the world was changing rapidly, he added, but in the Middle East "many think as before, that everything can be solved with the help of arms."[8] Since Syria obtained virtually all of its arms from the Soviet Union—an estimated $14 billion worth between 1982 and 1989—and its reputation as a regional power rested in part on the continued flow of these weapons, Moscow's suggestion that it might restrict arms supplies, or insist on full payment, caused profound alarm in Damascus. In September 1989, the Soviet ambassador to Damascus stated during a news conference that Syria's requests for military assistance for the next five years were being "scrutinized critically" and that "if there are any changes, they will be in favor of reductions" because "the Syrian government's ability to pay is not unlimited." In the past, he noted pointedly, Syria had paid for its weapons "maybe not to the full extent."[9] While the Soviet Union made it clear that it opposed Syria's goal of achieving strategic parity with Israel, it was willing to support a doctrine of "reasonable defensive sufficiency," providing Syria with the means to deter Israel from attacking. Thus, Moscow has indicated that it will not support any Syrian attempt to reclaim the Golan Heights through military action. In practical terms, Syria had lost its military option.

The Soviet Union's steadily improving relations with Israel under Gorbachev also caused much concern in Damascus and underlined how irrelevant some of Assad's most durable assumptions about the world had become. Assad had had absolutely no doubt about whose side the Soviet Union was on: in 1967 it had severed diplomatic ties with Israel, while Syria became one of its most favored allies. During Assad's visit to Moscow in April 1987, however, Gorbachev made a point of saying publicly that the absence of diplomatic relations between the Soviet Union and Israel was "abnormal." In effect, Gorbachev concluded that the Middle East would no longer be a zone of superpower confrontation and that the Soviet Union could win more influence in the world if it presented itself as a peacemaker. Improving relations with Israel was essential if it was to play such a constructive role. Subsequently, numerous high-level contacts occurred between the two countries: meetings between Shevardnadze and Israel's Foreign Minister, Moshe Arens, in Cairo in February 1989, between Gorbachev and the Israeli ministers of finance and science in Moscow in September 1990, and between Shevardnadze and Prime Minister Yitzhak Shamir in Washington in December 1990. Moscow agreed to reestablish consular ties in September 1990 and permitted the resumption of direct airline flights to Tel Aviv in October 1990. Full diplomatic relations were restored in October 1991, following Israel's agreement to attend a superpower-sponsored peace conference in Madrid.[10]

A particularly sore point for the Assad regime was Moscow's easing of emigration restrictions for Soviet citizens, which resulted in a massive influx of Soviet Jews into Israel. Whereas only 2,300 Soviet Jews entered Israel in 1988, approximately 181,000 did so in 1990, and as many as 400,000 more were expected in the two or three years following. Syria felt betrayed: here was its patron and ally supplying its foremost adversary with the demographic means to consolidate its control over occupied Arab territories and with the opportunity to widen farther its technological superiority over its neighbors. This was Assad's worst nightmare: one superpower supplied Israel with money and arms, the other provided it with people.

The collapse of the Communist regimes of Eastern Europe also had far-reaching consequences for Syria. Since the mid-1950s, these regimes had been supporters of the Arab cause, providing arms, diplomatic support, and economic and technical assistance. The creation of multiparty democracies in Eastern Europe was accompanied by a strong urge to renounce the friendships cultivated by the old regimes, particularly those with regimes that resembled the ones they had just repudiated. All of the Eastern European countries restored diplomatic relations with Israel, leaving Syria stunned and anxious. Assad, in a March 1990 speech commemorating the Ba'thist revolution, complained that Israel had been "the main beneficiary among all world nations from the international changes which have taken place." The Zionists, he said, were "active everywhere." Had anyone predicted ten years previously that Israel would have achieved such success in the socialist bloc countries, "we would have expressed our astonishment and utter rejection of such a possibility." He lamented, "How different is the situation today from yesterday."[11]

A Change of Direction

By the late 1980s, Syria's regional isolation and concerns about the reliability of Soviet support compelled the Assad regime to review its policies. One important outcome of this reassessment was the resumption of diplomatic ties with Egypt in late 1989. Assad sealed the reconciliation in July 1990 when he visited Cairo for the first time in almost fourteen years. The rapprochement signaled a major geopolitical realignment within the Arab world. The fact that it occurred entirely on Egypt's terms was enormously significant and could only be construed as a defeat for Assad's policy of tactical rejectionism and a sign that he was ready to explore new approaches to resolving the dispute with Israel. Evidently Assad calculated that involving Egypt on Syria's behalf would strengthen his hand in the peace process and open the door to improved relations with the United States. He also hoped that an alliance with Egypt would counter growing Iraqi power following the end of the Iran-Iraq War.

Assad was genuinely dismayed by Iraq's invasion of Kuwait in August 1990. Syrian media lambasted Saddam Hussein for providing the West with a pretext for massive intervention in the region, dissipating Arab energies, and squandering resources that could be used more profitably against Israel. At the same time, the invasion could not have come at a more fortuitous time for the Assad regime, providing it with a serendipitous opportunity to maneuver its way back to the center of things, consolidate its relationship with Egypt, ingratiate itself with Saudi Arabia and the Gulf sheikhdoms, punish its archrival, demonstrate its importance within the region to the West, and win the favor of the United States. In a world where Saddam Hussein was not much loved, Assad's credentials as an opponent of the Iraqi regime looked impeccable (even if to many outside the region the two seemed to have much in common). Most important, Assad correctly calculated that after the Gulf crisis had been resolved, the United States would face tremendous international pressure to turn its attention to solving the Arab-Israeli conflict.

Although the regime's stance in the crisis was risky and unpopular among many Syrians, the payoff for Assad was enormous and immediate and enabled him to reverse Syria's marginalization within the region with minimal effort. Syria's role in providing legitimating Arab nationalist cover for Western intervention in the Gulf was deemed so crucial that Assad calculated Washington would not stand in the way if he seized the opportunity to crush Michel Aoun's forces and consolidate Syrian influence in Lebanon. Jordan and the PLO, which had both sought Iraq's help in their efforts to avoid being drawn into Damascus's orbit, found themselves even more vulnerable to Syrian pressure, at least initially. With the destruction of Iraq's military power, Syria was once again the foremost Arab power in the Levant. After the war Syria and the PLO moved to mend their relations, although at the Madrid Peace Conference the much-weakened Palestinians showed more flexibility than anyone else and demonstrated their determination not to submit to Syrian pressure.

Syria also reaped immediate financial benefits for its stand during the crisis, receiving as much as $2 billion in windfall aid from Saudi Arabia and the Gulf states at a time when its economy was in difficulty and Soviet assistance could no longer be assured. The establishment of an Egyptian-Syrian-GCC bloc in response to the Gulf crisis triggered talk about the birth of a new Arab order in which moderate regimes would dominate the region and the marriage of the Arabian Peninsula's oil wealth with Egyptian and Syrian military power and political influence would create a new framework for stability and security and an opportunity to reduce the gap between Arab haves and have-nots. The March 6, 1991, Damascus Declaration gave formal expression to the alliance and signaled the so-called Group of Eight's intent to create a more permanent alliance following the war's conclusion. According to the pact, an Arab peacekeeping force would ensure the future security of the Gulf states. In return for their contributions to the force, Syria and Egypt would receive sharply increased financial assistance from the GCC states. But the Damascus Declaration was not the harbinger of a new Arab order, and each of those involved in the alliance had its own reasons to keep a certain distance from the others. There was little chance that the Gulf states would consent to a large Egyptian or Syrian military presence, especially when the need for such a deployment seemed less obvious. Nevertheless, the reconfiguration of the regional system as a result of the Gulf crisis created a political landscape far more congenial to Damascus.

Syria's participation in the anti-Iraq coalition was richly rewarded internationally: Britain resumed diplomatic ties, the European Community lifted economic sanctions, and, most important, relations with the United States warmed appreciably. Significantly, Assad met President Bush in Geneva in November 1990—his first meeting with a U.S. President in thirteen years—and the United States made Syria a focal point of its efforts to get the peace process moving after the war. Secretary of State Baker became a frequent visitor to Damascus, trying to find a way to get Syria to the negotiating table with Israel. On June 1, 1991, Bush sent letters to Syria and the other parties involved in the dispute outlining his proposals for convening a Middle East peace conference. On July 14, 1991, after six weeks of deliberation and intense consultation with Egypt, Saudi Arabia, Jordan, and the Palestinians, Assad characterized the U.S. proposals as "positive" and "constructive" and agreed that Syria would attend an international peace conference and open direct bilateral talks with Israel. In agreeing to the U.S. proposals, Assad showed new flexibility on a number of procedural points. Most important, he agreed to attend an international conference that bore little resemblance to the one he had long insisted upon: it did not involve the United Nations in any meaningful way, it was largely ceremonial in nature, and there were no workable provisions to reconvene it after the brief opening session. Indeed, the Palestinians accepted far less than had been offered to them at Camp David, which Assad had bitterly denounced for over a decade. In effect, Assad agreed to open separate and direct bilateral talks with Israel with only minimal international cover. He did so in large part because he believed that, in the wake of the Gulf War, the United States was serious about achieving a comprehensive settlement on all fronts, including the Golan Heights, based on UN Resolutions 242 and 338, as Bush stated in a speech before the U.S. Congress on March 6, 1991.

Whereas previous U.S. administrations had effectively excluded Syria from the peace process, or at least did not fully involve it, favoring sep- arate agreements between Israel and Egypt, Jordan, and the Palestinians over a comprehensive settlement, the Bush administration engaged Syria as a key participant in its post–Gulf War peace initiative from the outset. Assad also recognized that, with the end of the cold war and the collapse of Soviet power, Washington held all the cards. For Assad, that is what made the difference. He calculated that he had a better opportunity than ever before to recover the Golan Heights through diplomacy (and no chance at all of doing so through military action). At the same time, it is hard to see how he could have decided not to attend a peace conference without antagonizing the United States, the Soviet Union, the European Community, Egypt, and the GCC states and possibly reversing many of the gains he had made as a result of the Gulf crisis. The question that remains unanswered after the Madrid conference and the follow-up meetings in Washington is how long Syria will continue to talk with Israel if the Golan Heights really are nonnegotiable, as many Israelis assert (although one school of thought holds that Assad entered negotiations precisely because he was convinced Israel had no intention of returning the occupied terri- tories and consequently calculated that such talks would be futile). If Syrian-Israeli talks reach an impasse, a distinct possibility, and there is progress on implementing Palestinian autonomy on the West Bank, what will Assad's response be? He has devoted most of Syria's energies since the mid-1970s to fighting separate deals. The possibility that Syria may once again be shut out and marginalized is always at the back of his mind. Although the Syrians (and Lebanese and Palestinians) refused to attend the multilateral talks in Moscow in January 1992 on the grounds that there was no point in discussing regional issues like water until there was progress on a land-for-peace deal, they were un- able to prevent other Arab states from doing so, underlining their loss of leverage within the region. The irony was great: finally, multilateral talks, Syria's longstanding goal, were proceeding in Moscow—for three decades Damascus could not have hoped for a more favorable venue— and the Syrians were unwilling to participate and powerless to stop them.

Syria's Role in Lebanon

Lebanon has variously been described as Assad's Vietnam (by those who contend that Syria has let itself get bogged down there) and his Kuwait (by those who contend that its more powerful neighbor has swallowed it up, albeit with the mother of all bouts of indigestion, in accordance with some grand irredentist imperative). In fact, Syria's goals in Lebanon have been varied and complex since its direct military intervention in 1976. Assad clearly considers Lebanon part of historic Syria: the Lebanese and Syrians "are one single people, one single nation. . . . The feeling of kinship . . . runs deeper than it does between states in the United States."[12] In this respect, he reflects the views of most Syrians (although not most Lebanese). However, Assad views Lebanon primarily in strategic, not irredentist, terms, and considers it a buffer between Syrian and Israeli power, a "sisterly" country that rightfully belongs within Syria's sphere of influence, another front and pressure point in Syria's confrontation with Israel (Assad will not permit guerrilla attacks from Syrian territory, but it has occasionally suited his purposes to activate Palestinian or Shiite surrogates in Lebanon), and a possible Israeli invasion route (an offensive through the Bekaa Valley would outflank Syria's Golan Heights defenses and enable Israeli forces to attack Homs, where all of the key transportation lines in Syria converge). In addition, Assad has sought to contain Lebanon's sectarian strife—even as he has exploited it— and prevent it from spilling over into Syria, hurting his Alawi-dominated regime where it is most vulnerable.

One of Assad's fears has always been that Israel would exploit Lebanon's chaos to expand its power in the Levant at Syria's expense. The Israeli invasion of 1982 confirmed this fear. Thus, Syria spent most of the 1980s trying first to thwart Israel's ambitions by mobilizing the National Salvation Front, a coalition of Moslem militias and leftist parties, against the Israeli presence and then working to reassemble the country under its tutelage, despite strong opposition from the Maronites and a split within the Moslem camp over Assad's treatment of the PLO. As Lebanon's growing fragmentation made it increasingly ungovernable, Syria relied on a "balance of weakness" to maintain its supremacy, playing militias and factions off against one another, using proxies, and cutting down to size anyone who got too strong. Its heavy-handedness and inability to restore order further depleted its political capital with the Lebanese.

Nevertheless, Syria continued to profess that its goal was to assist in the reform and reconstruction of a unified and stable state—no easy task. Its efforts to impose a candidate in the 1988 Lebanese presidential elections were vigorously opposed by the Christians, with the result that Lebanon found itself without a president and divided between two rival governments. This provided an opportunity for General Michel Aoun to challenge Syria's presence in 1989. However, Aoun misjudged his strength and was forced to accept a cease-fire. The challenge set in motion the Arab-mediated Taif Agreement, which proposed many of the reforms Syria had long sought, including a more equitable sectarian distribution of power in Parliament and the cabinet and a reduction in the power of the Maronite president. Syria agreed to withdraw its forces to the Bekaa Valley within two years provided that the authority of the Lebanese government was restored. A pro-Syrian president, Elias Hrawi, was elected, but Aoun rejected the agreement, refused to accept Hrawi's authority, and tried to gain control of the Lebanese Forces militia, setting off bloody internecine fighting among the Maronites. Syria was initially reluctant to move against Aoun for fear that such an offensive might provoke Israeli intervention, win him more support among the Maronites, and undermine the Hrawi government's legitimacy. However, the crisis triggered by Iraq's invasion of Kuwait in August 1990, and Syria's support for the U.S. position, provided Assad with a perfect opportunity to strike. Aoun's defeat left Syria virtually unchallenged in most of Lebanon. Following Aoun's rout, the Hrawi government began to disarm the militias—with the notable exception of Hezbollah—and gradually established its authority over more of the country.

On May 22, 1991, the Syrian and Lebanese governments signed the unequal Treaty of Brotherhood, Cooperation, and Coordination, which effectively confirmed Syria's hegemony and institutionalized its control over Lebanon's foreign and security policies. By the time the Middle East peace process got under way, no one believed that Lebanon was making its own decisions about whether and when to attend talks with Israel. Although most Lebanese resent Syrian hegemony, by 1992 they felt more hopeful than at any time since the beginning of the civil war that the authority of the central government could be restored and Lebanon's problems resolved. Nevertheless, Lebanon's peace is fragile and its problems remain formidable. So long as Israel maintains a security zone in southern Lebanon, Syria will maintain a military presence in eastern Lebanon and Lebanon will remain the most likely flashpoint for a confrontation between Israel and Syria.

The Iranian Connection

One of Assad's most controversial and boldest foreign policies was to align Syria with Iran following the overthrow of the shah in

1979 and back it in its war with Iraq between 1980 and 1988. The alliance placed Syria outside the Arab mainstream and was bitterly criticized throughout the Arab world, as well as within Syria. But Assad saw the connection in strategic terms: an anti-Zionist and anti-imperialist Iran could be an important ally in the struggle with Israel (especially after Egypt broke Arab ranks and pursued a separate peace) and could increase his influence with Lebanon's Shiites. Moreover, the alliance seemed natural in view of Assad's bitter rivalry with Saddam Hussein. In 1982, Syria closed its border with Iraq and blocked the flow of Iraqi oil through the country. In return, Iran provided it with free or low-cost oil and became a major market for Syrian exports. By the mid-1980s, some 200,000 Iranians were visiting Syria each year.

In a region where alliances seldom seem to last long, the Syrian-Iranian friendship has proved to be remarkably durable and flexible, particularly in view of the striking dissimilarities between one of the region's most secular regimes and one of its most theocratic. The two countries have shown an ability to accept their differences and resolve their conflicts, and in that sense the relationship has a certain maturity and functionality. The strains have been numerous. Although Syria supported Iran in the Gulf War, it never wanted to see a fundamentalist Islamic regime in Baghdad. The two countries also have divergent interests in Lebanon, and squabbles between the rival Syrian-supported Amal and Iranian-supported Hezbollah Shiite organizations have been a recurring source of tension between their sponsors.

Syria's resumption of ties with Egypt in December 1989 following the end of the Iran-Iraq War and in response to the collapse of the Eastern bloc was initially opposed by Iran. However, Syria subsequently played a role in mediating a temporary end to the rift between Egypt and Iran, which also sought to reduce its international isolation following the end of its war with Iraq. The crisis brought on by Iraq's invasion of Kuwait added new potential strains to the relationship: although both regimes wished to see Saddam Hussein defeated, Syria seemed more ready to overcome its reservations and accept the deployment of U.S. forces in the region. Significantly, Assad visited Tehran for the first time since the 1979 Iranian revolution in September 1990 to coordinate the two countries' policies during the crisis.

Syria never seriously imagined that its decision to open peace talks with Israel in the wake of the Gulf War would jeopardize its relationship with Iran (Israel was, after all, a major source of weapons for Iran during its war with Iraq). Shortly before the Madrid talks, President

Hashemi Rafsanjani and Ayatollah Ali Khamenei loudly denounced Zionism at the International Conference in Support of the Islamic Revolution of Palestine meeting in Tehran. According to Iranian sources, Iran's foreign minister, Ali Akbar Velyati informed members of the Syrian delegation attending the Tehran conference that the Madrid conference was "obviously unilateral and serve[d] solely the interests of the Zionist regime."[13] Naturally, Damascus Radio's version was somewhat different: it reported Velyati had told the delegation that "we value Syria's stand on the peace conference. Iran is interested in and appreciates this stand."[14]

Prospects for Liberalization

The ease and speed with which the Communist governments of Eastern Europe and the Soviet Union collapsed could not have failed to impress Syria's yearning for political and economic change after almost thirty years of unbroken Ba'thist rule.[15] Moreover, few of the Syrian regime's many critics needed to be reminded of the obvious similarities—not to mention the intimate connections—between the reviled dictatorships of the Eastern bloc and the one whose demise they earnestly wished to see: the ills that Eastern Europeans complained about seemed altogether familiar. Shortly after the overthrow of the Ceausescu regime, which, with its praetorian guards, resembled the Assad regime more closely perhaps than any other in the Eastern bloc, a telling piece of graffiti appeared on the walls of Damascus: It said, quite simply: "Shamsescu" (Sham is the Arabic name for Damascus). Many Syrians allowed themselves to wonder: was the Ba'thist regime just as flimsy? Would political change finally come to Syria also? They did not need to look as far away as Europe for encouragement. A whiff of political liberalization also wafted into Syria from neighboring Jordan, where King Hussein opened up the political system and permitted relatively free elections. Since Jordanian television can be seen in Damascus, many Syrians were well aware of the changes occurring next door. Equally important, in Algeria the National Liberation Front, which had ruled single-handedly since independence in 1962 and faced many of the same criticisms that were leveled at the Ba'th, suffered ignominious defeat in local elections in 1990. How did the Assad regime respond to these changes, which created new pressures for reform in Syria?

The collapse of the Communist regimes of the Eastern bloc clearly

disconcerted the Syrian regime and forced it to look more carefully, if
not completely honestly, at some of its own deficiencies. Even the
most self-deluding and myopic Ba'thists had to entertain the possibility that they might be next on the chopping block. Within the elite,
therefore, there has been much discussion about Syria's future direction. Damascus has been awash in rumors of impending political reform. In 1991, the regime, apparently with no sense of irony, spoke
more frequently about the importance of freedom. Faruq al-Shar'a, the
foreign minister, stated in his address before the UN General Assembly in October 1991 that "the lessons that can be learned" from the
momentous changes in Europe were that "bread and freedom are two
basic needs for the individual and the society; they are inseparable,
and one cannot be sacrificed for the sake of the other."[16] Syrians, who
hunger for both, may justifiably have wondered exactly what he meant.
Shortly afterwards, an editorial in *Tishrin*, a Damascus newspaper,
suggested that "what happened in Eastern Europe and the Soviet Union
has rendered a great service to international socialist thinking" by revealing the "serious defect that has affected some aspects of socialist
practice." It went on to say that social progress and economic growth
could not occur "unless they are based on the principle of economic
and political pluralism. The disappearance of pluralism paralyzes great
capabilities of the community, makes the authority unaware of what is
happening, and separates the political movements from the masses."[17]
Subsequently, in December 1991, the regime announced its intention
to release 2,864 political prisoners, many of whom were Moslem
Brotherhood activists.[18]

Nevertheless, the prospects for genuine political liberalization in
Syria are poor. The Ba'thist regime has been reluctant to relinquish its
tight control over Syria and permit any serious challenge to its authority. Consequently, most of the changes that have occurred have
been minor and mostly superficial. Martial law regulations have been
abolished, but the various intelligence and internal security agencies
remain almost totally unaccountable. A few opposition figures were
invited to return to Syria in early 1990, but the regime's real foes remain imprisoned, underground, or in exile. The regime also permitted
the formation of two minor new political parties, the Nasserite Democratic Arab Party and a moderate Islamic party, but neither has an organized constituency or any credibility as a viable opposition party.
One exiled opponent of the regime dismissed the Islamic party with
the observation that "all its members do not amount to one row of

people lined up for prayer in the Umayyad Mosque." Assad has also pledged to broaden and strengthen the ruling Ba'thist-dominated National Progressive Front (NPF), a loose coalition of like-minded political parties. However, the NPF is little more than a cover for Ba'thist control; non-Ba'thist groups within the front have little real power, their constituencies are diminutive, and they have no right to recruit followers within the armed forces and the universities, which remain the exclusive preserve of the Ba'th. On the surface, the most significant opening up of the political system occurred in the May 1990 elections for the People's Assembly.[19] To increase representation by independents, the number of seats in the legislature was increased from 195 to 250. NPF candidates took 166, or 66 percent, of the contested seats, with the largest bloc—134, or slightly over half—going to the Ba'th. Independents won 84, or 33 percent, of all seats. Nevertheless, they do not constitute an effective, organized opposition which can challenge key government policies; their presence in the legislature should not obscure the fact that real power continues to be heavily concentrated in the hands of a small number of mostly Alawi officers. Despite Assad's assertion that voting had been conducted in a "free and democratic atmosphere," the elections were neither open nor fair.

A significant opening of the political system beyond what has already taken place seems unlikely. Assad has little genuine sympathy for political reform and evidently believes that he can get away with only minor tinkering with the political system: "We are satisfied with [the political system] and we have not built it to be despotic."[20] At times, his language has been Orwellian: "We have been practicing democracy for some time," he once asserted.[21] On another occasion, he claimed that Syria has long enjoyed "a multiparty system and political pluralism." The official position is that Syria does not need its own *perestroika* because it already had a corrective movement when Assad seized power in 1970. Syria was simply ahead of everyone else: "The Corrective Movement led by struggler Hafiz al-Assad . . . advanced the principle of political and economic pluralism almost two decades ago."[22] Therefore, what else was there to do? Assad's reelection in December 1991 by 99.9 percent of the electorate, following several days of massive orchestrated rallies to express support for the president, revealed the degree to which the regime controls life in Syria and highlighted its simultaneous concern about appearances and its complete contempt for them. It would have been only slightly more cynical, and certainly far cheaper and more efficient, to ask only those 360 Syrians who did not favor Assad's reelection to cast votes (especially since 334 of these ballots were reportedly cast at embassies abroad).[23]

At times, Assad has spoken more bluntly about the poor prospects for democracy in Syria so long as he is in power. In a key speech in May 1990, he laid to rest many Syrians' hopes for a Syrian *perestroika*: "Despite the fact that in many countries elections are held on a party basis; despite the fact that many in the world consider this method to be more advanced, more effective, more democratic, and more conducive to national unity; [and] despite the fact that many in Syria are convinced this is the best method . . . we are of the opinion that the phase through which our country is passing is not the most suitable for implementing this electoral system."[24]

The lesson Assad has learned from the upheaval in Eastern Europe and the Soviet Union is not that Syrians must have more political freedom but that giving them such freedom might result in the regime's downfall. Assad is, by nature, a profoundly cautious man who craves order and stability. As a despot, he cannot tolerate freedom, which he sees as a harbinger of chaos and disruptive nuisance that his foes will surely exploit. Assad claims that freedom needs to be controlled, and whatever limitations are imposed on it are actually designed to preserve it: "Regulating the practice of freedom means protecting it. . . . Freedom and its regulations belong side by side. If they are separated, anarchy and despotism will prevail. . . . Freedom needs order. . . . Freedom disappears if orderliness disappears. . . . And when the order is completely disturbed, freedom will be completely absent."[25] In a country where no criticism of the president, no matter how minor, is tolerated and where "no Syrian newspaper has printed a cartoon of Assad, even a favorable one, since he came to power,"[26] the suggestion that the Ba'thist regime is regulating freedom in order to protect it (and thereby save Syrians from despotism) lacks a certain plausibility.

The Assad regime has excellent reason to fear political liberalization. In both Jordan and Algeria, Islamist groups—the Ba'th's old nemesis—attracted a large vote in recent free elections. Such groups might not fare so well in Syria, a comparatively secular country by Middle Eastern standards, but Assad has not forgotten the role that religious fundamentalists played in the uprising against the regime between 1979 and 1982. Although Assad himself has a genuine, if narrow, base of support—many Syrians fear that there is no one else around at the moment who could protect Syria's regional interests so effectively—free elections would likely result in the repudiation of the Ba'thist regime and will therefore never be permitted. Ba'thists will not willingly surrender power in part because they know that if they do so, they will, for the first time in almost thirty years, have to answer for their many misdeeds. There are many scores to be settled.

In addition, free elections would inevitably produce a Sunni-dominated government and mark the end of the Alawi ascendancy within Syria. Fears among Alawis that they might be victims of a sectarian bloodbath under a majority Sunni regime are not entirely misplaced and provide them with powerful incentives not to relinquish power. The Syrian regime undoubtedly noticed that democratic reform in Eastern Europe and the Soviet Union was accompanied by the open expression of long-suppressed ethnic grievances and threats to the territorial integrity of several states. The lesson has been clear: the lid has to be kept on at all costs if national unity is to be preserved. So long as the military dominates Syria's political life and its upper ranks are controlled by Ba'thists and Alawis, the obstacles to political liberalization may be insurmountable. Even if the regime did not fear that opening up the political system might ultimately lead to a sectarian backlash and a settling of accounts, its obsession with the struggle against Israel and its equation between external and internal security make it deeply suspicious of democratization. Assad genuinely seems to believe that displays of discontent with the regime are invariably instigated by his regional adversaries, who would be the foremost beneficiaries of a weakened Syria. To be strong abroad—and that means, above all, in relation to Israel—he first has to be strong at home. So long as the conflict with Israel continues, the regime has a convenient excuse for stifling dissent.

While the Assad regime has resisted political liberalization, it has recently taken a number of important steps to open up the economy, largely because the regime's economic performance remains one of its greatest points of vulnerability.[27] On May 4, 1991, the People's Assembly passed the Law for the Encouragement of Investment (Law No. 10), the most significant and ambitious economic reform since 1970. The main purpose of the legislation was to attract foreign capital, especially from Syrian expatriates, and boost the private sector through a number of incentives, including investment protection, tax exemptions, the easing of import restrictions, and the right to transfer capital, profits, interest, and dividends overseas. In addition, foreign exchange controls have been relaxed; exporters are now permitted to retain 75 percent of their export receipts in hard currency. Eventually, all foreign exchange controls will be lifted and the Syrian pound allowed to float (or sink). In July 1991, the legislature passed a sweeping new tax law, which sharply lowered income tax rates in order to increase compliance. There have, therefore, been strong signs that the regime intends to move gradually in the direction of a market economy, although it is unlikely that large-scale privatization of state industries will be permitted. Some of the regime's efforts to nourish the private sector have already yielded positive results. In 1989, Syria achieved its first balance of payments surplus in thirty years, although official statistics, which do not record the huge volume of goods smuggled in from Lebanon, probably grossly overstated this surplus. In 1990, the trade surplus was even larger—$1.9 billion— because of growing exports of food and textiles from the private sector and booming oil exports. Indeed, the energy sector is one of the brightest spots in the economy: oil production increased from 270,000 barrels per day (b/d) in 1988 to an estimated 470,000 b/d in 1991, with 200,000 b/d available for export. Syria's total earnings from oil in 1990 were approximately $1.5 billion—an increase of almost 90 percent over 1989. Largely because of these gains, real gross domestic product (GDP) grew by an estimated 9.5 percent in 1990. Real GDP growth in 1991 is officially projected to be 6 percent, more than twice the rate of population growth.

Conclusions

By the end of the Iran-Iraq War in 1988, the regime of Hafiz al-Assad was isolated in the Middle East and uncertain about the backing of the Soviet Union, its superpower patron. The cornerstones of the regime's strategic paradigm had crumbled, and its standing as a regional power had been severely diminished. The prospects for recovering the Golan Heights through military or diplomatic means looked dismal. At home, things were no better. As political change swept through Eastern Europe and the Soviet Union, the regime's own gross deficiencies—its bloody repressiveness, corruption, narrow sectarian base, and economic mismanagement—were highlighted. After a quarter of a century of continuous Ba'athist rule, pressures to open up the political system and liberalize the economy were mounting once again. So severe were the regime's problems that some analysts wrote

Syria off as a declining power, contending that it could safely be marginalized and ignored. Yet barely two years later the epitaph seemed premature, and Syria was once again being characterized as a major power in the region, whose engagement was necessary if the region's key disputes were to be resolved. Assad had skillfully steered Syria back to the Arab mainstream, joining Egypt and Saudi Arabia to create a potentially formidable alliance at the center of the Arab world. As a result of its support for the U.S.-led coalition against Iraq in the Persian Gulf crisis, its relations with Washington were the warmest they had been in many years. Even the economy was beginning to take off. Despite its claim not to have compromised its principles, Syria's decision to attend the Madrid Peace Conference and open direct bilateral talks with Israel—under conditions that fell far short of what it had historically demanded—was a momentous step for a regime so entrenched in anti-Zionism. Assad has demonstrated a remarkable talent for turning crises into opportunities and for repositioning Syria more favorably in the Middle East just when its fortunes seemed to be at their nadir. The Persian Gulf crisis afforded him just such an opportunity, enabling him to maneuver Syria back into the center of things.

Notes

1. This point is especially well developed in two recent biographies: Patrick Seale, *Assad: The Struggle for the Middle East* (Berkeley: University of California Press, 1989), and Moshe Ma'oz, *Asad—The Sphinx of Damascus: A Political Biography* (New York: Weidenfeld and Nicholson, 1988).

2. For a fuller treatment, see Alasdair Drysdale and Raymond A. Hinnebusch, *Syria and the Middle East Peace Process* (New York: Council on Foreign Relations Press, 1991), from which this chapter draws.

3. The most explicit (and controversial) statement of this view is in Daniel Pipes, *Greater Syria: The History of an Ambition* (New York: Oxford University Press, 1990).

4. See Pedro Ramet, *The Syria-Soviet Relationship since 1955: A Troubled Alliance* (Boulder: Westview Press, 1990); Efraim Karsh, *The Soviet Union and Syria: The Asad Years* (New York: Routledge, 1988), John P. Hanna, *At Arm's Length: Soviet-Syrian Relations in the Gorbachev Era*, Policy Papers, no. 18 (Washington: Washington Institute for Near East Policy, 1989), and Helena Cobban, *The Superpowers and the Syrian-Israeli Conflict: Beyond Crisis Management*, The Washington Papers, no. 149 (New York: Praeger with the Center for International Studies, Washington, DC, 1991). See also Robert O.

Freedman, *Moscow and the Middle East: Soviet Policy since the Invasion of Afghanistan* (Cambridge: Cambridge University Press, 1991).

5. The origins of the dispute between the two regimes is detailed in Eberhard Kienle, *Ba'th v Ba'th: The Conflict between Syria and Iraq, 1968–1989* (London: I.B. Tauris, 1990).

6. *Foreign Broadcast Information Service: Near East/South Asia* (hereafter *FBIS:NESA*), May 17, 1990, pp. 27–28.

7. Efraim Karsh, *The Soviet Union and Syria: The Assad Years* (New York: Routledge, 1988), p. 92.

8. *FBIS:NESA*, February 24, 1989, pp. 12–19.

9. *Boston Globe*, September 19, 1989.

10. See chapter 3 by Robert O. Freedman in this volume.

11. *FBIS:NESA*, March 9, 1990, p. 34.

12. *New York Times*, December 4, 1983.

13. *FBIS:NESA*, October 23, 1991, p. 12.

14. Ibid.

15. For a comprehensive account of the regime's deficiencies, see Middle East Watch, *Syria Unmasked: The Suppression of Human Rights by the Assad Regime* (New Haven: Yale University Press, 1991).

16. *FBIS:NESA*, October 3, 1991, p. 29.

17. *FBIS:NESA*, October 4, 1991, p. 32.

18. *Middle East Economic Digest*, December 27, 1991, p. 36.

19. Volker Perthes, "Syria's Parliamentary Elections: Remodeling Assad's Political Base," *Middle East Report* (January–February 1992): 15–18.

20. *FBIS:NESA*, February 28, 1990, p. 45.

21. *FBIS:NESA*, May 8, 1990, p. 29.

22. *FBIS:NESA*, October 4, 1991, p. 32.

23. Judith Miller, "Syria's Game: Put on a Western Face," *New York Times Magazine*, January 26, 1992, p. 12.

24. *FBIS:NESA*, May 17, 1990, p. 27.

25. *FBIS:NESA*, March 9, 1990, pp. 29–30.

26. Middle East Watch, *Human Rights in Syria* (New York: Human Rights Watch, 1990), p. 138.

27. Volker Perthes, "The Syrian Economy in the 1980s," *Middle East Journal* 46 (1992): 37–58.

11

JORDANIAN POLICY FROM

THE INTIFADA TO THE

MADRID PEACE CONFERENCE

Adam Garfinkle

For Hashemite Jordan the period encompassing the outbreak
of the Intifada in December 1987, the denouement of the Gulf War in
early 1991, and the dramatic convening of the Madrid Conference in
late October and early November 1991 consisted of a long and frightful
roller coaster ride. Before the spring of 1991, Jordan went from a preci-
pice of deep economic crisis to one of political uncertainty and
watched from that dubious perch as a regional war nearly hurled Jordan
down to final disaster. But during the remainder of 1991, the diverse
fallout of the Gulf War and the dynamics of U.S.-led peace diplomacy
provided the context for skillful royal diplomacy that took Jordan from
near ruin to the point of diplomatic redemption.

Jordan's journey over this roughly four-year period is of interest not
only to Jordan but also to all of its neighbors. There cannot be peace
in the Middle East without active Jordanian participation, for Jordan
provides both shield and ballast for the sine qua non of a successful
peace process: genuine and politically sustainable Palestinian accommodation to the reality of Israel.

This essay takes an essentially chronological approach, looking
first at Jordan's considerable difficulties before the Iraqi invasion of
Kuwait, then at Jordan's diplomacy during the roughly eight months
of crisis and war over Kuwait, and finally at how Jordan navigated the
postwar situation to and just beyond the Madrid Peace Conference.

Jordan's Crisis

As the Bush administration began, Jordan was in the midst of a serious structural crisis that affected most aspects of national life. The economy was sputtering, Islam was increasingly militant and joining with romantic Palestinian nationalist extremism, and the East Bank constituency, which has ever been the backbone of the regime, was showing signs of changing direction on the future of Hashemite rule. Moreover, the king seemed tired and sick, the Israeli political scene was increasingly unfriendly to pragmatic moderation, and world attention was focused not on Jordan but on dramatic events in Europe and the Soviet Union.

Jordan's crisis of the late 1980s arose from the many regional and domestic political changes of the last thirty years, aggravated by some bad luck and an occasional lapse of royal skill. The crisis was composed of three interlocking parts: economic problems, political pressure, and the fallout from regional politics centered on the Palestinian problem.

The Economic Dimension

By the end of 1986, if not earlier, the Arab oil boom had clearly ended and was unlikely to recur. Ending with it was the largesse of Arab oil money given to Jordan. Pledges made to Jordan at the 1978 Baghdad Summit were never completely fulfilled, and each year Jordan received less money. The decline was particularly sharp between 1988 and 1989, when, according to World Bank figures, aid fell by fully one-third (a total of $178 million), from $536 million in 1988 to $377 million in 1989.

Remittances from expatriate Jordanian citizens in the Gulf, which at one time in the middle 1980s accounted for nearly a third of Jordan's income, were also affected negatively by the softness in the oil market. Meanwhile, rising expectations and the gradual evolution of a culture of consumption had bred a sharp increase in nonproductive imports that the government was reluctant to curtail. Between 1976 and 1982 Jordan's foreign trade gap between imports and exports increased by a factor of five.[1] The trappings of prosperity in Jordan nevertheless facilitated relative social amity and political calm, and a growing economic base worked doubly as a general palliative to soften the reality of grossly uneven income distribution and as a means to raise the lower strata of Palestinian society in Jordan into the mainstream.

Lean times, of course, had the opposite effect. When the oil bubble burst, the Jordanian government temporized, powerless to change the regional economic environment but afraid to announce and act upon the bad news. Jordan suffered a sudden and acute financial crisis in 1988, demonstrated dramatically by a plunge of foreign currency reserves to nearly zero.[2] As the crisis persisted, a two-sided reaction to the economic crisis developed: the government introduced stringent austerity measures to protect Jordan's capacity to borrow from international institutions until matters could be put right, and Jordan's nongovernmental intelligentsia, Islamist activists, professional associations, and new media elite all sharpened their sensitivity toward parvenu corruption by business fat cats and government officials.[3]

Part of the government program involved letting the Jordanian currency, the dinar, float in order to help correct the trade imbalance and satisfy World Bank demands for future borrowing. But the weakness of the dinar persuaded many expatriate workers to keep their discretionary funds abroad in other currencies, and persuaded other, wealthy Jordanians, to either keep or send their capital abroad as well. By the end of the 1980s, up to $10 billion in private Jordanian money was believed to be invested outside the country, a good deal of it sent out after the float of the dinar.[4] The amount exceeded Jordan's then external debt of about $8.5 billion.

In addition, Jordanian "disengagement" from the West Bank on July 31, 1988, contributed to economic troubles by accelerating the collapse of the dinar. The West Bank lost faith in both the value and convertibility of the dinar—a development that followed the Palestine Liberation Organization's (PLO) 1986 withdrawal of over $700 million from Jordanian banks in protest over Jordanian policy at that time.[5] The disengagement may also have been designed in part to attract those funds and others back to Jordan.

Jordan's economic trouble, whatever the proximate catalysts were, did not stem only from bad luck or poor management. It was, and remains, based on structural problems. Rapid population increase (3.5–4.3 percent yearly) in a country bereft of many natural resources and too small to support the infrastructure of a modern economy has threatened for years to drive the country to ruin. Indeed, that the mismatch of population with the natural carrying capacity of the land did not send Jordan spiraling into disaster earlier testifies to King Hussein's talent as a royal mendicant. But the reality of the kingdom's limits nearly caught up with it in 1988–89, and, unfortunately for the monarchy, it happened after the most affluent and economically optimistic era in the country's history.

Political Pressures

Beyond economic matters, Jordan's new, growing, better educated middle classes wanted to have more of a say in running the country. Jordan's population as a whole has become more educated, modern, and politically aware over the last few decades because of successful government policy, but, as in Iran in the 1960s and 1970s, opportunities to participate in public life failed to keep pace with the desires and capacities of new constituencies.

King Hussein was aware of this restlessness but nervous about allowing it full expression. In the mid-1980s he created a number of consultative councils with no real power, repeatedly hinted about reconvening Parliament, which had been suspended since just after the June 1967 war, and promulgated a new elections law in 1986.[6] More important, he also used his own brand of personal monarchical populism to convey the impression that even without genuine political pluralism, Jordan's government cared about and listened to its people.

But in reality, little changed. The king remained unchallenged at the pinnacle of power; next came the army and the *mukhabarat* (the internal security apparatus), the control of both vouchsafed to loyal East Bank supporters. Then came a group of business-government oligarchies, some of whom were Palestinian in origin. All aspects of public administration, from customs personnel to education ministry functionaries, were staffed through the tribes and the oligarchies. The same groups virtually controlled the print and electronic media, which never criticized the king or any important aspect of government policy. The Moslem Brotherhood was cautiously tolerated and modestly patronized; troublemakers were occasionally jailed but mostly co-opted, and that was that.

Withal, the demand to participate grew in intensity, and the groups making demands became more diverse. In addition to Palestinian merchants and East Bank technocrats there were professional groups, which, in lieu of political parties, became an organizational focus of the new middle-class political thinking and activism.[7] Also, ominously, fundamentalist Moslems, some far more militant than the Moslem Brotherhood had ever been, arose in the wake of the Iranian revolution. When the demand for political participation converged with the economic crisis, a sense of generalized discontent emerged and pressure for change reached the political elite. The monarchy bent; it reconvened Parliament and promised general elections in an effort to appease popular demands and, no doubt, to deflect the unpopularity of present and planned economic austerity measures onto others.

Perhaps most important, and most surprising to the king, epochal changes had been brewing in the kingdom's core East Bank constituency. The formative experience of the rising generations on East Bank is markedly different from that which came before. In all sectors of Jordanian society, political sophistication has been growing: there are more university graduates than ever before; new business and media elites are forming; and the general level of competence in all technical and managerial matters is much higher than a generation ago.[8] But the change is most striking in the support group most crucial to the monarchy, the East Bank. Thirty or forty years ago, most tribesmen could not read or write, and their education was restricted to memorization of Qur'anic verses and prayers. Faced with the general onslaught of modernity and the challenge of a more cosmopolitan and educated Palestinian group in the kingdom, East Bank residents were challenged to keep up. They have done so, and one result is that their capacity for reflection and critical thought about politics has increased radically even as former social stabilities have eroded.[9]

East Bank residents as a group are still loyal to the monarchy but their capacity to be effectively critical is new. Changes among them imply the relative politicization of the army and the intelligence services, too. Although such changes do not call into question the army's fundamental loyalty, they do suggest erosion of the traditional paternalism of the monarchy over the military.

To the extent that the upper ranks of the army and the security apparatus evolve different attitudes from those of the royal court, they are likely to be to the king's right when it comes to the central domestic political issue: controlling the effects of Palestinian nationalism in Jordan. This development was foreshadowed by the 1970 civil war, when high-ranking army officers pled with the king not to back down before the insulting hubris of PLO fedayeen groups; the king, ultimately, found that he had to listen to them. The independent tendencies of East Bank residents have become more pronounced ever since.

Related social changes in Jordan have to do with trends toward secularization[10] and urbanization. In conjunction with such trends, one of the most important developments in Jordanian society over the past two generations has been the relative decline in the cohesiveness and importance of tribal affiliations.[11] This is not to say that clan and family no longer matter at all; indeed, ascriptive characteristics still outweigh merit in most cases. But tribal ties are relatively less significant, and the reasons are clear: the settling of the bedouin and their recruitment into the army and from the army into the civil service had the effect of increasing personal mobility, breaking open the economic and social homogeneity of nomadic life, and thus diminishing the exclusive pull of tribal attachments.[12]

While specific primordial ties matter less to an increasingly urbanized, secularized, and culturally perforated society, East Bank society has not lost its sense of exclusivity. Instead, a transtribal East Bank political personality profile is emerging, and it appears to have strong anti-Palestinian aspects. Younger East Bank residents feel more antagonism toward those they consider aliens and interlopers, particularly as those of bedouin origin migrate to Jordan's cities only to find them economically controlled by Palestinians. Indeed, one cause of the April 1989 riots was young East Bank residents' perception that Jordan's middleman oil boom economy enriched only urban Palestinians and government oligarchies, while they were the main victims of the government's austerity program.

Regional Factors

Into this brew of economic stasis and social tension was thrown the spice of regional violence. The Palestinian Intifada had a major impact on Jordan as well as on Israel. Its outbreak in December 1987 immediately raised the worry that a romantic and violent form of Palestinian nationalism would once again spread to the East Bank, as it had in 1968–70. There was specific reason to worry. Leaflet Number 5 of the Unified National Leadership of the Uprising (UNLU) called on workers at the pro-Jordanian Jerusalem newspaper *An-Nahar* to resign. This led to attacks on the distributors of the paper in February 1988 and to the bombing of its offices. Leaflet Number 10, in March 1988 called for attacks on Jordanian Parliament members who dared cross the river, presumably to lobby for Jordan's interests in the occupied territories.

But after the first full year of the uprising, no real spreading of the Intifada to Jordan occurred. This resulted from bitter memories of the civil war and from the authorities' skill in suppressing the first sparks of a rising; also enough Palestinians in the East Bank had been sufficiently Jordanianized that they feared risking what they had for the sake of mere emotional demonstrations—what else could they accomplish?—for their brethren across the river.

This last was a crucial factor in the July 31, 1988, disengagement of Jordan from the West Bank. To say in the midst of the Intifada that Jordan was not Palestine, that it had a prior and separate agenda of its own, was testimony to the king's confidence that his Palestinian problem was manageable even if Israel's was not. From Hashemite Jordan's point of view, it was better to be farther away than closer to the havoc on the West Bank, but it was the regime's courage to act on this assumption that allowed the disengagement to proceed. The fact was that it did not require the army to "explain" the disengagement to the Palestinians in the kingdom, despite the fact that they had been told since birth that Jordan's role was to hold in safekeeping those parts of Palestine not taken by Israel in 1948 against the day of "the return."

Over time, however, the Intifada as well as the disengagement affected Palestinians in Jordan, although their reactions were paradoxical. On the rhetorical level the Intifada united Palestinian society in Jordan, but on every other it tended to sharpen differences among the demographic layers of Palestinians in the East Bank. Those most firmly established in Jordan, mainly from the generation of 1947–49 that never saw the inside of a refugee camp, were the most cautious; those more newly arrived (post-1967) with the least to lose were more prone to impatience and activism and in recent years increasingly united under the banner of militant Islam.[13] On balance, as control over the Jordanian status quo shifted away from the king in the last years of the 1980s and into 1990, a revived Palestinian nationalism emerged, as the initial support of Jordan's "street" for Saddam Hussein after August 2, 1990, clearly showed.

A final regional factor of note was the development of a Jordanian-Iraqi alliance during the 1980s.[14] Jordan's move toward Iraq had multiple propellants: it helped offset Syrian power and it put Saudi Arabia on notice that Jordan was not irrevocably tied to Arab moderates so as to extract aid from Riyadh. Most important, however, was Hussein's genuine fear of Iranian-inspired fundamentalism and his belief that only Iraq prevented it from lunging westward toward Jordan. In time, too, as the oil-based economy dwindled and Jordan became Iraq's indispensable land bridge to the world, a substantial economic dimension was added to the Jordanian-Iraqi partnership. As much as 80 percent of Jordan's oil came from Iraq, and most of its trade was also in time oriented toward Baghdad.[15]

Finally, by June 1990 many Jordanians feared that the new Israeli right-wing government was preparing to destroy the kingdom and set up a Palestinian rump state on the East Bank; Iraq thus became something of Jordan's defense-in-depth against such an eventuality. The king added to these fears by using the apocalyptical scenario of an Israeli invasion to shake loose financial assistance to "front-line" Jordan from the Arab Gulf states.[16]

Saddam Hussein, meanwhile, tried his hand at a roughly parallel fund-raising tactic, threatening to burn Israel with chemical weapons while simultaneously trying to shake down the same Gulf sheiks. Such rhetoric was immensely popular in Jordan, particularly among Palestinians, who by then had become increasingly frustrated that neither post-1988 declarations of PLO moderation nor the sacrifices of the Intifada seemed to be leading to any palpable change in the circumstances of their brethren under occupation.

It was not obvious at the time that Saddam Hussein was working to collect allies for a future adventure. The slow but continuous strengthening of Jordanian bonds to Iraq must have seemed on balance more useful than dangerous to King Hussein. Saddam Hussein, on the other hand, was not interested in Jordan's use of Iraq; he was, it later became clear, far more concerned with Iraq's use of Jordan.

Jordanian Politics before the Deluge

For the reasons sketched above, Jordan found itself beset with considerable political turbulence in 1990. But as bad luck would have it, Jordan's regime hit a historic low in stability at the worst possible time: August 1990. When the Iraqi invasion of Kuwait occurred on August 2, 1990, King Hussein exerted less control over Jordanian politics than at any time since the days just before the September 1970 civil war.

The July 1988 disengagement was Jordan's way of saying to the PLO, "You take the West Bank (if you can), but you have to leave me alone on the East."[17] Initially, the disengagement confronted Palestinians and their organizations with a question: to what extent and in which

ways should Palestinians in Jordan participate in a new era of Jordanian politics? But economic crisis, the heady symbolism of a protracted Intifada, the initial opening of the political system and particularly the press freedom it entailed, and the alliance with Iraq
encouraged the development of a self-confident and oppositional Palestinian self-consciousness in Jordan, precisely the reverse of what
the 1988 disengagement sought to produce. If the disengagement was
designed to make East Bank Palestinians choose—the king being rea-
sonably confident that they would choose to protect their concrete
stake in Jordan—then the period of Jordanian *glasnost* that came after
redefined what "choosing Jordan" meant in practical terms.

Although they were still technically illegal, Palestinian political activities and parties flourished in Jordan after July 1988, and there
seemed no price to pay for it. In late 1988, for example, Palestinian activists wondered whether, when political parties were legalized, PLO
member organizations should set up formal Jordanian affiliates. If the
king were to allow Palestinians to organize Palestinian political parties, would the regime find a way to use these parties to weaken and
co-opt the PLO? These questions were no longer compelling during
the heady period of the Kuwait crisis simply because the regime had
lost much of its leverage over the country's political processes. The
clearest signals of that erosion were the surprising riots in the southern part of the country in April 1989.

The disengagement signaled the king's desire to put the Jordanian
government on a more secure institutional political footing focusing
on the monarchy's core East Bank constituency.[18] If so, the king failed
to anticipate how much this core constituency, like the Palestinian
one, had changed. The April 1989 riots, centered near Ma'an, the region traditionally most loyal to the monarchy and most passively
long-suffering in hard times, brought home the point with alacrity,
and the king thereafter strove to accelerate his program.

After the riots the government of Zaid al-Rifai was made the immediate scapegoat; he was replaced by the king's cousin and a former
commander of the armed forces, Sharif Zaid bin Shaker. The new
prime minister moved swiftly and effectively to install new confidence in government, but Hussein knew that merely shifting cabinet
faces would not mollify angry citizens. He surely realized that pin-
ning Jordan's long-term hopes on this new breed of East Bank residents required more action. A plan to hold an election in November
1989 followed quickly on the heels of the April riots, and the regime

also broached the idea of a new National Charter that would legalize political parties and broaden participation in government. Both the election and the National Charter, which later gave birth to a new political parties law, were designed to accommodate Jordan's newly politicized East Bank constituency.

In preparation for the election, gerrymandering was tried by the regime to ensure that Palestinian representation was shaved in favor of East Bank representation, and it succeeded for the most part. But once again, social developments ran ahead of the king's tactics. What Hussein failed to anticipate was how well Islamic fundamentalists would do, nor did he guess the extent to which fundamentalism and Palestinian activism would merge and reinforce each other. A large protest vote looking for new names on the ballot also added to Islamist success because fundamentalist candidates alone were not associated with the recent malaise. The election results were so surprising in favor of Islamist candidates, which gave them roughly 40 percent of Parliament, that they gave the ruling elite more pause than the riots that had brought forth the election in the first place.

The Jordanian constitution is drawn so that the king retains the power to select his cabinet regardless of who wins the largest parliamentary bloc. King Hussein did so, but he made a concerted effort to introduce new faces into the cabinet as well.[19] But he could not undo the damage. Hussein had intended that the election produce a Parliament that would absorb discontent from unpopular economic measures to come; in other words, the election was supposed to siphon off pressure. But the election results, and the reported coincidental deterioration of the king's health, instead produced new pressures through a rogue element in the political status quo: a Parliament that, for the first time since 1956–57, imagined itself as having an independent political agenda and role in the country.

The Jordanian Parliament took on a life of its own and suddenly became interesting for the first time since the days of Suleiman an-Nablusi in 1957. Increasingly in 1989 and early 1990, a new and more open public life evolved faster than the regime's will or capacity to control it. What had started as deliberate, calculated royal restraint in exerting authority had gradually turned into a situation in which the regime would have to pay a significant price for reasserting its prerogatives. Parliament had turned into a political juggernaut while new press freedoms, and periodic scandals, (e.g., those concerning corrupt bankers), fed the heady new climate of political expression. Political parties arose before they were chartered legally.[20] Parliament called for a new eastern front against Israel, and unauthorized border incursions into Israel increased in frequency.[21] When public figures dared question the motive of the king's National Charter, it provided a stunning example of one public relations control mechanism (Jordan's press glasnost) doubling back, as it were, to attack a second (the National Charter idea.)[22]

A railroading metaphor might be of some use in capturing what had happened to society-state relations in Jordan after early 1988. The king prepared the locomotive of political change and commenced to build track to guide it, but the Jordanian street stoked the boiler with so much fuel that it was all the regime could do to lay new track fast enough to keep up. It was either that or throw on the brakes so hard it would shake every passenger aboard from head to heel and possibly cause the train to jump the track altogether.

The independent momentum of the new Parliament confronted the king with serious problems. The more secularly oriented members of Parliament, although an absolute majority, were too divided to offset the power of the Islamists, who now picked up the fallen torch of Arab political romanticism held in the 1960s and 1970s by Nasserites, Ba'thists, and communists. The Jordanian regime had never succeeded in creating a front political organization for itself to use in co-opting and outflanking such problems,[23] so the king allowed and even encouraged leftist elements, long banned from Jordan's public realm, to emerge as a counterpoise.[24] He also cozied up to Yasser Arafat, and the world saw the remarkable specter of two establishment politicians teaming up to oppose Islamists in their respective ranks.

The only other option open to the king was to confront the Islamists directly through use of the army and the General Intelligence Department (GID). But this was too dangerous, particularly since Islam had become so entangled with Palestinian activism that doing so might provoke a larger conflagration.

Jordan and the Kuwait Crisis

On balance, King Hussein acted calculatingly in 1988 and early 1989 but not boldly or quickly enough to prevent upheaval in 1990. Still, while the regime had been thrown back on its heels, it was still standing. It may even have made sense from the king's point of view to let Parliament find its way to that sense of responsibility that comes with real political experience, even if the exercise produced some unpleasantries. If Jordan were to evolve into a more stable polity with a reduced monarchy in the post-Hussein future, it would sooner or later have to get through a form of political adolescence. So, the king might well have reasoned, why not now?

The answer came on August 1, 1990, when King Hussein found himself beneath the falcon's wing of his erstwhile ally, Saddam Hussein. By then, the king had given the "street" in Jordan such a wide swath of self-expression and organizing energy that opposing its spontaneous support for Iraq was out of the question. The only way to have done so unequivocally was to call out the army to shoot demonstrators. Had the king gone that, even assuming the army's loyalty, all he had been trying to build in the event of his abdication or death would have been for naught.

The Kuwait crisis also worsened Jordan's economic situation. Aqaba was brought to a near standstill, income from tourism plunged to near zero, remittances were severely reduced, oil from Saudi Arabia was cut off, and Jordanian products were prevented from reaching the Gulf by Saudi diktat.[25] In addition, Jordan's Saudi subsidy was eliminated and special privileges formerly enjoyed in Saudi Arabia by Palestinians with Jordanian passports, such as being able to work without having a specific Saudi sponsor, were rescinded. As bad luck had it, the market for Jordanian phosphates was also depressed. Unemployment, hovering at around 15 percent before 1990, reached nearly 40 percent by the spring of 1991.[26] Most ironically, because of the crisis, Iraq had a good excuse not to repay what it owed to Jordan—which stood at about $835 million in the fall of 1989.[27]

As a result, the International Monetary Fund estimated that Jordan's GNP measured at market prices would shrink 16.5 percent when 1990 figures were accumulated, and projections for 1991 still expected negative rates. These predictions were too dire; the 1990 shortfall was 8.5 percent, and the economy did better in 1991 than most expected.[28] But there is no question that the Kuwait crisis hurt, and the impact of 280,000 Palestinians returning to Jordan from the Gulf by fall 1991,[29] and the continued shutoff of Saudi subsidies and trade, suggested to most analysts that the worst was yet to come.[30]

Moreover, the crisis furnished precisely what Jordan's Islamists needed in order to take the modest political space opened up by the November 1989 election and enlarge it. Until 1990, the Jordanian regime had been adept at co-opting and accommodating religious forces.

This was made easier by the fact that it is not noteworthy to be an orthodox Moslem in a traditional monarchy, and the general religious atmosphere in Jordan undercut fundamentalist criticisms. Although there was a logic for religious sensibilities to translate into political mobilization against the regime in the 1979–85 period[31]—rampant materialism, the ostentation of new suburbs around Amman, the fact that alcohol and immodestly dressed women coexisted in some areas of the capital with mosques and madrassas—a catalyst was lacking. On or about August 2, one arrived.

Radical scenarios seemed far-fetched before the Kuwait crisis because a thorough overturning of the status quo would have required four improbable things to happen simultaneously or in near sequence. One was a deep economic unraveling, with little help for the country from outside when it happened. Second, the regional environment would have had to be particularly crisis-prone either because of war, sudden regime transitions in nearby countries, or other equally serious dislocations. Third, there would have had to be a new cadre of united radical leadership. Fourth, the king would have had to die, fall seriously ill, or abdicate. The Kuwait crisis furnished the first three conditions in total or in part, and, conceivably, biology or a bullet might have provided the fourth before the war ended.

The question of an opposition leadership underwent the most dramatic change. Before 1989, it was hard to identify an incipient opposition leadership cadre to challenge the regime; political activism and violence were at a twenty-five-year low. Nor was it easy to find an East Bank cadre devoted to an Islamic revolution. Aside from Laith Shubailet, the maverick Islamic legislator, little was known about the new generation of politically minded Islamist activists.[32] But after the election and the Kuwait crisis, this new elite became more visible, and the rise of popular support for Iraq among the most disenchanted segments of Jordanian society propelled this new leadership forward with great speed. A united political front, led by Islamists, formed in August 1990, and it effectively operated not as a Jordanian government as such but as a power against which the palace could generally not operate effectively.[33]

By not applying royal influence in August 1990, the regime courted further challenges. In October, Parliament, led by Shubailat, demanded that the regime arm the people to confront the expected war with Israel.[34] Neither the king nor the prime minister, Mudar Badran, wanted to do that. In mid-May 1990 there had been serious riots by Palestinians in Jordan's refugee camps in the aftermath of the Rishon LeZion incident, when a deranged Israeli killed seven Palestinians on their way to work in Israel.[35] More important, Palestinian civilians with guns, even if trained by the army, raised memories of 1970 and further diminished the chance that, if needed, the army could or would defend the regime. The regime hit upon a compromise: the Palestinians would be given People's Army uniforms and trained by the regular army—but they would not be allowed to take their weapons out of the secured training areas such as Amman's football stadium.[36]

Then, on November 17, 1990, Jordan's lower house elected a fundamentalist as speaker over the opposition of secular leftists and liberals. This spelled trouble to come between Parliament and the king, but by the end of 1990 the trouble was still latent. As long as regime and street moved in the same general direction, a tense internal peace endured.

Thus, one can discount the hagiographic mumbo jumbo about Saddam Hussein that came from the Jordanian regime after the outbreak of the Kuwait crisis, dismiss reports about the deterioration of the king's health, and even de-emphasize the importance of Jordan's economic links to Baghdad and still understand the Jordanian reaction in the Kuwait crisis based solely on the exigencies of domestic politics as the king likely understood them. Some Bush administration officials seemed not to grasp this situation very well.

Jordan and the United States

The Jordanian king was criticized sharply by a range of U.S. observers for his pro-Iraqi tilt during the Gulf War, and initially even administration officials joined the chorus. There was, admittedly, much to be annoyed about.

At the least, Washington expected some Jordanian equivocation under the circumstances but did not really get it. Indeed, the president was so annoyed with the extent of King Hussein's early support for Iraq that he lost his temper, at a televised August 5 news conference, when ABC's Ann Compton began describing a pro-Iraqi interview given that day by the king. "I can read," Bush shot back, clearly more annoyed with the king than with Compton. It was the only time Bush lost his temper publicly throughout the crisis.

As the days passed, Jordanian behavior worsened from the U.S. point of view. In particular, the endlessly repeated Hashemite refrain that had it not been for the hasty introduction of U.S. forces an Arab solution could have been found annoyed officials in Washington, who knew it was just not true and found it difficult to believe that even the king himself took the argument seriously. And days after the invasion, as Bush was characterizing Saddam Hussein as a Hitler, King Hussein told NBC news that Saddam was "a person to be trusted and dealt with."[37] Thereafter, despite King Hussein's visit to Kennebunkport on August 16, Jordan's seemingly two-faced behavior with respect to sanctions, its complaints about the U.S. embassy monitoring the Jordanian-Iraqi border as the refugee problem grew in scope, its colorful, conspiracy-bedecked anti-U.S. rhetoric, and the king's gambit to bring the Europeans to undermine U.S. strategy—all of this annoyed Washington further throughout the nearly six months before the beginning of the air war on January 16, 1991.

In response to this, the U.S. Navy blockaded Aqaba and the administration urged Jordanian neutrality at the least.[38] After the air war began, it also sent Ambassador Richard L. Armitage to Jordan on January 23 to calm nerves and, with Lawrence Eagleburger in Israel, to try to prevent a second Middle East war from breaking out between Israel and Jordan.[39] This genuinely worried Jordan as well as the United States and Israel. Hussein was not exaggerating when he said on November 17 that Jordan was at a crossroads and that the Middle East was on the "verge of a catastrophe which would destroy our existence"; nor was Crown Prince Hassan just mouthing words when he said, "Plainly put, our small country of 3.5 million people is on the brink of destruction."[40] He went on to describe Jordan as "hell's firewood."

In addition to what Jordan was saying about the crisis, other irritations surfaced as well. There were unconfirmed claims that Jordan was training Iraqis on captured Hawk missiles, that Jordanian intelligence was aiding Iraq,[41] that Jordanian weapons had been sent to Iraq before and during the fighting,[42] that Jordan was laundering money for Iraq,[43] and that some Iraqi mobile SCUD launchers were hiding in Jordan despite the best efforts of coalition air forces to find them.[44] Meanwhile, Jordanian truck drivers were still plying the Iraqi-Jordanian desert highway in violation of the UN embargo, and, in early February, they too felt the brunt of coalition air attacks.

King Hussein delivered a particularly harsh anti-U.S. speech on February 6, seemingly triggered by the deaths of Jordanian truck drivers on that road.[45] The administration, in response, expressed its bitter disappointment with Hussein, suspended aid to Jordan, and commenced to review next year's aid allotment as well.[46] An unnamed senior administration spokesman, possibly Secretary Baker himself, told the *New York Times*, "'There is a war going on now. Americans are at risk, and what the king is doing is putting them more at risk. That is not the way friends behave—even friends under pressure. . . . We cannot be the ones always doing what we can to help him and then he goes and pockets that and doesn't care if he says things that make life more difficult for us. There are limits to our patience, and he needs to know that more clearly."[47]

The Jordanians, in turn, professed outrage, anger, and dismay at U.S. actions, and it appeared that U.S.-Jordanian relations had plummeted to their lowest point ever.[48]

However bad this looked, some of the anger and dismay was probably staged. The experts on the U.S. side knew how sharply Hussein's domestic situation limited his options. Hussein's need to posture for protection was doubtless understood to some degree even on the political level as was, more important, the sheer horror of contemplating a Hussein-less Jordan in the midst of the Kuwait crisis. Indeed, the day after the king's speech, Secretary Baker told the Senate Foreign Relations Committee that lines of communication with Jordan had to remain open because "when we look at alternatives we don't see what we perceive to be a particularly pretty picture."[49] And, while public evidence is lacking, it may be that a certain level of anti-Jordanian remarks by U.S. officials was expected to aid King Hussein in the court of Jordanian public opinion, where to be an enemy of the United States was to be a friend "of the people."

In this regard, U.S.-Jordanian discussions at Kennebunkport on August 16 and in the months thereafter may have led to more than just an exchange of sensitivities. Details are not public knowledge, but Thomas Friedman remarked in the *New York Times* on February 9, "Administration officials say they are ready to accept a certain amount of posturing by the king, *who has provided some useful intelligence on Iraq, and tacit military cooperation since the Gulf war began*" (emphasis added).[50] Moreover, the king's anti-U.S. diatribe of February 6 was motivated by an even more hoary motive than public relations posturing: literal self-defense. Saddam Hussein had gotten wind of Jordanian efforts to repair relations with Washington—this is perhaps where the gifts to which Friedman referred come into play—and had issued the baldest of personal threats against the king.[51]

Notwithstanding this diplomatic subtext to U.S.-Jordanian relations during the crisis, the U.S. cold shoulder persisted for a time after the war ended. Secretary Baker snubbed Hussein on his first two postwar trips to the region, and Policy Planning Director Dennis Ross dubbed the king "a master of strategic misjudgment."[52] At the same time, however, both the king and the administration were commencing efforts to patch up their spat. As early as his news conference on March 1, President Bush acknowledged difficulties with Jordan, but he cited extenuating circumstances and added, "Clearly we do not want to see a destabilized Jordan. I have no personal animosity towards His Majesty the King."[53] Later, on March 26, State Department spokeswoman Margaret Tutweiler said on the occasion of Adnan Abu-Odeh's trip to Washington that despite U.S. disappointment with Jordan during the Kuwait crisis, Jordan still had a very important role to play in the search for peace and security in the region. This statement was duly broadcast by Jordanian media.[54]

Luckily for Jordan, disappointed or not, the administration had even less interest in the PLO. It was clear by early autumn that there would be no renewed U.S.-PLO dialogue after the war. The president himself said on March 9 that he was not in any rush to restart direct talks with the PLO which, he said, had lost much credibility in the war by siding with Iraq.[55]

Even more important, the administration's approach to the peace process was first to concentrate on getting the Arab states engaged with Israel, then to address the Palestinian aspect of the process, which was when Jordan's role would become paramount—hence Baker's avoidance of Amman during his first two trips to the region after the Gulf War. The president said on March 9 that "it is high time that the combatants of the Arab-Israeli conflict recognized Israel's right to exist and we can *then* turn our attention to the unresolved Israeli-Palestinian conflict."[56] So the administration had not forgotten Jordan, and it knew it did not have the luxury of remaining angry at the king. Instead, though perhaps regretting the lack of alternatives, Washington waited for the right moment to recast U.S.-Jordanian ties and involve the king in the peace process.[57]

The coming of that moment was accelerated by an unexpected development: Congress's attempt in March 1991 to cut Jordan's aid package in a fit of pique by tacking on an amendment to the foreign aid bill. While the administration had come ineluctably to the conclusion that, as nasty as Jordanian policy had been during the war, the king was, frankly, indispensable, Congress resisted a similar conclusion. Acting on yesterday's news and emotions, Congress voted to turn Jordan's aid money—a pathetic $55 million a year though it was—into diplomatic bait. It warned Hussein to cooperate in the Arab-Israeli peace process or he would get no U.S. aid. The king did not deserve the treatment meted out by some senators like Don Nickles (R., Oklahoma): "What did we get in return for our generosity? We got more than a slap in the face. After billions of dollars of aid from the United States, Jordan actively opposed the United States and the United Nations by giving moral and political support to Saddam Hussein."[58]

The amendment passed, but not before the Bush administration won a provision within it allowing for a presidential waiver of the cutoff if, in the president's judgment, Jordanian policy contributed to the peace process. It was not easy, however, to get the waiver provision included, and the effort itself seemed to strengthen the administration's conclusion that the king had been less feckless during the crisis than frightened and was more important to prospective U.S. efforts now than ever before.

Jordan as an Ally of Diminishing Returns

When the peace diplomacy of the post-Gulf War period was truly joined, little about the Middle East was left unaffected. Jordan was swept up in the dynamics of producing a conference and sustaining the process thereafter, and those dynamics influenced both Jordanian foreign policy and internal politics in significant ways. Before describing those influences, it is important first to assay how the Bush administration viewed the Jordanian role in what was to come, how Jordan viewed administration plans, and how these two sets of perceptions fit together.

Matters of integrity and gratitude aside, administration experts, notably those in policy planning in the State Department, understood at the outset of the peace process that Jordan simply could not do as much to advance U.S. Middle East policy in the 1990s as it might have in the 1970s or earlier. No one in the administration pitched for the old idea that the king could play a key role in solving the Arab-Israeli crisis in a classical "Jordanian option." This enticing argument, where Jordan is the vehicle through which the Palestinian problem can be recontained as it was before the June 1967 war, has constantly eroded in the face of the consolidation of Palestinian nationalism. But the alternative to the classical Jordanian option is no Jordanian role at all, as many pundits mistakenly assumed after July 31, 1988. A more demur Jordanian option retained a strong logic for two basic reasons.[59]

First, administration experts knew that Israelis are far more inclined to consider territorial concessions to Jordan than to the PLO or any group of independently organized Palestinians. Second, and more to the point, they understood that Palestinian nationalism must eventually moderate its positions to set the stage for a stable settlement, and, just as important, that moderation must stick. (Contrary to some opinion outside government circles before the Kuwait crisis, genuine and stable PLO moderation was not an accomplished fact.) Jordan's role in advancing that process remained critical both because of its own Palestinian demography and because of its still considerable clout with those from the West Bank. Jordan was not only a shield to protect any future settlement from radical Palestinians and their Arab allies but also instrumental in the process itself. Specifically in this case, West Bank and Gazan leaders relied on Israel's need to use Jordan as a diplomatic address to accelerate the pace of their growing political status at the expense of Arafat and the Tunis crowd.[60]

Jordan's ancillary but still indispensable role, both present and future, explained the attraction for Israeli and U.S. diplomats of a joint Palestinian-Jordanian delegation to any peace conference. It also explained support among Labor party supporters in Israel and virtually all U.S. diplomats for a Palestinian confederation with Jordan thereafter. Without such a confederation no Israeli government would order its military to leave any part of the West Bank and Gaza, and without that, ultimately, there really could be no peace process.

It must have been clear, too, that in practice there was no real difference between the importance of Jordanian stability and Jordan's utility to the peace process. The two most likely alternatives to Hussein were plainly worse for U.S. interests, peace process or no peace process. A post–Hashemite bedouin regime based on the army and the security service would be weaker, so much so that it would not be a practical partner for Israel in a peace process. A Palestinian-Islamist revolutionary regime would be ferociously anti-U.S. and would not be a willing partner for peace. A third possibility, civil war with multipartite foreign intervention, was an outright horror.

Hussein's fall, then, would create a regional diplomatic crisis: those in Israel favoring territorial compromise in the protective nest of a Jordanian-Palestinian confederation would have the political rug pulled out from under them. A stable, potentially conciliable Jordan was a sine qua non for any practicable Israeli peace policy, Labor or Likud. Washington both hoped and expected the Israeli Labor party eventually to play some role in the process. Jordan's absence would have pushed the Labor party, already in the wilderness, either toward insoluble confusion or toward embracing a PLO solution. This, in turn, would have vaulted Labor into oblivion as far as Israeli electoral politics were concerned.

True, supporting the king after the Gulf War offered few opportunities for uplifting rhetoric—although Secretary Baker tried his hand at it anyway.[61] But the longer the peace process went on and the more success it achieved, the more indispensable the Jordanian role became. When in mid-November, after Madrid, Arafat and Assad joined forces to slow a process they disliked but that neither could stop by himself, Jordanian support for the newly emerging Palestinian leadership was absolutely crucial if Arafat and Assad were to be foiled.

Jordan and the Peace Process

Just as the United States had use for Jordan, Jordan had use for the United States and the peace process it created and shepherded. King Hussein had six good, interlocking reasons for wanting to partake in post–Gulf War peace diplomacy.

First and most important, while Jordan was weak, the PLO was even weaker. The chance to take advantage of Yasser Arafat while the PLO was down must have seemed irresistible to the king. Hussein and Arafat had been sparring for decades, before and after the 1974 Rabat Summit empowered the PLO, at Hashemite expense, as the sole legitimate representative of the Palestinians. After Rabat, the king fought a holding action against a rising tide of Palestinian nationalism that threatened Jordan's position in the West Bank and, ultimately, Hashemite rule in the East Bank. After the Gulf War, finally, the tables were turned and the king, though tottering, prepared to attack.

Second, with Syria and Israel likely to become the major focus of post–Gulf War diplomacy, Jordan did not want to be left out on the off-chance that a new peace process achieved success. And even if it did not, Syria was Jordan's once and perhaps future adversary after Saddam Hussein had been reduced. As always, the king wanted to head off trouble; he has always preferred to deal with danger by snuggling up to it rather than by confronting it.

Third, Hussein had to appear active diplomatically in order to raise money. The country was broke; and Amman needed all it could get and not only from Washington. It was through U.S. pressure, too, that the king hoped for a renewal of Saudi aid to the Hashemite kingdom.

Fourth, the king hoped that a helpful diplomacy would buy protection from Washington against future Israeli predations. The specter of "transfer"—a euphemism for expelling Palestinians from the West Bank and Gaza into Jordan—was foremost among Jordanian fears, albeit an exaggerated one.

Fifth, the very process of a peace diplomacy was useful to Hussein. It allowed Jordan to sidestep trouble with Washington over continuing Jordanian-Iraqi ties, including Jordan's importing roughly 55,000 barrels of Iraqi oil a day, about $400 million a year for Iraq. It helped drive Jordanian opinion toward moderation and thus helped the king isolate the Islamist challenge. It gave the king a reason to limit the more irritating manifestations of Jordanian democracy in the interest of a higher goal. It worked to help mend Jordanian-Saudi ties. It worked against extremism in Israeli politics, which Hussein greatly feared, and helped isolate Syrian rejectionism.

Last but hardly least, there were the benefits of peace itself, if only peace could be attained. For decades King Hussein has been waiting for a convergence of forces that would allow him to take prudent risks for peace, rather like a NASA scientist waiting for planets to align in such a way as to facilitate a successful space probe. In the denouement of the Gulf War, this convergence seemed to hover into view.

Hussein has always needed four keys in their locks, ready to be turned in sequence: the Arab key, the Palestinian key, the Israeli key, and the superpower key.[62]

As to the Arab key, Hussein has needed to know that no Arab state or group of states would veto his effort. Jordan remained concerned about Syria, but with Saudi Arabia and Egypt more or less in league, and with Arab radicals like Iraq and Libya on the sidelines, Hussein was buoyed. Indeed, the fact that Jordan was able to scorn Syria's insistence that Jordan and other Arab states stay away from multilateral talks after Madrid, and demur entering bilateral talks with Israel in the absence of U.S. and Soviet diplomats, proves that the tables have turned.

Hussein has also needed Palestinians to share the risk of compromise, lest he meet the fate of his grandfather Abdallah. After the Gulf War, the PLO's weakness and the Intifada-induced shift of the center

of gravity of Palestinian nationalism toward the more moderate Palestinians under occupation appeared to place this key in readiness. Arafat, in particular, was sidelined by the entire process, and West Bank
Palestinians inherently more amenable to Jordanian interests were
raised up in his stead. The king knew Arafat was not about to go
quietly into the Arab night as chairman-emeritus, but never had the
Palestinian national movement as a whole looked better from the
Hashemite point of view.

The Israeli key appeared not to be in readiness at Madrid, but the
·king had reason to be patient. An avid student of Israeli politics, Hussein knew that Israeli opinion—which favors land for peace by more
than half and which opposes the frenzied settlement policy of the
Likud government (as of this writing of November 18, 1991)—might,
under the right circumstances, bring to power in Israel a government
with that key in hand. (Such a government, led by Israel's Labor party,
was to emerge from Israel's June 1992 elections.)

Last, while Jordan disparaged both the skill and the seriousness of
the Carter and Reagan administrations, it had infinitely more faith in
the Bush administration's professionalism and determination.[63]

Hussein's Comeback

In short, King Hussein's planets were lining up, and, therefore,
both his hopes and his fears must have risen accordingly. In the spring
of 1991 unmistakable signs appeared that Hussein was trying to climb
back from the diplomatic, political, and financial abyss, and by the
end of the year he had succeeded, his effort demonstrating how all six
of the king's motives for joining the process had come into play.

In late February the king stated a willingness to reactivate the
Jordanian-PLO political agreement of February 1985, not, to be sure, to
save the PLO from oblivion but to subsume it beneath Jordanian interests.[64] The king also reportedly informed Israeli Labor party leader
Shimon Peres that he was ready to reinstate the London Agreement of
April 1987 between Hashemite Jordan and the Israeli Labor party.[65]
That agreement established a basis for a public diplomacy between Israel and Jordan, and terms of related agreements from the fall of 1985
presaged details of a formal peace between the two countries.[66]

Then, in early March, the king gave a coy interview to the *New
York Times* in which he said Jordan had a major role to play in a
peace process but that he would not substitute for the PLO unless Pal-

estinians asked him to do so.[67] At the same time, however, the king's court was quietly pressing Palestinians friendly to Jordan to ask him to do just that.[68] Before long, the Jordanian version of Jordan's utility to a peace process emerged in the Palestinian press, arguing that the king's popularity among Palestinians because of his support for Saddam Hussein had revived and legitimated his role.[69]

Toward the end of the month, the king's confidant, Adnan Abu-Odeh, visited Washington and spent more than an hour in conference with Secretary Baker. Israel's Dan Meridor, Egypt's Osama al-Baz, and Hanan Mikhail-Ashrawi from Birzeit University were in town at the same time. Shortly thereafter King Hussein visited President François Mitterand in Paris and let it be known that Jordan considered reviving the idea of a confederation between Jordan and the West Bank—if, Jordanian officials said, it would help relieve the area of Israeli occupation. Iraq's defeat, said the king, "opened a new window" for the peace process[70]—Jordan's interpretation, however, resembled far more closely old formulas designed to take advantage of the PLO's nadir in the wake of the Persian Gulf War. The king pursued this tack, arranging a meeting between Baker and Jordanian Foreign Minister Taher al-Masri in Geneva on April 12 and then received the secretary himself at Aqaba on April 21. In short, by the time U.S. diplomacy had advanced to the point where the question of Palestinian representation had to be tackled, Hussein was ready and waiting to lend his hand.

Jordan's gambit forced the question of how Washington should respond to Hussein's hints at diplomacy. The administration concluded that the king's direct participation in a peace process would be valuable only if two conditions were met—as eventually they were. The first concerned the PLO.

Much as Hussein wanted to subordinate Arafat to Jordanian purposes, it was risky business. Some administration experts feared that, for domestic political reasons, the king still would not negotiate with Israel without the protective garb of formal PLO approval. Some lower-ranking State Department officials may have been happy at the prospect of letting the PLO make a comeback, but administration principals looked dimly on the prospect of saving Arafat from the crushing marginalization he had brought upon himself and the PLO leadership, which, they felt, was richly deserved. The hope developed that if the United States insisted on Jordan's leaving the PLO behind, the king would agree, especially since there seemed some prospect of Egyptian, Saudi, and even Syrian help in so doing and, more important, some alternative Palestinian leadership in the territories developing. Clearly, there was no lack of incentives driving Hussein to involve himself in questions of an emerging Palestinian leadership that had begun to assert itself from the early days of the Intifada.

Administration hands also worried that the king might again demand prior Israeli agreement to territorial compromise as a precondition for Jordan's participation. But this would have retarded a peace process, not advanced it, so the Bush administration's response, although it clearly wanted an Israeli commitment to territorial withdrawal, was negative. Jordan, in a weak spot, was hardly in a position to offer much resistance.

After Syria's surprise agreement to the U.S. proposal for a regional peace conference in July 1991, attention soon turned to the perennial deal-breaker of regional diplomacy: Palestinian representation. As the foregoing analysis suggests he would, Hussein eagerly accepted the position of a joint Jordanian-Palestinian delegation, and most of July, August, and September was spent trying to get the PLO to acquiesce. This effort led, not surprisingly, to the restoration of U.S. aid to Jordan. Military aid was restored on September 27, economic aid some weeks earlier.

Syria helped, too, in early April 1991 by destroying the PLO's last stronghold in Lebanon.[71] Moreover, Palestinian nationalism—or at least significant elements of it—was then, arguably, more prone to compromise than ever before, including compromise over its leadership.[72] These new realities, the widespread acceptance of a joint delegation, and the appointment of Taher al-Masri, a Palestinian, as Jordanian prime minister in July, suggested a push either to displace the PLO with a more realistic Palestinian leadership or to watch as that new leadership drove PLO policy.[73] The latter, of course, is about what happened before Madrid, where more faxes went to Tunis than came from it.[74]

As usual, however, the king walked with care in relation to ties both with the United States and with the Palestinians. With respect to Washington, the king had to worry that continuing Jordanian ties to Iraq would get him in trouble. Jordan was still laundering money for Iraq and, as noted, providing cash for Iraqi oil in contravention of UN sanctions[75]—and this at a time when Iraq was actively deceiving UN inspectors trying to ferret out the truth about Iraqi nuclear weapons programs.

In addition, Jordan issued a white paper in September 1991, attempting to refute arguments that Jordan had been pro-Iraqi during the Kuwait crisis and Gulf War.[76] All in all, it was an unconvincing document, but the truth was that U.S. need for Jordan's help in the peace process overrode any inclination to come down hard on the king's dealings with Iraq.

As to the Palestinians, Hussein might have relished Arafat's total capitulation, but he abjured forcing it, waiting instead for a Palestine National Council meeting in mid-September. As everyone waited, questions naturally arose: would Jordan go to a conference without the PLO, and, if so, would it discuss Palestinian as well as more narrow Israeli-Jordanian matters? It was then, in the summer of 1991, that Hussein made it clear that the answer to both questions might well be affirmative as pressure on the PLO mounted from all sides.[77] The king also began making sharply anti-PLO remarks, saying that "a real Palestinian nationalist in my book is someone . . . who has been enduring hardship for years and years, much more so than someone who is sitting outside the territories pontificating about nationalist matters from a position of comfort. . . . People who have lived far from hardship that has lasted all these many years have no right to offer advice on what must or must not be done."[78] Hussein even suggested that once liberation was achieved, there would be no need for the PLO at all.[79]

Still, Hussein did help Arafat stay near the peace process. Hosting Arafat in Amman the weekend of October 18, the king agreed to a "high federal council" composed of Arafat and Hussein. This council was supposed to have ultimate authority over the joint Palestinian-Jordanian delegation in Madrid, but the actual relationship between the three tiers of Palestinian representation—Arafat, the advisory council headed by Faisal al-Husseini and Hanan Mikhail-Ashrawi, and the actual Palestinian delegation to Madrid headed by Haidar Abdel-Shafi—was not entirely clear. By the time the Madrid meeting had concluded, however, it seemed that Palestinian accomplishments had been achieved despite Arafat and not because of him. Both the advisory council Palestinians and the actual delegation had already concluded that as a result of their connections to all the other delegations, including those from Israel and the United States, they were prepared to take more responsibility for the political process than ever before.[80] They would inform Arafat and his colleagues in Tunis, but they were more disinclined than ever before to take orders.

The real significance of the eight-month road to Madrid and the achievements of the conference itself was the progress made in building up a new pattern and a new dramatis personae of Palestinian decision-making. Arafat is still around, but he can no longer call the shots in his imperious and devious way. One can argue that Hussein's allowing Arafat a way into the process via the "high federal council" was feckless and counterproductive—as was Soviet Foreign Minister Boris Pankin's meeting Arafat in Amman. But from Hussein's point of view, this was a means of dealing with Arafat from a position of strength; he was not helping Arafat but rather helping to deliver Arafat to a fundamentally more moderate constituency and one that, moreover, Arafat was losing control over day by day.[81] Besides, Hussein could count on and influence a political process that diminished Arafat far more than he could count on U.S. pressure to force Israel into territorial compromise; in other words, it was better to get something from the process while the getting was good.

The shift in the center of gravity of Palestinian nationalism toward moderation put it squarely within the parameters of Jordanian interests, an achievement the king has pursued since Rabat. The rhetorical dimension of Jordan's influence over Palestinians from days before the Jordanian civil war has changed dramatically, but the reality of that influence has changed much less markedly.

One final outcome of the Madrid Conference that concerns Jordan is worth noting. Between the opening sessions and the movement to bilateral meetings, Syria attempted to make the conference hostage to its own interests. Before the conference convened, Syria announced that it would not participate in multilateral meetings and urged the other Arab parties to follow suit. None did. Just before Madrid, all the Arab parties, including Arafat, met in Damascus and proclaimed a unified approach to the conference, but, as always with such matters, this proclamation was less than met the eye. Before the ink was dry, differences surfaced. Once in Madrid, the Syrians acted with a primitive sterility, dragging reluctant Lebanese behind, while the Jordanians, Egyptians, and the Palestinians took a more pragmatic approach. Syria clearly attempted to control the tempo of the negotiations, to slow them down so that full U.S. pressure could be brought to bear on Israel and more money extracted from Riyadh for Damascus. But Damascus could not control negotiations, and the prospect of being left alone to negotiate with Israel over Golan was not a cheerful one. Rather than the Syrians slowing down the Palestinians and Jordanians, it seemed more likely that the Palestinians and the Jordanians might speed up the Syrians.

From the Jordanian point of view, remembering the dark days of Jordanian-Syrian relations in earlier years, up through and including the mid-1980s, this may have been the best news of all. With Egypt, Saudi Arabia, the Palestinians, and the United States on Jordan's side, Syria effectively isolated itself at and just after Madrid. What was once a de facto Syrian veto over the peace process appeared to be a rapidly waning asset. Indeed, Assad and Arafat, long the two spoilers of the Middle East peace diplomacy, along with their Soviet sponsors, were left at the gate in Madrid—while the power of Mikhail Gorbachev, the leader of their former superpower patron, seemed to wither away. It was hard to think of a set of developments more beneficial to Jordan.

Home Alone?

As suggested, the value of U.S.-led peace diplomacy accrued not only to Jordanian foreign policy but also to the king's domestic situation. King Hussein survived the Kuwait crisis because he bent skillfully with the national mood. One writer put this particularly well with the title "Never So Popular, Never So Precarious."[82] He did this despite rationing and cutting back the work week to five days to save energy and despite what seemed the galloping devastation of the economy. Thanks largely to U.S. peace diplomacy, however, Jordan's internal situation a year after the end of the Gulf War was better in most respects than it had been a year before it.

First, the economy began a recovery, although longer-term prospects for growth remained poor. Returnees to Jordan slowly but surely were finding work, and the population seemed resigned to a lower set of expectations. Foreign workers were sent home as Jordanians accepted lower-paying and lower-status jobs that they demurred before (as for example, service station attendants and dock workers at Aqaba).

Second, the king's nationalist credentials, even among Palestinians in the kingdom, never shone more brightly, and Yasser Arafat's position among Jordan's Palestinians was never more parlous. Even former close PLO associates called for his ouster.[83]

Third, thanks to the Palestinian issue and the energies swirling around the U.S.-sponsored peace process, relations with the United States, Egypt, Syria, and even Saudi Arabia all improved—even as Jor-

dan continued to be Iraq's only window to the wider world—and the
Saudi angle contained a definite economic payoff. On October 17,
Saudi Arabia reopened itself to trade with Jordan, and most analysts
believed it only a matter of time before Saudi aid to Jordan would
begin again as well.[84]

Fourth, the radical threat to the monarchy receded, the Islamic fundamentalist threat in particular. Fundamentalism may wax or wane in
Jordan over the longer run; it is not clear which is more likely. But
there is no question that in the wake of the Gulf War, Jordanian Islamists were sent scrambling. Although superficially united with secular forces in late 1990, deep differences between fundamentalists and
secularists surfaced soon after Iraq's defeat. Also, Islamists unwisely
pushed their parliamentary power. In April 1991, the social development minister, Yusuf al-Athem—a member of the Moslem Brotherhood—ordered gender segregation at his ministry. Education Minister
Abdallah Aqayleh, also a Brotherhood member, banned male sports
teachers from instructing female students, and other Islamist deputies in Parliament introduced legislation banning all coeducational
schools.[85] The more Westernized strata of Jordanian society were appalled at all this and said so.[86] Rami Khouri, in the prodemocratic par-
lance of the hour, warned that Jordan might "make political history by
making the transition from autocracy to democracy to theocracy in
one smooth motion."[87] Even the king himself piled on, publicly criticizing Aqayleh in his speech proposing the al-Masri cabinet.[88]

The social backlash against the Brotherhood was strong, and the
depression caused by Iraqi defeat shrouded their parliamentary influence, at least temporarily. Mosque attendance dropped, in-fighting
appeared, the Jordanian *mukhabarat* acted against an armed cell of
the Islamists called the Army of Mohammed and harassed and arrested selected leftist politicians.[89] As noted, in July 1991 the king appointed Taher al-Masri prime minister, with no Islamists or prominent
leftists in the cabinet.[90] The Brotherhood tried to lead a no-confidence
motion to defeat the government's accession on July 19, 1991—and
failed.

Meanwhile, the monarchy took advantage of the decline of Islamists,
leftist factions, and anti-regime Palestinian political forces in the
country by promulgating a political parties law that posed explicit
constraints on any sectarian or externally connected political organization that would function in the kingdom.[91] Both the National Charter and the political parties law are designed to protect the regime

against an Islamic version of Suleiman an-Nablusi, and while no guarantee is foolproof these were well crafted to the purpose and will work as long as political willpower at the center holds fast.

Further, as Jordan approached the October 30 peace conference, King Hussein took other steps. In August, Parliament voted to oppose Jordan's participation in the peace conference, so the king now took steps to shut Parliament out of the process. The foreign minister, Dr. Abdallah al-Nusur, was a member of Parliament, so in a cabinet shuffle on October 3 the king dumped him, replaced him with Kamal Abu Jaber and had Abu Jaber lead the Jordanian delegation to Madrid. When the Jordanian delegation was finally formed, there was not a single member of Parliament in it.

Moreover, by a decree of September 25, the king delayed the meeting of Parliament from October 1 to December 1 so as not to allow anticonference forces a platform. Antigovernment forces threatened disruptions, but on October 10 Hussein banned an antigovernment rally organized by the Islamists for the day of a major royal address on the peace conference and shut down their newspaper, al-Ribat, as well.[92] As was widely known, too, the king had the border patrol with Israel beefed up to prevent terrorist infiltrations designed to throw a monkey wrench into the proceedings. There were some protests at all of these moves, but they were muted; there were a few incidents in which anti-Madrid rallies were broken up by what clearly were Jordanian mukhabarat operations. There were no deaths, but there was enough broken glass, bruises, and bloodstained clothing to suggest to the opposition that the regime was circling the wagons. If that were not enough to make the point, al-Masri resigned on November 17 amid speculation that Sharif Zaid bin-Shaker would again take over the premiership.

Ironically, Palestinians both in Jordan and in the occupied territories thought of still another reason to look again toward King Hussein: democracy. Palestinians in the West Bank and Gaza, increasingly desperate to save themselves politically after the debacle of the Gulf War, looked to Jordan partly because they believed it to be approaching democracy. Palestinians pride themselves on being democratically minded—although it is sometimes little more than a euphemism for the innumerable divisions of a political movement trying to operate in exile—and many persuaded themselves that being linked to a democratic Jordan is a qualitatively different fate than being linked to the old Jordanian autocracy.[93]

The truth of the matter is that the Jordanian regime and the more conservative East Bank leadership is not about to turn over their country to Palestinian rule just because there are more of them. Indeed, to many conservative East Bank residents, the idea of being saddled again with more than a million West Bank and Gazan Palestinians has the same appeal as a bad dream.

Conclusions

On balance, the comeback staged by the Jordanian regime under the guiding hand of King Hussein from March to October 1991 was little short of breathtaking. Before the Kuwait crisis, the essential question was whether the king would be on the throne when the social changes accumulating in Jordan exploded in crisis. If so, the country had a better chance of weathering the storm. During the crisis the question became whether the Kuwait crisis would elicit that explosion before its time and whether the king would even survive it. Clearly, the process of transformation, begun initially at Hussein's instigation, was for a time at the mercy of forces largely beyond his control. At the end of 1991, as Jordan's skies seemed to lighten, some asked instead whether there was any reason to worry in the first place.

The answer is yes, there was, and there still is. The dangers to the regime from the Kuwait crisis were exaggerated, mainly by those who did not know much about Jordan. But the longer-term dangers to the regime were underappreciated before the Kuwait crisis, and perhaps because of the king's masterful performance throughout 1991 they are liable to be underappreciated again.

The regime survived the Kuwait crisis and has managed to land on its feet, thanks in part to U.S. peace diplomacy and in part to the weakness of the PLO. But it remains to be seen how much control the king will retain in the long run over the top-down approach to constitutional devolution he began some years ago. A lot depends on the peace process.

If the peace process fails, or fails to move fast enough to improve significantly the conditions of Palestinians under occupation, the king could find himself back on the hot seat for having made public concessions to Israel while bringing back nothing to show for it. Basic political problems that beset the regime in the late 1980s persist and will be worsened by regional turbulence. The politicization of Palestinians in the kingdom will accelerate, as will that of young East Bank residents—but in an opposite direction. The future of Islamic fundamentalist power in Jordan, whether Palestinian-led or more ethnically ecumenical, is uncertain but will probably grow in rough proportion to economic hardship and frustration over the immobility of the peace process. As for the economy it is neuralgic at best, and Jordan's economic problems are so structurally rooted that salvation can come only, as it always has, from outside. For Jordan, as for so many other countries for so many centuries, there is money in peace but poverty in war. Even peace may not save the Hashemites for long, but, from the looks of things today, nothing else will.

In short, the monarchy's hold on power is likely to erode over time unless the peace process succeeds and Jordan finds a handy pot of gold at the end of its rainbow that would erase its $8.5 billion debt and provide capital for new investment. Beyond money, peace promises the solution to extremely pressing environmental problems, including water. For six months before August 1990, Ambassador Richard L. Armitage mediated serious discussions between Israel and Jordan over a riparian agreement that would allow World Bank financing of a dam on the Yarmouk River.[94] Those discussions were sidelined by the Kuwait crisis, but, as they communicated directly to Israel at Madrid, the Jordanians are eager to get them finished.[95] To underline the seriousness of the problem, it is worth pointing out that in the fall of 1991, residential water service in much of Amman was limited to two thirty-six-hour periods every two weeks. Private supplies could be purchased for about $20 per truckload, but only if the buyer had a place to store the water and only, of course, if he had money for that purpose.

If the peace process succeeds, it will do so because the Hashemite kingdom of Jordan is both willing and able to play a major role in buffering the fears of both Palestinians and Israelis. Palestinians under occupation want an independent state but may settle for confederation with Jordan if that is the only realistic way to get the Israeli military administration out of their day-to-day affairs. Nearly all Israelis oppose an independent Palestinian state, but some favor greater degrees of Palestinian self-determination to the extent that Jordan can be trusted to moderate the risks that such concessions bring. Jordan's role—and a role that only Jordan can play because of demography and location—is therefore to be likened to a bridge between antagonists who see their mutual relations, rightly or wrongly, in nearly exclusive zero-sum terms. Jordan can make it easier, and therefore more likely, for both parties to take the necessary risks to break the impasse and move matters forward.

If they do, the Palestinians would have neither mere autonomy nor full sovereignty but what, for lack of a better term, we may call sovtonomy—defined simply as something in between the two. As important, however, creating a form of sovtonomy that Palestinians can live with will advance the possibility of peace between Israel and the Arab states. And that, in turn and in time, may increase the level of trust and risk between Israelis and Palestinians. This triangular dialectic among Israel, the Arab states, and the Palestinians suggests the most promising operational means for bringing the Arab-Israeli conflict under diplomatic control. And while Jordan has gotten less attention in this regard than Syria, for it poses no military threat to Israel and Syria does, in the end its role is just as important, if not more so.

But however important Jordan may be, it cannot force Israelis or Palestinians to cross the bridge it provides. Jordan's weakness suggests that if general political comity in the area takes a decided turn for the worse, if the peace process in the end fails and gives rise to spasms of reaction toward extremism and violence, then Jordan stands to suffer greatly. And if Jordan suffers, so eventually will almost everyone else. Deepening hatred between the Israeli and the Palestinian political leadership will further divide Jordanian society between its Palestinian and East Bank parts, and relatedly between its Islamists and secularists; it will divide the Arab states and thus invariably create enemies for the Hashemites; and it will even threaten to destroy a quiet but pragmatic Israeli-Jordanian relationship of many decades' standing.

If the peace process succeeds, therefore, Jordan will not only be helping others but also helping itself. Peace is the only way the Jordanian regime can have good relations simultaneously with Israel, the United States, most of the Arab states, and, most important of all, its own people. From sheer self-interest alone it is clear that if the peace process fails, it will not be because Jordan wished it so.

Notes

1. This is derived from Jordan's *Monthly Statistical Bulletin*, published by the Central Bank.

2. See the charts in Valerie Yorke, *Domestic Politics and Regional Security: Jordan, Syria, and Israel* (Aldershot, England: Gower, 1988), pp. 64–66.

3. See "Hussein's Cash Crisis Is the Talk of the Souks," *The Independent* (London), May 30, 1990, p. 13.

4. See Isabel Kershner, "Why Jordan Needs Peace," *The Jerusalem Report*, November 14, 1991, p. 11.

5. Cited in the *Wall Street Journal*, July 21, 1986.

6. For a discussion, see Philip J. Robins, "Politics and the 1986 Electoral Law in Jordan," in *Politics and the Economy in Jordan*, ed. Rodney Wilson (New York: Routledge, 1991), pp. 184–208.

7. It is not surprising, therefore, that one of the leaders of a march to the Jordan River in April 1990 to support the Intifada and commemorate the "sad day" when Israel was established was Dr. Mamduh al-Abbadi, president of the Jordan Medical Association and of the Council of Jordanian Professional Associations. See Maryam M. Shabin, "Unionist Planning March to King Husayn Bridge," *Jordan Times*, April 12–13, 1990, p. 3. Nor is it coincidental that Laith Shubaileth, head of the Islamist bloc in Parliament, was once president of the Jordanian Engineers' Association.

8. One index of this change is studied in Mahbub Ahmad and Siham Muhammed Mahmud Hosain, "Length of School Life in Jordan," in *Aspects of Population Change and Development in Some African and Asian Countries* (Cairo: Cairo Demographic Center, Research Monograph Series No. 9, 1984), pp. 657–66.

9. One expression of this development was the 1991 creation of a so-called Jordanian Likud Party under the leadership of Abdelsalaam al-Majali. Put simply, the platform of the party is: the East Bank for East Bankers.

10. The rise in religiosity after 1978 is undeniable but is partly a response to broad trends toward secularization in the preceding thirty years. As a result, Jordanian society is more polarized today between the religious and the not-so-religious than ever before. See Fahmi Ghazwi and Steven L. Nock, "Religion as a Mediating Force in the Effects of Modernization on Parent-Child Relations in Jordan," *Middle Eastern Studies*, 25, no. 3 (July 1989): 363–69.

11. See Paul Juredeini and Robert McLaurin, *Jordan* (Washington: CSIS, 1984).

12. See Peter Gubser, *Politics and Change in Al-Karak* (Boulder: Westview, 1985), and Yorke, *Domestic Politics*, pp. 24–29.

13. Although the leadership of Jordanian fundamentalists is not Palestinian, up to 75 percent of its rank and file is. Generally, the leadership is evolutionist, the Palestinian rank and file impatiently militant.

14. See Amatzia Baram, "Baathi Iraq and Hashemite Jordan: From Hostility to Alignment," *Middle East Journal*, 45, no. 1 (Winter 1991).

15. The figure on oil imports comes from Ghadir Tahir, "Project to Deliver Iraqi Oil Via Saudi Pipeline," *Jordan Times*, April 25, 1990, p. 1.

16. The best example was the king's speech to the 1990 Arab Summit meeting in Baghdad.

17. This understanding was probably private but explicit; the matter was addressed publicly in considerable detail, as if it had been thought through. See Mustafa Abu-Lubdah, "Minister Says PLO Ties Reaching 'New Stage,'" *Al-Siyasah* (Kuwait) in *Foreign Broadcast Information Service: NearEast/South Asia* (hereafter *FBIS:NESA*), March 30, 1990, p. 15, and "PFLP Official Comments on Jordanian Ties, U.S.," *al-Dustur*, May 22, 1990, p. 11 (*FBIS-NESA*, May 24, 1990, pp. 6–7).

18. A similar argument is put by Valerie Yorke, "A New Era for Jordan?" *The World Today*, February 1990.

19. Of the twenty-three cabinet members, thirteen were new from the previous cabinet but only a few were new altogether; see "New Cabinet Named in Jordan," *New York Times*, December 7, 1989, p. A6.

20. One even had the temerity to decry "nepotism" in a hereditary monarchy. See "Democratic Unity and Justice Party Established," *Al-Dustur*, August 27, 1990, in *FBIS:NESA*, August 28, 1990, p. 43.

21. Mirmin Murad, "Lower House Calls for Reviving 'Eastern Front,'" *Jordan Times*, February 11, 1990, pp. 1, 3.

22. Badr'Abd al-Haq, "Deputies, Notables Question National Charter," *Al-Yawm al-Sabi'*, April 30, 1990, pp. 12–13, in *FBIS:NESA*, May 7, 1990, pp. 33–34.

23. It had tried in the period 1971–74 but with little success.

24. See Maryam Shahin, "Kings Meets with Members of Leftist Parties," *Jordan Times*, April 26–27, 1990, p. 1; Lamis Adoni, "King Hussein Meets JCP Leadership 15 April," *Jordan Times*, April 17, 1990, p. 1.

25. For a brief survey, see Judith Miller, "Jordan Economy Devastated by Effects of the Gulf Crisis," *New York Times*, October 21, 1990, p. 14.

26. *Middle East Economic Digest* (*MEED*), November 2, 1990, p. 15.

27. This figure is used in Joe Stork, "The Gulf War and the Arab World," *World Policy Journal* 8, no. 2 (Spring 1991): 369.

28. See Tony Walker, "Jordan on the Rebound after Gulf Conflict," *Financial Times*, May 31, 1991. This conclusion is strengthened in detail in *Jordan—Recent Economic Developments*, International Monetary Fund, SH/91/30, February 11, 1991.

29. *MEED*, August 30, 1991, p. 23.

30. See Fahd al-Fanik, "Economic Damage Has Yet to Come," *Jordan Times*, July 21, 1991, p. 4. See also "Jordan: Resettling returnees to cost $4.5 billion," *MEED*, September 20, 1991, p. 15.

31. For details, see Robert Satloff, *Troubles on the East Bank: Challenges to the Domestic Stability of Jordan* (Washington: CSIS, 1986), chap. 2.

32. Robert Satloff's *They Cannot Stop Our Tongues: Islamic Fundamentalism in Jordan* (Washington: Washington Institute, 1988), the result of fieldwork in Jordan, was virtually the only important exception.

33. "Islamists, Leftists Form 'National Front,'" *Jordan Times*, August 20, 1990, pp. 1, 4.

34. See Lamis Adoni, "Jordanians Clamor for Giving Weapons to People," *Christian Science Monitor*, October 18, 1990, p. 4.

35. For details, see "Fallout from Rishon Lezion Killing Reaches Jordan's Refugee Camps," *Al-Fajr*, May 28, 1990, p. 7.

36. For a pithy description and some color photographs of this training, see Joel Brinkley, "Divided Loyalties," *New York Times Magazine*, December 15, 1990.

37. Noted in Stanley Reed's "Jordan and the Gulf Crisis," *Foreign Affairs* (Winter 1990–91): 21.

38. See Eric Schmitt, "U.S. Views Threat by Iraq and Strategy to Split Critics," *New York Times*, September 25, 1990, p. A12.

39. Unknown to the press, Armitage had been to Jordan and Israel six times in the year before the August 2 invasion as the president's appointed mediator on a crucial water negotiation between Jordan and Israel. The king trusted and liked Armitage, making him the best liaison for such sensitive business.

40. Philip Shenon, "West Is Rebuked by Jordanian King," *New York Times*, November 18, 1990, p. 14; Hassan bin Talal, "Does the World Want Jordan to Vanish?" *Christian Science Monitor*, November 28, 1990, p. 18.

41. So claimed in *Al-Hamishmar*, January 30, 1991, p. 1.

42. See the photograph on p. A11 of the *New York Times*, February 28, 1991.

43. Amy Kaslow, "Jordan May Have Helped Iraq Pass Funds around International Freeze," *Christian Science Monitor*, February 27, 1991, p. 1.

44. *Ma'ariv*, January 28, 1991 quoting the London based *Al-Shaq al-Aswat*. This article was also mentioned on Radio Cairo, January 28, 1991. See *FBIS: NESA*, January 29, 1991, p. 36.

45. The full text can be found in *FBIS:NESA*, February 7, 1991, pp. 27–29. See also Alan Cowell, "Jordan Ends Neutrality, Assailing Allied War Effort," *New York Times*, February 6, 1991.

46. Thomas L. Friedman, "U.S. Reviews Aid to the Jordanians," *New York Times*, February 8, 1991.

47. Quoted in Thomas L. Friedman, "President Increases Pressure on Jordan to Stay Neutral," *New York Times*, February 9, 1991.

48. See "Anger and Dismay over U.S. Actions," *New York Times*, February 9, 1991, and Raniya 'Atallah, "King Says U.S. Misinterpreted Speech," *Jordan Times*, February 11, 1991, p. 1.

49. Friedman, "U.S. Reviews Aid," p. A10.

50. Friedman, "President Increases Pressure," p. 8.

51. Private interview.

52. Ross quoted in "Strategic Study Group Report of Meeting Number One, February 28–March 1, 1991," Washington Institute for Near East Policy, p. 11.

53. Quoted in the *New York Times*, March 2, 1991, p. 5.

54. "Tutweiler Cited on State's Postwar Role," Amman Domestic Service, March 26, 1991, in *FBIS:NESA*, March 26, 1991, p. 44.

55. Quoted in Paul Adams, "Palestinians Hope Deadlock Breaks," *Christian Science Monitor*, March 11, 1991.

56. Frank J. Murray, "Bush places Arab-Israeli Harmony First," *Washington Times*, March 8, 1991.

57. A good hint of this approach can be found in David Hoffman, "White House Weighs Jordan Role in Talks," *Washington Post*, March 27, 1991, p. A26.

58. Nickles quoted in Martin Tolchin, "Senate Backs Bill that Withholds $55 Million Aid Plan for Jordan" *New York Times*, March 21, 1991. For the full debate and the text of the amendment see the *Congressional Record—Senate*, March 10, 1991, S3633–S3646.

59. This section borrows from Garfinkle, "Allies of Diminishing Returns: The Hashemite Question," *The National Interest* 25 (Fall 1991).

60. I thank Ken Stein for insisting on this point.

61. Baker said in Amman on October 14: "I do not think anybody, your Majesty, has been more courageous in their support of peace, has been more forward leaning, or more helpful, than have you, sir." See "Baker, King Hold Joint Press Conference," Jordan Television, October 14, 1991, in *FBIS:NESA*, October 15, 1991, p. 47. As a Reuters reporter in attendance later told me, the U.S. and European reporters at the press conference could not believe their ears.

62. For more detail, see Garfinkle "The Importance of Being Hussein: Jordanian Foreign Policy and Peace in the Middle East," in *The Middle East from the Iran-Contra Affair to the Intifada*, ed. Robert O. Freedman (Syracuse: Syracuse University Press, 1991).

63. The king has been quite explicit about this. See his remarks in his interview with Rami Khouri on Jordanian television, translated and reprinted in *FBIS:NESA*, August 8, 1991, p. 27.

64. See "King Husayn's *LePoint* Interview Reported," *Jordan Times*, June 4, 1991, pp. 1, 5.

65. Judith Miller, "Jordanian King Is Said to Express Interest in New Talks with Israel," *New York Times*, March 5, 1991, p. A12. The story broke first in *Ma'ariv*, February 27, 1991, p. 1.

66. For details see Garfinkle, *Israel and Jordan in the Shadow of War* (New York: St. Martin's, 1992), pp. 121–23.

67. Judith Miller, "King Hussein Says He Won't Be PLO Substitute," *New York Times*, March 13, 1991.

68. See Jim Hoagland, "Palestinians: Starting from Zero," *Washington Post*, March 19, 1991, p. A19.

69. Maher Abukhater, "Jordan Seen Playing a Major Role in Future Plan for Mideast Peace," *Al-Fajr*, March 4, 1991, p. 1. See also the echo in George D.

Moffett III, "Jordan's Standing in Mideast Slips, but King Is Still Key to Peace Effort," *Christian Science Monitor*, March 27, 1991, p. 1.

70. See William Drozdiak, "Jordan Revives Proposal for Confederation," *Washington Post*, March 30, 1991, p. A10.

71. See Ihsan Hijazi, "Lebanese Cabinet Tells PLO Guerrillas to Disarm," *New York Times*, April 4, 1991.

72. See Ghassan al-Khatib, "Flexibility, Taking Initiative a Necessary Strategy," *Al Fajr*, March 25, 1991, p. 16.

73. See the analysis of Ehud Ya'ari, "Hussein's Game Plan," *The Jerusalem Report*, August 22, 1991, p. 38.

74. Thomas L. Friedman, "A Step Ahead in Madrid," *New York Times*, November 4, 1991.

75. See, for example, "U.S. to Investigate Jordan on Embargo," *New York Times*, March 1, 1991; Peter Beaumont and Julie Flint, "Jordan Serves as Pipeline," *Washington Times*, April 29, 1991; "Document Shows Jordan, Iraq Plan to Step up Cooperation," *Baltimore Sun*, June 25, 1991; and A. M. Rosenthal, "Praying in London," *New York Times*, June 25, 1991.

76. The text was published in *Sawt al-Sha'b*, September 10, 1991, see *FBIS: NESA*, September 11, 1991, pp. 29–36.

77. See Randa Habib, "Source on Participation in Talks without PLO," Radio Monte Carlo, August 15, 1991, in *FBIS:NESA*, August 16, 1991, p. 31.

78. See "News Analysis: Signs of New Tensions in Jordanian-Palestinian Relations: King Husayn's Criticism of PLO Arouses Questions in Cairo," *Al Sharq al-Aswat* (London), August 7, 1991, p. 3, in *FBIS:NESA*, August 15, 1991, pp. 6–7.

79. Smaller incidents illustrated still more pressure. Palestinian security officials persuaded their Tunisian counterparts to allow them to determine which Jordanian-Palestinian nationals could gain entry to Tunis and which would be denied. A Jordanian national of Palestinian origin visited Tunis in August and was kept waiting four hours at the airport for the approval of the PLO security chief, Hakem Bal'awi. The Jordanian ambassador to Tunisia, Haydar Mahmud, complained bitterly to both the PLO and Tunisian authorities. See "Jordanian Dispute with PLO Over Who Should Represent 'Passport Holders,'" *Sawt al-Kuwayt* (London), August 15, 1991, p. 1, in *FBIS:NESA*, August 20, 1991, p. 3.

80. These points come out clearly in Youssef M. Ibrahim, "For the Palestinians, Fading Euphoria," *New York Times*, November 5, 1991.

81. The same point is made by Ya'ari, "Hussein's Game Plan," p. 38.

82. *MEED*, September 14, 1990, p. 4.

83. "Fatah's al-Hasan Calls for Arafat's Removal," *KUNA* (London), August 10, 1991, in *FBIS:NESA*, August 12, 1991, p. 8.

84. See "Saudi Arabia to Lift Ban, Grant Travel Visas," Radio Monte Carlo, September 4, 1991, in *FBIS:NESA*, September 5, 1991, p. 33; and "Trade Rela-

tions with Jordan to Be Resumed," AFP Radio (Paris), October 17, 1991, in *FBIS: NESA*, October 22, 1991, p. 9.

85. *MEED*, April 12, 1991, p. 14.

86. See, for one example of many, "Minister's Decision on Sports Day Criticized," *Al-Ra'y*, May 9, 1991, p. 3, in *FBIS:NESA*, May 15, 1991, p. 26. See also the amusing column by Michael Sheridan, "Between Beacons of Islam and Tankards of Beer," *The Independent* (London), June 4, 1990, p. 13.

87. Rami Khouri, "Thank Heaven for Little Girls (in Shorts)," *Jordan Times*, May 7, 1991.

88. See the account in Simon Edge, "A New Image," *MEED*, July 5, 1991, p. 7.

89. See "Jordanian Authorities Arrest Youths Following Increase in Infiltration Incidents," *Al-Sharq al-Aswat* (London), April 21, 1991, p. 4, in *FBIS:NESA*, April 23, 1991, p. 25, and "Jordan: Arrest of Leftist Activists Angers Reformers," *Mideast Mirror*, June 13, 1991, p. 19.

90. Joel Brinkley, "Jordanian King Moves to Isolate Islamic Militants," *New York Times*, June 19, 1991.

91. The text of the political parties Draft Law ran in *Sawt al-Sha'b*, July 6, 1991, p. 3, translated in *FBIS:NESA*, July 9, 1991, pp. 47–51.

92. See Salamah Ni'mat, "Special," *Jordan Times*, October 10, 1991, p. 1. The king was already angry at the newspaper's editors for leaking a parliamentary report critical of the Jordanian secret police. See *al-Ribat*, September 10, 1991, pp. 2, 3, 14 in *FBIS:NESA*, September 12, 1991, pp. 37–40.

93. See the remarks of Hisham Awartani in *American Strategy after the Gulf War: The Soref Symposium* (Washington: Washington Institute for Near East Policy, 1991), p. 37.

94. For details, see Garfinkle, *Israel and Jordan in the Shadow of War*, pp. 164–69.

95. Interview, November 1991. Some of these communications might have been direct but not at Madrid. See *Al-Hamishmar*, November 7, 1991, p. 1. The official cited was Elyakim Rubinstein.

12

UNIPOLARITY AND EGYPTIAN HEGEMONY IN THE MIDDLE EAST

Louis Cantori

Nineteen eighty-nine, more than any other year in the past decade, was a benchmark for Egyptian diplomacy and a prelude to the promise and challenge which we see for the decade ahead. In May, we returned to full participation in the Arab League. Two months later President Hosni Mubarak was elected chairman of the Organization of African Unity (OAU). Then, in September, Egypt had the occasion to once again exercise major influence at the ninth summit of the Non-Aligned movement, of which it is a founding member.

    BOUTROS BOUTROS GHALI, former deputy prime minister for foreign affairs, Egypt, now secretary-general of the United Nations.

Naturally, Egypt has a pioneering and leading role whether we and others like it or not. Egypt has its history, culture and the ability to act. The fact is that I acted.

    PRESIDENT HOSNI MUBARAK, August 8, 1990

    The chapter epigraphs illuminate three persistent features of Egyptian foreign policy: the geopolitical arenas within which this policy acts, the destiny of Egypt to lead the Arab world, and the primacy of the executive in making foreign policy decisions.

    Ghali's comments about the significance of the year 1989 for Egyptian foreign policy is important not just for the events described but also for the demarcation of the Arab world, Africa, and the Third World as three arenas of diplomatic activity. With the additional area of the grouping of all Islamic states represented by the international organization of the Islamic Conference, these represent Egypt's perennial policy foci since 1952.[1] Each area represents potential for foreign policy prestige and status having a bearing on the Egyptian quest for leadership of the Arab state system as the most important of these arenas. A fifth focus in fact follows from the principle of nonalignment and positive neutralism of the nonaligned movement and that is the ability of Egypt to manipulate the great powers for economic and military benefit.[2] In addition, Ghali might have noted that 1989 was also the year the cold war ended, thus leaving the United States as the single superpower in the region. Also in that same year Iraq was emerging from its conflict with Iran only to become a competitor with Egypt for Arab world leadership.

President Mubarak's statement likewise is illuminating because speaking in the midst of an international crisis, he accurately portrays Egypt's foreign policy image of itself. Egypt possesses this sense of destiny expressed so clearly in his words. But while Egypt could perceive itself in this fashion and act to carry out its historical role in the Middle East region, the same interview revealed the constraints upon Egypt's effort to play the role. Mubarak went on to note that events after August 2 were being determined by the United States and that the Arab world must act quickly or it would be "humiliated and dictated to." Egypt, as erstwhile regional hegemon, also had to be wary of its U.S. patron.[3] In addition, the statement "I acted" suggests not only the autonomy of Mubarak's decision-making in foreign policy but also that of the Egyptian state itself.

The motivation for Egypt to reenter the Arab state system was a reflection of this unchanging self-image of cultural and historical destiny. However, the Middle East that Egypt reentered after ten years of ostracism because of its separate peace with Israel was itself transformed, and these very changes allowed Egypt's reentry. After all, Egypt had not changed; it still was at peace with Israel, and it still had a close economic and political relationship with the United States. It had in effect been invited back on its own terms. It was the Arab state system that had changed. There were many systemic changes in the Middle East subordinate system that had occurred in the 1980s, but the main one was the fragmentation of the Arab state system and the inability of the principal states of Syria, Iraq, and Saudi Arabia to engage in cooperative relationships. Specifically, Iraq was engaged in a bloody war with Iran until 1988. Syria had supported Iran in that war because of its animosity toward Iraq and was pursuing its own state interests in Lebanon. Saudi Arabia also reluctantly provided economic support to Iraq in order to contain Iran. What was unresolved as a result of the 1980–88 Iran-Iraq War were the remaining territorial losses of the 1967 and subsequent wars (Golan for the Syrians, the West Bank, Gaza, and East Jerusalem for the Palestinians, and South Lebanon for the Lebanese. With the decline in the late 1980s of the Soviet Union's influence as an Arab diplomatic alternative, it became clear that Egypt was needed to exert influence on the United States to get Israel to move on these issues. And Iraq, Saudi Arabia, and the Gulf states needed Egypt as a counterweight to Iran and as a supplier of Soviet weapons from its own production facilities. The catalyst for the realization of the need for Egypt's active participation was the outbreak of the Palestinian Intifada (Uprising) of December 1987. The fragmented Arab state system was in no position to react to the new circumstance when the Palestinian population in the occupied territories took the initiative from the external PLO leadership. Egyptian efforts at promoting the Palestinian cause had anticipated the Intifada, so the Egyptians possessed diplomatic momentum and leadership on the issue. The timing for Egypt's new prominence was further assisted by the end of the cold war in 1989 and the transformation of the Soviet Union from an adversary of the United States to, increasingly, a partner in the search for solutions to the region's conflicts.[4]

If Egypt's return to the transformed Arab state system was welcomed for the foregoing reasons, it was returning also to a changed set of power relationships. By the end of the 1980s, Iraq and Syria had acquired conventional arms capabilities and sizes of force to such a degree that Egypt lagged behind them in numbers and quality of tanks and numbers of aircraft.[5] Egypt by virtue of its U.S. connection did perhaps possess a superior electronic weapons capability, but Syria and Iraq had progressed in terms of missile technology and guidance systems as well as chemical and biological capabilities.[6] This more even military balance along with Saudi Arabia's financial strength created the multipolar configuration of the contemporary Arab world. Egypt's subjective sense of its own superiority now has had to deal with Arab actors more objectively equal in power. The result is that Egypt can now acquire power ascendancy only indirectly via its ability to lead an alliance consisting of Syria and Saudi Arabia, with U.S. backing of these two states.

Egyptian reentry into the Arab state system in May 1989, after ten years of isolation for having made peace with Israel, resulted from careful diplomacy. When Arab League headquarters returned to Cairo from its exile in Tunis with the former Egyptian prime minister Esmat

Abd al-Majid as its secretary general, the political stars of the Middle
East seemed to reposition themselves around Egypt as the political
center. Egypt has always been self-confident about its role, and to
some extent other Arab states continue to defer to Egypt. The fact is,
though, that changes in the international system in the aftermath of
the cold war and regional petrodollar prosperity have constrained
Egypt's return as regional hegemon. At a minimum, the end of the cold
war and the 1991 hot war of the Gulf have created a transitional period
of unipolarity at the international level and an alliance-dependent,
single-power dominance at the regional level that limits and constrains
Egypt's ambitions.

Post-Cold War Unipolarity

Egypt's reentry into the Arab state system in 1989 also coincided with the end of the cold war, with the result that the game of
the "Eastern Question," as described by L. Carl Brown, has become less
dynamic.[7] Rather than the bipolar international system of the rivalry
of two great powers—the British and French in the nineteenth century and the United States and the Soviet Union in the twentieth until the 1970s—which Egypt could manipulate to its advantage, there
exists the single power of the United States with whom the "Eastern
Question" is now played. The Israelis have had a singular relationship
to the United States until recently, but Israel must now share such a
relationship with Egypt and both face the rivalry of the Saudis and the
Syrians for U.S. attention. In its efforts to obtain the benefits of a
close relationship with the United States, Egypt has been successful
in getting sizable U.S. economic assistance. It has not, however, been
able to dominate other key Arab actors such as Syria, Saudi Arabia, or
even Iraq. Syria and Saudi Arabia have been able to use their ties to
the United States to assist in diminishing the potential Egyptian
hegemony.

It can be speculated that the end of the cold war has meant the destruction of the U.S. cold war policy prism. As a result it is now possible for the United States to pursue the goals of secure oil, a secure
Israel, and secure air and sea routes with primary attention to the
amelioration of regional disputes. This change has been expressed in
a more assertive policy that has set the security of the Gulf and the
stability of the region as a whole as key objectives. Thus from the last
year of the Reagan administration until 1992, U.S. policy has rather

doggedly pursued a settlement of the Palestinian question. This process was interrupted by the 1991 Gulf War but has been resumed.

The end of the cold war has had two somewhat unusual aspects in the Middle East. The cessation of the bipolar rivalry of the United States and the former Soviet Union has not resulted in an abrupt decline in their interest in the Middle East as it has, for example, in Afghanistan. Instead, U.S. diplomatic and military activities have increased rather than declined as policy has been focused on access to oil and oil pricing and the value of regional stability in maintaining the free flow of oil. In the last months of the Reagan administration a peace process was initiated and was pursued even more vigorously by the Bush administration. Even the 1991 Gulf War was only an interruption in this process. So, even as the cold war ended, the Middle East as a region within which U.S. policy had been driven by presumptions of Soviet expansionism gained new prominence as a factor in policy making. This prominence was to reinforce the closeness of the U.S.-Egyptian relationship which had begun with the Camp David peace treaty with Israel. In fact, events were to prove that what had begun as a way to secure Egyptian commitment to the peace treaty was to turn into a relationship of significant mutual interest.

The end of the cold war has not signaled the end of Soviet—now Russian—interest in the eastern Mediterranean either. The former Soviet Union had already changed its relationship with its former client states by insisting on hard currency payment for weapons shipments. Unlike other regions of the world, however, the end of the cold war still sees an active Soviet/Russian diplomacy.[8] It currently expresses itself more as a partnership with the United States in sponsoring the peace process and as support in pursuing the Gulf War. In the present transitional phase of the international and regional systems, the net effect of unipolarity has been to limit Egyptian diplomatic choices and maneuvers to the United States.

Thus our view of the Middle East has come to be defined by the participation of the superpowers in the Middle Eastern subordinate system and the interaction of these powers with regional actors.[9] The dynamic of the pursuit of their interests in the region by the great powers and by local nation-states results in either mutual or competing goals. As has been indicated, Brown defined this historical process as the "Eastern Question," arguing that the relationship has not always been one of great power domination but rather a more complex one of small states attempting to manipulate larger ones to their own advantage (e.g., the Syrian "tail" wagging the Soviet "dog" and Israel's similar relation to the United States).[10]

Egypt's objective in this period is to draw closer to the United States in order to gain economic and military advantages, especially since Egypt's military armaments are falling behind not only Israel but also Syria and Iraq. But this closeness has another dimension: ingratiation at the expense of other states, especially Israel. Egypt is a status quo state with an important interest in regional stability. By contrast the policy of Israel's Likud government of land annexation was destabilizing. Egypt serves U.S. interests concretely in that it is now a credible interlocutor with all of the Arab states, even with Iraq prior to the August 1990 invasion of Kuwait, in matters of peace and even more dramatically in the case of war.[11]

The Egyptian State and Foreign Policy

The concept of the autonomous state is important to the understanding not only of domestic politics but of foreign policy as well.[12] The autonomous state is an institutionalized state (i.e., one whose sovereignty is acknowledged both internationally and domestically). The international point of view is the broader one, namely the minimal requirement that there is authoritative exercise of control over territory irrespective of regime and government. From the foreign policy point of view, the autonomous state is one in which the regime and its basic policies and institutions are continuous even while its governments change. The autonomous state viewed domestically is a highly politically legitimate state. In the case of Egypt, the 1952 revolution and its institutions have come to be the ideology and structure of the Egyptian regime. In this respect, then, the changes in government from Nasser to Sadat to Mubarak have resulted in only a marginal redefinition of the regime. Not unexpectedly, therefore, Egyptian foreign policy has been more continuous than discontinuous over its forty-year history. It is a strong or hard state in the sense that its legitimacy strengthens its political ability to maintain order and extract an economic surplus.[13] It is a week or soft state in that the center does not perform religious, educational, industrial, and other functions.[14] In a politically hard state, foreign policy is an extension of the traditional imperative to maintain order (i.e., secure the nation's frontiers). In Egypt, foreign policy is also a source of economic and military enhancement. In this respect foreign policy making in the "traditional" Islamic state combines both order and taxation.

The autonomous Egyptian state's facility in foreign policy making is aided by the fact that the meaningful political groupings and individuals are located in the political class (i.e., the top 20 percent of the population who constitute the political class).[15] From this class, the ruling elite is recruited, and it makes the political decisions of the society. The political class in the autonomous corporatist Egyptian state is licensed (i.e., given monopolies over educational, agricultural, industrial, and other functions necessary for the maintenance of the state).[16] The devolution of these functions is what makes Egyptian state policy soft or inefficient. On the other hand, foreign policy decision making is what is reserved for the state and is ordinarily not susceptible to criticism. The corporatist state also possesses a conservative ideology that values the community over the individual; thus foreign policy is for the benefit of all and is not restricted to the advantage of a particular group or individual. This process legitimizes and stabilizes foreign policy. The consultative, as opposed to the representative, character of the state also facilitates it.[17]

In specific terms, this characteristic expresses itself in Egypt by an elitist parliamentary system. Not only the governing National Democratic Party supports foreign policy; it is also supported by members of the recognized political opposition (e.g., the New Wafd, the Labor Party, the Moslem Brothers, and so on). They have supported the peace treaty with Israel, the policy of pursuing a peace process on behalf of the Palestinians, and the relationship of Egypt with the United States. In the Gulf War, they supported opposition to Iraqi aggression in Kuwait, but they also opposed a role for the United States and the West in reversing it.[18]

The illegal opposition at both extremes of the political spectrum challenges a foreign policy consensus at the top and vehemently condemns U.S. policy. The opposition on the religious right has been consistently present since 1974. Its supporters have been involved in arson, communal violence against Coptic Christians, and assassinations, the most noteworthy that of President Anwar Sadat in October 1981. Domestically, they call for the creation of an Islamic state, including the instituting of Islamic law. In foreign policy they support the Palestinian cause, and during the Gulf War they opposed both what they regarded as aggression by the non-Islamic state of Iraq and the intervention of Western forces.[19] On the political left, an underground group of Nasserists under the leadership of Gamal Abd al-Nasser's son Khalid and the organization called Egypt's Revolution carried out armed attacks in the 1970s on Israeli diplomats they sus-

pected of being intelligence operatives and U.S. security personnel suspected of working with them. They have also been militantly supportive of the Palestinians and opposed in the name of anti-imperialism
to the prominence of the U.S. role in Egypt and the region, especially
as a supporter of Israel.[20] Mubarak is thus able to operate in foreign
policy terms fairly free from constraints by the political center in
Egypt while looking nervously over his left and right shoulders at
those groups and their constituencies. While the security apparatus
has repressed them with some efficiency, he also feels impelled to
diminish their appeal by the strength of his regionally hegemonic policy of Egyptian nationalism.

The popular centrist attitude toward the Gulf War was reinforced
by the experiences of as many as one million Egyptians, including
peasants, who had gone to Iraq during its 1980–88 war with Iran.
They provided much-needed replacements for the Iraqi labor force
mobilized in the war effort. In addition, Egypt sold Iraq Soviet weapons from its own weapons production center. Egyptian officers were
advisers, especially to the Iraqi air force, and many Egyptians were
recruited into the Iraqi army, suffering casualties and being taken prisoner.[21] When the Iraqi army was demobilized to a degree after 1988,
however, tensions arose between Iraqis and Egyptian nationals working in Iraq. Beatings and hundreds of deaths resulted.[22]

The violence was covered extensively in the Egyptian media and
created strong anti-Iraq sentiments. For this reason student demonstrations against government policy following the Iraqi invasion of
Kuwait were not very significant. More significant, but apparently
handled in a sensitive and quiet manner, was the reported unrest in
the officer corps against Western involvement in an "Arab" problem
and especially an invasion of an Arab country. The shortness of the
war prevented even the recall of the Egyptian field commander from
the Gulf from having further effects.[23] Mubarak's leadership role in
the coalition was maintained.

Pre-Gulf War Egyptian Foreign Policy

Egyptian foreign policy in the pre–Gulf War period was largely
concerned with the Palestinian question. In addition, however, Egypt
already had been invited by Iraq and Saudi Arabia to provide supplies,
military training, and military insurance in the struggle against Iran.
This role would assist significantly Egypt's gaining reentry into the

Arab state system.[24] Egypt still bore the burden, however, of having been willing to settle for its own territorial objective of recovering the Sinai in its 1979 peace treaty with Israel but failing to achieve the promise of autonomy for the Palestinians given in the 1978 Camp David accords. Mubarak, throughout the late 1980s, sought to relieve Egypt from this opprobrium and in doing so to use it as a ticket for acceptance back into the Arab states.

This focus on the Palestinian question coincided with the rekindling of U.S. interest in the problem in 1988, the last year of the Reagan administration, through the diplomatic activities of Secretary of State George Shultz.[25] That a U.S. administration should be so diplomatically active in the Middle East on the eve of a U.S. presidential election was in itself remarkable. Mubarak worked to sustain this effort even in the final two months of the campaign. On October 22, 1988, Mubarak met with King Hussein of Jordan and Chairman Yasser Arafat of the Palestine Liberation Organization (PLO) in Aqaba, Jordan. Following this meeting Mubarak and Arafat went to Baghdad to confer with Saddam Hussein. The dramatic result was the decision by the Palestine National Council (PNC) on November 15, 1988, to accept UN Resolutions 242 and 338, that is, agreeing to the principle of a two-state solution and the recognition of Israel.[26] This major diplomatic development in which Egypt had played an important role was consonant with U.S. policy. It illustrates Egypt's intent to retain its own policy independence but also to recognize the PNC declaration of an independent state of Palestine. This stand was contrary to U.S. policy, which still adheres to the Camp David principle of only autonomy for the Palestinians. The diplomatic momentum was sustained by Soviet Foreign Minister Eduard Shevardnadze's visit to the region in February 1989 and his support for an international conference. The new U.S. secretary of state, James Baker, in a meeting the next month with Israeli Foreign Minister Moshe Arens, also supported the idea of negotiations.[27]

The actual peace process was underlaid by the original Camp David formula of elections in the occupied territories, the creation of an elected Palestinian negotiating team, limited autonomy for a three-year period, and further talks in the third year to arrive at a final diplomatic solution at the end of five years on the basis of UN Resolutions 242 and 338. These were basically the U.S. plan and assumptions as set forth in an important speech by Baker to the U.S. Israeli Public Affairs Committee in Washington on May 22, 1989. In March, Prime Minister Yitzhak Shamir, in a visit to Washington, had laid out his version of this approach that was made concrete by the Israeli cabinet on May 14, 1989. While not agreeing to the principle of land for peace and ceasing the settlement process, it did call for elections and a five-year transitional period. Baker in his speech had alluded to the success of Egypt's peace treaty with Israel and Egypt's ability to reenter the Arab state system on its own terms as an indication of the changes in the Middle East. Shamir's plan explicitly called for Jordanian and Egyptian participation in the negotiations.[28] Egypt continued to play the role of facilitator of the peace process with the announcement of President Mubarak's ten points as a response to the Shamir plan. These points were largely devoted to the implementation of elections for the Palestinians. At the same time, however, the document stated, in agreement with U.S. policy but opposed to Shamir's, that the exchange of land for peace with an assurance of Israeli security was at the basis of the peace process.[29] In response, five points were presented in October 1989, as the Baker Plan. It explicitly recognized that Egypt and Israel had been in consultation with one another and that, while Egypt could not be a substitute for the Palestinians, it would consult with them in anticipation of a meeting with Israel and the United States. This meeting was to be held in late December in Washington and attended by the foreign ministers of the United States, Israel, and Egypt.[30] It did not take place, however. Within the Israeli Unity government, it was Labor, not Likud, that was most responsive to the U.S. initiative. The ensuing internal wrangling resulted in the fall of the Unity government on March 15, 1990. It was only on June 11 that Shamir was able to form a more rightist government on the issue of the peace process.[31]

With the peace process stalled, Egypt's ability to act as facilitator declined. The killing of seven Palestinians by a deranged Israeli in Rishon LeZion resulted in widespread retaliatory violence in the occupied territories. This violence, plus the stalled peace process, contributed to the ascendancy of radical sentiment among the externals in the PLO. An abortive PLO seafront raid on Israel on May 30 was followed by a statement of a PLO executive member that Iraq was now preferred to Egypt because the latter was hampered by its economic dependency upon the United States and its peace treaty with Israel. Iraq, on the other hand, was a growing power in the region and was said to be providing a "material base" for a peace settlement.[32] When the PLO refused to condemn the beachfront raid, the United States cut off contact with the PLO in Tunis. Egypt's role in the peace process had now ceased, and Iraq emerged as a rival to Egyptian efforts at regional hegemony. Following a meeting in Washington with the Egyptian foreign minister on June 27, a U.S.-Egyptian plan for the PLO to discipline those involved in the May 30 attack was rejected by the PLO. The peace process was at an impasse.

Egypt and Pre-Invasion Diplomacy

The period before Iraq's invasion of Kuwait on August 2 gave evidence of the relative decline of Egyptian foreign policy influence. In the 1980s widespread regional development had been created by subregional organizations perhaps to counteract the decline of Arabism and the sense of regional fragmentation. The first of these groupings was the Gulf Cooperation Council (GCC), formed in May 1981; it was followed, eight years later, almost simultaneously, by the Arab Cooperation Council (ACC), made up of Egypt, Iraq, Jordan, and Yemen, and the Arab Maghreb Union (AMU), made up of all the North African states, the former on February 16, 1989, and the latter the next day. According to the investigative reporting of Pierre Salinger and Eric Laurent, evidence began to emerge at the first annual meeting of the ACC in Amman on February 21, 1990, of animosity between Saddam Hussein and Mubarak when Saddam called those cooperating with the United States "cowards," and Mubarak and his delegation stormed out of the meeting.[33] The Arab summit in Baghdad on May 28 had been called to protest the influx of Soviet Jews into Israel, but in private remarks Saddam launched an attack on Kuwait for overproducing oil and depressing oil prices. It was this, plus Iraq's seeking the role of regional Arab leader, that again provoked Mubarak to anger.[34] Later, following the invasion of Kuwait, Egypt came to believe that Iraq had agreed to the creation of the ACC in order to alienate Jordan and Yemen from Egypt.[35]

Thus, by the summer of 1990 a momentary exhaustion of the opportunities for peace and the emergence of an assertive Iraq occurred simultaneously. Iraq was able to champion the Palestinian issue for the moment and combine it with pan-Arab rhetoric in order to cloak its grievances with Kuwait. As noted, Egypt encountered this militancy at the three-day Arab summit ending on May 30, 1990, which publicly condemned the arrival of Soviet Jews in Israel, while Saddam complained privately that Kuwait had victimized Iraq during its war with Iran. This was at a time when Iraq was burdened with the high costs of reconstruction after an exhausting eight-year war and was also facing Kuwaiti demands for the repayment of wartime loans.[36]

Egypt was aware of the growing Gulf crisis and saw the need to ameliorate it although seemingly without great urgency. Thus, all through July, while engaging in meetings and discussions with the two parties to the dispute, Egypt tended to make major foreign policy pronouncements dealing with the peace process rather than with the Gulf.[37] As we saw, the Arab summit of May 28–30, 1990, revealed the greater emphasis on the Palestinians and on the issue of Soviet Jews. After this, however, as the Iraqi military buildup became evident, a greater sense of urgency began to develop. On July 23, the Iraqi foreign minister met with Mubarak and King Hussein in Egypt, and Egypt suggested a four-point plan for resolving the conflict.[38] With continued urgency, Mubarak was in Baghdad on July 24. It is alleged that he had been told by Saddam that Saddam would not attack as long as negotiations were under way but that Mubarak chose to tell Kuwait and Washington that Iraq had said unconditionally that it would not attack.[39] That is, in effect he set up Iraq by decreasing the strength of concern about Iraqi behavior in the last days of fruitless efforts at an Arab solution prior to the invasion. Mubarak subsequently traveled to Kuwait and Riyadh with the expectation that media attacks would end and that Iraq and Kuwait would meet in Saudi Arabia in a few days.[40] The basis of the meeting would be Egypt's four points: that the less important issues would be considered first; that Sheikh Sabah and President Hussein would meet directly; that each side would communicate its positions to the other ahead of time; and that any continued disagreement would be mediated by Egypt and Saudi Arabia. In fact, when the parties met on July 31, they were represented by underlings and not by their leaders; insults were exchanged, and the Iraqi delegation left.[41]

Egypt was angered by the outcome, feeling that Iraq had not conducted itself in good faith and in accordance with the four points. This feeling of betrayal by the Egyptians was shared by the Saudis, who said that they had not been called in to mediate.[42] What is clear is that the Egyptians thought that they had developed a formula for defusing the conflict whereas, in the absence of the Egyptians in Jidda on July 31, the Saudis were left to carry the burden of shepherding the process. Clearly, efforts at an Arab solution had failed.

Egypt and the War

Mubarak's noting of the failure of the Arab efforts at mediation have been referred to. The U.S. action was to move quickly at the

United Nations for condemnation of the invasion and to call for a UN-sanctioned economic boycott. When Egypt inquired about further mediation, the United States said that it would continue with preparations for the boycott but that meanwhile Egypt could act if it wished.[43] In effect, events and the decisions of others had taken the initiative from the Arabs. As Mubarak noted, Egypt now had to act in unison with the United States and the United Kingdom, for "Egypt cannot lose its credibility before the entire world and thus lose the ability to mediate with any world country in connection with any issue. The U.S. and the U.K. were . . . doing as they please in our own area. If Egypt does not act, we will be as good as dead bodies. We will be humiliated and dictated to."[44]

King Hussein met with Mubarak in Alexandria, Egypt, on the day of the invasion. The former continued to attempt to broker an Arab solution to the conflict by asking that Egypt and the Arab League delay their condemnation of the invasion. Mubarak agreed that his foreign ministry and not he himself would issue the condemnation.[45] With the international community in the United Nations now having seized the initiative, Egypt felt impelled to move in concert with Saudi Arabia and the GCC states plus Syria to increase its leadership role and to give the Arabs a role in the crisis. There followed two important Arab League meetings that would crystallize the Arab alignment from then until the end of the war.

On August 3, the Arab League met in emergency session in Cairo, and by a two-thirds vote (fourteen of twenty-one states) both condemned the invasion and provided continued evidence of Arabism, by opposing intervention by non-Arab forces. Iraq, Yemen, the PLO, Mauritania, Sudan, Jordan, and, implicitly, Libya, which did not attend, refused to support the motion.[46]

Jordan was still attempting to broker a summit meeting with Saddam Hussein for August 4. Saddam Hussein had allegedly said that if the negotiations were successful, he would withdraw from Kuwait. Again, it is claimed that Mubarak passed word to the United States that in fact Iraq would not withdraw. The United States is said then to have communicated with Egypt that it was expected to condemn the invasion publicly.[47]

Jordan, along with Yemen, still continued to try to broker a summit meeting with Saddam Hussein for August 4, but this move was rejected by Egypt and Saudi Arabia apparently because they were under pressure from the United States to condemn Iraq.[48] When the Arab League summit did meet in Cairo on August 10 with Iraq in attendance, it would further crystallize the division in the Arab world over the crisis.

Egypt, on August 7, had already ordered up the first of what would become 30,000 troops to the Gulf (the second largest force in the coalition next to the United States). It had not only committed itself to the coalition against Iraq but had successfully persuaded the Syrians to join it. Egypt led the majority at the August 10 summit in a vote by twelve of twenty-one members to support UN Resolutions 660, 661, and 662 calling for Iraq's withdrawal. Thus Egypt, acting in effect as alliance leader, had succeeded in getting the summit to commit Arab troops for the defense of Saudi Arabia. In addition, Arab League Resolution 195 also endorsed the presence of foreign troops according to the UN Resolution 661 of August 6 in order to defend Saudi Arabia. Even with this emphasis upon defense, nine of the Arab League states would not support the resolution. Iraq, Libya, and the PLO voted against it (the PLO changed its vote the next day to abstention)—that is, they did not oppose the invasion of Kuwait. The others (with Algeria and Yemen abstaining, and Jordan, Mauritania, and Sudan having reservations) were mostly concerned with the introduction of foreign troops into what they regarded as an Arab problem.[49] This sizable feeling of Arabism would continue to characterize the important Arab state and domestic opposition to the later effort to oust Iraq by force.[50]

The Soviets attempted to mediate the conflict up to the UN-sanctioned outbreak of hostilities on January 15, 1991, but without success. Only Jordan and Arafat, already on the side of Iraq, were to continue to seek an Arab solution. The Arab coalition led by Egypt was committed to the use of force. The Egyptian and Syrian forces were to see little combat in the short war that followed, but they did secure the most Western flank of the coalition forces while the United Kingdom, France, the United States, and Saudi Arabia engaged the Iraqis in actual combat.

The Consequences of the War for Egypt

The conclusion of the war should have maximized Egypt's leadership role in the region. Egypt had after all once again found its interests coinciding with those of the United States. It was able to play the diplomatic leadership role in forging an alliance between the United States and the Arab states of the coalition in a military action, even one directed against a fellow Arab nation. Egypt had been successful in achieving this by playing the role of linchpin between Syria and Saudi Arabia. It was this axis that was able to form the coalition and that would remain important in the resumption of the peace process after the conflict. Iraq as Egypt's chief rival for regional leadership had been reduced. Moreover, Egypt's relationship to the United States had been strengthened because, as in the 1989–90 Baker peace process, Egypt functioned less as a state to be catered to because of its treaty with Israel and more as an ally. In this respect it also was able to draw ahead somewhat of Israel in a relationship with the United States. Israel, in the peace process and in the war, was either an increasing obstacle to U.S. policy or a burden because it had to be rewarded for holding back retaliation against the Iraqi SCUD attacks that killed thirteen Israelis and caused considerable property damage. In fact, however, while Egypt remains prominent in its relationship to the United States, its regional leadership has not dramatically increased in the aftermath of the war.[51]

On the other hand, some of the economic objectives of Egyptian foreign policy have been dramatically achieved. As much as one-half of its $40 billion debt has been forgiven by the United States, Saudi Arabia, Japan, the World Bank, Germany, and France, relieving it from an annual payment of more than $1 billion in debt servicing. In addition, Egypt has received in excess of $10 billion in compensation for its economic war-related losses (decline in tourism, worker remittances, and so on). In addition it has received at least $9 billion in new loans from the International Monetary Fund (IMF) and other agencies. It has also been once again temporarily relieved of the stringency of economic reforms by the IMF.[52]

The diplomatic and military prominence of Egypt's wartime role was not destined to be translated directly into an increase in its regional hegemony, however. At first, it appeared that it would be. The postwar Gulf was, after all, going to require a security arrangement to maintain the accomplishments of the war in reducing the Iraqi threat and to contain an expected resumption of Iranian efforts to dominate the area. Immediately upon the end of the war at a meeting of Egypt, Syria, and Saudi Arabia in Damascus on March 6, 1991, a declaration was issued stating that Egyptian and Syrian forces would collaborate with those of Saudi Arabia and the GCC in maintaining Gulf security.[53] In fact, however, the Saudis began to retreat from this "Arab solution" because, apparently given the possibility of Arab republican forces amidst the Gulf monarchies and the strengthening of Egyptian

hegemony, it decided that the more politically distant—but now militarily proven—U.S. "over the horizon" forces were preferable. Egypt
withdrew its forces from the Gulf on May 8, and a meeting in Kuwait
on July 5, 1991, did not rectify the situation.[54] Egypt's leadership position within the Syrian and Saudi axis had been weakened. A year or
more after the conclusion of the war, the Gulf remains without a security regime in place, other than the U.S. security guarantee for the
GCC.

The Resumed Peace Process

U.S. policy on the peace process was announced by President
Bush in a speech before Congress on March 6, 1991, using the declared conclusion of the war on February 27, 1991, to get on with the
interrupted peace process.[55] Israel, in anticipation of a visit by Secretary Baker, announced a recommitment to its own May 1989 peace
plan on March 10,[56] thus continuing to make Israel's own plan the
center of a resumed peace process. The new direction of U.S. policy
became evident when Baker met with Faisal Husseini and a delegation of Palestinian leaders from the occupied territories on March 12.
This signified that as the peace process was resumed, the United
States would deal directly with the internal Palestinian leadership and
Egypt would continue to deal with the PLO representing the externals. This plan has reduced Egypt's prewar prominence in the peace
process to a degree. It is also true, however, that the diplomatic rehabilitation of the PLO after its wartime association with Saddam Hussein remains vital to the peace process. The internal delegation, in its
formal statement at its March 12 meeting, reiterated the central authority of the PLO in any peace negotiations.[57] While the Egyptian
role is less visible, it remains vital to the authority of any peace
agreements. At the same time, however, Egypt continued to be con-
sulted by Secretary Baker in repeated trips in the spring and summer
of 1991 to set up a regional peace conference. Perhaps the most important task successfully undertaken by Egypt was to persuade Syria
to agree to attend an international peace conference. It was also able
to get Saudi Arabia to attend at least symbolically the opening session of the Madrid Conference in October 1991. By August 1 Israel
had also agreed, and the result was that all of the concerned states
agreed to attend the international conference to be held in Madrid in
October 1991.

Meanwhile, Egypt in its own effort at innovation in the peace process, would propose on July 19 an end to the Arab economic boycott of Israel, if the latter would halt construction of settlements in the occupied territories. Egypt was supported in this by Saudi Arabia, but Israel's Likud government ignored the offer.[58] (The Labor government, which came to power following the Israeli elections of June 1992, halted construction of all settlements except those in limited "security" zones.)

Conclusions

The end of the Gulf War and the beginning of the 1991–92 peace process in the Middle East has witnessed the institutionalization of Egypt as the first among equals of the Arab state system in general and in the Egyptian–Syria–Saudi Arabian axis in particular. While Egypt's military power has been equaled by Syria and prewar Iraq, it has gained authority and influence via the mechanism of the "Eastern Question" through its close association with the United States. In this fashion, international system unipolarity is linked to the intermediate role of Egypt within the Syrian-Saudi axis. The association is based on the mutual interests of the two states in desiring a solution to the Palestinian problem in order to stabilize the region. Egypt achieved—at least temporarily—the goal of gaining a degree of prominence over the Israelis within the U.S. policy sphere, thus expanding its military capabilities and giving it major economic advantages. Its continued ability to work with the Syrians and the Saudis ensures its hegemonical role. In the final analysis, however, Egypt's hegemonical ambitions will depend on a constructive outcome to the peace process. If solutions acceptable to the Palestinians, a settlement on the Golan acceptable to Syria, and one in Lebanon acceptable both to Syria and the Lebanese are worked out, then Egypt will continue to benefit as a guarantor of the agreements. It is noteworthy, however, that unlike the Nasser era of the 1960s, Egypt's regional foreign policy future will be in some kind of alliance, such as the current one with Syria and Saudi Arabia. Egypt is now less of a hegemon and more of a first among equals of the key Arab states. If no agreement is reached, then the volatile factors of the economic have-nots (Algeria, Tunisia, Morocco, Yemen, and Sudan) and the Islamic trend could come together to destabilize and radicalize the region. Iran has already shown a propensity to fish in troubled Arab waters by opposing the peace process. While Iran's post-Gulf War policy has been to improve its relations with Western Europe and the United States, its radical dimension continues to express itself. With the ending of the Republican Guard activities in Lebanon and the greater accountability of Hezbollah to the Syrians, both now appear active in the Sudan. There they have a base of operations which is already reaching out to the Islamic trend in Algeria and Tunisia, and especially in Egypt. In Egypt training has been given to the illegal Jihad organization, and its fugitive leader has been given asylum.[59] If Syria was to turn away from the peace process, it could come into association with Iran and contribute to this radicalization. Nuclear, ballistic missile, chemical and biological weapons represent latent factors in the situation. Egypt's foreign policy of an autonomous state operating within an elite consensus of what constitutes Egypt's historical hegemonical role and its particular national interest thus continues as a factor of regional stability. In the final analysis, Egypt's own domestic politics, and therefore its foreign policy, will be affected by events in the region. A successful peace process and provisions for the economic redistribution of Arab oil wealth are necessary for its continued stabilizing role in the region.

Epigraph Sources

Boutros Boutros Ghali, "Egyptian Foreign Policy in the Nineties," *Mediterranean Quarterly* 1 (Summer 1990): 26.

Hosni Mubarak, first press conference after the August 2 Iraqi invasion of Kuwait. Mubarak explained Egypt's role of attempted mediation in the immediate pre-invasion period. *Near East and South Asia, Foreign Broadcast Information Service*, August 8, 1990.

Notes

1. These are the arenas described by Gamal Abd al-Nasser in his *Egypt's Liberation* (Washington: Public Affairs Press, 1955).

2. This point is made by John Waterbury in analyzing the political economy of Egypt in its facility in almost routinizing international economic assistance benefits. See Waterbury, *The Egypt of Nasser and Sadat* (Princeton: Princeton University Press, 1983), chap. 2, pp. 21–40, where he argues, among other things, about the possibility of dependent development that can be the consequence of such a policy. This is also the argument in Ali Hillal Dessouki, "The Primacy of Economics: The Foreign Policy of Egypt," in *The For-*

eign Policies of Arab States, ed. Bahgat Korany and Ali Hillal Dessouki 2d ed. (Boulder: Westview Press, 1991), pp. 156–85.

3. News Conference, Middle East News Agency, August 8, 1990, in *Foreign Broadcast Information Service: Near East/South Asia* (hereafter *FBIS:NESA*) August 8, 1990. Historical geopolitical factors having to do with the strategic factors of the Nile River and the Mediterranean Sea dating from Pharaonic times to the present are summarized in Joseph Lorenz, *Egypt and the Arabs* (Boulder: Westview Press, 1990), pp. 1–13.

4. The preceding constitutes the analysis in Cantori, "Egypt Reenters the Arab State System," in *The Middle East from the Iran-Contra Affair to the Intifada*, ed. Robert O. Freedman (Syracuse: Syracuse University Press, 1991), pp. 341–66.

5. See Paul Noble, "The Arab System: Pressures, Constraints and Opportunities," Table 3.8, "Military Capabilities, Eastern Arab World, Mid-1980s," p. 70, in Korany and Dessouki, *The Foreign Policies of Arab States.*

6. Joshua Sinai, "Arms Sales to the Middle East: Security or Pattern of Destructive Competition?" *Armed Forces Journal* (August 1991): 40–44. For the explosiveness of the transfer of ballistic technology by diplomacy rather than necessarily indigenous technical development, see Janne E. Nolan, "World Wide Threats and Their Implications for the U.S. Force Structure: The Middle East and South Asia," General Accounting Office Conference on World Wide Threats, October 30, 1991, p. 3, and, more generally, Nolan, *Trappings of Power: Ballistic Missiles in the Third World* (Washington: Brookings Institution, 1991).

7. L. Carl Brown, *International Politics and the Middle East: Old Rules, Dangerous Game* (Princeton: Princeton University Press, 1984), pp. 16–18. In this book the historical concept of the "Eastern Question" is defined and operationalized as an analytical concept.

8. Robert O. Freedman, "Moscow and the Gulf War," *Problems of Communism* (July–August 1991): 1–19.

9. First developed as a concept in Louis J. Cantori and Steven Spiegel, *The International Politics of Regions* (Englewood Cliffs, NJ: Prentice-Hall, 1970).

10. Brown, *International Politics and the Middle East.*

11. In fact, both U.S. and Egyptian interests were compatible with preinvasion Iraq in that they viewed Iraq as a foil to Iran in the 1980–88 war and both gained economic advantages as well. See Ali E. Hillal Dessouki, "Egypt's Response to the Gulf Crisis," *Current History* (January 1992): 34 ff.

12. For a general discussion of the concept of state autonomy see Theda Skolpol, "Bringing the State Back In: Current Research," in *Bringing the State Back In*, ed. Peter Evans et al. (Cambridge: Cambridge University Press, 1985), pp. 9–20. For an Egyptian application, see Waterbury, *The Egypt of Nasser and Sadat*, pp. 12–17. The discussion here of Egyptian foreign policy follows the suggestion of Korany and Dessouki in emphasizing the domestic environ-

ment, foreign policy orientation, and the decision-making process. See "A Literature Survey and a Framework for Analysis," in Korany and Dessouki, pp. 18–22. The implication of the analysis here is the same as their own, that is, foreign policy in the Middle East is not necessarily idiosyncratic, institutionalized, or personalistic, e.g., "Third World." In fact, the autonomous state is a feature of all mature political systems.

13. The maintenance of order and the collection of essential taxes are the functions of the classical Islamic state. For a modern treatment of this distinction and others, see Khalid M. Ishaque, "Problems of Islamic Political Theory," in *State Politics and Islam*, ed. Mumtaz Ahmad (Washington: American Trust Publications, 1986), pp. 25–36.

14. This distinction of politics and policy clarifies the characterization of Egypt as a soft state by Waterbury. He is using the expression broadly when in fact in his argument it applies to policy (Waterbury, p. 11).

15. This class is what Leonard Binder, after Mosca, calls the "second stratum" in Egypt. See Binder, *In a Moment of Enthusiasm: Political Power and the Second Stratum in Egypt* (Chicago: University of Chicago Press, 1978). The 20 percent figure comes from table 28, "Income Distribution," *World Development Report 1985* (Washington: World Bank, 1985), p. 228. In 1974 the top 10 percent of households received 33.2 percent of income, and the top 20 percent got 48 percent.

16. Waterbury makes reference to Egyptian corporatism, pp. 309–12, and he and Allan Richards in *A Political Economy of the Middle East* (Boulder: Westview Press, 1990), pp. 337–44, expand the concept to the Middle East. Robert Bianchi, in his *Unruly Corporatism: Associational Life in Twentieth Century Egypt* (New York: Oxford University Press, 1991), has also employed the concept. My presentation of the concept differs from theirs in being more grounded in nineteenth-century German and French thought in which corporatism was a conservative political ideology. These ideas were set forth initially in *Comparative Politics in the Post Behavioral Era*, ed. Louis J. Cantori and Andrew Ziegler (Boulder: Lynn Rienner, 1988), pp. 75–77, 417–26.

17. The preceding is developed in my unpublished paper "Political Participation, Consultation and State-Civil Society Relations in the Middle East." The specific point about the restrictive nature of foreign policy making in terms (a limited number) of personalities and relevant organizations is made in Ali E. Hillal Dessouki, "The Foreign Policy of Egypt," in Korany and Dessouki, pp. 168–71.

18. On the political parties and their attitudes toward foreign policy, and the crisis in the Gulf, see Mona Makram Ebeid, "Political Opposition in Egypt: Democratic Myth or Reality," *Middle East Journal* 43 (Summer 1989): 423–36, and "Parties and Parliament in Egypt" in *Democratization in Egypt*, ed. Louis J. Cantori (Bloomington: Indiana University Press, forthcoming). See *FBIS:NESA*, September 19, 1990, pp. 9–10, for the Social Labor Party opposition.

19. On the Islamic organizations, see Marius Deeb, "Islam and Democracy in Egypt", in Cantori, *Democratization*, and Ebeid, "Political Opposition." In addition, the well-known theologian Muhammad al-Ghazal also noted the non-Islamic character of Iraq; see *FBIS:NESA*, September 26, 1990, pp. 8–9. See also Gehad Auda, "An Uncertain Response: The Islamic Movement in Egypt," in *Islamic Fundamentalism and the Gulf Crisis*, ed. James Piscatori (Chicago: American Academy of Arts and Sciences, 1991), pp. 109–30.

20. Ebeid, "Political Opposition," and Cantori, *Democratization*.

21. As late as January 1989, there were still 10,000 to 15,000 Egyptian prisoners being held by Iran. Middle East News Agency, *FBIS:NESA*, January 25, 1989, p. 10.

22. Hundreds of bodies were returned to Egypt, and the Egyptian press was full of stories regarding them. *FBIS:NESA*, September 7, 1990, p. 6, September 25, 1990, p. 7.

23. From September onward, there were press reports of officers not obeying orders, even of mutiny and the pensioning off of officers. *FBIS:NESA*, September 12, 1990, p. 2; December 19, 1990, pp. 24–25; January 16, 1991, pp. 7–8; January 17, 1991, p. 7.

24. See Cantori, "Egypt Reenters the Arab State System," in Freedman, *The Middle East*, and Abdel Moneim Said Aly, *Back to the Fold? Egypt and the Arab World* (Washington: Georgetown University Center for Contemporary Arab Studies, 1988).

25. William B. Quandt, *The United States and Egypt* (Washington, D.C.: Brookings Institution, 1990), pp. 27–28.

26. On Mubarak's meetings, see the *New York Times*, October 23, 24, 1988. For the text of the PNC communiqué see *American Arab Affairs* (hereafter *AAA*) 26 (Fall 1988): 185–92, and, for an analysis, see Muhammad Muslih, "Toward Coexistence: An Analysis of the Resolutions of the Palestine National Conference," *Journal of Palestine Studies* (hereafter *JPS*) 19 (Summer 1990): 24–27.

27. The Soviet conception of the international conference was described as identical with that of Egypt. Shevardnadze also met with Israeli Foreign Minister Arens in Cairo; see the *New York Times*, February 21, 1989.

28. See *AAA* 28 (Spring 1989), pp. 107–11 for the text of Baker's speech and pp. 113–16 for Shamir's plan.

29. For the text of Egypt's ten points, see *JPS* 19 (Autumn 1989): 144–45.

30. See the text of the five points of Baker, *JPS*, 19 (Winter 1990): 168–70.

31. On these developments and their role in the events leading to the position of the PLO and the Gulf War, see Ann Lesch, "Notes for a Brief on the Palestinian Question in the Context of the New International Regional Middle Eastern Order," Conference Group on the Middle East, American Political Science Association, Washington, August 31, 1991.

32. Abdullah Hourani, PLO executive board member, *Washington Post*,

June 5, 1990. On this point, see also Emile Sahliyeh, "The Gulf Crisis: Implications for the Palestinian-Israeli Conflict," American Political Science Association, Washington, August 31, 1991, pp. 9–10.

33. Pierre Salinger and Eric Laurent, *Secret Dossier: The Hidden Agenda Behind the Gulf War*, trans. Howard Curtis (New York: Penguin Books, 1991), p. 7. The second day of the meeting was canceled.

34. Ibid., pp. 29–33.

35. For the text of the agreement establishing the ACC, see *AAA* 28 (Spring 1989): 116–21. Clearly, Iraq, which had taken the initiative in forming the ACC, had attempted to use this organization for economic cooperation for its own political purposes. See Bruce Maddy-Weitzman, "The Inter-Arab System and the Gulf War," Occasional Paper Series (Carter Center, Emory University) 2, no. 1 (1992): 5. See also the *New York Times*, November 12, 1990.

36. The text of the final statement of the conference is in *JPS* 20 (August 1990): 152–59. See also Maddy-Weitzman, p. 10.

37. For example, as late into the crisis as July 21, Osama al-Baz, President Mubarak's political advisor, in an interview in *al-Watan* (Kuwait), talked extensively about the peace process. See *FBIS:NESA*, July 23, 1990, p. 10. Even more dramatically, in his annual Revolutionary Day speech Mubarak made practically no reference to the crisis, saying only that Saddam Hussein and his brothers would settle any differences. See *FBIS:NESA*, July 24, 1990, pp. 8–15, for text.

38. Agence France Presse, *FBIS:NESA*, July 23, 1991, pp. 8–9.

39. Salinger and Laurent, p. 45.

40. *FBIS:NESA*, July 24, 1991, pp. 26–29.

41. Radio Monte Carlo, *FBIS:NESA*, July 31, 1990, pp. 8–9, for the four points. According to Salinger and Laurent, pp. 65, 70, at the last minute the Emir of Kuwait decided not to attend and therefore Saddam declined as well.

42. Saudi Press Agency, *FBIS:NESA*, August 2, 1990, p. 24.

43. Middle East News Agency, *FBIS:NESA*, August 8, 1990, p. 11.

44. Ibid.

45. Middle East News Agency, *FBIS:NESA*, August 6, 1990, p. 20.

46. Text of the August 3, 1990, resolution is found in *JPS*, 20 (Winter 1991): 177–78. For the issue of Arabism, see Asad Abu Khalil, "A New Arab Ideology? The Rejuvenation of Arab Nationalism," *Middle East Journal* 46 (Winter 1992): 22–36.

47. The result was the scuttling of the proposed summit and the end of a possible Arab solution. See Salinger and Laurent, p. 112.

48. Radio Cairo, *FBIS:NESA*, August 8, 1990. p. 13. See note 47 above.

49. Text of the resolution is in *JPS*, 20 (Winter 1991): 178–79.

50. This was the basis of opposition to the Western role that swept the region and in the process gave evidence of popular and democratic sentiment. See Michael Hudson, "After the Gulf War: Prospect for Democratization in

the Arab World," *AAA* 45 (Summer 1991), and the contributions to Louis J. Cantori, "Democratization in the Middle East," *AAA* 36 (Spring 1991): 1–31.

51. Salah Basouny, former Egyptian ambassador to the Soviet Union, has stated the Egyptian case even more forcibly by saying that if Iraq had not been built up by the Gulf states and foreign powers and if Egypt's leadership role on the Palestinian issue had not been undermined by Western support for Israel, then Egypt might have led an Arab force to deter Iraq's invasion of Kuwait. In any case, Egypt seeks regional peace by being the leader of the regional balance of power. "The Dilemma of Egyptian Foreign Policy," *Middle East Papers*, "Special Dossier: The Gulf Crisis," National Center for Middle East Studies, Cairo, November 1990, pp. 6, 8.

52. The *Economist* Intelligence Unit, Egypt, Country File: Annual Survey of Political and Economic Background (London, 1990), pp. 44–47.

53. The text of the Damascus declaration is in *JPS*, 20 (Summer 1991): 161–63.

54. The Egyptians appear to have been miffed by the Saudis' reneging on the Damascus declaration. Egyptian blandishments denying anything unusual (*FBIS:NESA*, May 17, 1991) and the July 15 meeting (*FBIS:NESA*, July 16, 1991) could not obscure the unusual situation. *Al-Sha'b*, an opposition newspaper, even suggested that it was the United States that had told the Saudis that there could be no forces in the Gulf greater in numbers than those of the United States (*FBIS:NESA*, April 21, 1991).

55. Text of speech in the *Washington Post*, March 7, 1991, and excerpts in *JPS* 20 (Summer 1991): 180–81.

56. *FBIS:NESA*, March 11, 1991, pp. 41–42.

57. *FBIS:NESA*, March 13, 1991, pp. 24–33. The text of the "internals'" statement is also in *JPS* 20 (Summer 1991): 163–64.

58. *FBIS:NESA*, July 22, 1991, p. 8.

59. In fact, the assassin of Rifaat Mahgoub, the speaker of the Egyptian Parliament in October 1990, was said to have been trained in Khartoum. *Washington Post*, January 31, 1992.

CONTRIBUTORS

Eugene Brown is professor of political science at Lebanon Valley College. From 1989–91 he was visiting professor of foreign policy at the U.S. Army War College. His publications include *J. William Fulbright: Advice and Dissent*, as well as a number of papers, articles, and monographs on Japanese foreign policy.

Louis Cantori is professor of political science at the University of Maryland, Baltimore County. He is also a consultant to numerous agencies of the U.S. government, including the AID project in Egypt, and the Directorate of Planning of the Middle East headquarters of the U.S. Air Force. He is the author of numerous books and articles on the Middle East including *Local Politics and Development in the Middle East; Comparative Politics in the Post Behavioral Era*, and *The International Politics of Regions*.

Helena Cobban is the author of *The Palestinian Liberation Organization: People, Power and Politics*. She is currently research director of the Initiative for Peace and Cooperation in the Middle East.

Alasdair Drysdale is associate professor of geography at the University of New Hampshire and coauthor of *Syria and the Middle East Peace Process* and *The Middle East and North Africa: A Political Geographic Study*.

Marvin Feuerwerger has served as the acting director of the Pentagon's Policy Planning Staff and as director of regional policy in the Office of the Principal Deputy Undersecretary of Defense for Strategy and Resources. He is the author of numerous publications including *Congress and Israel: Foreign Aid Decision-Making in the House of Representatives, 1969–1976* and *Restoring the Balance: American Interests and the Gulf Crisis*.

Robert O. Freedman is Peggy Meyerhoff Pearlstone professor of political science and dean of Graduate Studies of Baltimore Hebrew University. Among his numerous publications are *Soviet Policy Toward the Middle East Since 1970*, now in its third edition, and *Moscow and the Middle East: Soviet Policy Since the Invasion of Afghanistan*.

Adam Garfinkle is a resident scholar at the Foreign Policy Research Institute in Philadelphia and a contributing editor to the institute's journal, *Orbis*. His latest book is *Israel and Jordan in the Shadow of War.*

F. Gregory Gause, III is associate professor of political science at Columbia University and a member of the resident faculty at the university's Middle East Institute. He is Fellow for Arab and Islamic Studies at the Council on Foreign Relations and is currently completing a project there on the monarchical states of the Gulf. He is the author of *Saudi-Yemen Relations: Domestic Structure and Foreign Influence* and numerous articles on Middle East politics.

Robert Hunter is vice-president for regional programs and director of European Studies at the Center for Strategic and International Studies. During the Carter administration, he was director of Middle East affairs at the National Security Council (1979–81), developing the Carter Doctrine and negotiating on autonomy for the West Bank and Gaza.

Shireen T. Hunter was a member of the Iranian Foreign Service from 1966 to 1978 and served in London, New York, and Geneva. Currently she is director of the Middle East program at the Center for Strategic and International Studies in Washington, D.C. Her *Iran and the World: Continuity in a Revolutionary Decade* is one of numerous books, including a major study, *Iran after Khomeini.*

Ilana Kass is professor of military strategy at the National War College, Washington, D.C. She has also taught at the Hebrew University of Jerusalem and the IDF Staff College. Among her publications are *Soviet Involvement in the Middle East: Policy Formulation* and *The Russian Military: Back to the Future?*

Laurie Mylroie, associate professor in the Department of Strategy and Policy of the Naval War College, is the author of numerous books and articles. Among her books are *The Future of Iraq*, *Saddam Hussein and the Crisis in the Gulf* and *The Soviet Position in the People's Democratic Republic of Yemen: Regional Challenges and Internal Vulnerabilities.*

Bard E. O'Neill is director of Middle East Studies and director of Studies of Insurgency and Revolution at the National War College. He is author of a number of books, including *Armed Struggle in Palestine* and *Insurgency and Terrorism.*

BIBLIOGRAPHY

Books

After the Storm: Challenges for America's Middle East Policy. Washington: The Washington Institute for Near East Policy, 1991.

Alpher, Joseph, ed. *War in the Gulf: Implications for Israel.* Tel-Aviv: Jaffee Center for Strategic Studies, Tel-Aviv University, 1992.

Aly, Abdel Moneim Said. *Back to the Fold? Egypt and the Arab World.* Washington: Georgetown University Center for Contemporary Arab Studies, 1988.

Bianchi, Robert. *Unruly Corporatism: Associational Life in Twentieth-Century Egypt.* New York: Oxford University Press, 1991.

Binder, Leonard. *In a Moment of Enthusiasm: Political Power and the Second Stratum in Egypt.* Chicago: University of Chicago Press, 1978.

Brown, L. Carl. *International Politics and the Middle East: Old Rules, Dangerous Game.* Princeton: Princeton University Press, 1984.

Cantori, Louis J., and Andrew Ziegler, eds. *Comparative Politics in the Post-Behavioral Era.* Boulder, CO: Lynn Rienner, 1988.

Cantori, Louis J., and Steven Spiegel. *The International Politics of Regions.* Englewood Cliffs, NJ: Prentice-Hall, 1970.

Cobban, Helena. *The Superpowers and the Syrian-Israeli Conflict: Beyond Crisis Management.* The Washington Papers, no. 149. New York: Praeger, with the Center for International Studies, Washington, 1991.

Conduct of the Persian Gulf Conflict: Interim Report to Congress. Washington, 1991.

Crisis in the Persian Gulf: Sanctions, Diplomacy and War. Hearings before the Committee on Armed Services of the House of Representatives, 101st Cong., December 1990.

Drifte, Richard. *Japan's Foreign Policy.* New York: Council on Foreign Relations, 1990.

Drysdale, Alasdair, and Raymond A. Hinnebusch. *Syria and the Middle East Peace Process.* New York: Council on Foreign Relations Press, 1991.

Economic Crisis in the Arab World: Catalyst for Conflict. Washington: Overseas Development Council, 1991.

Eisenstadt, Mike. *The Sword of the Arabs: Iraq's Strategic Weapons.* Washington Institute Policy Paper Number 21. Washington: The Washington Institute for Near East Policy, 1990.

Freedman, Robert O. *Moscow and the Middle East: Soviet Policy since the Invasion of Afghanistan.* Cambridge: Cambridge University Press, 1991.

————. *Soviet-Israeli Relations under Gorbachev.* New York: Praeger, 1991.

_____. *Soviet Policy toward the Middle East since 1970*. New York: Praeger, 1982.

_____. ed. *The Middle East from the Iran-Contra Affair to the Intifada*. Syracuse: Syracuse University Press, 1991.

_____. ed. *The Intifada: Its Impact on Israel, the Arab World, and the Superpowers*. Miami: Florida International University Press, 1991.

Frost, Ellen. *For Richer, for Poorer: The New U.S.-Japan Relationship*. New York: Council on Foreign Relations, 1984.

Gaddis, John Lewis. *Strategies of Containment*. Oxford: Oxford University Press, 1982.

Garfinkle, Adam. *Israel and Jordan in the Shadow of War*. New York: St. Martin's 1992.

Gorbachev, Mikhail. *Perestroika: New Thinking for Our Country and the World*. New York: Harper & Row, 1987.

Hanna, John P. *At Arm's Length: Soviet-Syrian Relations in the Gorbachev Era*. Washington Institute Policy Paper Number 18. Washington: The Washington Institute for Near East Policy, 1989.

Hart, Basil Liddell. *Strategy*. 2d rev. ed. New York: Praeger, 1968.

Holsti, K.J. *International Politics*. 5th ed. Englewood Cliffs, NJ: Prentice Hall, 1988.

Hunter, Shireen T. *Iran after Khomeini*. New York: Praeger/Center for Strategic and International Studies, 1992.

_____. *Iran and the World: Continuity in a Revolutionary Decade*. Bloomington: Indiana University Press, 1990.

Karsh, Efraim. *The Soviet Union and Syria: The Asad Years*. New York: Routledge, 1988.

Kawai, Kazuo. *Japan's American Interlude*. Chicago: University of Chicago Press, Midway Reprint, 1979.

Khalidi, Walid. *The Gulf Crisis: Origins and Consequences*. Washington: Institute for Palestine Studies, 1991.

Kienle, Eberhard. *Ba'th v Ba'th: The Conflict between Syria and Iraq, 1968–1989*. London: I.B. Tauris, 1990.

Kurdish Separatism in Iraq: Developments and Implications for the United States. Washington: Congressional Research Service, May 6, 1991.

Luttwak, Edward N. *The Pentagon and the Art of War*. New York: Simon and Schuster, 1984.

Ma'oz, Moshe. *Asad—The Sphinx of Damascus: A Political Biography*. New York: Weidenfeld and Nicholson, 1988.

Middle East Watch. *Syria Unmasked: The Suppression of Human Rights by the Assad Regime*. New Haven: Yale University Press, 1991.

Mirsky, Yehudah, ed. *American Strategy after the Gulf War*. Washington: The Washington Institute, 1991.

Morse, Ronald A. *Turning Crisis to Advantage: The Politics of Japan's Gulf Energy Strategy*. New York: The Asia Society, 1990.

Mylroie, Laurie, and Judith Miller. *Saddam Hussein and the Crisis in the Gulf*. New York: Random House, 1990.

Mylroie, Laurie. *The Future of Iraq*. Washington Institute Policy Paper Number 24. Washington: The Washington Institute for Near East Policy, 1991.

al-Nasser, Gamal Abd. *Egypt's Liberation*. Washington: Public Affairs Press, 1955.

Nolan, Joanne. *Trappings of Power: Ballistic Missiles in the Third World*. Washington: Brookings Institution, 1991.

O'Neill, Bard. *Insurgency and Terrorism*. New York: Brassey's, Inc., 1990.

Pipes, Daniel. *Greater Syria: The History of an Ambition*. New York: Oxford University Press, 1990.

Piscatori, James, ed. *Islamic Fundamentalism and the Gulf Crisis*. Chicago: American Academy of Arts and Sciences, 1991.

Quandt, William B. *The United States and Egypt*. Washington: Brookings Institution, 1990.

Ramet, Pedro. *The Syria-Soviet Relationship since 1955: A Troubled Alliance*. Boulder, CO: Westview Press, 1990.

Record, Jeffrey. *Revising U.S. Military Strategy*. Washington: Pergamon-Brassey's, 1984.

Reischauer, Edwin O. *The Japanese Today*. Cambridge: Harvard University Press, 1989.

Restoring the Balance: U.S. Strategy and the Gulf Crisis. Washington: The Washington Institute for Near East Policy, 1991.

Salinger, Pierre, and Eric Laurent. *Secret Dossier: The Hidden Agenda Behind the Gulf War*. Translated from the French by Howard Curtis. New York: Penguin Books, 1991.

Satloff, Robert. *They Cannot Stop Our Tongues: Islamic Fundamentalism in Jordan*. Washington: Washington Institute for Near East Policy, 1988.

————. *Troubles on the East Bank: Challenges to the Domestic Stability of Jordan*. Washington: Center for Strategic and International Studies, 1986.

Seale, Patrick. *Assad: The Struggle for the Middle East*. Berkeley: University of California Press, 1989.

Sicherman, Harvey. *Palestinian Self-Government (Autonomy): Its Past and Its Future*. Washington Institute Policy Paper Number 27. Washington: The Washington Institute for Near East Policy, November 1991.

Sifry, Micah L., and Christopher Cerf, eds. *The Gulf War Reader*. New York: Times Books, a division of Random House, Inc., 1991.

Simpson, John. *From the House of War*. London: Arrow Books, 1991.

Sims, Richard W. *Japanese Resource Dependency*. Monterey, CA: Naval Postgraduate School, 1982.

Summers, Harry G., Jr. *On Strategy: The Vietnam War in Context.* Carlisle Barracks, PA: U.S. Army War College, 1981.

Tzu, Sun. *The Art of War.* Translated by Samuel B. Griffith. Oxford: Oxford University Press, 1963.

U.S. Senate. Committee on Foreign Relations. *Civil War in Iraq.* Staff Report, 102d Cong., 1st sess., 1991.

The United States and the New Middle East: Strategic Perspectives after the Persian Gulf War. The Report of the Center for Strategic and International Studies Aftermath Policy Council. Prepared by Robert E. Hunter. Washington: CSIS, March 1992.

Waterbury, John. *The Egypt of Nasser and Sadat.* Princeton, NJ: Princeton University Press, 1983.

Waterbury, John, and Allan Richards. *A Political Economy of the Middle East.* Boulder, CO: Westview Press, 1990.

Woodward, Bob. *The Commanders.* New York: Simon and Schuster, 1991.

Yorke, Valerie. *Domestic Politics and Regional Security: Jordan, Syria, and Israel.* Aldershot, England: Gower, 1988.

Articles

Abu-Khalil, Asad. "A New Arab Ideology?: The Rejuvenation of Arab Nationalism." *Middle East Journal* 46 (Winter 1992): 22–36.

Ahmad, Mahbub, and Siham Muhammed Mahmud Hosain. "Length of School Life in Jordan." In *Aspects of Population Change and Development in Some African and Asian Countries,* 657–66. Cairo: Cairo Demographic Center, Research Monograph Series, no. 9, 1984.

Akhromeyev, Sergei. "Why Baghdad Suffered a Defeat." *Novoe Vremia,* no. 1 (March 1991): 22–25.

Aleksandrov, Yevgeny. "New Political Thinking: Genesis, Factors, Prospects." *International Affairs* (Moscow), no. 12 (1987): 87–95.

Andoni, Lamis. "The PLO and Syria: A Tricky Relationship." *Middle East International,* no. 401 (May 31, 1991), pp. 11–12.

"The Arabian Peninsula: U.S. Principles." *Current Policy,* no. 1292. Washington: U.S. Department of State, August 1990.

Arian, Asher. "Israel's National Unity Governments and Domestic Politics." In *The Elections in Israel—1988,* edited by Asher Arian and Michal Shamir, pp. 205–22. Boulder: Westview Press, 1990.

Aspin, Les. "The Role of Sanctions in Security U.S. Interests in the Gulf." Washington: House Committee on Armed Services, December 21, 1990.

Auda, Gehad. "An Uncertain Response: The Islamic Movement in Egypt." In *Islamic Fundamentalism and the Gulf Crisis,* edited by James Piscatori, pp. 109–30. Chicago: American Academy of Arts and Sciences, 1991.

Bogdanov, Rodimir. "From the Balance of Forces to a Balance of Interests." *International Affairs* (Moscow), no. 4 (1988): 81–87.

Cantori, Louis J. et al. "Democratization in the Middle East." *American-Arab Affairs* (Spring 1991): 1–30.

———. "Egypt Reenters the Arab State System." In *The Middle East from the Iran-Contra Affair to the Intifada*, edited by Robert O. Freedman, pp. 341–66. Syracuse, NY: Syracuse University Press, 1991.

Carswell, Robert. "Economic Sanctions and the Iran Experience." *Foreign Affairs* (Winter 1981–82): 264–65.

Cobban, Helena. "The Palestinians: From the Hussein-Arafat Agreement to the Intifada." In *The Middle East from the Iran-Contra Affair to the Intifada*, edited by Robert O. Freedman, pp. 255–59. Syracuse, NY: Syracuse University Press, 1991.

———. "The PLO and the Intifada." In *The Intifada*, edited by Robert O. Freedman, pp. 70–106. Miami: Florida International University Press, 1991.

Crow, Suzanne. "Legislative Considerations and the Gulf Crisis." *Radio Liberty Report* 2, no. 50 (1990): 2–3.

Danin, Robert M. "Moscow and the Middle East Peace Conference after the Coup." *Middle East Insight* 8, no. 2 (September–October, 1991): 4–8.

Dessouki, Ali Hillal. "The Primacy of Economics: The Foreign Policy of Egypt." In *The Foreign Policies of Arab States*, 2d ed., edited by Bahgat Korany and Ali Hillal Dessouki, pp. 156–85. Boulder, CO: Westview Press, 1991.

———. "Egypt's Response to the Gulf Crisis." *Current History* (January 1992): 34–36.

Ebeid, Mona Makram. "Political Opposition in Egypt: Democratic Myth or Reality." *Middle East Journal* 43 (Summer 1989): 423–36.

Freedman, Robert O. "Gorbachev, Iran, and the Iran-Iraq War." In *Neither East nor West: Iran, the Soviet Union and the United States*, edited by Nikki R. Keddie and Mark J. Gasiorowski, pp. 115–44. New Haven: Yale University Press, 1990.

———. "Religion, Politics, and the Israeli Elections of 1988." *Middle East Journal* 43 (Summer 1989): 406–22.

———. "Moscow and the Gulf War." *Problems of Communism* (July–August 1991): 1–19.

Garfinkle, Adam. "The Importance of Being Hussein: Jordanian Foreign Policy and Peace in the Middle East." In *The Middle East from the Iran-Contra Affair to the Intifada*, edited by Robert O. Freedman, 268–302. Syracuse: Syracuse University Press, 1990.

Ghazwi, Fahmi, and Steven L. Nock. "Religion as a Mediating Force in the Effects of Modernization on Parent-Child Relations in Jordan." *Middle Eastern Studies*, 25, no. 3 (July 1989): 363–69.

Inoguchi, Takashi. "Japan's Politics of Interdependence." *Government and Opposition* (Autumn 1990): 419–37.

Ishaque, Khalid M. "Problems of Islamic Political Theory." In *State Politics and Islam*, edited by Mumtaz Ahmad, 25–36. Washington: American Trust Publications, 1986.

Kemp, Geoffrey. "The Middle East Arms Race: Can It Be Controlled?" *The Middle East Journal* (Summer 1991): 441–56.

Kislov, Aleksander. "Novoe Politicheskoe Myshlenie i Regional'nye Konflicty" [New Political Thinking and Regional Conflicts]. *Mirovaia Ekonomika i Mezhdunarodnye Otnosheniia*, no. 8 (1988): 39–47.

Hudson, Michael C. "After the War: Prospects for Democratization in the Arab World." *The Middle East Journal* (Summer 1991): 407–26.

Hunter, Shireen. "Post-Khomeini Iran." *Foreign Affairs* 68, no. 5 (Winter 1989–90): 133–49.

Huntington, Samuel P. "The U.S.—Decline or Renewal." *Foreign Affairs* (Winter 1988–89): 76–96.

Kennedy, Paul. "The (Relative) Decline of America." *The Atlantic* (August 1987): 29–38.

Maddy-Weitzman, Bruce. "The Inter-Arab System and the Gulf War." Occasional Paper Series (Carter Center, Emory University) 2, no. 1 (1992).

Nolan, Janne E. "The Global Arms Market after the Gulf War: Prospects for Control." *The Washington Quarterly* (Summer 1991): 125–38.

_____. "World Wide Threats and Their Implications for the U.S. Force Structure: The Middle East and South Asia." General Accounting Office Conference on World Wide Threats, October 30, 1991.

Nye, Joseph S., Jr. "Soft Power." *Foreign Policy* (Fall 1990): 153–71.

Perthes, Volker. "Syria's Parliamentary Elections: Remodeling Assad's Political Base." *Middle East Report* (January–February 1992): 15–18.

_____. "The Syrian Economy in the 1980s." *Middle East Journal*, no. 46 (1992): 37–58.

Primakov, Yevgeny, V. Martnynov, and G. Duligenskii. "Nekotorye Problemy Novogo Myshleniia" [Some Problems of the New Thinking]. *Mirovaia Ekonomika i Mezhdunarodnye Otnosheniia*, no. 6 (1989): 5–18.

Rapkin, David. "Japan and World Leadership." In *World Leadership and Hegemony*, edited by David Rapkin, pp. 196–99. Boulder, CO: Lynne Rienner, 1990.

Robins, Philip J. "Politics and the 1986 Electoral Law in Jordan." In *Politics and the Economy in Jordan*, edited by Rodney Wilson, pp. 184–208. New York: Routledge, 1991.

Sadowski, Yahya. "Power, Poverty and Petrodollars: Arab Economies after the Gulf War." *Middle East Report*, no. 170 (May–June 1991): 4–10.

Sato, Hideo. "Japan's Role in the Post-Cold War World." *Current History* (April 1991): 145–48, 179.

Sato, Seizaburo. "The U.S.-Japan Alliance under Changing International Relations." *Washington Quarterly* (Summer 1990): 71–75.

Schlesinger, James. "Oil and Power in the Nineties." *The National Interest* (April 1990): 111–15.

Schuler, G. Henry M. "A Petroleum Forecast: The Impact on U.S.-Arab Relations in the Coming Years." *American-Arab Affairs* (Winter 1986–87): 83–87.

Sick, Gary. "Slouching toward Settlement: The Internationalization of the Iran-Iraq War, 1987–1988." In *Neither East nor West: Iran, the Soviet Union and the United States*, edited by Nikki R. Keddie and Mark J. Gasiorowski, pp. 219–46. New Haven: Yale University Press, 1990.

Sinai, Joshua. "Arms Sales to the Middle East: Security or Patterns of Destructive Competition?" *Armed Forces Journal* (August 1991): 40–44.

Skolpol, Theda. "Bringing the State Back In: Current Research." In *Bringing the State Back In*, edited by Peter Evans et al., pp. 9–20. Cambridge: Cambridge University Press, 1985.

Tamamoto, Masaru. "The Japan that Can Say Yes." *World Policy Journal* (Summer 1990): 493–520.

Trofimenko, G.A. "Novye Real'nosti i Novoe Myshlenie" [New Realities and New Thinking]. *Ssha*, no. 2 (1987): 3–15.

Weisberg, Jacob. "Gulfballs." *The New Republic*, March 25, 1991, pp. 17–19.

INDEX